CENTRAL EUROPE SINCE 1945

The Postwar World
General Editors: A.J. Nicholls and Martin S. Alexander

As distance puts events into perspective, and as evidence accumulates, it begins to be possible to form an objective historical view of our recent past. *The Postwar World* is an ambitious new series providing a scholarly but readable account of the way our world has been shaped in the crowded years since the Second World War. Some volumes will deal with regions, or even single nations, others with important themes; all will be written by expert historians drawing on the latest scholarship as well as their own research and judgements. The series should be particularly welcome to students, but it is designed also for the general reader with an interest in contemporary history.

Central Europe since 1945

Paul G. Lewis

Longman
London and New York

Longman Group UK Limited,
Longman House, Burnt Mill,
Harlow, Essex CM20 2JE, England
and Associated Companies throughout the world

Published in the United States of America
by Longman Publishing, New York

© Longman Group UK Limited 1994

First published 1994

ISBN 0 582 03609 7 CSD
ISBN 0 582 03608 9 PPR

British Library Cataloguing-in-Publication Data

A catalogue record for this book is
available from the British Library

Library of Congress Cataloging-in-Publication Data

Lewis, Paul G., 1945–
    Central Europe since 1945 / Paul G. Lewis.
        p. cm. – (The Postwar world)
    Includes bibliographical references and index.
    ISBN 0–582–03609–7 (cased). – ISBN 0–582–03608–9 (pbk.)
    1. Central Europe–History.   I. Title. II. Series.
    DAW1050.L49   1994
    943–dc20   93–32588
                                                                CIP

Set by 7BB in 10/12 New Baskerville roman
Produced by Longman Singapore Publishers (Pte) Ltd
Printed in Singapore

Contents

List of Maps

Abbreviations and Acronyms

AFD	Alliance of Free Democrats (Hungary)
AK	(Polish) Home Army
AVH	State Protection Authority (Hungarian secret police)
CDP	Civic Democratic Party
CDU	Christian Democratic Union (Germany)
CF	Civic Forum (Czechoslovakia)
CMEA	Council for Mutual Economic Assistance; also COMECON
COCOM	Coordinating Committee (Economic arm of North Atlantic Treaty Organization)
COMINFORM	Communist Information Bureau
COMPSTEP	Comprehensive Programme for Scientific and Technological Progress
CPSU	Communist Party of the Soviet Union
DBD	Democratic Farmers' Party (Germany)
EC	European Community
FDGB	Confederation of Free Trade Unions (East Germany)
FIDESZ	Alliance of Young Democrats (Hungary)
FRG	Federal Republic of Germany
GDR	German Democratic Republic
GRU	Main Intelligence Directorate (Soviet military intelligence)
HSP	Hungarian Socialist Party
HSWP	Hungarian Socialist Workers' Party
INF	Intermediate-range Nuclear Forces
KLD	Liberal Democratic Congress (Poland)

KOR	Workers' Defence Committee (Poland)
KPCz	Communist Party of Czechoslovakia
KPD	German Community Party
KPN	Confederation of Independent Poland
KPP	Polish Communist Party
LDP	Liberal Democratic Party (Germany)
MDF	Hungarian Democratic Forum
MDP	Hungarian Workers' Party
MDS	Movement for a Democratic Slovakia
HSWP	Hungarian Socialist Workers' Party
MVD	Soviet Interior Ministry
NATO	North Atlantic Treaty Organization
NDPD	National Democratic Party of Germany
NEM	New Economic Mechanism (Hungary)
NKVD	Soviet Security Organization
NSZ	National Armed Forces group (Poland)
OKP	Citizens' Parliamentary Club (Poland)
ORMO	Volunteer Citizens' Militia Reserve (Poland)
OPZZ	National Trade Union Accord (Poland)
PAV	Public Against Violence (Slovakia)
PCC	Political Consultative Committee (of the WTO)
PCF	French Communist Party
PDS	Reformed Communist Party
PPR	Polish Worker's Party
PPS	Polish Socialist Party
PSL	Polish Peasant Party
PUS	Polish Social-Democratic Union
PZPR	Polish United Workers' Party
ROAD	Citizens' Movement for Democratic Action (Poland)
SD	Democratic Party (Poland)
SdRP	Social Democracy of the Polish Republic
SED	Socialist Unity Party (East Germany)
SMAD	Soviet Military Administration in Germany
SMERSH	Soviet military counter-intelligence organization
SNB	National Security Corps (Czechoslovakia)
SPD	(West Germany) Social Democratic Party
UD	Democratic Union (Poland)
VdgB	Farmers' Mutual Aid Association (East Germany)

VONS   Committee for the Defence of the Unjustly
               Persecuted (Czechoslovakia)
WAK   Catholic Election Action (Poland)
WTO   Warsaw Treaty Organization
ZSL   United Peasant Party (Poland)

Editorial Foreword

The aim of this series is to describe and analyse the history of the World since 1945. History, like time, does not stand still. What seemed to many of us only recently to be 'current affairs', or the stuff of political speculation, has now become material for historians. The editors feel that it is time for a series of books which will offer the public judicious and scholarly, but at the same time readable, accounts of the way in which our present-day world was shaped by the years after the end of the Second World War. The period since 1945 has seen political events and socio-economic developments of enormous significance for the human race, as important as anything which happened before Hitler's death or the bombing of Hiroshima. Ideologies have waxed and waned, the industrialised economies have boomed and bust, empires have collapsed, new nations have emerged and sometimes themselves fallen into decline. While we can be thankful that no major armed conflict has occurred between the so-called superpowers, there have been many other wars, and terrorism has become an international plague. Although the position of ethnic minorities has dramatically improved in some countries, it has worsened in others. Nearly everywhere the status of women has become an issue which politicians have been unable to avoid. These are only some of the developments we hope will be illuminated by this series as it unfolds.

The books in the series will not follow any set pattern; they will vary in length according to the needs of the subject. Some will deal with regions, or even single nations, and others with themes. Not all of them will begin in 1945, and the terminal date may similarly vary; once again, the time-span chosen will be appropriate to the question under discussion. All the books, however, will be written by expert historians drawing on the latest fruits of scholarship, as well as their own expertise and judgement. The series should be particularly welcome to students, but it is designed also for the general reader with an interest in contemporary history. We hope that the books will stimulate scholarly discussion and encourage specialists to look beyond their own particular interests to engage in wider controversies. History, and particularly the history of the recent past, is neither 'bunk' nor an intellectual form of stamp-collecting, but an indispensable part of an educated person's approach to life. If it is not written by historians it will be written by others of a less discriminating and more polemical disposition. The editors are confident that this series will help to ensure the victory of the historical approach, with consequential benefits for its readers.

A.J. Nicholls
Martin S. Alexander

The publishers would like to thank the following for permission to reproduce copyright material: Wadsworth Publishing Co. for Table 3.2 from *Politics in Eastern Europe* by I. Volgyes; Harvard University Press for Table 4.1 from *The Soviet Bloc: Unity and Conflict* by Zbigniew K. Brzezinski, Cambridge, Mass. (Harvard University Press, Copyright © 1960, 1967, by the President and Fellows of Harvard College); NATO Office of Information and Press for Table 5.5 from *The Economies of Eastern Europe Under Gorbachev's Influence,* published in Brussels in 1989; PWPA (Paragon House) for Table 10.3 from *The Uncertain Future. Gorbachev's Eastern Bloc* (1988) by (eds) N.N. Kittrie and I. Volgyes; Routledge, New York for Table 10.4 from *Economic Integration in Eastern Europe* (1989) by J. van Brabant.

The publishers were unable to trace the copyright holders for permission to reproduce the following: Table 5.1 from *Economic History of Eastern Europe 1919–75 – Vol III: Institutional Change within a Planned Economy* (1986) by M.C. Kaser & E.A. Radice (ed.) published by Oxford University Press; Table 5.4 from *Eastern Europe Since 1945* (1984) by L.P. Morris published by Hutchinson; Table 6.3 from *Socialism's Dilemmas. State and Society in the Soviet Bloc* (1988) by W. Connor published by Columbia University Press, and Table 10.2 from *Eastern Europe in the 1980s* (1981) by (ed.) S. Fischer-Galati published by Westview Press. We would be grateful for any further information that would enable us to establish the copyright owners of these tables.

Preface

Considerably after the event, I learnt that I had been born the day after Danzig and Gdynia had been liberated from Nazi rule by the Red Army and during the night the last V-bomb of the Second World War fell on London. I am, then, very much a member of the generation that has lived through the "long peace" of the post-war period and experienced the lengthy period of stability in Europe that the post-war settlement brought into being. The cost at which that stability was obtained, however, was not always fully appreciated by the nations of the West and it is only recently that some of its implications have become more fully apparent. The peace and stability enjoyed by many Europeans like myself was accompanied by the imposition of considerably less advantageous conditions on the peoples to the east of the former Federal Republic of Germany. It was precisely the ambiguous form taken by the liberation of towns like Gdynia and Danzig (Gdańsk in Polish) that underwrote the oppressive nature of the stability imposed on much of Central Europe and the coerced peace that the period of communist rule brought to the region. Only much later did signs of the ultimate collapse of the communist system also become apparent in Gdańsk with the emergence of a solidly organized free trade union movement under the leadership of a hitherto unknown shipyard electrician called Lech Wałęsa.

The experience of post-war Europe has, therefore, been a diverse one and it is only after a near-half century of division and separation that the implications of that diversity are becoming more clear. Nowhere has the anomaly of this separation been more obvious than in the countries of Central Europe, which were particularly ill-suited to the situation that developed following the division of the continent into clearly demarcated eastern and western portions. It is the task of this book to chart the role of the different forces that have, during this period, acted on the region and interacted to produce the complex condition of post-communism, tentative democratization and problematic capitalist development that has emerged during the 1990s. Their history did not, of course, begin in 1945 and so, while the main focus is directed to the events of the communist period, attention is also paid to developments before 1945 and the pre-war history of the region. The book ranges, therefore, from the pre-communist period, through the years of Soviet-sponsored rule, to the recent period of post-communism – although by far the larger part is devoted to an account of developments under communism in Czechoslovakia, East Germany, Hungary and Poland.

It aims to provide a general survey of the key events that marked a near-half century in the life of a sizeable portion of European society (some 80 million people in the 1980s – roughly the size of the unified Germany that was formed soon afterwards). It is, then, by no means a specialist work and presents a narrative and general analysis of major developments in political, economic, social and cultural spheres. As such, it should be accessible to students from a variety of disciplines as well as the more generally interested reader. Covering a broad geographical area and a lengthy historical period it also draws on a range of sources, only some of which can be listed as formal references. A wide-ranging literature, many discussions of a formal and informal nature, and numerous visits to the region since the 1960s have contributed to the general view of Central Europe presented here. More specific acknowledgements and individual debts are acknowledged in the text, although I should also like to express gratitude for the helpful comments and careful reading of earlier drafts by the general editors of this series. Any remaining errors and peculiarities of judgement must remain my responsibility.

For Nicholas and Simon

CHAPTER ONE

Introduction and General Survey

PERSPECTIVES ON CENTRAL EUROPEAN HISTORY

The writing of this book spanned the period during which the grip of communist power over Central Europe, for several post-war decades a seemingly immovable barrier to political and, increasingly, economic change, weakened and then suddenly disappeared completely. As a contribution to a series of books on the post-war world this volume suddenly assumed, therefore, a different status. It had initially been conceived as setting out to depict a course of events and describe the situation they created within a different framework – one in which a major part of Europe had emerged from Nazi rule only to be plunged into a further, more prolonged period of dictatorship and political oppression whose end was surely overdue but whose removal hardly appeared in imminent prospect. Until the very end of the 1980s Central Europe had the appearance of an historical region still submerged by the post-war flow of Cold War currents and which only with difficulty maintained a shadowy, if distinct, identity within a broader area of Sovietized Europe.

Suddenly, however, much of the nature and experience of post-war Central Europe became 'historical' in the sense of forming part of a closed chapter in the history of the region – one characterized by social conditions, forms of rule and economic organization whose ineffectiveness and unnatural basis seemed not just inappropriate and wasteful but now also archaic. From an existing social system which, whatever the judgments passed on it, had an undeniable existence and worked (despite its many shortcomings) to a greater or lesser extent, European communism

1

rapidly took on the appearance of a museum exhibit whose relevance to the activities of the contemporary world was becoming increasingly doubtful. If by the early 1980s, as Martin Malia suggests, the Soviet Union had become a vast, Eurasian 'Stalin mausoleum', by the early 1990s the illustrious corpse had also been removed and European communism had lost virtually all self-respect and any residual meaning and legitimacy it might have retained.[1] Yet, as in many other cases, this sudden change and shift in perspective, although exhilarating, also gave rise to conflicting and, in some cases, quite misleading views. Soon after the collapse of communism in Central Europe during 1989, perspectives on the historical nature and implications of the transformation also began to change quite rapidly. The lifting of communist dictatorship was greeted, not surprisingly, with joy and satisfaction by most of those concerned and certainly by the great majority of Western observers. A swift passage to political democracy and free market economics – and then to levels of relative affluence markedly higher than those achieved during the communist period, if somewhat less elevated than those of Western Europe and the more advanced capitalist Western nations – was anticipated by many, particularly (though not exclusively) amongst the inhabitants of Central Europe themselves. An ill-defined, and often rather confused, idea of a 'return to Europe' summed up many of these expectations and provided something of a spurious historical basis for them.

Consequences of the integration of the former German Democratic Republic (GDR) with the Federal Republic (FRG), which followed union on 3 October 1990, though, gave a first indication of the dire consequences that full exposure to the direct force of the Western economies could have on the run-down and poorly equipped structures of production and distribution found in Central Europe. Further evidence of the rocky road to growth and economic recovery was soon provided by the radical programme of stabilization and market development put into operation in Poland, where inflation was indeed curbed and greater market stability achieved – but at considerable cost in terms of living standards and with disappointingly fewer signs of economic growth than anticipated.

The transition to political democracy in Central Europe also soon proved to be more difficult than expected, not least because of the onerous economic conditions just mentioned under which the process had to occur. Taxi-drivers and transport workers struck in Hungary and blockaded Budapest streets in October 1990, threatening the stability of the recently elected government, as an austerity programme was introduced and fuel prices were sharply raised. Support in Poland for the trade union and social movement 'Solidarity' plummeted as the government it had helped install led the economy into recession and many of its members into unemployment. In presidential elections held during November and December 1990, little more than a year after the establishment of a non-communist government, Tadeusz Mazowiecki, the first post-communist prime minister, lost ignominiously not just to Lech Wałęsa but also to Stanisław Tymiński, a little-known but politically ambitious émigré. Parliamentary elections a year later in October 1991 saw only a 43 per cent turnout and marked disenchantment on the part of electors, both with the political process and with many of the new institutions and parties struggling to become established in the wake of communist rule. A similar reluctance to vote and disillusion with political life could be seen in Hungary. Turnout (at 96 and 83 per cent) was high in the Czechoslovak elections of 1990 and 1992 and it appeared at the outset that Czechoslovakia would have a relatively unproblematic future in view of its developed and well-ordered society and extensive experience of democratic ways before World War II. However, the more general course of post-communist development in Czechoslovakia also proved to be quite stormy as prospects for harmonious relations between Czech and Slovak areas deteriorated and the survival of the unified state itself became threatened.

It soon became apparent that the demise of the communist system by no means meant its automatic replacement by liberal democracy, the development of smoothly functioning free market economies or an immediate transition to the orderly affluence of more advanced Western countries. History, despite the extensive publicity which had been given to views propounded in an article written in 1989 by US Department of State official Francis Fukuyama,[2] had not come to an end. The principles of liberal democracy (as was the case with those underlying processes which were supposed to lead to the creation of appropriate economic conditions for economic development), while embraced with considerable enthusiasm in Central Europe, did not prove so easy to realize as many had at first thought. One consequence of these developments was a strengthening of the historical perspective and refocusing of attention on the Central European past – though less on the period immediately preceding and more on the experiences of the 1930s and the pre-war period. The problems of sustaining democratic government in semi-developed societies still marked by traces of political dictatorship and authoritarian practices suddenly assumed greater relevance, as did the threat posed by entrenched backwardness, recession and prolonged economic stagnation.

Conditions in the 1990s could in no way be seen as identical to those of the 1930s – but growing recognition of economic difficulties and the emergence of social tensions which had, on previous occasions, proved to be incompatible with the maintenance of democratic institutions and processes prompted a resurgence of interest in the region's history. The renewal of ethnic tensions between Hungarians and Romanians, Czechs and Slovaks (and others concerning the place of Hungarians in Slovakia), and the strengthening of nationalist sentiments in Poland (including the ominous resurfacing of anti-semitic currents) were one element in this situation. In combination with the rapid onset of disillusion with the slow-moving procedures of a reborn parliamentary democracy these tendencies raised considerable disquiet. Further parallels with the pre-war record could be seen in the re-emergence of a highly fragmented, multi-party legislature following the 1991 general election in Poland, and the return of the populist-urbanist division characteristic of Hungarian political life before the Second World War.

Correspondingly less attention was initially paid to the communist period, as it was felt that this was a chapter of Central European history now emphatically closed. Apart from its unfortunate legacy in terms of rusty and inefficient production facilities and a threadbare social fabric, it was considered of limited relevance now that what people understood to be a 'return to normality' was possible and the way open to rejoin the mainstream of Western social development. It soon became evident, however, that the experiences of the communist period could not be neatly tidied away and relegated to the status of museum piece and that its influences, too, formed part of the reality of post-communist Central Europe. Firstly, the economic transformation of post-communist societies was proving to be a more complex and long-drawn out process than originally envisaged as it became evident that the monopolistic structures of the communist economy could neither be dismantled nor privatized with the speed some had initially thought possible. It became clear that many of the economic structures characteristic of the communist system with, inevitably, their attendant problems and social consequences, would be around for some years.

Nor was the political legacy of communist rule inconsiderable. The communist party in Czechoslovakia retained a significant presence and, although far behind Civic Forum, remained one of the major smaller parties in parliament after the free elections of June 1990. This reflected the experience of the pre-war republic where, in contrast to the other countries of Central Europe, the communist party remained legal and had achieved a steady level of electoral support. But even in Poland (of all places) the Union of the Democratic Left, a grouping composed of forces derived from the recently dissolved communist party, emerged as one of the largest parties in the freely elected parliament of 1991. This was partly a reflection of the high level of fragmentation of political forces and the organizational experience of the Union, but it also showed – apart from a certain (if limited) basis of continuing communist or post-communist political support – the level of disillusion caused by the austerity and material deprivation imposed on parts of Polish society during the process of economic transition. The appeal of earlier forms of collective material provision in terms of pensions and social benefits under such conditions was by no means negligible.

There were also more diffuse features of the legacy from the communist years. Alienation from the post-war political domination of society and the decades-long supremacy of 'the party' discouraged people from regular participation in political activity of any kind, and made them hesitant to embrace the very idea of a political party. The important role played by broad-based social movements like Civic Forum in Czechoslovakia and New Forum in East Germany, as well as Solidarity in Poland, reflected the value people placed on alternative forms of organization and social consensus, an objective that soon began to recede as the normal processes of political life and conflict over policy and its implementation began to surface. While such cultural tendencies were by no means just the product of the communist period, they had certainly been strengthened by it and the experience of party dictatorship that had been such a central feature of those years. The persistence of such tendencies served to reinforce the historical links between the communist period and the rather confused years that immediately followed it.

As historical links between the communist and post-communist periods in Central Europe have became more apparent as well as those with the pre-war years, so the question of evaluation and historical judgment has emerged as a more complex one. With the collapse of the communist system and subsequent revelations about the extent of the activity of security organs, the prevalence of corrupt practices among the elite and the thoroughgoing nature of its economic failure, wholesale rejection and condemnation of the communist years was only too easy. Yet, in view of the instabilities of post-communist transition and the general obstacles to constitutional government and economic development within Central Europe, it also became important to exercise caution in terms of appraising social outcomes and avoid any rush to historical judgment. As the problems of assuring economic development according to principles of economic liberalism emerged and signs of social breakdown and public disorder multiplied, so the benefits of collective solutions to common problems, planned conditions of large-scale socio-economic change, and the advantages of state continuity and processes maintaining public order – all areas in which the approach of communist decision-makers made at least some contribution – continued to merit consideration. A broader judgment on the post-war period and the part it played in the development of Central Europe will take some time to emerge. In this sense only the future, as E.H. Carr pointed out, can provide the key to interpretation of the past.[3]

While elements of historical continuity between the pre-war years and post-war Central Europe emerge as factors to complement the undoubtedly striking contrasts between the different periods, so judgments on the different periods need to be qualified not just by awareness of the relations and diverse linkages between them but also by reasonably comprehensive analysis of the region's history. It is to the understanding of one of the areas, the post-war history of Central Europe, that this book is designed to make a contribution. As a history of Central Europe since the ending of the Second World War in 1945 it primarily presents a narrative of developments during the post-war period and an account of the main features of the different phases the region passed through in those years. But in doing so, as well as recording the major events, the book also aims to provide some understanding of the nature of the particular course taken by developments in Central Europe and offer some basis for the analysis and evaluation of the outcomes reached.

THE HISTORICAL DEVELOPMENT OF CENTRAL EUROPE

In seeking to provide these insights the account presented here does, of course, impose its own structure on events and provide a particular foundation on which to develop the historical narrative. It begins, in Chapter two, with a consideration of the foundations of the post-war order in Central Europe. The lengthy social and cultural traditions of the region's peoples placed them at the centre of a series of major historical conflicts and fostered a sense of European identity (based on a common Roman Catholic faith and early ties with Western Europe) in the face of external threats and incursions like those of the Mongols and the Ottoman empire from the east. The post-war expansion of Soviet power in this area could hardly fail to draw on such memories and become associated with the legacy of earlier conflicts. But the location of Central Europe in terms of the ill-defined divide between West and East, one that moreover tended to shift during the course of history, was by no means fully clear and has been, indeed, the subject of considerable debate. Some have identified a fundamental division within Europe that links the fate of Poles, Hungarians, Slovaks, the inhabitants of the eastern areas of modern Germany and perhaps Czechs (whom others would see less ambiguously as a Western nation), as well as Russians, Ukrainians and the Balkan peoples, predominantly with the traditions of an Eastern Europe.

It was certainly relevant to their fate that the Central European nations did not develop the political form of the modern state that arose first in Western countries like England and France (it was only much later that one emerged even in Germany) and that they generally became members – mostly unwilling ones at that – of extensive multi-ethnic empires. The idea of Central Europe in anything more than a purely geographical sense thus sits uneasily with established notions of West and East, and with general conceptions of an historic Europe in relation to eastern and southern neighbours and, frequently, opponents. Hungarians and Poles, who saw themselves as outposts of European civilization in the face of an uncultured East, were themselves often viewed in similar terms by western neighbours, who were, moreover, often content to leave them subject to the rule of the eastern powers. The modern idea of a Central Europe was first expressed in more developed form with the rise of German power and the growth of a unified empire assembled under Prussian auspices, but this idea of

Mitteleuropa was rather different from that held by Czechs, Hungarians, Poles and Slovaks which is broadly the one which concerns us here. That later conception of Central Europe was one developed by peoples and, eventually, nations located between the greater powers and more extensive states of Germany and Russia. In this sense, the idea of Central Europe is one that is more political and cultural than geographic in origin. It is a region that does lie in the middle of Europe (if the easily traversable Ural mountains – whose peaks are little higher than those of the Scottish highlands – are taken to mark Europe's eastern border), but geographical form has not been its most important characteristic.

The notion of post-war Central Europe employed in this book is certainly a predominantly political one, proceeding from the westward expansion of Soviet power into Europe as a result of armed conflict and the settlement reached after the Second World War. Central Europe, in this sense, refers to the northern countries lying to the east of Western Europe and outside institutions like the North Atlantic Treaty Organization and the European Community founded during the post-1945 period. It is that part of Europe within the Soviet zone of post-war influence (or, more simply, subject to the dictates of Soviet power) which was not taken to form part of the Soviet Union itself. This book is concerned, then, with post-war developments in Czechoslovakia, Hungary and Poland – but also with those in the German Democratic Republic, or East Germany, which was severed from the parts of post-war Germany occupied by the Western powers and which for much of the post-war period mostly shared the fate of other countries dominated by the Soviet Union. After the unification of the two parts of the country in 1990 the former GDR simply became part of a larger Germany and its history rejoined that of the West, departing from the course taken by the other countries of Central Europe and not, therefore, forming part of the final section of this narrative. Following the events of 1989 and 1990, this Central Europe regained much of its former identity. With the collapse of communism in Central Europe and the dissolution of the Soviet Union soon after, in 1991, the countries of Central Europe moved closer to their former, pre-war status – nations with a distinctive identity and close relations with the west of Europe, but separate from neighbouring states like the Baltic republics, Finland, Belorussia, the Ukraine and the western portion of a still extensive Russia, which could reasonably be called Eastern Europe.

The fate of Central Europe between the two world wars had not, however, been a very happy one – although the fact of national independence was the basis for considerable nostalgia after 1945 as Soviet rule became established throughout the region. The rich ethnic mixture and number of contested borders threatened the stability of the newly established states from an early stage, although the resurgence of German power soon proved to be a greater danger. Its growing military power was enhanced by economic influence which, in a situation of world recession, the countries of Central Europe were in no position to resist – particularly as the Western powers offered little assistance in this respect. The German threat soon turned into outright aggression for Czechoslovakia and Poland (with Slovakia preserving an independent existence as a German puppet state), while Hungary strove to maintain a greater measure of autonomy before entering the war on the German side. But the overall situation changed with Germany's attack on the Soviet Union and, particularly, with the Soviet success at Stalingrad during the winter of 1942–43 in beginning to push back the German army and set Soviet forces on their long advance to the west.

The role of the Soviet Union in engaging German forces and, eventually, securing their defeat was responsible for the acquiescence of the Western powers at an early stage in Soviet aspirations and intentions in Central Europe – although the full extent of Soviet aims took some time to emerge. Britain, in particular, was also more concerned with its interests in the southern Balkans than in prospective developments to the north. The rigour with which the Soviets were determined to pursue their policy objectives and their insistence on imposing power structures commensurate with their interests in Central Europe was also not anticipated. But the consolidation of communist rule in Central Europe, at least in the carefully programmed Soviet form it eventually took, was not quite the inevitable process it later appeared. Its origins and outcome in terms of political and economic processes provide the subject-matter of Chapters three, four and five. Coalition governments, subject to varying degrees of Soviet influence and communist intimidation, were set up in the initial stage – but in most cases any claims to genuine political representation had become very thin by the beginning of 1947. The coalition phase lasted slightly longer in Czechoslovakia, where communist forces had stronger domestic roots, but this too was superseded by full communist control in 1948 as a result of communist intrigue and political misjudgments on the part of other

9

groups. But by this stage the outcome had already been largely decided by changes occurring both in the international sphere and in neighbouring countries.

Throughout 1948 the degree of communist control intensified and the qualified participation of selected non-communist forces in government was rapidly eliminated. The idea of the post-war Central European regimes as People's Democracies, an intermediate political form initially accepted by Soviet leader Joseph Stalin and subject to less rigorous communist control, soon lost its allure. Controls within the Soviet camp intensified and, by the end of 1948, Soviet control of Central Europe was virtually complete. But there was still a difference between communist rule and the predominance of Soviet power, on one hand, and the introduction of full Stalinism on the other. Intensified domestic repression and the imposition of direct Soviet rule followed somewhat later. The dictatorship of the single party was fully established and the exercise of power increasingly restricted to a small group of party leaders, Soviet representatives and security chiefs. Bureaucratic control and a complex network of institutional surveillance developed to keep social forces and all spontaneous social activity in check.

Party purges and show trials soon followed. As many as a quarter of party members fell victim to processes of intensified organizational control in Czechoslovakia, but the purges were also significant elsewhere. As this movement gained strength, the role of the security police was also enhanced – and this also helped increase the influence of Soviet agencies. The Stalinist period thus saw multiple channels of Soviet control over Central Europe: direct leadership links, the prominence of the role assigned to the Soviet ambassador, the proximity of the contacts maintained between organs of party control and their Soviet counterparts, and the direct (and often unacknowledged) penetration of the institutions of communist rule in Central Europe by Soviet counterparts. The exercise of Soviet power over the individual countries of the region was further facilitated by the effort made to maintain the isolation of the People's Democracies from one another. But the changes that reflected the onset of Stalinism in Central Europe were far from being restricted to areas of political control.

Planned economic growth, socialist industrialization and the priority development of heavy industry were also major elements of the Soviet model applied in Central Europe. International factors played a significant role in this. The rate of capital accumulation, already high in comparison with the immediate post-war years, was further raised under the pressure of the Cold War and the influence of the outbreak of hostilities in Korea. These developments had a decidedly negative effect on living standards, although the worst consequences were mitigated following the death of Soviet leader Joseph Stalin on 5 March 1953. But even under the rigorous economic conditions of crash industrialization, the lot of individuals and their families was often improved by the high rates of occupational mobility and the opportunities for social advancement these opened up. Industrial development, if not always planned in the best way, nevertheless had a marked influence on living conditions and basic indices like levels of food consumption showed a clear improvement throughout Central Europe during the late 1950s and early 1960s.

REFORM IMPERATIVES AND COMMUNIST RESISTANCE

The socio-economic effects of rapid industrialization could not be sustained and the rate of increase in Gross National Product began to decline in the second half of the 1950s, a process that continued during the 1960s. A fundamental barrier to sustainable growth was the rapid industrialization model derived from the pre-war experience of the Soviet Union (where it had had greater applicability), which was not well suited to the development needs of Central Europe. Some areas, like East Germany and parts of Czechoslovakia, were already far more advanced economically than had been the case during the equivalent phase of communist rule in the Soviet Union, and they received little benefit from the crude methods of economic administration transplanted from there. Plans for and processes of economic reform thus became a major preoccupation of government decision-makers during the years that followed Stalin's death. Continuing emphasis on the principle of centralization, however, closely associated with the foundations of communist rule and the operation of the political system, persistently undercut reform initiatives.

The acceleration of economic processes had, not surprisingly, a major impact on the fabric of Central European society and its structure in terms of the situation of major social groups. These changes are examined in Chapter six. An important feature was the

11

reduction in the proportion of the work-force employed in agriculture and the shrinking social role of the peasantry, previously the most numerous group in the underdeveloped areas of the east of Europe. This had repercussions for the conditions of life experienced by the urban population, particularly in terms of the social and material environment and matters like housing provision, which became a major problem throughout Central Europe. The emergence of a significant group of 'peasant workers' was both a response and partial solution to this problem. In this sense, as well as others, communist rule produced its own sources of equality and inequality within society. The emergence of a well-documented 'new class' was one consequence of this, although the implementation of some policies of economic reform also began to produce further signs of inequality.

Accompanying the features of economic and social change which followed the death of Stalin were certain elements of political relaxation. These dimensions are explored in Chapters seven and eight. By way of immediate response, the role of the secret police was reduced, the pace of forced economic change reined back and the weight of Soviet influence diminished. Problems of economic adjustment soon entered into the situation also. Monetary reform in Czechoslovakia led to riots in Pilsen in June 1953 and more extensive demonstrations broke out two weeks later in East Berlin, which spread throughout the whole of the German Democratic Republic. These outbreaks were soon contained, while the potential for more serious conflicts gradually developed in Hungary and Poland. Polish developments were relatively restrained, although violent demonstrations were staged in Poznań during June 1956. Prolonged conflict within the the Hungarian leadership, however, culminated in a major crisis during 1956 and resulted in decisive Soviet intervention, following which all thoughts expressed earlier about the neutrality of the Hungarian state and the establishment of a multi-party system were expunged.

The Soviet invasion of Hungary and defeat of the revolution that had broken out there marked the end of the first stage of post-Stalinist change in Central Europe and set limits on the degree of reform that might be tolerated by the Soviet leadership. Overall communist rule and the maintenance of a decisive Soviet influence were clearly to remain as the major conditions of further development, although they also acted as a brake on other aspects of social and economic change. The process of restoring communist power in Hungary lasted for some years before a policy of reconciliation and a mood of openness to reform emerged during the 1960s. The apparent liberalism and sensitivity to national sentiments initially detected in Poland soon disappeared there, too, as Władysław Gomułka conformed to orthodox Soviet lines and committed himself to the maintenance of a Soviet-style system. Post-Stalin changes in Czechoslovakia were slower to make themselves evident and those that did emerge were carefully managed by the party leadership to avoid affronting Soviet sensibilities. But this effort, too, ultimately proved to be unsuccessful and a further Soviet invasion of the region was mounted in 1968, though without the extensive hostilities and bloodshed that had been seen twelve years earlier in Hungary.

The limits on change in Central Europe thus proved to be quite tight – indeed, considerably more so than even the relatively cautious Czechoslovak leadership had judged to be the case in 1968. The maintenance of strict Soviet control, however, provided no solution to persisting social tensions and the signs of opposition that continued to emerge. Following the outbreak of opposition in East Germany during 1953, affairs there had been kept under tight control. But the economic situation continued to deteriorate and in August 1961 the Berlin Wall was erected to prevent the continuing departure of skilled refugees. Despite its uncivilized effects, this act was followed by the revival of the GDR's economic fortunes and a period of relative affluence during the rest of the 1960s. Later, however, Party leader Walter Ulbricht fell foul of the Soviet Union's changing policy towards the Federal Republic of Germany and was replaced in 1971. Leadership change also took place in Poland in late 1970, as Gomułka's hold over power weakened and renewed worker opposition broke out over price rises and preparations for further economic reform.

The record of leadership stability was not so grim in other countries of Central Europe, though. In Hungary, after the inauspicious beginnings of János Kádár's career as leader in 1956, his position was consolidated and he proved strong enough to introduce both a more conciliatory political approach in the early 1960s and the economic reforms encapsulated in the New Economic Mechanism (NEM) of 1968. But this strategy, too, eventually ran out of steam and Kádár was ignominiously ditched by his party colleagues in 1988. In Czechozslovakia, the 'normalization' policy applied after 1968, however unpalatable in political and moral terms, also assured a lengthy period of political stability and some success in terms of economic growth. As part of a common pattern, though, the differing strategies employed to preserve basic principles of communist rule all eventually petered out and each of the policies finally ran into the buffers. There was throughout communist Central Europe a fundamental problem of system reproduction in terms of social development, economic growth and political stability that was never fully addressed and which seemed to be largely insoluble within the parameters of the post-war system.

The economic and political situation was most critical in Poland where Edward Gierek, Gomułka's successor, sought to bolster living standards and sustain growth by using extensive foreign credits. Apparently successful for a period at the beginning of the 1970s, the strategy soon showed its limitations and the Polish economy ran into severe difficulties both domestically and in terms of its international situation well before the end of the decade. Political conditions also began to change, while the public mood was transformed with the election of Cardinal Karol Wojtyła of Cracow as Pope and his triumphant visit in that capacity to Poland during 1979. Further economic difficulties in 1980 and attempts to raise food prices were followed by a series of strikes and the eventual formation of the free trade union, Solidarity, in Gdańsk by Lech Wałęsa. Although an agreement was signed with the party-state leadership, relations between Solidarity and the political authorities remained difficult and in December 1981, several weeks after the accession of General Wojciech Jaruzelski to the party leadership, a 'state of war' was declared under which the free trade union and the activities of many other organizations were suspended and martial law imposed as a means of assuring political stability.

But, even though the free fall of the Polish economy was halted and a surface calm imposed on public life, the conditions for effective development and national recovery were not in place. Following increasing signs from the Kremlin that new possibilities of change had opened up, a more radical view of reform possibilities emerged. Measures were taken to re-establish Solidarity as a legal entity and permit elements of free choice in the parliamentary elections of 1989. The dramatic success of Solidarity-sponsored candidates in the seats they were able to contest – the level of support coming as something of a shock even to Solidarity activists themselves – changed the face of Central Europe in no uncertain way. Although Solidarity candidates only gained a minority of seats in the parliament, the nominated communist prime minister found it impossible to form a government that would gain the approval of the legislative chamber and it fell to Tadeusz Mazowiecki, respected journalist, committed Catholic and Solidarity activist, to form the first non-communist led government in Central Europe since the 1940s. Developments in Hungary were not far behind and, once Kádár was eased from office in 1988, the process of reform and increasing disengagement from the Soviet model gained considerable impetus there also. The Hungarian Socialist Workers' (communist) Party (HSWP) dissolved itself in October 1989, before its Polish counterpart, and Hungarians, too, showed themselves unwilling to tolerate any delay in moving away from their subjection to communist rule.

REGIONAL BASES OF COMMUNIST POWER

The account of developments in post-war Central Europe that follows will, then, be largely narrative and sequential in the early chapters. It aims to present a fairly straightforward historical account. Following this introduction and general survey, the broad contours of the region's history are sketched out and the foundations of the post-war order delineated. The mechanics of the communist assumption of political power and the transformation of the countries of Central Europe into People's Democracies are outlined. Descriptions of the progressive Stalinization of political life and the imposition of a rigorously organized communist political system follow. The account of socialist industrialization and processes of economic development, however, outlines not just the policies adopted with the installation of a Stalinist political system but also the outcome of the system of economic development and administration established. This is followed by a general survey of the processes of social change that accompanied these political and economic innovations and were largely engendered by them.

The following chapters focus on the institutions of political, military and economic power that held sway over the countries of Central Europe and the societies that had developed under the agencies of communist rule. The course of political development during the post-Stalin period is examined first and the nature of the restrictions involved in continuing communist party control outlined. Subsequently, in Chapters nine and ten, the structures of military and economic integration and control that went with the exercise of communist political authority are examined. Political, military and economic agencies of communist rule were all part of the institutional complex of Soviet-sponsored domination that took hold in Central Europe after the Second World War. The fact of post-war Soviet control over Central Europe is an obvious one and does not take much effort to establish. But to understand the way in which Soviet power was exercised and the role of the regional institutions with which it was associated requires a little more analysis.

For example, while the role of Soviet armed forces in maintaining communist rule in Central Europe was clear in general terms, the precise way in which military power was exercised was much less so. The main organ of communist military integration, the Warsaw Pact (or Warsaw Treaty Organization), only came into being in May 1955 – well after the period when Soviet military power had shown itself to be decisive in determining the fate of the Central European nations. Care was nevertheless later taken to indicate its role in the largely Soviet-mounted invasion of Czechoslovakia in 1968. Warsaw Pact exercises and the leading personnel of the organization also played a prominent role in the Polish crisis of 1980–81. The nature of the Pact's activity in underpinning communist power was, therefore, evident but the details of its role somewhat unclear. In many ways it seemed that the Warsaw Pact was concerned more with matters of regional political organization than with affairs of military integration – and that its effect was to separate the leaders of the Central European countries from the armed forces they formally controlled rather than to consolidate any form of concerted joint action.

The regional economic framework in which the Central European countries were located, the Council for Mutual Economic Assistance (COMECON), was also somewhat ambiguous in its character and consequences. While formally a supranational body and an agency of international organization, it in fact tended to enhance national economic isolation, maintain rather outdated forms of autarchic economic organization and help support unproductive patterns of trade. The early years of the organization (which coincided with the years of accelerated socialist industrialization) were marked more by passivity than by any signs of economic activity. After the death of Stalin and the accession of Nikita Khrushchev to power in the Soviet Union, steps were taken to co-ordinate national economic plans, enhance processes of production specialization and expand the volume of trade between COMECON countries. The practical consequences of these actions were, however, limited and Soviet leader Leonid Brezhnev launched a further integration programme in 1971. While largely un-successful in achieving this objective, economic links within COMECON nevertheless remained much more significant for member states than those with countries outside the communist network. For much of the post-Stalin period this connection was by no means disadvantageous for Central Europe, although from the second half of the 1970s the terms of trade increasingly came to favour the Soviet Union.

COMMUNISM AND AFTER

The later years of communist rule were characterized by increasing obstacles to stability and effective political development throughout Central Europe, problems arising in the pursuit of economic growth and balanced budgets and the heightened role of military power in maintaining Soviet control of the region. But, even as attempts to broaden the base of political support were made, communist rule crumbled with startling rapidity at the end of the 1980s. Military support was required to sustain the position in Poland in 1981, but this did not prove to be very effective and an accommodation with opposition forces was entered into at the first available opportunity in an effort to stabilize the situation. In Hungary Kádár's introduction of some elements productive of political stability and a more advanced mode of economic development associated with the New Economic Mechanism also proved to be unsuccessful in terms of the attempt to preserve the communist system. The existing order thus collapsed as rapidly in Hungary as it did in Poland.

The situation in Czechoslovakia and East Germany was rather different. Czechoslovakia, effectively 'normalized' since 1968, had begun the communist period at a high level of economic development and provided its population with a relatively high level of affluence and acceptable living standards for a number of years. The GDR also assured reasonably high living standards for its population, although special relations with the Federal Republic and the European Community (EC) were crucial here. But even in these countries matters had by no means progressed satisfactorily and currents of opposition, if relatively restrained, were developing beneath a politically controlled surface. The visit of Soviet leader Mikhail Gorbachev to East Germany in October 1989 and his obvious dissatisfaction with Erich Honecker made an important contribution to the process, while the growing propensity of the Czechoslovak population to demonstrate its feelings and organize meetings of opposition to the authorities was a further sign of waning communist power in the area.

A number of tendencies, outlined in Chapter eleven, thus came together in the second half of 1989. The Polish situation had produced a series of political and economic problems which proved to be virtually insoluble within the structures of the communist system. Hungary, despite its more thoroughgoing economic reforms and policy of relative political liberalism, also ended up with a situation of major leadership conflict and disillusion with the established party chief which was compounded by growing economic problems. Poland and Hungary therefore led the way to the demise of communism in Central Europe. But the other countries were not far behind. Erich Honecker was given a firm push towards political change by Gorbachev during his visit to the GDR made, ironically, to celebrate the fortieth anniversary of the founding of the German communist state. As part of the process of accelerating political change, Honecker was rapidly eased out of the leadership and, a matter of greater significance, the Berlin Wall itself breached on 9 November 1989. Little more than a week afterwards, demonstrations in Czechoslovakia gained mass proportions and pressure on the communist leadership mounted, forcing it to reform and then quietly relinquish positions of authority. By such measures, the communist period finally came to an end in Central Europe.

But while the removal of communist power now seemed assured, the region's future remained an uncertain one. The ending of communist rule, as noted at the beginning of this introductory survey, by no means guaranteed the establishment of political democracy or the opening of a smooth path to economic development and the operation of a free market economy. The pre-war and post-war experience of the individual countries continues to exert an influence on later developments, making its own contribution to the formation of a post-communist Central Europe and illuminating contemporary processes of change there. The history of Central Europe, like that of any other part of the world, cannot be neatly separated into discrete segments. While many inhabitants of the region were initially more inclined to distance themselves from the communist years and hasten post-communist development, they will certainly not be able to escape the continuing effects of the lengthy period of Soviet-imposed rule.

At the time of writing, this process is relatively little advanced, and in Chapter twelve of this book only the major changes can be indicated and some factors sketched out which bear on the direction of change. They include the nature and sequence of the developments that were associated with the end of communism in the different countries. In political terms this points particularly to the role of social movements like Solidarity in Poland and Civic Forum in Czechoslovakia in the process of transition. They, to varying degrees, played a part in mobilizing opposition to the communist system, its leaders and institutions, and provided much of the organizational framework during the immediate post-communist period. The unity first of Solidarity and then of Civic Forum soon disappeared however, once the original enemy was eliminated. Conflicts over the pace and nature of post-communist development surfaced – as well as all-too-normal signs of frustration and personal anatagonism between political leaders.

These factors, along with cultural inheritances and more diffuse consequences of communist rule, have not always helped the process of democratic transition. Leaving aside East Germany, which formed part of a unified German nation less than a year after the opening of the Berlin Wall, all the countries of the region experienced significant problems in the development and operation of democratic processes and structures. Historic problems concerning the relations between Czechs and Slovaks re-emerged with a new intensity and, by 1993, had brought into existence two separate, independent states to succeed the unified post-communist republic. The electoral process and path of parliamentary development ran a somewhat smoother course in Hungary, where careful attention had been paid to areas in which problems emerged more urgently elsewhere. In Hungary, too, though, there were signs of political crisis like those surrounding the taxi-drivers' strike in 1990, symptoms of authoritarian populism and suggestions that, by attempting to avoid some of the disruptive consequences of the radical economic policy pursued in Poland, the government was tending to hang back from taking any major decisions in this area at all.

The problems of political transition and economic transformation have, therefore, been tightly linked – and it is by no means clear how or even whether the tensions between the processes can be overcome. The end of communist dictatorship and the onset of liberal democracy were associated with the resurrection of free market forces and the promise of eventual economic success. An initial paradox, however, was that the early stages of economic transformation meant more social dislocation and a further reduction in living standards. This had immediate implications for the problematic process of early democratic transition – whose major requirement was more, not less, social and economic stability. In both economic and political terms, then, the problems of Central Europe by no means disappeared with the elimination of communist rule. Global and international pressures were also highly significant and exercised further constraints on national development. For the first time in the post-war period, however, the countries of Central Europe were able to confront national and regional problems on their own terms and did not have to cope also with the direct interference in their affairs of their more powerful neighbour to the east.

NOTES AND REFERENCES

1. Malia, 'To the Stalin mausoleum', p. 322.
2. Fukuyama, 'The end of history?'
3. Carr, *What Is History?*, p. 123.

CHAPTER TWO

Foundations of the Post-war Order in Central Europe

CENTRAL EUROPE: HISTORICAL BACKGROUND AND MEANING

In contrast to the thirty years that followed the outbreak of the war in 1914, Central Europe after the Second World War experienced almost half a century of stability. The earlier period began with the collapse of several empires and saw the establishment of new states and their slide (in several cases) into authoritarianism or worse, the accompanying rise of the Nazi dictatorship and the bloody aftermath of its attack on Stalin's Russia, and finally the sweeping back of a victorious Soviet army. Post-1945 Central Europe was characterized by stable borders and the continuity of its political regimes. This all changed, of course, with the collapse of communism in 1989 – but the speed and radical nature of that change was at least in part itself a consequence of the decades of stability. It was not a half-century of tranquillity or peaceful evolution, however. The imposition of the political regime, strategies of accelerated heavy industrial development and rigidly centralized processes of economic administration developed in Stalin's Russia did not suit the more sophisticated societies and developed economies of the Central European countries.

Czechoslovakia, East Germany, Hungary and Poland all saw the rise of opposition or popular revolts against the regime imposed during the Stalin years and the modified systems that developed after the death of the Soviet dictator. The outbreaks of opposition that occurred soon after the death of Joseph Stalin on 5 March 1953 were followed by related developments in 1956, 1968, 1970, 1976 and 1980. The Hungarian revolution of 1956 and its bloody

21

suppression by the Soviet army was the most dramatic case of national revolt and constituted the most fundamental onslaught on structures of communist power. But that challenge was swiftly repulsed and the essentials of the regime gradually restored. In contrast to the thirty years between the outbreak of war in 1914 and the arrival of the liberating Soviet army in 1944, the years after the Second World War saw (at least until the major step of German unification) permanent state frontiers and, for a lengthy period, relatively unchanging political, economic and social structures. Indeed, in the eyes of the great majority of those who lived under them, these systems were characterized by an excessive degree of stability.

This stability was the consequence of the rise of Soviet power and its extension into the European heartland. The years between 1914 and 1944/45 may well be compared with the Thirty Years' War of the seventeenth century which ended with the Treaty of Westphalia in 1648. More than one historian has described the events that unfolded in the region between 1914 and 1945 as an extended European civil war. The treaty that ended the Thirty Years' War is linked with twentieth-century developments in another way, as it laid the foundations for the development in Europe of a political order that lasted for nearly three centuries. It established the basis of the modern European state system that was to persist, in its essential characteristics, until the formation of the German Empire and the outbreak of the First World War. As the rise of German power made a fundamental contribution to the ending of that system and the turmoil in Europe during the first half of the twentieth century, so the rise of Soviet power and its extension to the west brought a new kind of stability to Central Europe. It was one based on the relations that developed between the superpowers and was, from an early stage, associated with the conflicts of the Cold War. It was a stability sustained by broadly non-European or semi-European forces and one that by no means fully suited the traditions of the Central Europe or the inclinations of its peoples. Their ideas and traditions, however, were far from extinguished and they survived the long years of unwanted Soviet dominance.

The cultural and political traditions of Central Europe are lengthy ones and reach back to the middle ages. While the modern nation-states of Central Europe were established after the demise of the multi-ethnic empires of Austria-Hungary and Romanov Russia, the roots of the contemporary political formations generally ran far deeper. For example, Czechoslovakia as a modern state, was a unit formed from fragments of the former Austrian empire. Although the union between Czechs and Slovaks was indeed a novelty in terms of the particular political relationship that was established, the former group at least could look back to the Kingdom of Bohemia and Moravia whose capital of Prague in the fourteenth century was one of the leading cultural, political and scientific centres in Europe at that time. While the partitions of the late eighteenth century had put an end to Poland as an independent state, its history is conventionally traced back to the end of the first millenium. An ancient Hungarian state had also been eliminated in the sixteenth century following defeat by the Ottoman Turks and occupation of much its former territory. Hungary only regained a measure of autonomy within the Habsburg Austrian empire in 1867. Compared with these established state traditions, the part of Germany included in this historical survey had a far shorter record in terms of shared experience within the German Empire formed under Prussian leadership in the nineteenth century. Nevertheless, its social and cultural antecedents extend back considerably further and also draw on the currents of mainstream European history. The states of Central Europe had extensive historical roots, and the reaffirmation of their values and resurgence of some of their traditions within the Soviet empire confronted leaders in the Kremlin with the challenge of specifically European conceptions and aspirations.

The lands of Central Europe have therefore been associated with long-established regional traditions and with the shifting pressure of forces from both east and west. The dominant influence after 1945 was, of course, that of the Soviet East – although this had been foreshadowed by that of the Ottomans and Mongol Tatars, the Magyars and by the migrations of the Slavic peoples themselves. This eastern influence was countered and qualified by others deriving from the increasingly dynamic civilizations of western Europe, in particular the German peoples who established settlements throughout Central and Eastern Europe. The dominant religious influence was that of the Catholic Church, with its seat in Rome and association with the authority of the Holy Roman Emperor. The spread of these influences and their admixture was encouraged by geographical factors. The North European Plain dominates the north of the region and runs along the Baltic coast. It provides easy access through Germany to the Russian lands, as well as facilitating movement from the other direction. This has been reflected in the name given to the inhabitants of the lands that lie between these two powers – 'Poles', meaning 'the people of the field' in early Slavonic form.

The flatness of the country enhanced the importance of waterways as significant features of the landscape, and they also form some of the region's natural borders. The western border of the Polish Republic thus rests to the north on the River Oder and continues directly south along the Neisse (or in Polish the Nysa Łużycka; the Nysa Kłodzka, which flows into the Oder further to the east, was reported to have been initially confused with it by leading figures within the Western alliance during war-time negotiations. This error may have given the Soviet leadership a misleading impression of Western views on the nature of post-war Poland.) The River Elbe also functioned as a border, a stretch of it dividing East Germany from the Federal Republic. (It had been the meeting point of the Soviet and Western armies in 1945, although the latter subsequently withdrew to the west along agreed demarcation lines for the zones of post-war occupation.) The western frontier of the former GDR followed the Elbe only for a short distance before continuing south to meet the Weser. After German unification on 3 October 1990, that border ceased to have any international significance and now reflects only an administrative division within the enlarged German state.

The region's highlands also act as national borders. The division between Poland and Czechoslovakia runs along the Carpathian and, to the west of them, the Sudeten mountains – whose earlier inhabitants of German origin played an important part in the developments leading up to the German dismemberment of Czechoslovakia following the Munich agreement of 1938. Beyond the mountains is the broad plain through which the River Danube flows. The higher reaches of the river lie to the south of the Czech lands; it touches on Slovakia at Bratislava, and forms the Slovak-Hungarian border for a stretch before turning south towards Budapest. Beyond the Hungarian capital, the plain extends southwards until it encounters the highlands of Slovenia and the former Yugoslavia. To the east, it continues until interrupted in Romania by the Transylvanian Alps.

The geography of Central Europe has been associated with the openness of the region to movements of population and the effects of demographic pressure. The early arrival from the east of Germanic peoples and Asian migrations dispersed the Slavs and forced them north, south and west from their original locations. Successive migrations (the Magyars arriving relatively late, occupying the lands of Hungary in the ninth century) brought further conflict and encouraged tribal interchange. This contributed to the ethnic diversity that came to characterize the region and laid the basis for the extensive multi-ethnic empires that were formed in the early modern period. Later incursions found the Central European peoples more resistant to further occupation of their territory: it was only the eastern Slavs who succumbed to the Mongol invasions of the thirteenth century and became isolated from the major European developments taking place to the west, a factor whose continuing influence even modern Russia was unable to escape. Southern Slavs fell under the control of the Ottoman empire, as did much of the Kingdom of Hungary, although the Turkish invasions were halted outside Vienna. Later rulers played a more active role with respect to some ethnic groups. Jews were offered the protection of the Polish crown in expectation of the benefits to be gained from their economic and commercial services; Germans were offered settlements in south Russia and the Ukraine by Catherine the Great, with a particular view to assisting agricultural development. Commercial and economic benefits also underlay the spontaneous movement of German settlers through many areas of Eastern Europe. Others groups were less welcome, had fewer resources, or simply arrived too late – like the gypsies, who entered Europe in the fourteenth century but nevertheless succeeded in preserving their community and maintaining a social existence into the twentieth century.

Central Europe thus developed as a region of considerable ethnic variety and has, throughout much of its recorded history, been the arena of extensive cultural competition and territorial conflict. Different groups have exerted greater strength and influence at different times; alternative solutions to the problems of ethnic, social and cultural diversity have been tried through the centuries – and have met with varying degrees of success. Throughout much of Central and Eastern Europe the multi-ethnic empire held sway until the early years of the twentieth century. The subsequent effort to nurture the nation-state in Central Europe between 1918 and 1939 met with little success, while the German attempt to combine principles of empire and nation produced a far worse disaster. After 1945 the situation was in one sense simplified with the displacement of entire national minorities and large-scale population movement, which in at least some cases created conditions of unprecedented national uniformity in terms of ethnic composition. Nevertheless, the potential for national tension and ethnic conflict within Central Europe was by no means eradicated.

Beginning in 1945, the Soviet Union effectively reimposed an imperial framework on Central Europe, albeit one articulated through the rhetoric of Marxism-Leninism. This pattern, too, eventually came apart under the pressure of the contradictions that lay within it. While the threat of foreign incursions and external military forces may now have passed, and much of the force has been taken out of internal ethnic tensions, Central Europe has remained an arena of social and political conflict and maintained many of its cultural traditions. The creation by the Soviet Union of an empire in Central Europe, whose structure was sustained by the political, military, and economic mechanisms it had developed, served to reinforce earlier fears and anxieties about the influence of aggressive forces from the east. Having survived and defeated the Nazis – modern barbarians emanating from the heart of Europe itself – Central Europeans also recalled their role as defenders of European civilization and the stand taken at various times against eastern antagonists and invaders during earlier periods of their history. Such occasions ranged from the Mongols and defeat of Turkish forces outside Vienna in 1683 to the 'miracle on the Vistula' which preserved Poland – and perhaps the rest of Central Europe – from the Red Army in August 1920. The Polish writer Aleksander Wat, himself a prominent communist during the 1930s, wrote that he regarded such opposition of Europe to Asia 'merely empty anti-Soviet propaganda, a nineteenth-century issue'. But when he encountered Soviet troops in Lwow after the invasion of Poland in 1939 'there it was – pure Asia'.[1] The ties that bind Central Europe with the West and strengthen the contrast with eastern neighbours received greater emphasis with the decline and eventual collapse of communism and are frequently those which receive emphasis today.

Others, taking an equally broad historical perspective, have directed attention to divisions that run through the centre of Europe itself and suggest the existence of major ambiguities in the character of Central Europe and the people who live there. The western border of the Soviet zone of occupation in Germany in 1945 lay very close to the line which separated Charlemagne's empire of early European Christendom from the Slav 'barbarians' in AD 814, a fact that some saw as having particular significance in the context of post-Second World War developments. As this Catholic/feudal society developed it monopolized the very idea of Europe although between the eleventh and thirteenth centuries, the frontier of this 'Western Europe', shifted to the east to take in groups more recently converted to Christianity, including the inhabitants of the lower Danube, the eastern Carpathians and the forest area separating Poles from Russians.[2] This cultural frontier is one that contemporary Central Europeans are often prone to emphasize. In socio-economic terms another, more recent but still long-established, division can be detected which shifts the major fracture to a line running from the Elbe down to the Mediterranean at Trieste. This is 'perhaps the most fundamental frontier in European history' and is one which divides areas where serfdom disappeared in the fifteenth and sixteenth centuries from those in which it was introduced during the later period or survived until the nineteenth.[3]

None of these ancient cultural and socio-economic distinctions could be regarded as invalid in the twentieth century and even the oldest, relating to the eastern borders of Christendom, retained considerable significance for a Central Europe bordering the Soviet Union which proclaimed atheistic adherence to Marxism-Leninism. Early ideas focused on the distinction between eastern and western Europe – or Europe proper and the land and peoples beyond. More recent conceptions of Central Europe overlaid this with the concerns and realities of subsequent European history. The growing strength of Germanic power in the centre of the continent came to exert a major influence in the nineteenth century and gave the idea of Central Europe a particularly Germanic connotation.[4] Since this had emerged more recently than the Russian regional presence it was in distinction to the German conception of *Mitteleuropa* that a contrasting modern conception of Central Europe was developed. Its development was associated with the establishment of the new nation-states after the First World War, and the Central Europeans in question were the subjects of the independent states sandwiched between the major regional powers of Germany and the Soviet Union.[5] In the north of this area were thus located Poles, Czechs, Slovaks and Hungarians.

Just as the borders of western and eastern Europe – and, indeed, the location of 'Europe' itself – have changed over the centuries, so it seems reasonable here to reformulate the idea of Central Europe in terms of contemporary and recent historical experience and to take particular account of the particular conditions of post-Second World War Europe. Thus we shall understand the borders of contemporary Central Europe in terms of the post-1945 European settlement and the fundamental division drawn across Europe by the Cold War. If Germany has been the hinge in the modern

European structure,[6] post-war Central Europe can be regarded as that major portion which was broken off but contrived not to be built into the Soviet edifice. It will be treated here as the area whose western frontier for most of the post-war period was the Federal Republic of Germany and which was bordered in the east by the Soviet Union. This is a conception that accords with the political realities and socio-economic experience of the now lengthy post-1945 period.

INTERWAR DEVELOPMENTS AND THE ONSET OF HOSTILITIES

As this brief survey might suggest, the meaning and most appropriate conception of any modern Central Europe has not been an easy one to pin down. The concept has been a highly mobile one and, as has been observed, 'Central/eastern Europe is no place for the tidy-minded'.[7] Following the collapse of the multi-ethnic empires at the close of the First World War, the interwar experiment which attempted to give concrete political form to a contemporary conception of Central Europe and saw the establishment of a number of nation-states in the region also proved to be largely unsatisfactory. While nationality had acquired considerable legitimacy and mass popularity as a major principle of political life by the beginning of the twentieth century, successful application of the principle as a basis for political order proved to be enormously difficult. Nationalism had certainly been a major factor in the conditions that led to the outbreak of the First World War and this was recognized with great clarity by many of the relevant policy-makers at the time. The post-war attempt to create political structures that would satisfy nationalist sentiments and aspirations, promoted with particular enthusiasm by US President Woodrow Wilson, however, produced conditions hardly less destabilizing than those that had characterized the pre-1914 period. One problem was the sheer diversity of nationalities and number of ethnic groupings in Central and Eastern Europe. While Eastern Europe, in the sense of the lands lying to the east of the predominantly German- and Italian-speaking areas, had roughly the same area as the western portion, it contained three times as many different nationalities.[8]

A second complicating factor was the dispersal of national groups throughout large areas and the rich ethnic mixtures that were found in many parts of Central Europe. This made a particular contribution to the problems of state-formation and consolidation after the First World War and was clearly apparent in the ethnic composition of the new states (see Table 2.1). Some rulers had made specific invitations of settlement to non-indigenous nationalities, such as the Russian ruler Catherine the Great with German settlers and the Polish monarch with Jews. Spontaneous migration, and the effects of successive waves of immigration from the east (compounded by a long-established German tendency to settle attractive or sparsely populated areas in the east), was also a major factor, though, and produced multiple layers of settlement and many small ethnic enclaves within broader national areas.

Table 2.1 Population by ethnicity in terms of language (groups comprising more than 1 per cent of population), 1930/31

Ethnic group	Population	Percentage of population
Czechoslovakia		
Czechoslovak	9,688,770	66.9
German	3,231,688	22.3
Magyar	691,923	4.8
Ruthenian/Ukrainian	549,169	3.8
Hebrew and Yiddish	186,642	1.3
Hungary		
Magyar	8,001,112	92.1
German	478,630	5.5
Slovak	104,819	1.2
Poland		
Polish	21,993,444	68.9
Ukrainian	3,221,975	10.1
Yiddish	2,489,084	7.8
Ruthenian	1,219,647	3.8
Belorussia	989,852	3.1
German	740,992	2.3

Source Rothschild, *East Central Europe*, pp. 36, 89, 192

This was reflected in the different view taken of the same area by different nations and governments – none of which could necessarily be described as wrong (although the territorial claims made on their basis were often highly exaggerated). The Soviet occupation of Eastern Poland in September 1939 is thus described by Nikita Khrushchev in his memoirs as the recuperation of lost Ukrainian territory (and that of Western Belorussia). The areas disputed by Poland and the Ukraine were, indeed, ethnically quite ambiguous. Polish nobles and landlords had ruled for a lengthy period over Ukrainian and Belorussian peasants, for example, while essentially Polish towns like Lwów (or Lviv) were set in a surrounding Ukrainian countryside. But it was, according to Khrushchev, 'an artificial majority. Ukrainians were barred from jobs in the cities; they weren't even given roadwork. This discrimination had been practised as a matter of policy to make sure that Poles dominated the cities.' In this view, the Soviet Union 'gained practically nothing except what we were legally entitled to'.[9] The problems of drawing ethnic frontiers were demonstrated as much by the post-Munich solution applied by Germany in Czechoslovakia as by the problems of the 1918–39 period that led up to the Czechoslovak crisis and provided Hitler with a pretext for annexation. Even when Hitler was in a position to pursue the principle of 'ethnic justice' there, around half-a-million Germans and Magyars remained in the rump Czechoslovak state while more than a million Czechs and Slovaks were transferred to foreign rule.[10] There were no neat borders to be drawn that would have satisfied national claims to exclusive territories in pre-war Central Europe.

A third problem was the dissatisfaction engendered by the treaties signed after the First World War at Versailles, Riga and Trianon, and the vehement desire of many national groups to secure revision of the post-war settlement. This was, naturally enough, felt most strongly by the defeated nations. East Prussia, for example, was separated from the bulk of the German state by the corridor which gave the new Polish state access to the Baltic sea at the Free City of Danzig (now Gdańsk). Areas of Silesia, valuable for their deposits of coal, were disputed by Poland and Germany, the matter eventually being put to a plebiscite conducted by the League of Nations, whose outcome the Poles nevertheless refused to recognize and which was therefore followed by partition. Hungary, as part of the defeated Austro-Hungarian empire which had been in alliance with Germany, emerged from the post-war settlement stripped of much of its territory. Two-thirds of its former lands and 60 per cent of its former population were taken from it, most passing to Czechoslovakia, Romania and Yugoslavia. In 1920 around 30 per cent even of ethnic Hungarians (Magyars) lived outside the post-war state. Russia had, of course, been one of the Entente powers of the victorious alliance in 1914 but had collapsed in revolution in 1917 and suffered defeat by the German army. Victory over the Germans in the west, however, did not restore the Russian position and, following the Polish-Soviet conflict of 1920, the Soviet border was set considerably more to the east than either the Soviets were willing to accept or the western powers deemed appropriate.

Nor were the apparent victors, or those favoured by the victorious powers, necessarily fully satisfied with the settlement. Poland and Czechoslovakia disputed the city of Těšín (Cieszyn) and the surrounding area which the Poles finally seized in 1938, following the example of Nazi Germany in the aftermath of the Munich agreement. But ethnic tensions during the interwar period were not restricted to international relations and conflicts between states. The territorial provisions made for the new Czechoslovak state meant that it included nearly three million Germans. This caused considerable domestic difficulties and made it particularly vulnerable to the German expansionism which developed under Hitler and became transformed in 1938 into direct aggression against the Czechoslovak state. Although Czechoslovakia was the only Central European state during the interwar period that could mount any claim to have maintained and put into practice the democratic principles that prevailed in the immediate post-war period it was, in one view, the pattern taken by internal ethnic relations that placed this claim in the greatest doubt and the demographic composition of Czechoslovakia that 'compounded all the other weaknesses of the state'.[11] In a broader perspective, though, Czechoslovak practice had much to recommend it. Government policy elsewhere in this sphere was certainly not more moderate or justly conducted. Poland's experiences with its large Ukrainian and Ruthene minorities, which made up 14 per cent of the population, and its Belorussians, played an important part in that country's move towards increasingly dictatorial methods of rule.

But, rather than internal weakness or domestic tension, it was the threat posed by the power and policies of the resurgent German state in combination with the consolidation of Soviet power that posed the greatest threat to the independence of Czechoslovakia, Hungary, and Poland – and to their survival as autonomous political units. That of Czechoslovakia was brought to an end by the German occupation of Bohemia and Moravia in March 1939. The challenge to the continued existence of the independent states was directly associated with their history as former territories of the dominant, but temporarily weakened, political forces of the region. This was most obviously the case with Poland, where war was declared over the question of German control in Danzig and the issue of the 'Polish Corridor'. After the non-aggression pact signed between Germany and the Soviet Union in August 1939 and the Soviet invasion of eastern Poland in September when Germany had virtually completed its military campaign, Poland was once more removed from the map of Europe as a national entity. It had the singular misfortune to be a prime target of German aggression and to include large areas that had earlier formed part of the Russian empire, a fact that gained increasing relevance as Soviet power grew and the German threat to European stability as a whole became apparent. Czechoslovakia, too, had a sizeable German minority which attracted Hitler's attention at an early stage and stimulated his appetite for aggression, an appetite which – after the Munich agreement of 1938 and in early 1939 – he was able to satisfy without provoking international conflict or armed resistance on the part of Czechoslovakia.

Hungary, as a territorial loser and revisionist nation on its own account, was not directly concerned in this manner as German aspirations and military strength grew. It was, however, affected in other ways. Having revisionist claims itself and vehemently asserting its rights to ethnic and historic Hungarian territories outside the current state borders, it was faced by a coalition of antagonistic neighbours – the Little Entente of Czechoslovakia, Romania and Yugoslavia. This overwhelming enmity on its borders made it highly receptive to German influence, as well as that of Italy, which had its own reasons for taking advantage of regional enmities and had extensive ambitions in Yugoslavia. The ties were strengthened in the economic field, as they were with most countries in the region, by the impact of the Depression and the response of the Western powers to it. Levels of Eastern indebtedness in the 1930s were high (a tendency foreshadowing developments that began to show themselves during the 1970s) and the Central European economies were badly hit by the West's deflationary policies and import restrictions. Hungarian interest payments as a proportion of its exports were the highest in the area, and in 1931 stood at 48 per cent. The West refused further credit facilities and, by such actions, encouraged the impoverished Eastern countries to turn to Germany which, in sound recognition of its regional interests if hardly altruistically, offered capital goods, technical assistance and a market for agricultural produce. This, in turn, was only possible because, with the Nazis in power, the German government had nothing to fear in terms of political opposition or an electoral backlash from the farmers' lobby.[12] In the absence of the kind of German territorial threat that faced Czechoslovakia and Poland, Hungarian satisfaction at the strengthening of these relations was relatively unqualified.

The influence of Germany grew enormously throughout Central Europe in the 1930s and it appeared well set to achieve many of its objectives without recourse to warfare or running the risk of precipitating a general European conflict. The submission and dismemberment of Czechoslovakia after the Munich agreement confirmed this view, while the signature of a non-aggression pact with the Soviet Union on 23 August 1939 appeared further to strengthen the German position. By the time German forces invaded Poland on 1 September 1939, Czechoslovakia was already subdued and Hungary comfortably within the German sphere of influence. Within two weeks the German command recognized the success of their campaign and the inevitability of victory, and therefore began the transfer of troops to the west even before the entry of Soviet forces on 17 September and the partition of Poland in accordance with the agreement concluded in August. With the invasion of the Soviet Union on 22 June 1941 all pre-war Polish territory fell under German control, and it was not until February 1944 that Soviet forces again crossed the 1939 border, this time to begin the liberation of Polish territory from Nazi domination.

In Hungary the situation took longer to reach a critical resolution in terms of its relations with Germany and the government maintained, though with increasing difficulty, a significant measure of autonomy. Forces of the radical right had gained considerable political momentum in the 1930s, while successive governments had attempted to improve relations and strengthen links with the Western powers. The latter process was not halted by the outbreak of war in 1939, although Hungary's freedom of manoeuvre became even more restricted and the extension of German power gave increasing satisfaction to Hungarian revisionism and its demands for territorial realignment. But the maintenance of a position of neutrality and some balance between the major powers became increasingly difficult, and the problems associated with this process led to the suicide of one prime minister, Count Pál Teleki, in April 1941. By the end of the year Great Britain had declared war on Hungary, itself already engaged in hostilities with Germany against the Soviet Union. Hungary then followed Germany in announcing that it was also at war with the United States. Nevertheless, Hungary still held to a virtually neutral position in the armed confrontation between the Axis and the Western powers (though not that with the Soviet Union) until 1944, and was initially more preoccupied militarily by the reformation within the German sphere of influence of a Little Entente composed of Slovakia, Romania and Croatia. The situation only changed significantly in this respect in March 1944, when German forces finally undertook the occupation of Hungary.

THE WAR-TIME ORIGINS OF MODERN CENTRAL EUROPE

The implications of the war for the future character of Central Europe were a matter of uncertainty and debate, often conducted with considerable acrimony, for some years – although by the middle of 1945 the general direction developments were likely to take was becoming quite clear. One of the major indications of the pattern that was finally to emerge was the course the war took a couple of years earlier, far to the east of the Central European area. At Stalingrad, to the east of the Black Sea, the German army suffered a major reverse and, by the time the battle ended in February 1943, the victory of Stalin's forces appeared finally to have set the Soviet Union on the path to its post-war emergence as a world power. Immediately after the German attack on the Soviet Union on 22 June 1941 there had been serious doubts on many sides as to whether German military forces would not prevail within Soviet territory as completely as they had to the west of the European continent. But by the end of the year the advance had been halted outside Moscow, even if this was only achieved in the very suburbs of the Soviet capital. The following year the German front line did not advance in the north, although progress was made in the south along the eastern shore of the Black Sea towards the Caucasus, reaching as far as Stalingrad in the east. It was here, on the Volga, that Soviet forces began to turn back the invaders.

When the Western allies – primarily, at that stage, Great Britain – joined with the Soviet Union in armed conflict with the Nazi dictatorship, their initial priority in practical terms had been to keep the Soviet ally in the war, prevent its defeat (Lend-Lease was to prove particularly significant in helping to remedy the chronic

Soviet deficit of motor vehicles) and discourage any thoughts of a separate peace. More general war aims had, however, been set down in the Atlantic Charter signed by Franklin Roosevelt and Winston Churchill on 14 August 1941, nearly four months before the United States entered the war. These included a commitment to national sovereignty and the principle of self-government, international co-operation and the prospect of establishing some general security organization, and free and equal access of all countries to international resources. Pre-eminent among Stalin's objectives were the preservation of the frontier of the Soviet Union operative at the beginning of June 1941 (thus including the territorial gains made in agreement with Nazi Germany) and alleviation of the military burden placed on the Soviet Union by a campaign to maximize the Western military effort, particularly important here being the opening of a second front in Europe.

The first of Stalin's objectives presented Britain and the United States with a major problem, particularly over the question of Poland. It was the country over which Britain had gone to war in 1939 the day after the German invasion and it remained, of course, a military and political ally. The Soviet Union, however, had been attacked nearly two years later when German forces crossed its western frontier, which at that time extended well into what had been Polish territory in 1939. It was understandable that the Soviet Union intended to regain the frontiers it possessed at the outset of the hostilities in which it had become engaged. Unfortunately, however, not only did Britain (generally in this matter at one with the United States according to the agreement reached in the Atlantic Charter) have different objectives from those the Soviet Union seemed to have, but their wars had actually started at different times, so, while sharing the same enemy, they were in a sense engaged in different conflicts.

These differences would turn out to be of paramount importance for the future form and character of Central Europe. Soviet ideas of an appropriate Central European settlement were very different from those of the Western powers. Only at the very beginning, as the German forces threatened Moscow in July 1941, it seemed, was Stalin able to consider abandoning the gains achieved on the western border through the Nazi-Soviet Pact of 1939 – and even then a *Pravda* article provided a correction a few days later and suggested that the 1941 frontier should still be adhered to. In December 1941, Stalin was reported to have admitted to General Władysław Sikorski, prime minister of the émigré Polish government, that Lwów and the surrounding area should indeed be recognized as Polish, but there is no record of any further such statements in this vein. Stalin's view and that of Soviet government representatives (there is no evidence of any discrepancy between the two) were remarkably consistent on such issues. In view of the context in which the Soviet Union entered the war, the concentration of German military might that the Soviets faced on the eastern front and the problems involved in starting up a second front in northern Europe, it is hardly surprising that the Western allies treated Stalin's objectives in a relatively distant Central Europe with considerable respect. Churchill's response was to subordinate the contradictions involved to the greater necessity of defeating Nazi Germany and thus to tolerate Stalin's aims on pragmatic grounds. Roosevelt, it seemed, was inclined to a more Machiavellian approach. He was happy in 1942 to commit himself to opening a second front in order to avoid building territorial commitments into the military alliance with the Soviet Union – although it was obvious that the only second front he could envisage was that in North Africa, not what Stalin had in mind at all.

While the military conflict on the eastern front remained finely balanced, the implications of such conflicting views and contradictions in the allies' policy could be viewed with a measure of distance and allowed to some extent to remain in the realm of speculation. Once the military tide had turned in the east, resolution of these issues became more urgent and they began to take on more practical implications. The Soviet military victory at Stalingrad, momentous as it was in those terms alone, also had considerable significance in structuring relations between the allies and shaping the form that negotiation between them was to take – and thus in determining the post-war future of Central Europe. Material considerations by this stage also played an important part in the shifting balance of power. The emphasis in Soviet policy on heavy industrial development during the 1930s seemed to have paid off. Despite early losses, the confusion created by war-time conditions and the enormous demands made of it, Soviet industry proved capable of producing the weapons needed and turning out military supplies at the level required. In conjunction with American engagement in the European war and the major contribution its powerful economy was able to make, this meant that the long-term outlook for Nazi Germany had become a stark one. Soon after Stalingrad, in the early summer of 1943, it could be concluded that a balance was reached whereby the Germans could no longer count on winning the war and the Russians, in the long run, could hardly lose it.[13]

Significant developments in relations between the allies took place around the same time. The second front in the form of a cross-Channel invasion, which had been timed provisionally for the late summer of 1943, was now postponed until 1944. Shortly before this decision was taken, the Germans announced the discovery of mass graves of Polish officers at Katyn, an important clue to the fate of the entire Polish officer corps interned by the Soviets in 1939 and not heard of subsequently. The Polish call for an international commission to investigate this finding was regarded by Soviet authorities as an act of hostility and used, within a matter of days, as a pretext for severing diplomatic relations with the government-in-exile in April 1943. Such was the sensitivity of this issue (which could well have brought into question the fundamental legitimacy of the Polish communist state) that it was only in October 1992 that President Yeltsin made public documentary evidence of overall Soviet responsibility for the murders.[14] At the beginning of 1943 a Polish national committee had been set up in Moscow; after the Katyn episode this became the basis for the establishment of a Polish fighting force to operate with the Soviet army and act as an alternative focus for the new post-war Poland whose creation was envisaged by the Soviets. In July the Germans launched a final mass offensive against Soviet forces at Kursk and it was following the important Soviet victory there, which confirmed the direction that military operations had taken since Stalingrad, that Stalin prepared for the first 'Big Three' summit meeting in November 1943 in Teheran. It presented him with a major diplomatic and political opportunity which he was able to exploit to the full. British and American policy had not been fully agreed beforehand, and Roosevelt excused himself from any formal commitment on the future of Poland because of a forthcoming election in which the Polish vote was likely to be crucial to his success. He was, in any case, inclined to leave territorial issues for decision after the conclusion of hostilities.

In the event, Stalin was granted in essence what he wanted over the border with Poland and gained a firm commitment on the opening of the second front. Two months after the meeting at Teheran, Soviet forces crossed the former Polish border and began the liberation of Central Europe from Nazi domination, although it was some time before any important centres were taken. Early reports indicated satisfactory military relations between Soviet forces and the Polish underground. Soviet progress on certain parts of the front was rapid, and towards the end of July military detachments neared the suburbs of the Polish capital on the east bank of the Vistula, across the river from the centre of Warsaw. Dismayed by the outcome of Western treatment of the Polish issue, and apparently faced by the imminent Soviet liberation of the capital, the Polish underground (with some encouragement from Soviet broadcasts) rose against the Germans on 1 August 1944 and launched their own liberation. Initially relatively successful, they were soon faced with unexpectedly fierce German retaliation, while assistance from the Soviet side was significantly unforthcoming.

There were certainly some practical reasons for Soviet passivity, though it was difficult to understand why aircraft from western bases were not even allowed to drop supplies and land behind Soviet lines. Having established the nucleus of a pro-Soviet Polish government in Lublin during July on territory Stalin was happy to acknowledge as authentically Polish, he was clearly unlikely to extend much sympathy to the Warsaw insurgents or recognize the validity of the political objectives they undoubtedly had. While attempts to offer military support were made by Polish forces fighting under Soviet command (actions for which their commander was subsequently punished), the Soviet army remained inactive across the river as the German army, including some particularly murderous SS detachments, methodically put down the insurrection (at the cost of some 200,000 Polish lives) and then razed the city.[15] The Western powers' obligation to accept the full consequences of the need to maintain the military alliance with the Soviet Union eventually had dire consequences for their less powerful allies. Soviet behaviour in Poland, in combination with the full-blooded pursuit of their interests in the Balkans, soon gave rise to the conviction in the West that a 'fundamental change of policy had taken place in Moscow' and that the principles that had underpinned the military alliance had virtually disappeared.[16] It was also relevant that the second front in northern Europe had finally opened with the Normandy landings in June 1944, and that Stalin now had little to gain in this area from further negotiation of a more diplomatic nature with the Western allies.

Poland was not the only country in which a national bid for liberation was made. The conditions of German occupation in Czechoslovakia differed from those established in Poland, and the invasion of Czechoslovakia had been followed by the establishment of a puppet state in Slovakia. In 1944 its armed forces staged an uprising against German rule. By April 1944 advancing Soviet troops had reached the borders of Slovakia. In the aftermath of the 1938 Munich settlement, whose consequences had been so catastrophic for Czechoslovakia and its prospects of independent statehood, President Edvard Beneš had been eager to maintain and develop cordial relations with the Soviet Union. As a result, the Soviet Union had far better relations with the Czechoslovak émigré government than had been established with the Poles. There were clear signs, though (for example, in connection with the drafting of the war-time alliance in 1943), that the Soviet leadership was not only willing to respond to the friendly approach of the émigré government but felt quite unconstrained about adapting it further to suit its own interests. There was, to say the least, some ground for suspicion that the Soviets treated the co-operative attitudes of the Czechoslovaks with as much ruthlessness and cynicism as they did those of the more suspicious Poles.

In mid-1944 Soviet groups and the émigré government in London began making preparations for armed struggle, but the critical plans were those made by the underground Slovak National Council and by army leaders in the Slovak Ministry of Defence who concealed them from pro-fascist forces. The situation got out of hand, however, and communist guerrillas acted prematurely in late August 1944, attracting an effective German counter-attack. The mountainous terrain hampered the advance of Soviet detachments undertaken to relieve Slovak forces (although other, less favourable, reasons have also been adduced to account for Soviet tardiness), while continuing negotiation and disagreements between the émigré government and Soviet representatives prevented swift co-ordination of the military relief effort. By the end of October the bloody suppression of the uprising, under the direct supervision of Heinrich Himmler, was almost complete. In two countries of Central Europe, then, the critical consequences of their dependence on Soviet forces and vulnerability to the lack of political agreement amongst the allied powers had been made clear to the indigenous population before the end of 1944.

Developments in Hungary took a different course. German troops did not occupy the country until March 1944, and soon afterwards Hitler decided to make a major military stand at Budapest. Fighting was fierce and the Soviet army took seven weeks to liberate the city, achieving that objective only in mid-February 1945 and having the effect of destroying much of it in the process as the tenacious German resistance was gradually overcome. An even higher level of destruction had already been inflicted on the Polish capital, Warsaw, following the abortive uprising of August-September 1944. The extensive conflict and lengthy occupation of Poland had been responsible for a proportionately higher level of casualties than those seen in either Yugoslavia or the USSR (where the toll was also enormous) and produced there the greatest rate of fatality of all the countries occupied by German forces – 22 per cent of the 1939 population – while 38 per cent of the Polish national wealth had been destroyed. Conditions were considerably less extreme in Czechoslovakia, though even here an uprising was staged in Prague as late as May 1945 in which two thousand Czechs died. In this case, too, Stalin bore considerable responsibility for the losses incurred, as General Patten's US army was already in Pilsen but was not permitted to go to the aid of the insurgents.

SOVIET POLICY AND AGREEMENTS BETWEEN THE POWERS

Such experiences during the war gave an indication of the pattern that was likely to emerge in Central Europe and the course that future developments might take. This vision gained further definition during the discussions held at Yalta. The second of the 'Big Three' meetings (and the last to bring Churchill, Roosevelt and Stalin together), it was held during February 1945 in the Crimea. In relation to Central Europe in particular, 'Yalta' became a symbol and shorthand for an arbitrary process of decision-making by distant power-holders unconcerned for the nations and people whose fate they were deciding. It should now be clear, however, that much of the Yalta agreement was based on decisions already effectively taken and on the *de facto* military situation that prevailed in the region. In many areas, there was little scope for the Western partners to take decisions that would change the course that developments in Central Europe were already taking. The fact that, by the time of the previous meeting at Teheran, Soviet forces were nearing the frontier of pre-war Poland meant that, even by that stage, Britain and the United States had relatively little capacity to influence the Soviet decision on whether the border should be recognized; the Soviet refusal to allow virtually any support for the Warsaw uprising might, too, be deplored by the Western powers but it could hardly be countered by them. In other areas, moreover, notably the occupation of the Balkans and the policy pursued in Romania, Stalin had been given a free hand in return for Soviet non-interference with respect to British actions in Greece. This *quid pro quo* had been the origin of the 'percentages' agreement about spheres of relative post-war influence proposed by Churchill in Moscow during October 1944. It was subsequently extended to other Balkan countries (but not to Poland or Czechoslovakia further north) – although it was not very clear what status the agreement had or what its precise implications were.

What was made clear at Yalta was that Stalin fully recognized the primacy of the rights and demands of the 'Big Three', as the leading victorious powers in the struggle against fascism, in relation to smaller powers. He articulated further his refusal to compromise any major Soviet interests in relation to Poland, and spoke strongly in favour of the dismemberment of the German state after surrender. (This position became of particular interest when Roosevelt announced that American troops were not likely to stay in Europe for more than two years after the war – information that apparently came as news as much to the British prime minister as it did to Stalin.)[17] Most of these points were not new, however, and had already been conceded in earlier exchanges. Roosevelt, too, was not inclined to press the Soviet leader on his demands during the negotiations as the primary American interest lay, in Roosevelt's view, in securing Soviet agreement to and participation in the projected international organization that would later take form as the United Nations Organization. Further weaknesses were the wishful thinking that had characterized Western (and particularly US) approaches on various occasions and, particularly, their failure to develop or articulate clear national policies and a firm strategy of post-war development. This area had certainly not been neglected by Stalin, as British officials had come to recognize by 1945.[18] Victory over the Axis had clearly been Stalin's major objective but for much of the time he had far more than this in mind.

While, then, the imperatives of war and the limited influence the Western powers were able to exercise were major factors in the generally unfavourable situation that emerged in Central Europe, they were not the whole story. The Western powers had been less well prepared and were less consistent in terms of their political strategy. This was not without significance for the direction that events took. Even if, by late 1944, the Soviet intention and capacity to acquire an empire in Central Europe had been established beyond any real question, there still remained the important issue of how it should be integrated within the international order in ways compatible with Western ideas and established procedures. To Maxim Litvinov, war-time Soviet ambassador to the United States, it was clear that 'Anglo-American support of any settlement his government would wish to support in east central Europe was indispensable for Russia's true security'.[19] Here was an area where the West could have exerted a greater influence even at a relatively late stage. Litvinov's emphasis on security concerns was of particular relevance, as these emerged as a major priority in Stalin's thinking and might well have been worked on to secure the imposition of some qualification on the use of the extensive power resources amassed by Stalin which were now being increasingly deployed beyond Soviet borders.

The acquisition of guarantees for the future security of Soviet borders was certainly one of Stalin's fundamental objectives. This goes a long way to explaining his emphasis on the Soviet interest in imposing what he regarded as the appropriate borders of the post-war Polish state, particularly to the east. Ensuring the protection of the Soviet Union, and particularly the Russian heartland, against the kind of attack from the west such as that mounted both in 1914 and 1941 was an understandable objective. It also helps to explain why Stalin was also eager to see a Poland that was 'friendly' to the Soviet Union – effectively, one that was not likely to enter into an alliance with Germany or permit the transit of military forces through its territory towards the east. It was a conception based almost wholly on perceived security needs. Any notion of an authentically 'friendly' regime, as had been fore-shadowed in the approach of the émigré Czechoslovak government or was apparent in Yugoslavia following the victory of Tito's communist partisan army, was evidently out of the question in Poland. Polish-Soviet relations had never been able to sustain a true collaboration and the communist base in the country was very weak, not least because Stalin had himself dissolved the communist party there in 1938. Security concerns in the normal sense, however, do not readily explain Soviet attitudes and behaviour in the Balkans after the summer of 1944. They seem to fall more readily into more traditional directions of Russian foreign policy in terms of the push to the south and long-held hopes of gaining control over the Dardanelles.

Soviet security objectives appeared, in fact, to be potentially almost limitless and were linked to the high degree of paranoia that Stalin was prone to display. The problem was compounded by the fact that he did not seem to recognize the validity of the desire of other countries to guarantee their security or the legitimacy of others' aspirations to maintain a reasonable degree of national autonomy.[20] While Stalin's security concerns were in principle comprehensible and by no means wholly unreasonable, they were in practice excessive and beyond normal requirements and levels of acceptability.

The Soviet vision of post-war Central Europe and the objectives pursued in that region were also influenced by the perceived threat of ethnic divisions within the Soviet Union. The desire to enclose all Ukrainians and Belorussians within the Soviet border and seal the Soviet nations from what might be regarded as potential external contamination was another of Stalin's major concerns. This helps to explain the primacy he attached to deciding the future borders of Poland and Romania and a greater willingness to hold back on final decisions concerning the form that the 'friendly' post-war governments might take.

THE EMERGING PATTERN OF COMMUNIST EUROPE

As conditions within the Grand Alliance deteriorated and relations between the major powers worsened, the end of the war in Europe approached. German forces surrendered and a general capitulation became effective on 9 May 1945. By this stage the Red Army had advanced to the west of Berlin and Soviet forces were established in positions of strength throughout Czechoslovakia, Hungary, Poland and Eastern Austria, as well as in the Balkans. The political conflict that had developed over the future of Central Europe was now accompanied by worsening social conditions in the area. The severity of the warfare in Central Europe, high levels of material destruction and enormous social dislocation combined with extensive population movement in terms of the migration of refugees, liberation of prisoners of war, forced labourers and the displacement of national groups, to produce a situation of massive devastation and disruption. A representative of the United States Control Commission thus wrote of the 'complete economic, social and political collapse' in Central Europe as one which probably had no parallel since the end of the Roman Empire.[21] The 'initiative groups' (composed of German communists) which were despatched to Berlin immediately after the Soviet conquest painted a Dantesque picture of the hellish conditions prevailing in what remained of the city.[22] Russian writer Lev Kopolev, arrested and sentenced in the course of his military service as an anti-Soviet agitator for objecting to the excesses committed by Soviet troops in the liberation of German-held territory, compared the condition of the country to one not seen since the Thirty Years War.[23]

The final summit meeting held by the war-time Big Three powers, which opened on 16 July 1945 outside Berlin in Potsdam, developed little in the way of practical solutions to these problems. Following the death of Franklin Roosevelt on 12 April 1945, vice-president Harry Truman had assumed his role and took the lead at the conference in identifying some of the major points of contention. These included the failure to apply satisfactorily all parts of the Yalta agreement and delays in formulating policy for the treatment of post-war Germany. Continuity in the representation of the other Western power was also limited as Winston Churchill and foreign secretary Anthony Eden were only present for one week, leaving when the Conservative defeat in the British national election became known. They were replaced by Labour leader Clement Attlee and his colleague Ernest Bevin and the latter proved to be an informed and able source of support for Truman in his efforts to deal with Stalin's mounting demands.

Many of these focused on Germany and concerned the determination of the Soviet Union to maximize the level of economic reparations they drew from the occupied territories. It had previously been agreed that Germany was to be treated as a single unit by the joint occupying forces and this was confirmed in the Potsdam agreement. In the atmosphere of growing allied suspicion which accompanied the meeting of their forces in the centre of Germany and the assumption of positions within agreed zones of occupation, application of the principle met with considerable resistance. The maintenance of Germany as a single unit was attractive from the Soviet point of view in terms of the potential exercise of political influence and more immediate hopes of reparations (it was the British sector that held most industrial plant, for example). The two aims were, however, bound to come into conflict and Soviet authorities were in any case loath to relinquish the control they already had over the eastern part of Germany. The question of Poland's western border and the fate of East Prussia also remained to be decided. In the event, the Potsdam talks ended very much in stalemate and reflected the compromise that had already evolved in allied relations on the basis of the existing disposition of military forces within Europe. This gave developments in Central Europe their own momentum and showed early signs of confirming Stalin's well-known statement to Yugoslav communist Milovan Djilas in April 1945 that whoever occupies a territory now 'also imposes on it his own social system'.[24]

This principle was rapidly put into effect in the Soviet zone of Germany. Former leaders of the German Communist Party returned from Moscow to the Soviet zone before Berlin fell to Soviet forces, and proceeded to organize the formation of a new local administration. The Soviet occupation forces led the other allies in granting permission for the revival of political parties. The Communist Party was the first to take advantage of this decision and, with a view to consolidating its political position and improving prospects for future development, was already pressing in early 1946 for unification with the socialists. (This process was assisted by Soviet military representatives who imprisoned the less enthusiastic members of the socialist party.) Despite considerable reluctance on the part of many socialists, the unification process was pressed through and formalities completed by the end of April. The majority of rank-and-file members, in so far as their opinion could be established, appeared to be resistant to unification – although the evidence was somewhat ambiguous and there seemed to be more sympathy for a less tightly organized form of co-operation. Signs of the rapid emergence of the communist pattern was not restricted to the political sphere. An equivalent transformation of the economic structure was occurring as estates of ex-Nazis and then all those over one hundred hectares in area were taken over and redistributed according to the provisions of a land reform programme promulgated in September 1945. Legislation on more general nationalization was agreed by referendum in June 1946 in Saxony (where 40 forty per cent of the zone's industrial potential was located), and similar acts were prepared by the other regional authorities.

Such direct methods were hardly possible elsewhere in Central Europe. Nevertheless, as the bitter struggle for the liberation of Budapest was being fought, measures were already being taken to shape the future structure of post-war Hungary. A National Independence Front was founded in Debrecen, near the Romanian border, before the end of 1944. It was composed of representatives of a number of political organizations, only about 30 per cent of whom actually supported the communist party directly. The party's political influence, however, was broader than this and, naturally enough, it tended to grow as Soviet power was established throughout the country and became consolidated in the region as a whole. An early move was that taken in January 1945 by Imre Nagy, the communist minister of agriculture, to enact a land reform which eliminated large estate owners from the countryside and removed the traditional base of their extensive power. In the 1930s 43 per cent of the farm area had been held by one per cent of owners in estates of over 500 acres, and such land reform spelt major change in the social structure of the Hungarian countryside.

The influence of the peasantry also grew in the political sphere, and in free elections held in November 1945 the Smallholders' Party won 57 per cent of votes cast. The communist and socialist parties each received 17 per cent of the vote, representing a distribution of political support conditioned by the longstanding refusal of both communists and socialists to countenance the distribution of farm-land to individual peasants for private ownership. As the communists had attempted to moderate their policies to suit Hungarian conditions, the election results were a considerable disappointment to them. Following this defeat, the leaders of the communist party turned to a range of less open and more manipulative means of gaining power. It was the outcome of this election that led to the adoption of what gained notoriety as 'salami tactics'. By their use, portions of opposing political forces were targeted and sliced off by the communists, steadily reducing the strength of antagonistic groups. Tactical alliances with the left wing of the Smallholders' and Social Democratic parties were established and attempts made to reduce the authority of the right and centre. They also uncovered 'conspiracies' which linked prominent figures with foreign agents and representatives of the pre-war dictatorship, thus securing their removal from political life.

The situation was different in Czechoslovakia where the pre-war communist party, while lacking a revolutionary tradition, had commanded a significant level of electoral support. It had polled 13 per cent of the vote in the parliamentary elections of 1925 (less only than the Agrarians' share), and 10 per cent in 1935. In the absence, too, of the territorial conflict and historical antagonisms that bedevilled Russo-Polish relations, the war-time relations of the Czechoslovak government with the Soviet leadership were quite different from those of their northern neighbour. Nevertheless, following clear signs that the Soviet leadership showed little compunction in exploiting the pro-Eastern sentiments of the

Czechoslovak government and after the sorry experience of the Slovak uprising, the approach taken in Prague became more cautious. Before the end of 1944 Beneš was becoming very worried about Soviet behaviour in Ruthenia (or sub-Carpathian Ukraine), in the eastern extremity of his country. Like the territories of eastern Poland Stalin seemed determined to absorb it and place it under firm Soviet control. As in other liberated areas, Stalin was also showing signs of preparing to take reparations and impose a Moscow-formed government on post-war Czechoslovakia – unexpected behaviour with respect to a firm war-time ally. Up to the 1946 election the prime minister was Zdeněk Fierlinger who was nominally a Social Democrat but known to be a communist puppet. In local government, too, communists moved quickly to occupy positions of power.

The Soviet approach to liberated Poland was no less decisive. A Polish Committee of National Liberation had been established in Lublin on the first portion of liberated territory the Soviet authorities regarded as indisputably Polish and had published its political manifesto on 22 July 1944. It was recognized at Yalta as Poland's provisional government, and finally reconstituted as the basis of one that could receive the full recognition of the Western powers in June 1945. Stanisław Mikołajczyk, leader of the Peasant Party, had resigned as prime minister of the Polish government-in-exile in November 1944 in anticipation of some eventual arrangement with the Moscow-backed Poles. He now entered the Warsaw government, as deputy prime minister (under the socialist Edward Osóbka-Morawski) and minister of agriculture, in anticipation of the free elections agreed to at Yalta and with the hope that he would be able to exert more influence on developments once based in Poland. But proper elections were not held until January 1947, and then the conditions of the vote were far from being free and unfettered as promised in the Yalta agreement. Nevertheless, a referendum was held in June 1946 on issues which included the land reform programme and the fate of the Polish senate, and this seemed to give some promise that the contrasting political views evident within the country might be given some democratic expression. Mikołajczyk attempted to distinguish his party's position on the basis of these issues, and thus to demonstrate the level of support it could command. Intimidation and falsification of the results, however, produced an official victory for the communist-led 'democratic bloc'. Only after party archives were opened in 1990 was it possible to establish that 73 per cent of votes had in fact been cast against the proposals of the communist regime.[25] The events clearly demonstrated, however, the poor democratic prospects of the 'friendly' Poland that Stalin had long been determined to create.

NOTES AND REFERENCES

1. Wat, *My Century*, p. 99.
2. Berend, 'Historical evolution of Eastern Europe'.
3. Polonsky, *The Little Dictators*, p. 3.
4. Judt, 'The rediscovery of Central Europe', p. 24.
5. Ash, *The Uses of Adversity*, p. 167.
6. Wiskemann, *Europe of the Dictators*, p. 12.
7. Okey, 'Central Europe/Eastern Europe', p. 104.
8. Pearson, *National Minorities in Eastern Europe*, p. 1.
9. Khrushchev, *Khrushchev Remembers*, p. 122.
10. Rothschild, *East Central Europe*, p. 132.
11. Pearson, *op. cit.*, p. 151.
12. Calvocoressi, *Resilient Europe*, p. 44.
13. Erickson, *The Road to Berlin*, p. 114.
14. *RFE/RL Research Report*, 22 January 1993.
15. Leslie, *History of Poland*, p. 273.
16. Mastny, *Russia's Road to the Cold War*, p. 212.
17. Erickson, *op. cit.*, p. 653.
18. Thomas, *Armed Truce*, p. 311.
19. Mastny, *Russia's Road to the Cold War*, p. 223.
20. Gaddis, 'The emerging post-revisionist synthesis'.
21. Thomas, *Armed Truce*, p. 461.
22. Dennis, *German Democratic Republic*, p. 1.
23. Kopelev, *No Jail For Thought*, p. 112.
24. Djilas, *Conversations with Stalin*, p. 90
25. *Rzeczpospolita* (Warsaw), 16–17 January 1993.

CHAPTER THREE

The Communist Takeover and Consolidation of Power

SOVIET INFLUENCE AND COMMUNIST POWER

Once history has travelled its course, the past often takes on a distinct appearance of inevitability. The long years of Soviet domination in Central Europe after the Second World War seemed to suggest that no other outcome had really been possible. Consolidation of communist rule, and even its rapid assumption of a fully Sovietized Stalinist form, were soon interpreted as an unavoidable process that flowed directly from the disposition of allied military forces on the ending of hostilities in Europe in 1945 and the general international conditions that prevailed at that time. Djilas's report of Stalin's comment that occupation now meant the imposition of a particular system also seemed to lend support to this view and, further, to the idea that Stalin did have fairly detailed plans for the areas that fell under Soviet influence. It would, however, be misleading to assume that all immediate post-war developments in Central Europe took place as part of a clearly articulated pattern or that Soviet intentions themselves did not change as a result of international and domestic developments. The outcome was not so predetermined as it later appeared and significant areas of uncertainty could be detected. Stalin's policies towards the region as a whole were quite tentative well into 1947.[1]

In certain respects, however, it was clear that Stalin had such definite priorities that they did cohere into a rigidly applied plan of action once the initial shock of the German invasion of 1941 had been weathered. This was certainly the case with the western frontier of the Soviet Union and the borders of post-war Central Europe. As had been evident since 1941, a particularly difficult dimension of allied relations was the securing of agreement on the borders of post-war Poland. Stalin had been remarkably insistent in his claims on the eastern territories of pre-war Poland, and the Western powers soon realized that they had little chance of changing the Soviet leader's mind on this score. Even here, though, final decisions on Poland's western border were postponed as a result of the wider problems involved in securing allied agreement on the general form of post-war Europe and the nature of its development. In recompense for the loss of the eastern territory that went to the Soviet Union, Poland received territory to the west of Danzig (now Gdańsk). It also assimilated much of East Prussia – with the exception of the ancient German city and port of Königsberg together with its hinterland, which went to the Soviet Union and was renamed Kaliningrad. In terms of international law, however, many of Germany's eastern territories were left 'under Polish administration' and their status only received final ratification following agreement between the governments of Poland and the Federal Republic of Germany in December 1970, with a formal treaty being signed in 1972.

The Soviet Union and its newly promoted communist allies in Central Europe faced fewer territorial uncertainties over the treatment of Germany's defeated allies. Hungary, as one such ally, naturally lost the territorial gains made after 1938, which had nearly doubled the area allocated to it under the Trianon agreement of 1920. Part of this change involved the return of Slovak territory and the reinstatement of Czechoslovakia's pre-war border in this area (Czechoslovakia also restored its authority over the small area occupied by Poland in 1938). A significant exception to the reformation of the Czechoslovak state as it had existed before German aggression, though, was the occupation of Ruthenia (sub-Carpathian Ukraine) by Soviet forces and its subsequent annexation. These developments provoked considerable disquiet on the part of the Czechoslovak government but it had little choice other than to acquiesce. Both Poland and Czechoslovakia, then, emerged in 1945 reduced in area but with more homogeneous populations (Table 3.1), which was a political advantage. This higher level of uniformity and ethnic homogeneity of their populations was a significant feature of the post-war period and helped the countries of Central Europe avoid some of the sources of instability that had created problems before the Second World War. Some ethnic diversity remained, however, and a number of minorities could still be identified in the 1980s (Table 3.2).

Table 3.1 The countries of Central Europe, area and population

	Area, sq. km		Population m.	
			1948	*1989*
Czechoslovakia	127,869		12.339	15.639
East Germany	108,299	(1953 estimate)	18.318	16.630
Hungary	93,030		9.165	10.578
Poland	312,520		23.970	37.963

Source Skilling, *Governments of Communist East Europe*, p.9; GUS, *Rocznik Statystyczny 1990*, p. 521

Table 3.2 Minority populations in Eastern Europe

	Population	Percentage of total population
Czechoslovkia		
Hungarians	500,000	3.25
Germans	100,000	0.65
Ruthenians	80,000	0.52
Poles	70,000	0.46
East Germany		
Sorbs	30,000	1.78
Hungary		
Germans	205,000	1.91
Slovaks	120,000	1.12
Southern Slavs	110,000	1.03
Romanians	25,000	0.23
Poland		
Ukrainians	200,000	0.55
Belorussians	200,000	0.55
Russians	150,000	0.41
Germans	50,000	0.14

Source Volgyes, *Politics in Eastern Europe*, p. 12

This degree of post-war ethnic homogeneity was only achieved, however, in consequence of the tragic fate of the great majority of the region's Jewish population and the expulsion of the Germans from Czechoslovakia, as well as that of virtually the whole of the indigenous population from the areas of Germany placed under Polish administration. In Czechoslovakia, Hungary and Poland alone 3.6 million Jews died, the majority of them in Poland where 91 per cent of the country's 3.3 million pre-war Jewish population were put to death.[2] Of the German population, 0.8 million left Czechoslovakia of their own accord before the end of hostilities and all but 30 per cent of the 2.7 million that remained were expelled during the rest of 1945 and 1946.[3] Arguably, the very nationalism of Edvard Beneš, the Czech president, and his eagerness to settle scores with the Sudeten Germans played a major part in consolidating Czechoslovakia's increasingly subordinate status within the Soviet sphere of influence.[4] The takeover by Poland of large areas of eastern Germany in recompense for land lost to the Soviet Union meant the displacement of an even larger number of Germans. Of a pre-war population in those areas of between 8 and 9 million, only 1 million remained by 1948 and 4.5 million Poles had been moved in from other regions to take their place.

These changes were of considerably more than demographic significance. With them Germany lost a major part of its agricultural area, a change that upset allied plans for the occupied country to feed itself after the war. It also set in place a major additional source of tension in German-Polish relations which was by no means fully eliminated with the formal signature of a treaty between Poland and the Federal Republic in 1972. Problems arising from the treatment of the Sudeten Germans, who had been settled in northern Bohemia for many centuries, also lingered and came into greater prominence following the collapse of the communist regimes.

In contrast to developments in other countries within the Soviet area of influence, the formation of a post-war state in eastern Germany followed the shaping of internal power structures and emergence of the mechanisms of communist rule in institutional form. Socialist and communist parties merged in April 1946 to form the Socialist Unity Party (SED according to its German initials), three years prior to the establishment of the GDR. In October 1946 the SED fought provincial elections and gained 249 seats against the 254 won by the Christian Democratic Union (CDU) and the Liberal Democratic Party (LDP), which gained 133 and 121 seats respectively. The CDU, in particular, resisted proposals made by the SED to the other parties for closer co-operation in support of the Soviet position during negotiations with the Western powers. In doing so, the CDU incurred the wrath of the Soviet Military Administration in Germany (SMAD), who dismissed two of its leaders, Kaiser and Lemmer, in December 1947. Its position was further weakened by the creation of two new 'bourgeois' parties – the National Democratic Party of Germany (NDPD) and the

Democratic Farmers' Party (DBD) – as further members of the anti-fascist bloc, within which their stance served to enhance the dominance of the SED.

An area of continuing uncertainty was the future of occupied Germany as a whole, both in territorial and more general political terms, and the fate of its different zones of occupation. This had particular implications for the German capital, Berlin, which was also subject to four-power occupation but which lay well away from the other Western-occupied areas, some 150 kilometres inside the Soviet zone. Resolution of these uncertainties tended to emerge from changes in the general tenor of Great Power relations rather than from more focused negotiation and specific decisions. Relations between the war-time allies continued to deteriorate during 1946 and 1947 and exerted a strong influence on the attitudes of the different powers in occupied Germany. In May 1946 General Lucius Clay, commander of US forces in Germany, suspended reparations from the American zone to the Soviet Union in response to escalating Soviet demands and a refusal to supply food and agricultural goods to the western areas. Towards the end of the year the United States initiated measures to advance the economic integration of occupied Germany, and the British and American zones were merged at the beginning of 1947.

The process of economic development and integration in the west of the country gained further impetus with the formulation of the Marshall Plan which provided substantial US aid for European recovery, and the introduction by the Western powers of a new Deutschmark in June 1948. The process had been facilitated by the withdrawal of the Soviet representative from the Allied Control Council, and plans now went ahead to draft a constitution and create a separate West German state. The Soviet response was to suspend transport links between Berlin and the West, a threat that was countered by the organization and maintenance of a mass airlift which lasted for nearly a year until the Soviet blockade was lifted in May 1949. By that stage the events of the past year had played a major part in consolidating the Western alliance, dispelling any remaining doubts that the US might once more divest itself of European responsibilities as it had after 1919. In April 1949 ten European nations joined the US and Canada in signing the North Atlantic Treaty which formed the Organization henceforth known as NATO.[5] Soviet behaviour also helped accelerate the establishment of a West German state and the agreement of its constitution, which came into force in May 1949. Around the same time in the Soviet zone, the People's Congress elected a People's Council which in turn agreed a draft constitution and proclaimed the foundation of the German Democratic Republic (GDR) in October 1949. The path of German development for the coming decades was now decided, and separation of the former Soviet zone of occupation from the areas controlled by the West thus completed.

In other parts of the region, however, Soviet power could not be applied so directly and communist influence was exerted in more diverse ways. The regional presence of the Red Army was, of course, a major background condition to post-war developments, and Soviet military dominance was an important factor in Western acceptance of the post-war settlement and acquiescence in the extension of communist power. But, apart from the part it played in the occupation of Germany and the direction applied by SMAD to developments in the eastern zone, the Red Army's role in the communist takeovers in Central Europe was largely indirect or its power exerted behind the scenes. Soviet forces were withdrawn from Czechoslovakia early on, in December 1945, and they played only an indirect part in the political process of establishing communist rule in Hungary and Poland (although they did not withdraw from Hungary until 1947, after the demise of anything like an authentic parliamentary regime).[6] However, as members of the war-time alliance, both Poles and Czechs had formed substantial armies on Soviet territory and they were on hand to act as an important force in the newly liberated states. The Polish army commanded by General Rola-Żymierski numbered some 400,000 in May 1945 (among whom, however, were 16,000 Soviet officers – generally of Polish descent), while General Svoboda stood at the head of a substantial army as defence minister in Czechoslovakia.[7] Their activities and organization were, needless to say, under close Soviet surveillance and control.[8]

The establishment of communist power was also facilitated by the gradual elimination of armed anti-communist groups and reduction of the active opposition they were originally able to mount. Competing national forces became steadily less prominent, a development whose significance was greatest in Poland. Following the tragedy of the Warsaw Uprising, the extensive and battle-hardened Polish Home Army (AK) was formally disbanded in January 1945 – a process in some cases brutally assisted by Soviet forces. In March 1945, for example, 16 members of the resistance leadership were invited to Moscow where they were then seized for trial and sentenced, several dying in captivity. While some groups decided to maintain a policy of armed opposition, it was mostly the small extreme right-wing National Armed Forces group (NSZ) in combination with Ukrainian partisans who continued to fight Soviet forces and maintained a significant military presence, mostly in south-east Poland, for several years after the end of the war.

Communist sources claimed that 25,000 men continued to offer armed resistance after the amnesty of August 1945. In all, armed conflict between anti-communist and Soviet-sponsored forces was probably responsible for some 20,000 deaths in the immediate post-war years, and it is beyond doubt that a significant level of violence was involved in the establishment of communist rule in Poland. While, broadly speaking, this involved Polish rather than Soviet forces, the distinction was not always an easy one to make. General Karol Świerczewski, killed in action by Ukrainian partisans in March 1947, was known as General Walter, commander of the International Brigade in the Spanish Civil War, and had played an important part in the activities of the international communist movement. Similarly, apart from the informal influences exerted by Soviet agencies over the national security organizations, Soviet operatives frequently occupied significant positions in notionally Central European institutions and it was clear that the strings of power were pulled very effectively behind the scenes. According to a former employee, ethnic Poles occupied only 15 per cent of the posts in the national security agency.[9]

COALITION POLITICS IN CENTRAL EUROPE

The establishment of communist power in Central European countries was thus a complex and gradual process, with Soviet and domestic communist influence being exercised in a variety of ways and through diverse institutions. The direction of change, set in a hardening international context, was nevertheless quite clear and the immediate post-war years saw a steady strengthening of Soviet control over the region. With Mikołajczyk's resignation from the London government to join the new ruling group in Warsaw after its recognition by the West in June 1945, and in the light of the poor showing of the communists in the Hungarian elections of November 1945, the scene was set for a period of wide-ranging political conflict and a complex pattern of power-struggles. It was, however, a period when genuine government coalitions were established and allowed to operate. They were succeeded by the stages of more direct Sovietization which involved the appearance of bogus coalitions, composed mostly of communist front representatives, and only later the eventual imposition of a monolithic communist regime. A three-stage model of political change could therefore be identified, and communist power was established according to a fairly well-defined sequence of events.[10]

The first electoral test of communist support in Central Europe occurred in Hungary at the end of 1945. After the elections the leader of the Smallholders' Party, Zoltán Tildy, became prime minister and then, following the proclamation of a republic, president. His place as premier was taken by Ferenc Nagy, also one of the Smallholders. As the government was formally constituted as a coalition, this gave the communists grounds to press for occupation of the ministry of the interior (a frequent claim in the region, as it ensured control over police and internal security forces), and Imre Nagy moved from agriculture to take the job. The post-war reduction in Hungarian territory meant that the civil service was due to be trimmed, and the communist assumption of the interior ministry placed party agents in an advantageous position to use political criteria in purging the bureaucracy. Salami tactics came into use as moves were made to slice away at the Smallholders' majority, an early achievement being the removal of Desző Sulyok, a lawyer who criticized the abuse of police powers. Sulyok and his associates in parliament were expelled from the main party in March 1946.

Soviet occupation forces also intervened in parliamentary developments, exercising their right of veto over government bills and encouraging the build-up of security forces. A full-scale onslaught on the Smallholders' Party was mounted following the discovery of an alleged conspiracy which implicated some of its members. Its general secretary, Bela Kovács, was taken into custody (one of the rare direct political interventions of the Soviet military forces) and removed to the Soviet Union. By mid-1947 Ferenc Nagy, the prime minister, had also become implicated and was forced to resign. Pro-communist members of the Smallholders were appointed to government posts and the party's political independence was eliminated. Similar pressures were exerted on the National Peasant Party and the Social Democrats. The conditions under which further elections were held on 31 August 1947 were far more restrictive than those operative in 1945. The Communist Party this time gained 22 per cent of the vote, and allied parties a further 38 per cent, giving them a joint majority over opposition groups who received 35 per cent of the vote.

Greater caution in testing public opinion was shown by the authorities in Poland and, discounting the ambiguous national referendum of 1946, it was only in January 1947 that elections were held. This was associated, amongst other things, with the fact that Mikołajczyk refused to accept non-competitive elections with seats already assigned to the different political parties unless the party he headed, the Polish Peasant Party (PSL), was awarded three-quarters of all parliamentary seats. Communist representatives, meanwhile, were already moving into key positions. Internal affairs were the responsibility of two ministries, one of which – Public Security, concerned with all police activities – was run from the outset by Stanisław Radkiewicz, a prominent communist. In view of the continuing armed resistance to communist forces in Poland its role was a particularly important one, and it expanded its activities in April 1946 by establishing a Volunteer Citizens' Militia Reserve (ORMO) with a membership exceeding 100,000.

At the end of 1945 a separate Ministry of Regained Territories had also been set up to oversee the resettlement and development of the areas of eastern and northern Germany taken over by Poland and placed under its jurisdiction. The Ministry was headed by the leading communist Władysław Gomułka, general secretary of the Polish Workers' Party (PPR), and the territory he administered virtually became a communist fiefdom and a major power-base in the post-war state. With the steady growth of the communist base in Poland in political, institutional and numerical terms, the Peasant Party (still forming part of the governing coalition) was increasingly becoming the focus of political opposition and the object of growing harassment with some of its leading figures being kidnapped and murdered. 100,000 of its members were reported to have been imprisoned during the campaign preceding the 1947 elections, in which the Peasant Party officially won 28 seats and the government bloc awarded itself 394. A new, Soviet-influenced constitution was adopted in February 1947 and, faced with growing threats to his life, Mikołajczyk fled the country in October (supposedly in the boot of the US ambassador's car – although this account was later challenged). The era of genuine coalitions was clearly passing in both Hungary and Poland, although the authenticity of that in Poland had always been dubious in the absence of elections and with the armed conflict that was a major feature of the immediate post-war period.

Unlike the situation in Poland, where historic enmity and long-standing disagreements produced problems for communist forces from the outset, or in Hungary, where the Soviet Union occupied the territory of a defeated enemy, in the case of Czechoslovakia the Soviet authorities had enjoyed relations with a co-operative émigré government. It was, moreover, a country in which the Communist Party had developed significant electoral support before the war and occupied a position of considerable authority in the immediate post-war period. In the National Front, whose position had been articulated in the Košice programme of March 1945, communists held the Ministry of the Interior (in the person of Nosek) and had a strong base in the National Security Corps (SNB). They also occupied the Ministries of Agriculture, Information and Education. As in Poland, communist representatives controlled areas cleared of the former German population, which gave them the opportunity to expand their power by distributing the resources and land that came under their jurisdiction.

Local communists were therefore in a position of strength in Czechoslovakia at an early stage and consolidated this with a positive result in the parliamentary elections of May 1946, gaining 38 per cent of the vote – by far the largest single share. They clearly received extensive support from the peasants, who had benefited from the distribution of land expropriated from the German population. A further relevant consideration, however, was the fact that the Agrarian Party was not allowed to take part in the election because of its previous position and the attitude taken towards the Germans after 1938, and was completely banned from public life in post-war Czechoslovakia. The level of support for the communists nevertheless differed throughout the country, and they gained 42 per cent of votes in the Czech lands but only 30 per cent in Slovakia.[11] After the election, communist leader Klement Gottwald became prime minister and the coalition government operated quite smoothly until July 1947 when, having accepted an invitation to a preliminary conference on the Marshall Plan – as had the Poles – they were immediately required to reject it, on Soviet orders. This certainly impressed on key figures like Foreign Minister Jan Masaryk the extremely strict limits now imposed on their freedom of action.

This was followed by general demands from Moscow for a closing of ranks on the left, which in some respects conveyed a direct threat to post-war Czechoslovak democracy. In international terms it led to the establishment of the Cominform, or Communist

Information Bureau, which was designed to promote the transition to a common path of development in the Soviet zone of influence. At its initial meeting 'the complete victory of the working class over the bourgeoisie in every East European land except Czechoslovakia' was formally noted.[12] Domestically it brought about stronger links between communists and social democrats, a move required to forestall any possibility of the expulsion of communists from the government (a rather unlikely development in Central Europe by this stage) as had happened in France and Italy. The Social Democrats in Czechoslovakia were, however, satisfied with existing coalition arrangements and resisted the establishment of closer relations. A series of crises increased the political tension. Domestic communist forces did not regard a political confrontation with disfavour at this time for other reasons, as they were becoming fearful that forthcoming elections were unlikely to see a repetition of their strong performance in 1946. With the intention of preserving their existing position, they launched a campaign to organize the next elections (due to be held in May 1948) on the basis of proportionately organized single-party lists that would be presented to the electorate for approval. The salami tactics developed in Hungary were also put into operation in Slovakia, where leaders of the Democratic Party were accused of involvement in an anti-state conspiracy in the autumn of 1947 and forced to accept a government restructuring in which communist forces gained control.

Conflict was heightened by growing criticism of the way the police force was being stacked with communists by minister of the interior Nosek, a process which gave them direct access to arms stores. When he ignored a cabinet decision on 12 February 1948 to halt this process (and reinstate the police commanders in eight Prague districts who had been replaced by communist nominees), ministers from the Czech People's, National Socialist and Slovak Democrat Parties resigned from the government. They were not, however, joined in this by the Social Democrats, who had previously voted with them and increasingly held the political balance in the country. Since they had failed to secure the support of the Social Democrats or an assurance that President Beneš would not accept their resignation, this response opened the way to their rapid departure from the political scene. In the crisis this action precipitated, characterized by mass demonstrations of politically committed workers, the appearance of 'Action Committees', diverse forms of extra-parliamentary pressure, and all the other accoutrements of a stage-managed incoming revolutionary tide, the coalition goverment was rapidly undermined. Little resistance to this process was offered or suggested by the minister of defence, Ludvík Svoboda, nominally a social democrat but not lacking alternative political commitments. He had, it was reported, previously offered his services to the Communist Party but had been assured that, by remaining outside it, his political contribution to its interests might be that much greater. The classical concept of the Trojan horse once more proved its worth in modern Central Europe.[13] President Beneš was himself also swayed by the strong communist influence and he now sanctioned the formation of a firmly communist-dominated government.

ECONOMIC CHANGE AND POST-WAR RECOVERY

Czechoslovakia was the last Central European country to maintain a reasonably authentic form of coalition government, and by the time that had been eliminated the conditions of social life that prevailed in the region at the end of the war had changed significantly. The situation had been transformed at several levels – national, regional and international – and while political change was in many ways to the fore in the process of establishing communist rule in Central Europe, it was not just the nature and form of political life that was revolutionized as Soviet influence became stronger. The industrial and agricultural work-force were critical groups for the communist movement, and changes in their position were an important aspect of the post-war transformation of Central Europe. The growing influence of communist forces was associated with important shifts in economic policy and the forms of socio-economic organization. The changes in political life and social structure that occurred as a result of the war meant also that further radical development in those areas was unavoidable in the years after 1945.

The economic experiences of the 1930s had impressed on a broad public the need for a new approach in a number of areas, industrial organization being one of the most important. Nationalization was an early item on the post-war timetable in Hungary: in early 1946 the mines were taken over and major industrial concerns were taken into the state sector later the same year. In January 1948 the banks were included and a general nationalization law passed in March, covering all factories with more than 100 employees. Nationalization in the allied countries of Czechoslovakia and Poland was facilitated by the fact that German ownership and control had become dominant during the war. Following the German defeat, a nationalization law was also passed in Czechoslovakia during October 1945 which covered banks, insurance companies, mines, munitions and many iron, steel and chemical plants. In addition, the legislation covered all factories employing more than 400 persons. In Poland a nationalization law was passed in January 1946 with respect to all enterprises having shifts of more than 50 workers. By the end of the year state-employed workers produced 91 per cent of all goods and materials.

The occupation of Germany itself, as a defeated country, left it open to even greater economic change. Reparations were a priority area for the Soviet government, which was responsible for the dismantling of about a quarter of industry's capital assets in its zone of occupation. Combined with reparations payments and other losses, industrial capacity declined there by 40 to 50 per cent from pre-war levels.[14] Reform of the industry that remained in the Soviet zone began on the orders of the occupation forces in October 1945 and gained pace the following year. 25 per cent of productive capacity was directly taken over and transferred to the title of Soviet companies.[15] By early 1948 firms which accounted for 40 per cent of industrial production were under the control of local authorities or administrative bodies subject to the occupation forces.

In countries like Poland and Hungary, where the Peasant Party and the Smallholders offered the greatest opposition to communist forces, land reform was an issue important in both economic and political terms. In Czechoslovakia, too, the Agrarian Party would have been a likely focus of opposition if it had been allowed to reorganize after the war. Unlike the policies of collectivization and farm amalgamation that were soon to follow, however, reform during the early post-war period led to land being transferred into the hands of the peasants themselves. In Poland agrarian reform meant the expropriation of all holdings over 100 hectares and of arable land over 50 hectares. 6 million hectares were distributed to the peasants, a process which meant the end of the land-owning nobility and the demise of the gentry as a class. In some areas, though, this led to the passage of 1.5 million hectares to state or collective ownership and, in others, to the proliferation of non-economic holdings. The Polish Workers' (Communist) Party (PPR), nevertheless, maintained opposition to mass collectivization until mid-1948. In Hungary reform was implemented as the

Germans were driven out and by 1947 only 20 per cent of land (including that in state hands) was held in packages of over 100 acres (approximately 40 hectares). The redistribution of land previously held by Germans in Czechoslovakia (particularly in the Czech lands to the west) also contributed significantly to the level of support the Communist Party derived from the peasant sector at the time of the 1946 election.

The changes in the structure of economic life and the organization of production took place against an overall process of post-war economic recovery. The degree of war-time destruction had not been uniform throughout Central Europe and the post-war economic situation differed according to country – both for this reason and because pre-war levels of development had also varied. Czechoslovakia, for example, marked in its western areas by a high level of economic development before the war, was relatively favoured and emerged from it 'more confused and disorganized than devastated'.[16] More serious here than material destruction were human losses, and their concentration in key groups like the intelligentsia. By 1948 levels of production and the standard of living in Czechoslovakia were way ahead of those in neighbouring Central European countries, not to mention the Soviet Union and the Balkans. On the completion of the Czechoslovak Two-Year Plan in 1948, industry was producing slightly more than in 1937 – although performance in the consumer goods sector was weaker and drought in 1947 caused a serious shortfall in agricultural production (a weakness which fed directly into the developing political crisis later that year). A Three-Year Plan of economic reconstruction was introduced in Poland at the beginning of 1947. Industrial production increased by 33 per cent that year and a further 37 per cent in 1948. By June 1948 the real wages of manual workers had risen above pre-war levels, although the general standard of living remained below that of 1937. During the period covered by the Plan as a whole national income rose by 219 per cent and consumption by 226 per cent.

Such levels of recovery were impressive not just in comparison with pre-war performance but also in view of the overall disruption in the region, the extent of territorial and population exchange, and the demands imposed by Soviet occupation forces. In the defeated Axis countries particularly, the costs of economic reparations were severe. Reparation payments in Hungary during 1946 and 1947, for example, accounted for 26 and 18 per cent of state expenditure respectively. Even the latter figure constituted 71 per cent of Hungary's exports, and these conditions imposed strict limits on the country's capacity for economic recovery.[17] In 1946 workers' wages stood at just one-half of their pre-war level and industrial productivity just 60 per cent. By 1949, nevertheless, the production of electricity was well above 1937 levels in Hungary as well as in Czechoslovakia and Poland, while the extraction of coal had also been increased, particularly in Poland. In the Soviet zone of occupation in Germany losses in terms of pre-war capacity were serious between 1945 and 1948. Industrial output overall in the Soviet zone in 1946 was down to 42 per cent of the 1936 level, while occupation costs took 26 per cent of its income. A further problem was the dislocation of previous patterns of production and distribution in Germany as a whole. The Soviet zone, for example, had formerly produced only 2.3 per cent of Germany's hard coal and 5 per cent of iron ore, but 68 per cent of textile machinery and 82 per cent of its office goods. Within the Soviet occupation zone, then, production in 1946 was drastically down on the levels of ten years earlier in areas like vehicle output (from 60,849 to 1,439 units), steel (from 1.2 million tons to 0.15), and cement (from 1.7 million tons to 0.57).

CONSOLIDATING COMMUNIST POWER

Political transformation in the immediate post-war years was therefore occurring in a context of diverse kinds of economic change, in countries where levels of development before the war had been markedly different and where there had been major contrasts in the material impact of the war. All these dimensions had some influence on the processes of political change and the consolidation of communist power in Central Europe. Developments in the countryside in particular helped to reduce the strength of opposition to the communist takeover. In urban and industrial areas the rapid pace of post-war reconstruction and the social mobility that accompanied it tended to reduce stability but also offered considerable opportunities for occupational advancement.

The process of immediate post-war recovery broadly coincided with the period during which genuine government coalitions were in existence – although in countries like Poland and Hungary conditions for the survival of independent political forces and expression of their preferences were rapidly becoming less favourable. The coalition governments that were formed as a result of the elections held in Poland in January 1947 and later the same year, in August, in Hungary were far less authentic and had been more subject to communist manipulation. The Czechoslovak coalition held until February 1948 and collapsed with the resignation of most non-communist ministers, after which the pattern of increasingly monolithic communist rule was followed in Czechoslovakia too. In the Soviet zone in Germany the coalition element in the provincial councils had been qualified earlier, following the elections of October 1946. By the time a People's Council was elected there in 1949, prior to the establishment of the Democratic Republic, the political situation was under far more rigorous political control.

After the 1947 Polish elections leading communist Politburo member Bolesław Bierut was elected President of the Republic, while the government was headed by socialist Józef Cyrankiewicz. The post-war Polish Socialist Party (PPS) was, however, a different political body from its influential predecessor before the war. Its post-war revival was only tolerated by the Soviet Union on the condition that former leaders were not reinstated. Some had been killed during the German occupation, others stayed in the West and remained attached to the émigré government, and one (Kazimierz Pużak) had been among the resistance leaders kidnapped by the Russians and transported to Moscow. The post-war PPS had thus committed itself to loyal co-operation with the Workers' Party from the outset and an alliance between the two was formed as early as November 1946. Following the 1947 elections, the governmental role of members of the PPR Politburo was strengthened. Jakób Berman, under-secretary of state in the prime minister's office, played a major role in security, foreign affairs and ideology. Hilary Minc dominated economic matters as minister for industry. In March 1948, following the *coup* in Czechoslovakia, and probably with an eye to developments in Hungary, Cyrankiewicz announced (without consulting the party's national executive committee) that it was time to amalgamate the two organizations. PPR membership had grown rapidly with the extension of communist power, and there was considerable scope to tighten up on party discipline. Purges of local branches had been carried out in 1946 and 1947, but the pace quickened during 1948.

Developments elsewhere contributed to the imposition of

stronger party discipline, and the distinctive position of Yugoslavia was particularly important. More than any other European communist regime, Yugoslavia could claim to have made its own revolution and established a regime which had authentic social roots. Under the leadership of Josip Broz Tito it was already pursuing radical Stalinist policies before the end of 1945. Precisely because of this domestic strength, though, Stalin soon began to show his suspicions of Yugoslav loyalty (as well as the growing arrogance of the country's leader). Tito, meanwhile, grew increasingly resentful of Soviet interference in the internal affairs of his country. Relations rapidly worsened after the foundation of the Cominform in 1947 and, in June the following year, the Yugoslav Communist Party was expelled from the organization amidst charges that it encouraged anti-Soviet criticism and failed to exercise proper political leadership.[18] Despite the growing condemnation of Tito's nationalist heresy in Yugoslavia and moves to strengthen the unity of the international communist movement (which was also a contributory factor to the coup in Czechoslovakia), in Poland PPR general-secretary Gomułka nevertheless maintained his commitment to a Polish road to socialism. This meant continuing emphasis on the importance of taking account of specific national conditions in the construction of socialism.

Both Gomułka's ideological position and Stalin's suspicions were influenced by the fact that he, like Tito, was a 'native' rather than a 'Muscovite' communist, having spent the war years in occupied Poland rather than taking advantage of the refuge offered by the Kremlin. Having extensive experience as an active trade unionist, he had attended the Lenin School for communist cadres in Moscow during the 1930s, but was arrested on his return to Poland in 1935 and spent the following four years in prison. On the ill-wind principle, it should be noted that this had the advantage of protecting him from the ravages of Stalin's purges, which were particularly lethal in the case of the Polish Communist Party (KPP). This was dissolved wholesale by Stalin in 1938, ostensibly for its political unreliability, but more likely because it would prove to be an embarrassment if plans for a tactical alliance with Nazi Germany and the dismemberment of the Polish state came to fruition (as they did in August 1939). Although Gomułka had never shown signs of disloyalty and was by no means a 'soft' communist, he had greater experience of the Polish communist movement than most of the Muscovites and more distinctive personal views. Pre-eminent among these was a recognition that Stalinist orthodoxy would be particularly difficult to impose in Poland of all countries and a reasonable belief that communist rule should take some account of national conditions. This particularly concerned the avoidance of rapid agricultural collectivization and the need to take into consideration the interests and strength of Poland's numerous independent peasants.

Following the restatement of his views in June 1948, Gomułka's position rapidly weakened within the party's leadership and in September he was replaced as PPR secretary by Bierut (himself a 'Muscovite'). The following day, a commitment to the collectivization of agriculture was announced and a purge of those who sympathized with Gomułka's 'nationalist deviation' begun. Unification of the purged parties finally occurred in December 1948. A Polish United Workers' Party (PZPR) was formed with Bierut as leader and a new party statute laid down which closely followed the standard Soviet model. This effectively inaugurated a period of one-party rule, although auxiliary parties remained in existence. One was the United Peasant Party (ZSL), based on the pro-communist Peasant Party (SL) which had been formed in 1944 and was merged in November 1949 with the remaining members of Mikołajczyk's Polish Peasant Party (PSL). The same year a Democratic Party (SD), targeted on the retail trade and craft sector, was formed. In the years that followed neither made any contribution to the formation of genuine political coalitions. They played, rather, a limited role in creating a vaguely pluralist image for the increasingly unitary process of communist rule. SD leader Chajn had, for example, been a political officer in the Soviet-organized Polish army and had joined the SD and entered its leadership on the direct orders of the Communist Party.[19]

Although the outcome of the Hungarian elections of August 1947 was also coerced, the formal victory of the communist bloc was still less than overwhelming. Lajos Dinnyés, a member of the Smallholders' Party but also a communist collaborator, remained prime minister (a role he had filled since the forced resignation of Ferenc Nagy). Further moves were soon made against the opposition parties. The Independence Party, led by Zoltán Pfeiffer who had earlier been expelled from the Smallholders' at the communists' request, was dissolved in the autumn after being denounced for its reactionary character by communist vice-premier Mátyás Rákosi. The Democratic People's Party, a progressive Catholic organization, was dissolved later in the year, while the Catholic Primate, Cardinal József Mindszenty, was himself arrested in December. There remained, in name at least, the Smallholders' Party, now led by István Balogh, a Catholic priest who had been on good terms with the communist authorities. In 1949 he moved to join the government bloc. In 1948 growing pressure was exerted on the social democrats, whose right wing had already been crushed in 1946. Those who continued to resist the pressure for amalgamation with the communists were also expelled and a unified Hungarian Workers' Party (MDP) set up in June 1948. The compliant leader of the social democrats, Árpád Szakasits, became president of the republic. Government reorganization brought in communists Mihály Farkas and István Kossa; László Rajk became minister of foreign affairs and János Kádár took over the interior. Even this government disappeared in April 1949, elections with no opposition candidates at all then being held for a new assembly. The era of monolithic communist rule in Hungary had clearly arrived.

Matters also came to a swift conclusion in Czechoslovakia during 1948. Key posts in the government installed after the February coup were held by communists, with most other parties having only one representative – each chosen by the communist majority. The left-wing social democrats were also well represented, the group which was under the leadership of Fierlinger and in favour of closer collaboration with the communists having taken control of the party's headquarters – with communist action groups in attendance. Jan Masaryk, son of Tomáš, the founder of modern Czechoslovakia, remained in charge of the ministry of foreign affairs, but was found dead beneath his office window on 10 March. Suicide was the official verdict, but there were suspicions of Soviet security involvement. An investigation into the matter during 1968 was curtailed by the Soviet invasion, but it was becoming increasingly clear to some at least that the explanation of suicide was not an accurate one.[20] Political purges of diverse social organizations followed throughout 1948, and compliant leaders were appointed in the non-communist parties. During the summer the Social Democratic Party merged with the communists. Parliament was dissolved in May and non-competitive elections on a joint list held to form a new one. Beneš resigned on 6 June (and died on 6 September), being replaced by Gottwald as President. Former trade-union leader, the communist Antonín Zápotocký became prime minister. As in Poland and Hungary, the fusion of socialist and communist parties in Czechoslovakia during 1948 marked the onset of the period of monolithic communist rule throughout Central Europe, the transition being given a final touch in Hungary and Czechoslovakia by the holding of non-competitive, acclamatory national elections.

In East Germany, the SED had already been formed in April 1946 by merging social democrat and communist organizations within the Soviet zone. This body, further, controlled the Farmers' Mutual Aid Association (VdgB) and the Confederation of Free Trade Unions (FDGB). The extension of its power over the administrative structure, however, depended on the nature of international developments and the rate at which the combined western sectors moved towards independent statehood. The meagre results achieved by successive conferences of foreign ministers, one held in Moscow during March and April 1947, another in London during November and December of the same year, brought the final outcome closer. The failure of the ministerial conferences encouraged the Soviet authorities to bring into greater prominence the 'German People's Congress' it had decided to set up. In early 1948 they handed over new powers to a German Economic Commission which held responsibility for the Soviet zone, this being under the leadership of the communist Heinrich Rau.

The emphasis on the separate economic development of the Soviet zone was furthered with the announcement of a Two-Year Plan by SED leader Walter Ulbricht to the Central Committee of the party in June 1948. A review and purge of the SED membership followed later in the summer, while a new centralized system for public education and propaganda was also established. After elections held on a single list dominated by the SED, the People's Congress approved a constitution which was claimed to be valid for the whole of Germany. The People's Council it produced also established a government, with Otto Grotewohl as prime minister and Ulbricht as first vice-premier. In October 1949 this government, while consolidating the strong hold it had established over the former Soviet zone, now claimed authority over the whole of Germany.

THE DEVELOPMENT OF THE PEOPLE'S DEMOCRACIES

The character of the developments that took place in the Soviet zone of occupation in Germany was a mixed one, often based on a response to events rather than on the initiation of policy in terms of state formation and political development, but aggressive and ambitious in seeking to maximize communist influence and make claims for Germany as a whole. This reflected a broader ambiguity in the process of change within Central Europe during the immediate post-war period. There was a rapid shift from what appeared to be relatively moderate Soviet policies in some parts of Central Europe, involving the acceptance of genuine political coalitions and the holding of free elections (Hungary and Czechoslovakia in 1945 and 1946, as well as others in the Soviet zone of Austria), to outright communist aggression and political manipulation. This seemed to represent a duality of outlook within the Soviet leadership – if not sheer duplicity in terms of political manoeuvring.

This ambivalence was also partly a response to changing international conditions and shifting views within the communist movement about the most appropriate policies to adopt. It was equally reflected in the conception of the post-war order that was being constructed in Central Europe and the theory that was elaborated to account for its development. Considerable thought was expended on the appropriate theoretical view to be taken of the regimes in the newly liberated areas. They were clearly not (despite some later, cruder formulations) the revolutionary consequences of a purely domestic upheaval, and the standard Marxist-Leninist conception of the dictatorship of the proletariat did not fit the new state forms. In short, Russian and Soviet experience was not directly applicable to Central Europe, if only because the role and presence of the Red Army was itself a major factor in the establishment of what came to be termed People's Democracies.

The term was first used by Tito in 1945 with reference to Yugoslavia, and it appeared with increasing frequency during 1946 in the statements of Polish leaders as well as in the views of former Comintern leader and Bulgarian politician Georgi Dimitrov. It provided an appropriate conception of shared power-holding both in the formal sense relating to the composition of political coalitions and to the mixed class base (worker, peasant and significant sections of the bourgeoisie) of the new systems. It also permitted some recognition of a national component in the new regimes and the need to adapt policy to suit specific social and historical circumstances. Little wonder, then, that Tito and the Poles showed an early attachment to the concept – and that the strength of their views soon led them into conflict with the Soviet Union and, in the case of Polish leader Gomułka, condemnation by the rest of the national leadership. Soviet leaders showed less inclination to pronounce publicly in terms of the People's Democracy formulation and it was only towards the end of 1947, after the establishment of the Cominform and when any semblance of genuine coalition had been expunged in Poland and Hungary and was clearly faltering in Czechoslovakia, that they made greater use of the term. It was, even then, employed with a distinctly different emphasis. The timing suggests, in terms of Central Europe at least, that in policy terms the Stalinism that drove the course of events there should be celebrated less as a particularly skilful and sophisticated application of Marxist-Leninist dialectics, than defined as an extremely cautious approach to relations within the region in which tactical conceptions dominated the grand strategy.

It was, of course, an approach that was also open to inter-pretation as cynical manoeuvring, although it would be mistaken to claim that the 'entire period of relative institutional and ideological flexibility had been a well-timed hoax'.[21] Indeed, some elements of a more open Soviet position persisted under conditions that were rapidly becoming unfavourable to any notion of international agreement or the expression of Western sympathy with Soviet aims. The Soviet leadership was reluctant to foreclose on any path of change that might further its interests. Even as the brief period of coalition government came to an end and monolithic regimes were imposed with increasing firmness, the 1949 German constitution elaborated by the SED stated that eastern Germany was to be a 'democratic republic' rather than a People's Democracy. This was not just because it fitted the cautious approach to political development and domestic change taken within the Soviet zone of occupation, but also because it continued to hold to the increasingly unlikely possibility of forming a united Germany. As the separate paths of development taken by West and East Germany further diverged in the early fifties, though, domestic arrangements within the GDR grew closer to those in the other Soviet bloc states.

Implementation of the principles that underlay the idea of the People's Democracies was dependent, as indeed was that embodied in any specific political form, on developments within a broader context and the evolution of relationships in a complex pattern of political, social and economic forces. One of the reasons both for the tolerance shown by the Soviet Union of the original form taken by the People's Democracies in Central Europe and its imperm-anence was the very strength of the Soviet position in the region at the end of the war and the relative ease with which non-communist forces could be handled.

Western response to the situation that developed had been mixed. Although there was no formal agreement, a reasonable level of understanding seemed to have been reached with the former allies about the Soviet position – largely on the basis that they could do little about it – and about the kinds of activity the Soviet Union would be able to initiate and maintain without active opposition or interference from the Western powers. Growing Western criticism of Soviet conduct was therefore accompanied by considerable tolerance of the Soviets' actions in practice.[22] They appeared on this basis to have been given extensive freedom in Central Europe. Western forces had foreshadowed this tolerance by not pressing forward with the force they could have mustered for the liberation of Berlin or Prague – and even withdrawing away from the Elbe in the south out of the areas that would later maintain the industrial viability of the Soviet zone and the future GDR (Saxony and Thuringia). This understanding was given further weight when the Americans showed signs of contemplating a swift military withdrawal from the European continent.

Their apparent tolerance gave communist theoreticians the chance to develop new ideas about the nature of the post-war coalitions within Marxist-Leninist categories. It also gave them the possibility of forcing political practice in a more extreme direction when the opportunity presented itself – and as international and domestic developments showed less promise for further political progress along the lines of the original coalitions. But, although Western behaviour did not greatly change, tolerance of Soviet intransigeance had clearly begun to evaporate as the war neared its end and the position of the western allies was bolstered by the success of the atomic weapon. This tendency was strengthened by the problems experienced in developing an effective collaborative relationship between the four occupying powers in post-war Germany. The development of an integrated Western pattern of action finally took shape after the adoption of the Truman doctrine, whose anti-communist principles were spelt out in a speech made by the US president on 12 March 1947, and the formulation of the Marshall Plan. Such initiatives, in combination with growing Soviet doubts about the course political developments were taking in Central Europe (like, for example, the capacity of the Czechoslovak communists to emerge creditably from another free election) prompted change in communist practice and the categories within which it was understood.

For the Soviet leadership, issues of the adequacy of control over developments in the region were paramount. Even before much was heard from Soviet leaders about the idea of People's Democracies in Central Europe, signs were emerging from the Kremlin that they were not fully satisfied with the performance of communist leaders in Central Europe. Once in action in post-war Central Europe, communist leaders, not surprisingly, became increasingly sensitive to local conditions and more preoccupied with domestic issues. This gave rise to the tendencies towards 'domesticism', which soon began to trouble Soviet leaders. The problems encountered in the construction of socialism in the Central European countries – by no means the ideal location for such an enterprise – naturally directed the attention of local activists to the significance of national conditions and prompted them to review past policy errors. The question of nationalism emerged in Poland during 1947, while echoes of similar preoccupations were also detected amongst Czechs, East Germans, and Hungarians.

Attempts had earlier been made to combine national forces in order to strengthen the position of the communists. They originated from the ideas of Tito and Dimitrov about a Balkan Union but soon spread to Poles, Czechoslovaks and Hungarians. These now encountered Soviet criticism too. Poles and Czechs also looked further afield and responded positively in July 1947 to American proposals to participate in the Marshall Plan. Moscow, however, directed Central European communists to concern themselves more fully with the development of forces within their own countries – while avoiding, of course, the encouragement of excessively domesticist orientations. The task of striking the right balance was clearly difficult, but the question was not really one of applying ideological principles correctly or just developing the right policy. Stalin told Tito directly that the problem was not that of whether mistakes were being made: 'the issue is conceptions different from our own'.[23]

The foundation of the Cominform in September 1947 was the major Soviet response to this set of problems. Only Gomułka, who continued to stress the importance of the experience of Polish socialists in tackling the tasks facing contemporary communists and held different views on the advisability of a collectivization policy, declared himself against the establishment of the new organization. His persistence in these views led to what was interpreted as the degeneration of a tendency towards domesticism into the graver deviation of national communism, an error for which he was duly censured and punished by the Polish Central Committee in September 1948. Most other leaders, however, did not just accept the Soviet initiative but received it with some relief as the accelerating pace of change and enhanced political conflict in Central Europe was in any case leading to greater dependence on the Soviet Union. In the same way, the foundation of the Cominform helped to dissipate the illusions of some fellow-travellers and clarified the strength of the Soviet conception that underlay the process of building socialism in Central Europe. It also led to reinterpretation of the idea of a People's Democracy. Increasing stress was placed on the role of communists within the broader political coalition and the idea of the dictatorship of the proletariat was reintroduced as part of a broader conception of political change.

The foundation of the Cominform also meant the end of a phase of diversity and the beginnings of full-blown Stalinism, the period of near-total conformity in relations among communist states. By some kind of dialectic of its own, it seemed, the post-war coalition phase in Central Europe had become transformed into the era of the political monolith. Communist forces had, of course, sought to establish and maximize their power from the outset. The aim of the Soviet leadership to extend its influence and consolidate power in Central Europe provided the underlying dynamic. But the objective had not been pursued blindly and the process had not been an unconditional one. Options remained partly open over the German question, if only to give the Soviet Union the possibility of extending its influence further west if the opportunity presented itself. A government coalition remained in existence longer in Czechoslovakia than elsewhere in Central Europe – and it was, in fact, the non-communist ministers who incautiously excluded themselves from power and precipitated the crisis that ended the transitional phase. The communist leadership in Hungary had itself complicated the issue by organizing the free elections in 1945 that showed up communist weakness. In Poland, it was the otherwise dogmatic Gomułka who proved to be sufficiently responsive to national conditions to resist the tide flowing from the Kremlin and thus lost his position in the national leadership.

The communist takeover in Central Europe was not, therefore, a smooth or uncontentious process. The international context had initially served to restrain communist domination but then, ironically enough, as the Western powers expressed more firmly their resistance to the communist advance, to accelerate it. The consolidation of Soviet power in Central Europe was clearly signalled by the establishment of the Cominform. The communist takeover of the social democratic parties, most of them in the following year, firmly established the monopoly on the left, while the organization of non-competitive elections provided the phoney parties with a spurious legitimacy. Communist uniformity in Central Europe made a further advance with the establishment of the German Democratic Republic in 1949. The *Gleichschaltung* between Central Europe and the Soviet Union now made the incorporation of the People's Democracies into the USSR a feasible option and this did present itself at the time as a real possibility. It was, however, an unlikely prospect as Tito had already made such a proposition and been roundly condemned for it. Further, it would not enhance the prospects of communist movements in other countries and would hardly be welcomed by Mao Tse Tung in China. Arguments from within the communist world thus militated against a yet tighter Soviet embrace, while that already achieved between 1945 and 1949 was certainly sufficient to impose a strongly Stalinist pattern on the Central European societies in the following years.

NOTES AND REFERENCES

1. Zeman, *The Making and Breaking*, pp. 229–30.
2. Pearson, *National Minorities in Eastern Europe*, p. 200.
3. Turnock, *Eastern Europe*, p. 125.
4. Rupnik, *The Other Europe*, pp. 88–89.
5. Young, *Cold War Europe 1945–1989*, p. 7.
6. Pethybridge, *History of Postwar Russia*, p. 89.
7. Morris, *Eastern Europe Since 1945*, p. 19.
8. Kaplan, *The Short March*, p. 13.
9. Checinski, *Poland*, p. 50.
10. Seton-Watson, *The East European Revolution*, p. 169.
11. I am grateful to Gordon Wightman for drawing this, as well as other points concerning Czechoslovak developments, to my attention.
12. Tigrid, 'The Prague coup of 1948', p. 407.
13. Carrère d'Encausse, *Le grand frère*, p. 351.
14. Dennis, *German Democratic Republic*, p. 128.
15. Childs, *The GDR*, p. 13.
16. Bradley, *Politics in Czechoslovakia*, p. 1.
17. Hoensch, *History of Modern Hungary*, p. 175.
18. Stokes, *From Stalinism to Pluralism*, pp. 58–60.
19. Torańska, *Oni*, p. 193.

20. Charlton, *The Eagle and the Small Birds*, p. 76.
21. Brzezinski, *The Soviet Bloc*, p. 45.
22. Harbutt, *The Iron Curtain*, p. 283.
23. Brzezinski, *op. cit.*, p. 57.

CHAPTER FOUR

The Politics of Stalinism

STALINISM AND THE ECLIPSE OF NATIONAL COMMUNISM

The unity of the Soviet bloc was progressively strengthened following the establishment of the Cominform in 1947. Internal political uniformity within the Central European states was enforced with the amalgamation of the communist and remaining socialist parties in 1948 and the elimination of any lingering political significance attached to the government coalitions that survived. Although the different areas of Central Europe had been exposed to Soviet influence and experienced the rigours of communist dictatorship well before 1947, the establishment of Stalinism as an international system encompassing the region can be dated from the middle of that year. Its onset meant the strengthening and more direct exercise of Soviet power within Central Europe; growing uniformity and social regimentation; stronger central control over political and all social organizations (involving purges of their membership) the development of mechanisms of detailed surveillance; greater repression and ultimately terroristic intimidation of the population; growing prominence of the leadership cult, both around Stalin and national leaders; and policy changes which involved the acceleration of industrial development and collectivization of agriculture.

The imposition of Stalinism in Central Europe contained its own paradoxes, however. As one-party communist rule became firmly established the party became less significant as an institution – its discussions and meetings were ridiculously formal, official internal procedures fell into disuse and governing bodies ceased to meet, while members – and particularly many of its leading personnel – were increasingly subject to police surveillance and victimization. Ideological dogma and mass propaganda monopolized public life, but they evoked little positive response among the population and carried less and less credibility. Constant propaganda and official enthusiasm produced private cynicism; the promotion of inter-national communist amity was accompanied by growing national isolation and fostered popular resentment; and many Central Europeans became disillusioned and bitter about the outcome of the 'liberation' they had so recently experienced. When possible, individuals tended to retreat from public life and protect the values and private interests that remained to them. The atmosphere this created struck party activist and Comintern agent Adam Rayski on his return to Poland from France in the early 1950s: 'Man was degraded. The harshness of the everyday battle for life carried him back several centuries . . . An egocentrism which had nothing in common with the individualism of bourgeois society and was rent by the laws of competition dominated everyday relations.'[1] By the time George Orwell's *Nineteen Eighty-Four* was published, in June 1949, many of the features of the society he depicted – evident for some years within the Soviet Union – could be detected in Central Europe.

The key features of Stalinism were, of course, ineradicably linked with the actions and outlook of the Soviet leader, whose power had steadily grown in the years following the revolution of 1917 but was extended more dramatically after Vladimir Lenin was incapacitated by a series of strokes and died in 1924. By 1928 Stalin's dominance and style of rule had evolved to the point where it was possible to identify a Stalinist system in the Soviet Union, a situation that lasted until his death in 1953. Orthodox Soviet historiography never referred to Stalinism as such but rather to a 'cult of personality'. In fact, matters went considerably beyond that, and Stalinism was much more than a personal dictatorship. Its origins and essence were, however, the subject of some controversy. Some saw it as a natural culmination of Bolshevism and a particular strand of the socialist tradition, while others regarded it as a pre-eminently Russian phenomenon and part of a specific cultural tradition. The latter interpretation was lent some support by Stalin's own views and his self-identification with the tyrannical Tsar Ivan the Terrible. This was the origin of Sergei Eisenstein's famous film which had originally been intended by the modern tyrant to portray the sixteenth- century dictator as a great and wise ruler.[2]

Stalinism was also intimately linked with the Bolshevik project of social modernization, and the obstacles and problems it encountered once the prime assumption on which the Russian Revolution was based – that the Bolshevik seizure of power would be sufficient to spark off world revolution – proved to be illusory. The onset of Stalinism can thus be identified with the beginnings of the collectivization of agriculture in 1928 and the attempt to secure the means for forced industrialization by reducing the peasantry to something like the condition of serfdom from which it had been liberated in 1861. Occurring in a situation where all democracy had been eradicated from party practices and Soviet political life, the single-minded pursuit of economic goals with complete disregard for human suffering and welfare rapidly led to further abuses. It was not just dictatorship but tyranny, a system of untrammelled excess: 'Genghis Khan with a telephone' in one version or, perhaps more appropriately, Ivan the Terrible with a modern and far from humane police force. Stalinism, wrote Stephen Cohen,

> was not simply nationalism, bureaucratization, absence of democracy, censorship, police repression, and the rest in any precedented sense . . . Instead, Stalinism was excess, extraordinary extremism, in each. It was not, for example, merely coercive peasant policies, but a virtual civil war against the peasantry; not merely police repression, or even civil war-style terror, but a holocaust by terror that victimized tens of millions of people for twenty-five years; not merely a Thermidorian revival of nationalist tradition, but an almost fascist-like chauvinism; not merely a leader cult, but deification of a despot.'[3]

It was, paradoxically, also a war against Bolshevism in the sense that the older generation of leaders and Lenin's collaborators were virtually wiped out in the purges of the 1934–38 period. Of the 1,966 delegates present when the 17th Congress of the Soviet Communist Party (CPSU) opened in January 1934, 1,108 died in the terror unleashed by Stalin. As many as 98 of the 139 members of the Central Committee elected by the congress were to perish. Indeed, as the carnage proceeded and spread to the armed forces it began to threaten the security of the Soviet state as well as proving to be counter-productive economically. Despite the transition to a war economy in response to the growing dangers evident in the policies of Nazi Germany, there was no growth in steel output between 1937 and 1939 as qualified managerial staff disappeared and production became increasingly disorganized.[4] It was only recognition of the threat this posed to the survival of the Stalinist system itself that caused some of the worst excesses to be checked and presaged the restoration, in a strange sense, of some notion of social normality following the German invasion. After the allied victory, however, many of the features of the former Stalinist rigour were restored in the Soviet Union.

The development of the Stalinist system after the consolidation of communist power in Central Europe took some time and not all of its features immediately became apparent. While the communist regimes were firmly established by 1947, fully-fledged Stalinism did not really appear in Central Europe until the 1950s. Uniformity was not immediately imposed; social institutions retained some autonomy (in the case of the Polish trade unions, for example, until the merger of the PPR and PPS in December 1948); national control was maintained over the armed forces; and even police activity in political life was reduced following the defeat of the PSL in the 1947 Polish elections. It can be maintained, then, that the consolidation of communist power in Central Europe was, at least initially, a matter primarily of national communist activity, although made possible, of course, by the extension of Soviet power over the region. It has, further, been suggested – by, significantly, a Polish writer and observer of the process in that country – that one can detect a definite reluctance on the part of Central European communists to impose the full Stalinist pattern.[5]

That did not mean that they failed to develop and apply the pattern of communist rule with greater firmness. The unification of the socialist and communist parties was a major step in this direction. Nationalization also gathered pace in 1948 and by the end of the year embraced 80 per cent of the economy in Czechoslovakia, Hungary and Poland. Part of this process involved an attack on private entrepreneurs and capitalist elements in the trade and distribution network. This took the form in Czechoslovakia of an attempt to impose a 'millionaires' levy' (a measure first proposed in 1947) and in Poland of a 'battle for trade', which was also associated with a reduction in the role of the co-operative sector. New steps were also taken in Czechoslovakia towards agrarian reform. An initial emphasis on national, at least partially autonomous roads to communism could, nevertheless, be detected in terms of differences in economic strategy between the plans developed and put into operation in 1948–49 and the amended versions that emerged in 1950–51. While the original plans represented ambitious and highly demanding projects for industrial growth, they did not threaten the degree of economic imbalance or reflect the disregard for the population's living standards that was evident in the final variant.

In the case of Hungary, the amended version provided for a 60 per cent increase in investment in heavy industry over the 1950–54 period. The investment increase in East Germany was relatively modest at 6 per cent, but more marked in Czechoslovakia (around 50 per cent) and similarly high in Poland. The priority attached to heavy industrial investment meant that agriculture, light industry, services and housing could not fail to be neglected and that living standards were correspondingly lowered. While policies of agricultural collectivization, too, were adopted in 1948, the intentions behind them appeared to be more moderate than the form they took when pressed forward in the early 1950s. The reluctance of Central European leaders to apply the full Stalinist pattern is suggested by their eagerness to restrain the collectivization drive when opportunities presented themselves: to a limited extent in 1951 and, more significantly, following Stalin's death in 1953. Although the rule of the new communist elites had been imposed on the Central European countries with considerable brutality and they were undoubtedly dictatorial in their actions, it is at least possible to argue that throughout 1947 and 1948 they were developing and applying policies that took some account of national conditions. It was really after 1949 that Stalinism came into full prominence and rose to the status of a universal model. Clear indications of the path to be taken and the nature of the model that would be applied nevertheless existed before that date. One major sign was the fate of Gomułka following his resistance to Polish collectivization and the foundation of the Cominform.

Gomułka's emphasis on the need to take account of national conditions in the construction of socialism had already led him to oppose the foundation of the Cominform (an event which in fact took place in the Polish hill resort of Szklarska Poręba). As Tito's resistance to the strengthening of Soviet control stiffened, Stalin's antipathy to communist 'domesticism' also grew and he became increasingly sensitive to the threat of nationalist deviation. It was for this error that Gomułka was censured and removed from the leadership of the Polish Workers' Party (PPR) in September 1948. The case mounted against Gomułka introduced several themes that were to receive fuller expression as Stalinism took form in Central Europe. He was charged with distorting the role played by the party and undermining the 'class struggle content' of the socialist transformation of the countryside by refusing to support an anti-kulak policy. (The 'kulak', or fist, was officially an exploitative capitalist producer who relied on hired labour, but the term was often applied more generally to better-off peasants.) Notwithstanding this, Stalin was reported to have assured the party leadership in 1946 that there would be no need to collectivize agriculture in Poland.[6] The growing rigidity of Soviet control was suggested both by the accusation that Gomułka had not taken enough account of the role of the Soviet Union and by references to the worsening international climate, in particular 'the increasing polarization of forces in the world between the imperialist and anti-imperialist forces'. The September 1948 plenary session of the PZPR Central Committee thus sharpened the focus on what were defined as the central issues facing communists in East Europe and what was the 'correct' position to take under Stalinism.

While the Gomułka case gave a good indication of Stalinism's ideological themes and the form that it was to take in Central Europe, the consequences were relatively restrained and the treatment of the former Polish leader lacked the rigour and ruthlessness that was soon to emerge elsewhere. He remained a member of the Central Committee and at the unification congress in December 1948, to the surprise of many delegates, was again proposed by the Politburo for membership of it.[7] He thus remained a CC member into 1949 and retained a position in the central government administration. At a subsequent plenum in November 1949, however, he came under sharper attack, this time accompanied by references to the activities of enemy agents and with accusations of treachery. During it he was removed from the Central Committee and (it later transpired) was expelled from the party, although he remained in employment for some time afterwards. Nevertheless, more recent historical investigation has confirmed the close involvement of his successor, Bolesław Bierut, in the investigation and removal of Gomułka from public life rather than the prominence of Soviet pressure.[8] But the course of the Gomułka affair in general supports the idea that the Stalinist grip on Central Europe really tightened during the course of 1949. In May 1949 László Rajk, the Hungarian foreign minister, who, until his transfer in 1948, had also been in charge of the ministry of the interior, was arrested and charged with espionage and nationalist deviation. Like Gomułka, he had not spent the war years in the Soviet Union. He was tortured, tried in September 1949 and, in association with two other political leaders, executed in October. This gave a more accurate foretaste of full-blown Stalinist practice.

DIMENSIONS OF ONE-PARTY RULE

While the international dimension was clearly a major component of Central European Stalinism,[9] for the population as a whole it was the dominance of the national communist parties, the cult of their leaders and the repetitive promulgation of Soviet-inspired ideology that were its most striking features. Fusion between the communist and the socialist parties was achieved by the end of 1948 and the scene was then set for the more insistent expression of the dictatorship of the proletariat. Opposition parties had been defeated and neutralized politically but it was, in most cases, thought useful to keep them in existence, partly to give the impression of broader public support for the minority communist dictatorship and partly to emphasize the distinction from the more advanced Soviet model of communist party rule. Alongside the Communist Party of Czechoslovakia (KPCz) were the Czechoslovak Socialist Party, the Czechoslovak People's Party, the Slovak Freedom Party, and the Slovak Renaissance Party. Accompanying the East German Socialist Unity Party (SED) were the Christian Democratic Union, the Democratic Farmers' Party, the Liberal Democratic Party and the National Democratic Party. The Polish United Workers' Party (PZPR) coexisted with the Democratic Party and the United Peasant Party. Maintaining the form, if not the reality, of coalition government, the party organizations in Czechoslovakia, Germany and Poland were bound together in National Fronts, which served to sustain the myth of social and political unity in the regularly organized non-competitive elections. Hungary, ruled by the Hungarian Workers' Party (MDP) boasted a Patriotic People's Front, which did not have individual members but was meant to draw on the traditions of the anti-fascist movement.

The pretence of coalition government did little to qualify the practice of one-party rule or the cult of the party leader. Party leaders also occupied major offices of state and held key posts in the government. A system of interlocking political positions strengthened communist party rule. Bierut, secretary-general and chairman of the Polish United Workers' Party after the removal of Gomułka, was president and then (in 1952) prime minister. Mátyás Rákosi, Hungarian communist leader (MDP secretary general) from 1944, also took over the premiership in 1952. Czech Communist Party chairman Klement Gottwald (who had been its secretary general from 1929 to 1946, when he was succeeded by Rudolf Slánský) assumed the presidency in 1948 and assigned the prime ministership to fellow-communist Zápotocký. Wilhelm Pieck and Otto Grotewohl, SED Chairmen from 1950, became in 1949 the East German president and prime minister respectively, although Walter Ulbricht wielded greater power as secretary-general from 1950. But despite emphasis on bureaucratic formality and the introduction of ceremonial constitutions throughout Stalinist Central Europe, the party was rarely mentioned in the key documents of state and the central relations within the structures of power received little formal expression. Even party statutes only alluded in a relatively restrained way to the role of party organs in directing the work of communists in other institutions.

Nevertheless, the central political role of the communist party in society was a major feature of Stalinism. The rapid rise to power of the communist parties (even if they had not actually been called such) during the few years that followed the end of the war had been accompanied by a massive expansion of membership (Table 4.1). Only in Czechoslovakia, moreover, had there been a mass communist party undertaking public activity immediately prior to 1939. The Polish party had refused to register for legal political activity during the first year of the existence of the inter-war republic, while the Hungarian party had been banned following the

Table 4.1 Party members, including candidates

	1945	1947	1949	1954
KPCz (Czechoslovakia)	712,776	1,281,138	2,311,066	1,489,234
MDP (Hungary)	150,000	700,000	1,200,000	864,607
PZPR (Poland)	235,296	820,786	1,200,000(ap.)	1,297,000
SED (East Germany)	511,000(1946)	2,000,000(ap.)	1,773,689	1,413,313

Note Initials of post-unification party names used where changes made; pre-unification CP membership totals shown in 1945 and 1947 entries for Czechoslovakia, Hungary and Poland, 1945/6 in the case of Germany

Source Brzezinski, *The Soviet Bloc*, p. 86

short-lived rule of the Hungarian Soviet government in 1919.[10] The extensive organization of the German communists was also driven underground by Hitler. Rapid post-war growth was further augmented by the amalgamation with social democratic parties, a process that brought the communist organizations into greater prominence and was hardly qualified at all by the change of name that accompanied the unification that occurred in most countries. The growth of the parties during the consolidation of communist power and their assimilation of what was left of the membership of the former socialist parties also gave leaders the chance (and often necessity) to exercise more rigorous discipline over what was now a mass membership. The imposition of tighter Soviet control over Central Europe and the national communist parties was accompanied by the further strengthening of central power within the Central European organizations.

The openness previously shown towards all who had wanted to join in the immediate post-war period was now no longer necessary, and a more selective approach could be adopted towards the rank and file. (The fate of leaders like Gomułka and Rajk suggests, however, that it would be naive to suppose that it was predominantly those who joined for opportunistic reasons who were excluded.) Socialists who retained too much allegiance to the democratic roots of their party could also be dispensed with. Thus numbers in the Polish party were already declining in 1949 following unification at the end of 1948, and the membership total also fell in East Germany after 1948. Communist ranks similarly shrank in Czechoslovakia and Hungary from early 1949. The communist parties, nevertheless, now occupied a central position in terms both of numbers and power resources far removed from their status in Hungary and Poland before the war. The primacy of the party was, in any case, not just expressed in the acquisition of a mass membership and the occupation by its representatives of the major offices of government and state.

While formally distinct and separate from the government structure, the party's assumption of a 'leading role' within the social, economic and political system as a whole was accompanied by a claim to be authorized to intervene in virtually all public (and many private) matters. This was facilitated, firstly, by the fact that posts of national and, increasingly, local significance were occupied by party members. Jobs of any importance in the administration, economy or social organizations were invariably now taken by party members. The party leadership also commanded a growing body of full-time party officials, the political 'apparatus', whose structure paralleled that of the state administration and whose members supervised its work in all areas of activity. This body of officials soon grew to encompass some 15,000 individuals in Poland, and in a smaller country like Czechoslovakia probably around 9,000. It acted as something of a shadow administration which generally wielded more power than the formal organization it was supposed to oversee.

Thirdly, party leaders took special account of appointments to all major posts and public offices, and ensured that the 'right' people (with regard more to political suitability than specialist qualifications) were placed in them. This involved the systematic identification both of a wide range of important jobs and lists of the right kind of people to fill them. Those appointed by the matching of these lists gained their status by the process of *nomenklatura*, a mechanism developed to assert and retain political control over the organization of social life whose principle of operation, it has been claimed, could be traced back and discerned in the practices of feudal systems.[11] The state thus became the property of the privileged few and the mass of the citizenry little more than their chattels. In Czechoslovakia this powerful group ultimately grew to involve people occupying 100,000 different posts and in Poland to something more like 250,000. This patronage gave party leaders enormous powers of potential control, although it also opened up the possibility of an awesome degree of bureaucracy and confusion due to overlapping competences and demands.

The extensive powers also provided fertile ground for the exercise of personal patronage, the creation of networks of political friendship and influence, the development of numerous cliques, and the formation of diverse relations of mutual advantage and clientilism. While it was not actually supposed to be the party's business to govern or administer directly (although this often did happen), it did regard it as a major responsibility and prime aspect of the leading role to supervise and check on the operation of all significant matters: to exercise 'control' over public affairs as it was generally put (following Soviet practice) in party terminology. The diverse aspects of the party's leading role outlined above, and the various functions it performed within the social system as a whole, gave it an extensive capacity to exercise this 'control'. The impetus within the Stalinist system to maximize central control meant that the party tended not just to supervise and check, but to usurp government and administrative functions and take over their work, too.

THE NATURE OF STALINIST DICTATORSHIP

Given the nature of the process by which communist power in Central Europe was established, and the degree of carefully organized central party control, there was little scope for parliamentary activity or the exercise of constitutionally established legislative authority. Elected assemblies formally retained their traditional role and constitutional status (even if this had not been particularly prominent before the war) but played little part in effective decision-making, which became the prerogative of the party leadership. This was a further aspect of the process by which constitutional forms and procedures fell into abeyance and the rule of law was eclipsed by the arbitrary exercise of political power. Party members generally held over half the seats in the representative assemblies, but it was not through these that the party's power was primarily exercised. The assemblies were only convened a few times each year and the sessions were generally short, lasting only a few days. The programme was carefully planned, debates lifeless and uncontroversial, and the proceedings largely ritualized, being mostly restricted to endorsement of decisions taken elsewhere and merely fulfilling the function of the metaphorical rubber stamp. The assemblies' Councils of State, or Presidia, seemed to show more activity, as did the Councils of Ministers (the central organs of government) which were also elected by the assemblies, but membership of these bodies was similarly dependent on the individual's position within the party. The principles of representative democracy were now clearly subordinate to the alternative criteria of democratic centralism associated with the proletarian dictatorship.

Although power and the means of its exercise were clearly concentrated around the central party leadership, its precise location and the key processes involved in its exercise remained uncertain. The national party leader obviously played a dominant role, but he also owed his position in large measure to the predominant influence of the Soviet Union and the decision of its supreme leader. The national communist leaders were, as Gomułka later put it, satellites of the supreme body, illuminating their societies only with the reflected light of the Soviet power-source. Nevertheless, the national leader (Bierut, Gottwald, Rákosi or Ulbricht) was dominant in his own country and on that basis the appropriate cult of personality, with the accompanying images, slogans and plaudits, was created. The composition of the slightly larger, but still highly restricted, inner circle of power was also not easy to pin down. It was closely associated with the top party leadership, but it was not reducible to the party's leading executive organ, the Politburo, as there were long stretches during the Stalinist period when it met irregularly, if at all. Some, but not all, of the leading figures within the Politburo would certainly form part of the national power centre. At one stage in Czechoslovakia it may well have been identified with the Central Committee's Political Secretariat. The Hungarian power elite of the 1950s could be described in terms of four individuals: Rákosi, the party chief; Gerő, in charge of the economy and Rákosi's eventual successor; Farkas, minister of armed forces and head of the security police; and Révai, in charge of ideology and cultural affairs within the Politburo.[12] Key Soviet representatives – the ambassador, major security operatives, individuals with particular national backgrounds like Marshal Rokossovsky (Polish minister of defence but a member of the Soviet communist party since 1919) – might also be critical.

The mix varied according to national conditions, the channels of Soviet influence and, doubtless, the character and personality of the leaders involved. In general, though, power-holding and the exercise of power under Stalinist conditions was a secretive and often conspiratorial business. Wherever it was to be found, power did not flow through the party's formal procedures. The Czechoslovak Central Committee, for example, was not convened at all under Gottwald between 1949 and 1952, and the frequency of its Presidium's (later Politburo) meetings also declined in 1952 and 1953.[13] One secretary of the Polish Central Committee later pointed out that the political characteristics and deformations that arose in the early fifties were, indeed, specifically Stalinist in character and should not be linked with the leading role of the party and its practice – these produced their own problems at a later stage of communist development.[14]

The network of power under Stalinism was therefore extensive and diffuse, but its critical areas were often mysterious and undetectable from the viewpoint of the public. Within the government structure, ministries proliferated to produce a complex which combined those of a traditional nature, covering the standard areas of government activity, with others concerned, along Soviet lines, with the detailed execution of economic plans. For example, it was believed that the top decision-making body in Poland (the party Politburo), once concerned itself with the issue of whether lard should be sold in retail outlets loose or pre-packed.[15]

The number, range and status of ministries and government commissions changed frequently. The size of the cabinet in all countries nevertheless grew steadily and came to represent some 30 to 40 ministries. The number of lower-level functionaries increased accordingly. Somewhat later it was estimated that Czechoslovakia contained one administrative employee for every three workers and that over 10 per cent of the work-force was involved in administration. In Hungary, too the number of white-collar collars rose considerably – by 41 per cent between 1949 and 1980 – and came to represent 27 per cent of all wage-earners.[16] Throughout post-1945 Central Europe, administrative personnel made up a much higher share of the work-force that they had before the war.

People were eventually confronted by Kafkaesque jungle of institutions and organizational controls, interlinked by party and other agencies, behind which stood an extensive yet ultimately ill-defined apparatus of power. It was hardly surprising that the writings of that earlier resident of Prague, Franz Kafka, were regarded with considerable suspicion as if they represented a form of premature political criticism. Stalinist bureaucracy thus presented a public face that combined red-tape, inefficiency and menace. For, alongside the party and its auxiliary organizations, the police apparatus and security organs constituted a second major pillar of the Stalinist system. Having taken care to secure control over the interior ministries at an early stage, communist leaders did not neglect development of the police forces and leant heavily on their activities to enhance close political control. Special security forces and para-military units were also built up, the size of the latter representing from one quarter to one third of the strength of the regular armed forces by the early 1950s. Political conformity was combined with direct repression as dual components of the social control mechanisms that emerged to dominate Central Europe society at that time. The tone of such security operations was initially set by the kind of attention paid to party leaders like Gomułka and Rajk.

IMPLICATIONS OF THE PURGES

Apart from major economic initiatives in terms of industrialization and collectivization, the pattern of Stalinism in Central Europe contained two main strands.[17] One was implementation of the theory of the political supremacy of the party and assertion of the dictatorship of the proletariat. The political supremacy of the party had grown steadily through the period of the post-war coalitions and had been consolidated, organizationally and numerically, with the absorption of the social-democratic parties. The importance of the doctrine of the dictatorship of the proletariat had, too, become more prominent in Central Europe during this period. By the end of 1948 it was a major feature of the people's democracy concept, an idea which previously had seemed to stand in some contrast to the more forthright and aggressive connotations of proletarian dictatorship. The second component of Stalinism was the intensification of the class struggle, directed not just to the confrontation of known hostile classes but also to the identification, unmasking and elimination of those enemies who had infiltrated the communist movement. The isolation of and sanctions applied to Gomułka and Rajk were early signs of what the intensification of the class struggle in Central Europe was to entail under the political conditions of Stalinism.

Gomułka was specifically charged with undermining the 'class struggle content' of the socialist transformation of the countryside by failing to embrace the anti-kulak policy. In Soviet eyes Gomułka also took insufficient account of the international dimensions of the class struggle and the increasing polarization that was occurring between imperialist and anti-imperialist forces. The international dimension was also to the fore in the Rajk case. At the time of his arrest he was Hungary's Foreign Minister, and the charges against him included espionage (on behalf of US Central Intelligence Agency head Allen Dulles and Yugoslav police chief Ranković). During his trial the prosecution maintained, indeed, that sentence was also being passed on the Yugoslav 'deserters and traitors to democracy and socialism', who were supposed to have been bought by American and British intelligence services during the Second World War in preparation for a third which would be waged against the Soviet Union.[18]

Claims of treacherous international links were also apparent in the more extensive purge that occurred in Czechoslovakia a little later. Accusations against leading Jewish communists were prominent here and, apart from openly anti-semitic attacks, charges of subversive links with Israel were made. Plans for an anti-semitic trial in Poland, prevented only by the death of Stalin, were also rumoured.[19] The Czech purge began in early 1950 with the removal mostly of officials responsible for foreign policy and trade, but also of the editor of *Rude pravo*, the official party daily. Foreign Minister Clementis, a Slovak, was soon involved and other leading members of the Slovak Communist Party also fell under suspicion. By 1951 the purge had reached the Czech leadership and in November Rudolf Slánský, previously secretary-general of the party, was arrested. There was some hope that this meant a return to moderation and lawfulness, as Slánský's actions after the 1948 coup had been so ruthless and terroristic.[20] This, however, was not to be the case.

The trial opened in November 1952 and eleven of the accused were hanged the following month. The Czech purge was, moreover, a widespread one. The original trial was followed by eight others. 50 of the 97 Central Committee members and six of the seven CC secretaries were removed. Numerous officials in the bureaucracy were affected, as was much of the army. In terms of Central Europe, it was the experience that seemed most to replicate the purges and show trials that had been held in the Soviet Union some fifteen years earlier. Less violent change occurred in the party leadership of East Germany, as it had earlier in Poland. Some important expulsions took place in 1950 in Germany, but they were not accompanied by the ideological furore or the doctrinal criticism that was evident elsewhere.

Purges in the party organization and accelerated turnover in the party membership were widespread throughout Central Europe at this time. Roughly a quarter of party members were purged and, while the total was highest in Czechoslovakia (550,000), the number of removals was also substantial in Poland (370,000), East Germany (300,000) and Hungary (200,000). Many found themselves assigned to forced labour and transported to the concentration camps which also became more numerous after 1948 (199 having been identified in Hungary, 124 in Czechoslovakia and 97 in Poland). A reduction of party membership was hardly unexpected at this stage, as party numbers had grown enormously since the end of the war and totals had further been swollen by amalgamation with the socialist parties and the inclusion of many who had not in fact initially opted to join the communist parties. Some had joined for the sake of social and political advancement and revolutionary zeal was by no means always dominant in the party organization.

The expansion of the parties and their growing importance in political life had tended to transform them into more diverse organizations with groups representing quite different traditions and viewpoints. This was certainly evident in the parties' leading groups, with war-time underground communists vying with Moscow-based émigrés and others who had spent the war in the West or had seen military and political action during the Spanish Civil War. With the drive towards greater uniformity these differences took on greater political significance. Although within the communist parties the intensification of the class struggle had great relevance to the political rank and file and the less highly placed officials, it was allegations made against higher officials and leaders susceptible to suspicions of unorthodoxy that carried the greatest ideological charge and were sustained by accusations of treachery and class betrayal. The ideological form taken by elite conflicts and the major leadership purges masked more concrete differences between the groups. In particular, they reflected the career and political contrasts that had developed between the domestic communists who had remained in their country during the war and the Moscow émigrés. This was certainly a major factor in the Polish and Hungarian developments. The importance of the Soviet link in this form emerged *within* the communist leaderships and served to differentiate between groups forming part of the communist elite itself.

In this context the secret police and security organs of the newly established communist states also took on particular importance and developed considerable freedom of manoeuvre. They soon loosened the reins of party control and became semi-autonomous, subject only to direct Soviet control. While they tended to act in the interests of the dominant Moscow group within the national leaderships, they were also closely linked with and under the overall supervision of senior Soviet partners. In some cases the security organs not only performed a Soviet-defined role but were also staffed as outposts of the Soviet power apparatus. *Informacja*, the Polish counterpart to the Soviet military counter-intelligence organization SMERSH, was itself largely a Soviet organ and Poles made up no more than a small minority of its staff. The Czech Ministry of Public Security contained 26 Soviet advisers whose influence and decision-making powers, were certainly greater than those of the minister himself and proved critical during the period of the purge trials.[21]

The privileged access of the security organs to Soviet power-holders thus gave them considerable autonomy *vis-à-vis* their nominal superiors in Central Europe. But that does not absolve some Central European communist leaders from the major responsibility they bore for the murderous show-trials. Gottwald is reported initially to have resisted the idea that Czech party secretary-general Slánský was guilty of the charges made but soon yielded to the continuing pressure exerted by Stalin and acquiesced in his judgment although no evidence was provided. He seems, on the other hand, to have drawn appropriate personal conclusions from the murderous escalation of charges and counter-charges that took place, for he was reported to have become so scared of Stalin that he was afraid to visit the Soviet Union in case he did not return.

The Polish leadership, on the other hand, appears to have resisted later Soviet pressure to put Gomułka on trial and succeeded in saving the PZPR from the fate that befell the Czech party. While Stalinism clearly meant the strengthening and more direct exercise of Soviet power within Central Europe, then, the pursuit of Soviet interests and desires did not run at the same pace or with the same intensity in all areas. There was also scope for local autonomy and national influence to be exercised. This often involved predicting what Stalin would favour or require and acting accordingly (Rákosi and Bierut appeared to be particularly effective in applying the principle of 'anticipated reaction'), but there was some scope for more independent decision-making. This scope, however, seemed to diminish as Stalinism strengthened as an international order and Stalin's paranoia deepened in the years immediately preceding his death. Signs of the onset of a renewed wave of purges and the rising strains of anti-semitism were symptoms of this. His later ideological pronouncements also placed a stronger emphasis on the priority of Soviet interests in the development of Stalinism as an interstate system.

STALINISM AND THE REALITIES OF SOVIET CONTROL

The exercise of Soviet power over Central Europe during the Stalinist period was a complex and somewhat contradictory affair. Rather like the bureaucratic party dictatorship in the individual countries which neglected the formal procedures of party life, so the development of international Stalinism as a political mechanism and interstate system tended to bypass the formal channels of international integration. A series of bilateral political and cultural treaties were concluded between the Central European states and the Soviet Union, and between the states themselves. But, apart from this, there was relatively little conventional diplomatic activity between the interested parties. Even the Cominform, whose establishment in 1947 had been a major political landmark, did not prove to be much of a focus for subsequent activity and it did not hold any meetings after that of November 1949. Formal signs of regional integration and common sentiment were nevertheless prominent with the all-pervasive proclamations throughout Central Europe of gratitude and loyalty to the Soviet Union, respect for its communist party and admiration of its leader, Joseph Stalin, himself. Such manifestations were, of course, presented as spontaneous and authentic expressions of social feeling.

In reality, as the minuscule numbers of active communists in countries like Poland and Hungary towards the end of the war suggest, they were no such thing: the spontaneous expressions of international amity were carefully organized and the manifestations of social feeling strictly formalized. Great pains were taken to promulgate the myth of Soviet leadership. The mass media were dominated by products of Soviet origin; much effort was devoted to the promulgation of Soviet culture, while school-children spent many hours in Russian classes. As the inability or reluctance of many contemporary Central Europeans to speak that language suggests, much of this effort bore little fruit and the attempt to resocialize whole societies met with scant success. The realities of Soviet leadership were quite different, and it was behind the public façade that the real mechanisms of Soviet control and regional integration operated.

Five main links in the chain of Soviet control could be identified.[22] The first was direct bilateral consultations between Central European leaders and Moscow (although, in common with other processes established in the international movement, bloc party meetings fell into desuetude and no top-level multilateral communist consultations were held from 1949 until the 19th Congress of the CPSU in October 1952). A second link was the permanent supervision and influence exercised by the Soviet ambassador. His reports were a prime source for Kremlin decision-making and he also acted on occasion to transmit policy direct to the Central European leaders. Some, like ambassador Lebedev in Poland (1946–53) were widely thought to have played a strongly interventionist role and to have sponsored intraparty intrigues. Access to the ambassador was therefore a prime political resource and the maintenance of unauthorized personal links with him could on occasion be sufficient reason for strong party sanctions and even expulsion from the Central Committee.

A third form of Soviet control was the maintenance of close contact between key party bodies and the employment in positions of Soviet-trained personnel. The growing dominance in Central Europe of the 'Moscow' communists after 1948 and the purging of their home-based rivals was one reflection of this. In Poland, for example, apart from party leader Bierut, who had worked for the NKVD, the Soviet security organization, Jakób Berman had been active in the Comintern and Politburo member Franciszek Mazur was understood to maintain links with the MVD, the Soviet interior ministry. Collaboration and 'comradely links' were also maintained between a range of professional, political, scientific and cultural groups.

The fourth avenue of control, that of direct Soviet penetration of Central European institutions, was particularly critical with respect to security organs and the military. Although there were suggestions that Czechoslovakia was the exception to this and was able (or allowed) to manage its own affairs and cope largely on its own account, after 1949 and the trial of Lázló Rajk in Hungary, the role of Soviet 'advisers' became considerably more prominent in Czechoslovakia. The Hungarian security organization, the AVH, was advised by a minimum of twelve Soviet officers (a number which on occasion could rise to forty). In the Polish Ministry of Public Security, too, eight of the twenty departments were headed directly by Soviet officers and three enjoyed the services of their own Soviet 'advisers'. Minister Stanisław Radkiewicz had Soviet officers as his personal guards. Soviet security officials often had their own powers of arrest in the Central European states. This was true of East Germany and other former enemy countries like Hungary, and was certainly the case on occasion in Poland. As steps were taken after 1948 to build up the Central European armed forces, appointments were made to ensure an appropriate level of control there too. Mihály Farkas, actually a Soviet citizen, was appointed Hungarian minister of defence in 1948, while Soviet army officer Konstantin Rokossovsky was appointed to the Polish ministry of defence in November 1949 and also became a member of the Politburo.

The fifth means by which Soviet control was maintained and enhanced was the unusual isolation of the Peoples' Democracies from one another. The dominance of bilateral links with the Soviet Union meant the severe curtailment of horizontal relations within what was supposed to be an international socialist community. This was, however, an accurate reflection of the principles of democratic centralism at the supranational level. The publications of the Central European parties were often not available in neighbouring countries, nor were the pronouncements of party leaders or even party decisions publicized elsewhere. Individual movement was of course severely restricted, and economic development and exchange tended only to strengthen relations with the Soviet Union or enhance national autarchy.

Post-war Stalinism therefore developed as a national and inter-state political system characterized by a diverse mix of formal and informal structures. The national and international relations that developed during the period seemed, at almost every turn, to attempt a synthesis of apparently contradictory principles and conflicting processes. The consolidation of one-party rule was followed by the increasing neglect of party procedures, while the ethic of the collective was supplemented by the cult of an individual personality – notably that of Stalin, but one reprised also in derivative national forms. The concept of people's democracy soon embraced proletarian dictatorship, and the defeat of former ruling groups and the destruction of the old class system was superseded by an intensification of the class struggle. As part of this process, national communist leaders were frequently unmasked as spies and traitors. Stalinism clearly brought some kind of revolution to Central Europe, but though it was far-reaching it was also perverse and contradictory, both in its guiding principles and social consequences.

One of the major principles and priorities of Stalinism was that of modernization and social progress, based on a supposedly rational understanding of social processes and involving the application of advanced technology. This was embodied in the policies of accelerated industrialization which were formulated by the communist leaders on their accession to power and significantly upgraded with the onset of the Stalinist period proper. It might, indeed, be argued that these economic policies and their particular bias towards heavy industry have been among the most tenacious and ineradicable features of Stalinism and one of its most lasting consequences. Yet the degree to which this process actually facilitated the modernization of Central Europe and advanced its social development was later open to considerable doubt. It is this feature that we shall next examine, tracing the evolution of the framework established by Stalinist policies into later periods and establishing the economic contours that shaped the societies of contemporary Central Europe.

NOTES AND REFERENCES

1. Rayski, *Nos illusions perdues*, p. 240.
2. Tucker, *The Soviet Political Mind*, p. 174.
3. Cohen, 'Bolshevism and Stalinism', p. 12.
4. Elleinstein, *The Stalin Phenomenon*, p. 116.
5. Brus, 'Stalinism', p. 244.
6. Torańska, *Oni*, p. 304.
7. Bethell, *Gomułka*, p. 159.
8. Wąsowicz and Socha, 'Z archiwum Bolesława Bieruta', p. 80.
9. Dawisha, *Eastern Europe*, p. 70.
10. de Weydenthal, *Communists*, p. 10; Heinrich, *Hungary*, p. 108.
11. Davies, *Heart of Europe*, p. 53.
12. Molnár, *Budapest 1956*, p. 23.
13. Kaplan, *Communist Party in Power*, pp. 28, 103.
14. Zambrowski, 'Dziennik', p. 94.
15. Andrzejewski, *Gomułka i inni*, p. 126.
16. Heinrich, *op. cit.*, p. 104.
17. Brzezinski, *The Soviet Bloc*, p. 84.
18. Stokes, *From Stalinism to Pluralism*, pp. 68–9.
19. Checinski, *Poland*, p. 82.
20. Rothschild, *Return to Diversity*, p. 135.
21. Skilling, 'Stalinism', p. 274.
22. Brzezinski, *op. cit.*, pp. 116–22.

CHAPTER FIVE

Socialist Industrialization and Economic Development

BASIC FEATURES OF SOCIALIST INDUSTRIALIZATION

Planned economic growth and the priority development of the industrial sector were central features of the socialist model as it evolved from the experience of the Soviet Union and came to be applied in Central Europe. The contours of this model sharpened as Stalinism tightened its grip and the Cold War intensified with the outbreak of hostilities in Korea on 25 June 1950. Ambitious economic plans were reformulated and geared to a faster rate of growth and higher levels of production. Although the Stalinist phase was relatively short in Central Europe, it was during this time that the basic features of central control and detailed administration of the economy were established. Some changes and a certain relaxation were to come after Stalin's death, but these concerned the intensity with which the principles that underlay the model were pursued rather than any major change in structure. The fundamentals of the economic structure imposed under Stalin persisted throughout the communist period in Central Europe. More thoroughgoing changes were contemplated but never enacted in Poland, and reform was not allowed to progress far in Czechoslovakia. Concerted reform measures were taken in Hungary but it became evident in the course of the economic difficulties encountered during the 1980s that even these were not sufficient to overcome the fundamental problems of the command economy and many features of the initial Stalinist economic model remained.

Table 5.1 Percentage share of socialized sector in industrial output and retail turnover in 1952

	Industry	*Trade*
Czechoslovakia	98	97
GDR	77	54
Hungary	97	82
Poland	99	93

Source Kaser, *Economic History*, p. 8

The patterns of economic life established soon after the consolidation of communist power in Central Europe, then, set the context for many of the developments seen during the following forty years. The foundations of the Stalinist economic model were put in place, and the nationalization of economic production units that progressed as communist power was consolidated which enabled the pattern to be applied and its content quickly developed. Reform of industrial organization in the Soviet occupation zone of Germany gathered pace in 1946, and by early 1948 firms within the state or local authority sector accounted for 40 per cent of industrial production. Nationalization legislation was passed in Czechoslovakia, Poland and Hungary between 1945 and 1948 with the consequence that, by January 1948, all major production units lay within the state sector. At the end of the year it embraced 80 per cent of the economy in those three countries. Four years later (Table 5.1), with the partial exception of the GDR (which kept some special characteristics in this respect through to the 1970s), the state sector accounted for the overwhelming bulk of industrial production and much of retail trade.

Table 5.2 Socialization of the agricultural area: percentage in collective and state farm ownership

	1952	*1953*	*1954*	*1955*	*1956*	*1957*	*1958*
Czechoslovakia	43	43	42	43	49	68	87
GDR	3*	30	28	33	30	34	90
Hungary	37	39	31	34	39	12*	77
Poland	17	19	19	24	22	13	13

* percentage under collective ownership

Source Kaser, *Economic History*, pp. 52, 80

An equivalent process in the rural sector was the adoption of a policy for the socialization of agriculture on the Soviet model and, particularly, the decision to accelerate collectivization after 1949 (Table 5.2). Aware of the dire consequences that had followed the Soviet collectivization campaign twenty years earlier (not the least of which had been widespread famine in 1932–33), Central European leaders were not eager to rush the process. This was particularly true in Poland and, to a lesser extent, Hungary. Gomułka's sensitivity to the significance of national conditions in the construction of socialism and, particularly, his resistance to the imposition of the Soviet model on the Polish countryside were major elements in his removal from power. The relatively tentative imposition of the Soviet model in the GDR also had a moderating influence and the adoption of the New Course in the Soviet Union following the death of Stalin further served to slow down and even, in some cases, reverse the socialization process in the agricultural sector. Finally, the revolutionary uprising in Hungary during 1956 and the analagous, though more peaceful, developments in Poland were accompanied by the spontaneous dissolution of collective farms in those countries. In the case of Poland, the mass collectivization policy was never readopted.

Table 5.3 Percentage of net material product generated in the socialist sector

	1950	1955	1960	1965
Czechoslovakia	78.9	92.0	98.5	99.2
GDR	56.8	69.9	84.6	86.0
Hungary	65.7	70.8	91.0	97.0
Poland	54.0	70.3	62.5	77.5

Source Kaser, *Economic History*, pp. 50, 83

As a result of the policies adopted both for industry and agriculture, the level of overall production (or net material product) generated in the socialist sector rose markedly, but took some time to become overwhelmingly dominant even in the countries that had earlier been in the lead, like Czechoslovakia and Hungary (Table 5.3). The disappearance of most of the Polish collective farms in 1956 meant a sharp reduction in the level of 'socialist production' in Poland, although steady development and rising production in the rest of the economy meant that the earlier level was quite soon exceeded. Nevertheless, in the mid-sixties, Poland continued to show differences in production structure that were reflected in the overall pattern of production, as did the GDR, which in 1965 derived 14 per cent of industrial production from the non-state sector.

The rise in the proportion of output deriving from the socialist sector was accompanied by growth in the percentage of the national (net material) product derived from the industrial sector (Table 5.4). In the case of Poland the association was a particularly direct one, as the growing role of the industrial sector qualified the reduced part played by socialized production in agriculture and reversed the trend initiated in 1956. The rapid dominance of production in the socialist sector elsewhere, though (91 per cent or more in Czechoslovakia and Hungary in 1960, 86 per cent in the GDR by 1965), was by no means just the product of socialist industrialization, though it was the most prominent feature of the Stalinist economic model. Even by 1963 only Czechoslovakia and the GDR derived more than 60 per cent of their net material product from the industrial sector.

Table 5.4 Percentage of net material product derived from industry

	1950	1958	1963	1967	1975	1980
Czechoslovakia	48.5	58.8	66.8	67.3	64.4	75.5
GDR	53.6	61.5	66.0	65.4	62.2	75.1
Hungary	41.9	50.8	59.1	63.3	47.0	60.1
Poland	34.6	44.6	49.9	53.5	52.1	64.0

Source Morris, *Eastern Europe Since 1945*, p. 104

The socialist industrialization drive initiated in the late 1940s and the general programme of communist development associated with it showed quite high rates of growth in the early stages. More balanced analysis, however, suggests that they were nothing like as high as those claimed at the time by Central European governments in terms of net material product indices (Table 5.5). In most countries growth rates were highest in the 1950s. The pattern of growth in Czechoslovakia, where industrial development had already been advanced and war-time destruction largely absent, was somewhat different. One major economic problem was the acute shortage of labour – a short-fall of 200,000 workers was calculated for 1945 (particularly evident in the light industries) – a factor closely related to the high number of German workers expelled.[1] Recalculations also suggest a somewhat lower growth rate for East Germany during the early 1950s as well.[2] It has, indeed, been suggested that East German statistics were even less reliable than those published by the rest of the communist camp, partly at least in order to avoid odious comparison with the FRG. While growth rates may generally have been overstated by some 2 per cent, those in the GDR could well have been inflated by as much as 8 per cent.[3] The growth that did occur was achieved at considerable cost throughout the region, particularly in terms of the high levels of capital investment involved. The share of capital accumulation in national income was suddenly increased by 30–40 per cent compared with the immediate post-war reconstruction period, while investment levels were further raised in 1950 under Soviet influence in response to the growing Cold War pressures that followed the outbreak of the Korean War. International factors were therefore of prime importance during this critical period. While the US contributed substantial resources to the reconstruction of Western Europe under the provisions of the Marshall Plan, the Soviet Union actually extracted roughly the same amount from the regions of Europe it controlled.[4] The combined influence of these elements imposed substantial costs in other areas.

Table 5.5 Estimated annual growth rates in gross national product

	1950–55	1955–60	1960–65	1965–70	1970–75	1975–80
Czechoslovakia	3.0	6.3	2.0	3.5	3.4	2.2
GDR	6.4	5.0	2.9	3.2	3.5	2.4
Hungary	4.7	4.6	4.3	3.1	3.4	2.3
Poland	4.6	4.5	4.1	3.8	6.6	0.9

Source Alton, 'Comparison', p. 40

Table 5.6 Changes in real wage levels, 1950 = 100

	1951	1952	1953	1954	1955	1956	1957
Czechoslovakia	96	95	95	104	110	118	122
Hungary	89	81	85	101	104	117	138
Poland	100	92	92	104	110	124	133
GDR	136	157	177	207	227	234	248

Source Kaser, *Economic History*, p. 64

The factors responsible for the high growth rates in the early communist period, for one thing, had a decidedly negative effect on popular living standards. The strong flow of capital investment meant that investment funds for agriculture, consumer goods and housing were all cut. During this period, wages fell in many areas in real terms from an already low base and inflation levels rose, largely in consequence of the growth in employment and the failure of consumer goods supplies to keep up (Table 5.6). Rationing was introduced – during 1950 in Poland, for example. The same country had a high rate of inflation, with consumer prices rising by 80 per cent between 1950 and 1953. In Hungary they rose by 70 per cent and in Czechoslovakia by some 20 per cent. In the GDR consumer prices fell after 1950 – but on the other hand rationing was maintained there until 1958, whereas in Czechoslovakia, Hungary and Poland it was abolished in 1953. Monetary reform (introduced in Poland during 1950 and 1953 in Czechoslovakia) had the effect of further reducing public purchasing power. Living standards were also kept low by the failure to invest in housing and urban infrastructure at a time when rates of rural emigration and industrial construction were high.

Wage levels thus fell markedly in real terms during the early 1950s: by 5 per cent in Czechoslovakia between 1950 and 1953, 8 per cent in Poland and 15 per cent in Hungary (where they were even lower in 1952). Conditions differed in the GDR, as some remedies were developed to cope with the devastation of the immediate post-war years. In the region as a whole, though, conditions improved with the adoption of the New Course in the Soviet Union after Stalin's death. The proportion of net material product devoted to accumulation was cut back and living standards were permitted to rise. Other measures also relieved the burdens placed on the economies of Central Europe. The Soviet-Hungarian joint companies were dissolved in 1954, pressures to maintain collectivization eased and incentives to increase agricultural production were introduced. Real wages rose throughout the region after 1953. Even in the early 1950s, though, the pattern of socio-economic change did not always have quite such negative consequences as the indices might suggest.

Considerable emphasis was placed on general and vocational education, opportunities were opened up for underprivileged groups and new paths of social mobility appeared. The market for farm produce was strong and agricultural underemployment declined. In Hungary peasant incomes grew rapidly from the mid-

1950s and by the late 1960s were broadly at the same level as those of workers.[5] One major effect of Kadarism was to compensate the peasantry for the sacrifices it had to make during the 'construction of socialism'.[6] There was extensive migration from rural areas to the towns. Between 1950 and 1955 off-farm employment rose by 15 per cent in Czechoslovakia, 20 per cent in Hungary, 24 per cent in the GDR and 34 per cent in Poland. Manual workers were promoted to foremen and advanced managerial positions. The needs of industrial construction and demand for building workers helped to improve their earning capacity and reduce wage inequality. An increasing proportion of women found employment outside the agricultural sector and undertook work in industry (although this tendency was limited in Poland, where the labour demands of small-scale agriculture remained strong).[7] The period of dynamism in the economy undoubtedly had positive effects, although the balance of investment and implications of the overall pattern of development meant that the process of change soon encountered major obstacles.

THE COMMUNIST ECONOMIC MODEL IN CENTRAL EUROPE

The policies of socialist industrialization were thus formulated and the Stalinist model of economic development applied with considerable rapidity. Major economic changes were carried through within relatively few years. Post-war conditions (including the inheritance of enterprises formerly under German control) and the expropriation of former ruling groups, as well as pre-war traditions of state ownership and economic influence in some areas, facilitated state intervention and the introduction of measures of nationalization from the immediate post-war months. Such changes in the economic sphere accompanied the establishment and consolidation of communist power from the outset, the full pattern crystallizing swiftly at the end of the 1940s and its features receiving further emphasis during 1949 and 1950. Soon after Stalin's death in March 1953, however, steps were taken to modify some of the more exaggerated features of the model which had already caused serious economic imbalances and whose continued existence threatened further problems. This particularly concerned the maintenance of high levels of capital accumulation, the concentration of resources in the heavy industry and defence sectors, and growing difficulties caused by the neglect of consumer needs and popular living standards. More attention was paid to consumer industries, the pressure of collectivization was eased and wage levels rose. Significant improvements in living standards were already evident in 1954 and carried through to the 1956–60 period, though this development did not continue during the following decade.

In the early stages and in terms of its consequences for an impoverished post-war population, the Stalinist model was not without several quite significant virtues. Before the war there had been extensive rural overpopulation in relation to the needs of agricultural production and the employment it offered. This was particularly true of countries like Romania, but it had also been a major problem in Poland and Hungary. The rapid development of heavy industry and the demands of construction work associated with it helped to provide the necessary demand for this reserve of labour and the products of the agricultural sector. Post-war policies also pointed the way to a radical improvement in structures of land ownership and the possibility of much needed agrarian reform. Before the war rural poverty in Central Europe had been exacerbated by the falling price of agricultural produce and denial of access to West European markets. The Depression held back regional economic development and the growth of domestic markets. As market forces did not seem to be capable of producing the structural changes required for the shift of capital and labour resources needed to produce growth, the directive processes characteristic of the command economy (strongly supported and reinforced by the political conventions of the Soviet system) were able to play a positive role in this area. Highly centralized government processes and political leadership provided means for the accumulation and movement of capital resources to facilitate this form of development. A certain level of urban infrastructure was provided within the communist system to accompany the growing industrial centres. More town-dwellers increased demand (all too often unsatisfied) for food and agricultural products, as for other consumer goods.

The Stalinist model of socialist industrialization was, nevertheless, one that had been developed and fully articulated in the Soviet Union during the 1930s. The model was one that favoured heavy industry over light and consumer industries, quantity over quality, traditional technology over more advanced variants, and the exercise of strong control over the economy to the detriment of innovation. As applied in the Soviet Union, the policy of socialist industrialization was one designed to catch up (and eventually overtake) the developed capitalist nations. It contained, however, little capacity for more complex adaptation or recognition of the fact that the objectives and processes of the modern economy were themselves subject to change. Its defects were already becoming evident once the initial phase of industrialization had passed soon after the war. These problems became severe in Central Europe as early as the 1950s and persisted during subsequent decades. Areas like East Germany and the Czech lands of Bohemia and Moravia were already well developed and bore little resemblance to the relatively backward, peasant-based economy in which the Stalinist model of accelerated industrial development had originally been articulated. The crude pursuit of basic plan targets was a process little suited to the operation and further development of relatively mature industrial societies. Adoption of the Soviet model in Czechoslovakia, particularly in the exaggerated post-Korea version of the early 1950s, thus represented a 'great leap backward'. This entailed an irrational restructuring of the economy, directing it to an over-emphasis on heavy engineering to satisfy immediate Soviet demands and cutting it off from the Western markets from which it might have derived further benefits in terms of continuing technological innovation.[8]

Central Europe contained, too, smaller countries with an established place in world trade patterns and the international division of labour. Some industries were already highly developed and had been well integrated in regional or world trade structures before the war. Their separation from Western markets or, in the case of East Germany, from other portions of their own nation, caused considerable dislocation which could hardly be remedied within the Soviet-imposed framework of autarchic national development. In addition, the imposition of a uniform model of economic development on such areas made necessary the creation of industrial sectors for which the raw materials were often lacking locally. The emphasis on heavy industry was unsuitable for countries ill-supplied in sources of energy and raw materials. Poland and Romania could draw, respectively, on extensive supplies of coal, oil and natural gas, but the region as a whole had little iron ore on which much of the drive for heavy industrial development depended. In the late 1940s the growth potential of Czechoslovakia was the highest of all the Central and South-East European countries, but while its strengths lay in the production of industrial goods its particular weaknesses were identified with the poor supply of raw material resources.[9] The erection of the Iron Curtain and reorientation of Central European economies in many spheres towards the needs and policy preferences of the Soviet Union, therefore, presented them with limited prospects of real development or sustained growth. Oil supplies from the Soviet Union made up a quarter of total GDR imports. In the early 1960s the USSR accounted for nearly half the country's foreign trade, although efforts at diversification meant that this proportion was brought down to less than a third in 1974.[10] Dependence on the outdated model presented by the Soviet Union meant that while, for example, most countries had by 1980 overtaken Britain in areas like the extraction of coal and iron production, they still tended to lag behind in the provision of a basic flexible energy source like electricity.

Patterns of growth throughout the communist period clearly suffered from the rigorous application of the Stalinist model during the early years. While high rates of growth were achieved in the early 1950s, this was associated with factors like the rapid mobilization into the industrial sector of former agricultural workers and was not something that could be replicated. Despite the relaxation that took place after 1953 and the attempt to apply a more balanced model of development, growth rates tended to fall in most countries during the second half of the decade and declined further in the early 1960s (Table 5.5). In terms both of living standards and overall growth rates, then, the economic pattern that took shape in the early years of communist power soon showed signs of considerable strain and gave cause for dissatisfaction on a number of grounds. A certain stabilization in growth rates nevertheless took place in Czechoslovakia and the GDR between 1965 and 1975, and some recovery was evident in Hungary after 1970 (as it was in Poland, where it occurred under unusual and artificial conditions). However, this could not be sustained in the changing economic environment and global recession that took hold later in the 1970s. Rates of economic growth thus slackened generally between 1950 and the late 1980s, but this was particularly true of the period following 1975.[11]

Nevertheless, by 1980 significant steps had been taken towards the establishment of modern industrial economies, high rates of production had been reached in major industrial sectors and the supply of energy resources had been greatly increased. But it was also becoming evident that the objectives and concepts of modernity embodied in the Stalinist pattern no longer accorded with patterns that had developed elsewhere. Indeed, the Stalinist claim to have constructed any form of modernity at all was open to considerable doubt.[12] The capacities of the communist economies were, in particular, increasingly outstripped by the demands of the high-technology revolution of the late twentieth century, which involved primarily an information revolution based on the extremely rapid acquisition, processing and retrieval of enormous quantities of data made possible by computers and micro-electronics.[13] Instability in relations with developed Western countries meant that the deficit could not be made up from that source. Although there was considerable expansion in Western technology imports in the early 1970s, growth was not maintained and Western technology had a relatively weak impact, largely because of the systemic problems afflicting the Central European economies.[14] Within an international frame of reference, East Germany was the only Central European country to suffer a decline in relative position when the economic record of thirty-two major states between 1937 and 1960 was examined. The GDR slipped from eighth to sixteenth place, probably because of the burden of reparations, other transfers to the Soviet Union, inability to benefit from the Marshall Plan, and the extensive loss of skilled human resource before the construction of the Berlin Wall. Between 1960 and 1980, however, it was the decline of Czechoslovakia that was most marked, although some slippage could now also be seen in the position of Poland and, still, the GDR.[15]

The post-war model of economic development applied in Central Europe thus had serious drawbacks that soon made themselves felt. Its prime characteristic was the organization of the economy on the basis of central planning, in which leading decision-makers had the power ultimately to control the operation of every factory or enterprise within the socialized sector. Relations between all production and retail units, increasingly diverse and fast-moving within a complex modern economy, were formally mediated by the central authorities and at least potentially controlled by them. Relatively small numbers of private production enterprises or retail organizations, and the larger sector of private agricultural production (including the plots of collective farmers or state farm employees), lay outside their detailed guidance – although, of course, they were subject to the extensive rules and regulations governing all economic activity. Most wages and prices were centrally determined, as were the supply and allocation of the great majority of goods and services (housing, education, transport, health services). In principle, organization and administration served many functions performed within capitalism by the market. The control of economic and social processes was one of the system's prime values. This was officially because of its greater rationality and the capacity it gave to plan social development, but it also constituted a major power resource, which accorded with the totalitarian drive that underlay the Stalinist political system. The idea of the command economy reflected this aspect of the model, although the proliferation of individual commands that the model entailed meant that many were ignored, delayed or not carried out properly.

In practical terms, the development of whole economies along these lines meant an enormous and rapid expansion of administrative processes and institutions. In several senses, the economies became bureaucratized. National planning organs were all transformed and reorganized in 1949 along the lines of the Soviet Gosplan, and their leadership placed under firmer Politburo control. Ministries proliferated to exercise direct and detailed control over all aspects of economic life. None of the countries had fewer than ten economic ministries and at one stage Poland had as many as twenty-six (including three for construction and three for transport). Central government expanded as the number of vice-premiers was increased to oversee the work of the different ministries. A similar process took place in the party and its apparatus as 'party leadership' took a more detailed form and individual officials assumed specific responsibility for particular areas of activity. The development of a planned economy thus meant an enormous expansion of administrative organizations, their staff and activities. In fact, as the newly established communist regimes were dedicated to rapid and extensive change, formal administrative processes were often ignored or bypassed and priority was attached to a few particularly important production targets and activities. The characteristics of the command economy meant that key targets could be identified and resources directed towards them, while others received far less attention than they were supposed to. In this way pronounced imbalances could develop with alarming speed, and the Stalinist economies became critically slanted to investment in heavy industry and satisfaction of its virtually limitless demands.

Problems also occurred in the detailed operation of the system. The principles of effective planning and appropriate decision-making depended on the availability of accurate information. The interests and material advantages of those who provided this were dependent on what was done with it, however, so it was hardly surprising that the information supplied was governed less by questions of accuracy than by its likely future impact on the unit supplying it. Plant directors, for example, often presented enterprise activity in such a way as to show that targets had been met and great achievements made, but otherwise were happy to minimize past achievement so as not to have higher plan targets imposed in the future. Accurate information might well be prominent by its absence.

Problems of detailed planning led to a concentration on gross output and lack of attention being paid to its quality and assortment. There was less concern for inputs and production costs. Stockpiles and the hoarding of resources (both of labour and materials) could be considerable to help managers build security into future production processes. These were often balanced by unsold output, credit for whose production had already been acheived but which attracted few or no customers. Obedience and predictability were sought from producers and there was little encouragement of innovation. In this process it was the consumer who received least attention, a consequence that ran throughout the entire system and affected not just the interests and level of satisfaction of the public but also those of industrial consumers at intermediate stages of production. This tendency was further strengthened by the conscious policy emphasis placed on heavy industry and its rapid development as the foundation of the whole process of economic development.

ECONOMIC CHANGE AND LIVING STANDARDS

Despite shortcomings in the economic strategy pursued in Central Europe and problems experienced in the process of rapid industrial growth, extensive development did take place and a large increase in output was achieved over the post-war period (Table 5.7). Comparable output figures for the United Kingdom are also given, although they cannot be taken as direct equivalents and permit only a broad idea of relative production levels. The 1980 figures have also been recomputed on a current population base (column eight) to give a more realistic idea of production levels in the given

Table 5.7 Production of Selected Industrial Items

	1949	1954	1960	1965	1970	1974/5	1980	1980 per capita	1987 per capita
Electricity (MWh):									
Czechoslovakia	8	14	25	34	45	59	74	0.49	0.55
GDR	15	24	40	54	68	85	99	0.59	0.69
Hungary	2	5	8	11	15	21	24	0.22	0.28
Poland	8	15	29	44	65	97	122	0.34	0.39
UK	51	74	121	178	229	252	282	0.50	
Coal/Lignite (m tons):									
Czechoslovakia	42	58	85	101	106	114	123	0.80	
GDR	113	182	226	252	261	247	258	1.54	
Hungary	11	22	27	31	28	25	26	0.24	
Poland	76	98	104	142	173	212	230	0.65	
UK	215	224	195	189	150	131	124	0.22	
Pig iron (m tons):									
Czechoslovakia	1.6	2.8	4.7	5.9	7.5	8.9	10.3	0.67	
GDR	0.2	1.3	2.0	2.3	2.0	2.3	3.0	0.18	
Hungary	0.4	0.7	1.2	1.6	1.8	2.3	2.4	0.22	
Poland	1.2	2.7	4.6	5.8	7.3	8.2	11.6	0.33	
UK	9.5	11.9	15.8	17.5	17.7	13.9	11.8	0.21	

Source Morris, *Eastern Europe Since 1945*, p. 81; *Polityka – Eksport – Import* (Warsaw) 1989, 26

society. Column nine provides equivalent figures for per capita electricity generation in 1987. They demonstrate, among other things, the high (and almost certainly excessive) output of a traditional fuel like coal in preference to such a flexible energy source as electricity. Iron production in Central Europe rose considerably, too, while Britain took steps to reduce output levels. Such proportions lend support to the idea that the communist economic model locked Central Europe into a dynamic, but ultimately limited model of development.

The balance of communist economic development should by no means be viewed wholly in negative terms, though. In giving priority to the development of heavy industry, previously the major motor of development in the West and in the Soviet Union, socialist industrialization achieved impressive rates of growth. This gave a marked boost to less developed economies like Hungary and Poland. Major steps in social development took place – as, indeed, also happened after 1945 in Western Europe (with the consequence that most countries of Central and Eastern Europe, apart from Czechoslovakia, were still below the average European per capita income level in 1973 by 9 to 15 per cent).[16] It had a major impact on the living standards of the mass of the population and on elements like food consumption and housing (Table 5.8). Meat came to play a much larger part in the population's diet between 1950 and 1965 and levels of cereal consumption fell somewhat. Considerably more sugar was also eaten. The degree to which these developments can be regarded as an improvement and a contribution to health standards may be open to some doubt, but it was certainly the case that many Central Europeans came to regard increased food consumption, particularly of meat and related products, as a leading index of socio-economic advance and a major criterion by which to judge the performance of their rulers. Whatever the GDR's other failings, meat consumption there was on a par with that in the Federal Republic in the 1980s.[17] For these, as well as other reasons, extensive state subsidies of food products became widespread and the question of raising food prices was a serious political problem, particularly in Poland. Housing and the provision of accommodation was a further major problem, associated both with the rapid growth of towns and the changing values and aspirations of new generations. Trends during the early 1960s show less improvement here, although the situation in the GDR was not so negative as it appears, due to the lower rate of marriage and a higher level of residential provision in relation to the rate of household formation. East German consumption rates in general were judged to be 'clearly superior to all other European communist states in virtually every conventional category'.[18]

Table 5.8 Aspects of living standards

| | Per-capita food consumption (kg) | | | | New dwellings per 1,000 inhabitants | |
	1950	1960	1965	1984	1960	1965
Czechoslovakia						
Cereals	124	126	130		5.4	5.5
Meat	33	57	62	85		
Milk	146	173	180			
Sugar	26	36	38			
GDR						
Cereals		102	100		4.7	4.0
Meat	22	55	59	94		
Milk			105			
Sugar	20	29	30			
Hungary						
Cereals	142	133	136		5.8	5.4
Meat	34	48	52	76		
Milk	112	114	97			
Sugar	16	27	30			
Poland						
Cereals	166	147	143		4.8	5.4
Meat	37	50	56	67		
Milk	212	363	367			
Sugar	21	28	33			

Source Kaser, *Economic History*, pp. 131, 133; Dennis, *German Democratic Republic*, p. 75

Table 5.9 Annual percentage increase in real wages

	1956–60	1961–65	1966–70	1971–75
Czechoslovakia	4.6	1.2	3.5	3.4
GDR	7.4	2.5	3.7	3.8
Hungary	8.0	1.7	3.5	3.4
Poland	5.1	1.5	1.9	7.3

Source Kaser, *Economic History*, pp. 95, 150, 152

As industrial output rose, wages also increased and sustained the improvement in living standards reflected in higher consumption levels and more food purchases (Table 5.9). After the rigours of the early industrialization process, overall incomes rose throughout much of the period, although at different rates, reflecting the fluctuations and a general slowing down process evident in economic developments (Table 5.5). The improvements seen in real wages during the 1950s following the relaxation of the original industrialization drive in fact turned out to be the greatest of the whole period. They were succeeded by a period of relative stagnation in the early 1960s and limited improvements thereafter (with the partial exception of Poland, where the costs of more striking increases in the early 1970s were fully repaid during later years).

REFORM IMPERATIVES AND THE PROBLEMS OF CHANGE

In view of the range of problems involved in the operation of the communist economic model, and with the growing threat to political stability posed by popular dissatisfaction and the opposition that began to surface in 1953 after several years of stringency and falling living standards, it was not surprising that reform measures were sought only a few years after the onset of Stalinism in Central Europe. The subsequent fate of economic reform was a lengthy and somewhat strange one. The need to depart from the excessive emphasis on growth and industrial development was recognized at an early stage but found to be remarkably difficult to achieve. Despite modifications, the central elements of the model introduced in the late 1940s persisted and the changes made failed to tackle fundamental economic problems. The subsequent influence of global recession and the difficulties associated with international debt that became critical towards the end of the 1970s also served to underline the continuing gravity of the economic situation and the partial nature of the departure from Stalinist principles in the economy. There remained major obstacles to the introduction of effective reform and even Hungary, where the most thoroughgoing and apparently effective reform was relaunched at the beginning of the 1980s, encountered further problems in the middle of the decade, which prompted consideration of the need for more radical change.

The difficulty of reconciling two key objectives of economic policy became apparent at an early stage. It had soon been possible to secure high overall growth (as had been the case until 1953) or to achieve higher living standards (as happened during the New Course of 1953–56), but it proved hard to assure the conditions for progress in both directions at the same time. For a period after 1955 it seemed that the objectives could be reconciled. But the process soon turned out to be more complex than first thought. Early attempts at rationalizing the system of central planning made its operation even less efficient. Material incentives for plan fulfilment were reinforced by administrative regulations; the reduction or removal of administrative pressures made existing incentives even weaker.[19] A further problem that soon made itself felt was the imposition of a post-1956 political 'normalization', most obvious in Hungary after the Soviet invasion but also present to an increasing extent in Poland under the influence of Gomułka. The reformist outlook that had seemed to accompany his return to power soon evaporated. The reassertion of political control, moreover, made it difficult to modify the economic command system and reduce centralized control of the economy. While an official commitment to the introduction of substantial economic reform still existed in Poland in 1957, the advisory Economic Council that was supposed to research and formulate the necessary policies was ignored by central party and government leaders and soon ceased to exist. Declining rates of growth in Poland and a particularly poor record in terms of Polish living standards during the 1960s were a clear consequence of these developments and the failure to implement earlier reform proposals (Table 5.5, 5.9).

Czechoslovakia was the second country to prepare (at the end of 1957) reform plans which were intended to reduce detailed central supervision and increase the role of economic incentives. But the reform process was half-hearted here, too, and most of the changes that had occurred were scrapped by 1961–62. In consequence, growth rates in Czechoslovakia were particularly low during the early 1960s, and it was here that the first absolute decline of the post-war period in national income was recorded in 1963. The first wave of economic reforms after 1956 thus bore little fruit. The shortcomings of the conventional communist model and the economic problems they had been designed to tackle persisted, however, and a renewed concern for reform activity emerged in the mid-1960s.

Five characteristics can be identified in connection with the second reform wave that surfaced in the region. Firstly, the reforms were implemented more fully than had been the case in the earlier period. Secondly, they all provided for a fuller devolution of decision-making and a greater role for market mechanisms. In order to retain a necessary degree of control they also, thirdly, contained provisions for industrial concentration and enhanced the status of the intermediate tier of economic administration. A fourth characteristic of the second reform wave was the inclusion of socialized agriculture and measures to reform planning procedures, increase the role of market-type methods of exerting control over production, and raise the level of farm incomes. However, a fifth feature was that, as before, the reforms lost momentum and their influence tended to peter out.[20]

In terms of the reform measures introduced during this period, it was Hungary that brought forward and implemented the most important proposals. Preparations for the New Economic Mechanism began in 1965 and full implementation was introduced at the beginning of 1968. Enterprise autonomy was increased in terms of investment and the capacity to respond to incentives; price mechanisms were overhauled and made more realistic; and the role of market forces was generally enhanced. By 1973, however, steps were being taken (both for economic and political reasons) to weaken the impact of these changes, a tendency that was strengthened by the pressure exerted by international constraints associated with the sharp rise in energy and raw material prices.

Changes made elsewhere remained within the limits imposed by the more conventional conceptions of established centralist procedures. New economic guidelines were drawn up in the GDR in 1963 which also provided for a significant reduction in the number of plan indicators and the allocation of a greater role for profit in guiding economic decision-making. But signs of reluctance to press on with the changes became evident in 1967 and they were beginning to be reversed by the beginning of the 1970s. Similar changes were projected for Poland, but their implementation was interrupted by the worker unrest of December 1970, provoked by measures to realign price structures and prepare the way for a new incentive mechanism. The reform was, therefore, only partially implemented and soon overshadowed by the growing tensions caused by Gierek's loan-fuelled expansionist policy. The fate of Czechoslovak plans for economic reform was similarly intertwined with the political changes which were increasingly seen as necessary to secure effective change in any major portion of the communist economy. Again, the political aspect soon became dominant and reform was generally held back after 1968. After Husák's election to the Czechoslovak party leadership, the reform movement was halted both because of the ideological proclivities of the post-Dubček équipe and the emphasis on strengthened central control occasioned by the chaos and political tension that followed the August invasion.

Table 5.10 Estimated annual growth rates in gross national product

	1980	1982	1984	1980–85	1986	1987
Czechoslovakia	1.7	1.4	2.2	1.4	2.1	1.3
GDR	2.4	0.0	3.0	1.7	1.5	2.2
Hungary	0.5	1.5	1.3	0.9	2.1	1.2
Poland	–3.2	–0.6	3.4	1.2	2.8	–2.5

Source Dawisha, *Eastern Europe*, p. 135; Alton, 'Comparison', p. 40

The pervasive centralism and emphasis on institutionalized mechanisms of control in general made it remarkably difficult to achieve effective economic reform within the orthodox structures of the communist system and under the conditions of strict political discipline that lay at the heart of it. Little appetite for extensive reform was shown in the GDR – and, indeed, the level of economic performance there was not so disturbingly low as it was in some other countries (Table 5.5). When, too, development conditions became particularly unfavourable for the Central European economies in the 1980s, the closer relations that had developed with the Federal Republic became particularly advantageous in helping it secure loans at favourable rates and in facilitating access to EC markets (Table 5.10). The GDR was the only East European country in the first half of the 1980s to escape having a year of 'negative growth', or economic shrinkage.[21] During this period Czechoslovakia remained subject to the spirit of post-1968 'normalization' that followed the Soviet invasion both in the political and economic spheres. Living standards had been generally maintained throughout the 1970s and the leadership showed no desire to disturb the order that had been imposed either by political or economic experimentation. Even the replacement of Czechoslovak leader Gustav Husák in December 1987 did little to change this. The leadership remained resistant to Gorbachev's bolder initiatives for *perestroika* and broader ideas of political and economic reform.

However, draft principles for the restructuring of the economic mechanism were approved in 1988 and, six months later, a law which provided for the creation of workers' councils came into effect.

Poland, following the political and economic debacle that resulted from Edward Gierek's policies during the 1970s, experienced a similar period of normalization that began with the imposition of martial law in December 1981. While a programme of reform was notionally still in force, little effective change was achieved and an attempt to relaunch the reform process from the end of 1987 petered out the following year. Only Hungary succeeded in pursuing the objectives of economic reform it had set and renewed its commitment to further change in the late 1970s. The more flexible economic model it developed helped it survive the vicissitudes of the late 1970s and early 1980s with a fair degree of success, but a combination of economic and political tensions combined to threaten the continuity of the Kádár leadership from 1986. Even this, the most consistent attempt to modify the model developed and maintained since the Stalin period, thus found it impossible fully to escape the limitations of the orthodox communist legacy.

NEW PERSPECTIVES ON ECONOMIC CHANGE

As we have seen, the persistence of the principles and processes that flowed from the centralized economic model were closely associated both with the continuing imposition of the political structures that had grown out of Stalinism and the general importance attached to the idea and practice of central control within the communist system. A further significant factor here was the emphasis placed on the role of economic factors in social development and Marxist-Leninist notions of economic determinism. The priority attached to the rapid development of heavy industry was strengthened by ideas about the historical development of modern economies as well as by ideological conceptions concerning the prime role played by the working class in the construction of socialism. The preference for the direction of resources to the heavy industry sector was, therefore, not just a matter of economic calculation. It also formed part of a general ideological conception and the political dogma with which it was associated. Conceptions of the economy went far beyond ideas about the production and distribution of essential goods and services and its development was presented as a critical factor in the course of social and political development. This identity strengthened elements of resistance to reform and economic change and made it difficult for communist decision-makers to view the systems of production and distribution they had imposed just in economic terms and to set about removing the major obstacles to their more effective operation.

It was, therefore, only under the conditions of general crisis during the 1980s that issues of political and economic change emerged in a form that took account of the interrelation between the two areas and began to open the possibility of radical alternatives to established practices being taken. Half-measures that attempted to tackle particular economic problems in isolation and which were separated from more general issues of centralization and political control had made little impact and were watered down before any real improvement could be made in economic processes.

Conditions imposed by the international environment also played a major role in determining the possibilities of change.[22] The policies pursued by the Soviet Union and imposed on individual Central European countries were clearly of great importance in the immediate post-war period. The opportunities for greater international integration that emerged in the 1970s were significant, although their consequences (particularly for Poland and Hungary) were by no means wholly positive. But the new climate that followed the accession of Gorbachev to the Soviet leadership brought with it the possibility of real change in the Central European economies. The initiation of *perestroika* opened up new perspectives on the role of the structures and processes involved in the operation of the communist economies. A major aspect of the reappraisal this involved was the different view taken by the Kremlin of international relations and the place of the communist economies in the broader world system. The phase of national autarchy inaugurated by Stalin was clearly over.

The opening up of the communist economies to the influence of international trade and production processes thus became a major aspect of the conceptions of economic reform that emerged in the 1980s. Closer contact with international money markets during the previous decade had already brought some of the communist economies into close, and often painful, relations of dependence with the capitalist world. Despite the unfortunate consequences of this relationship, it soon became clear that tighter integration with the world economy was a precondition for the restoration of economic equilibrium and any economic recovery that was possible. Departure from the practices of the Stalinist economic model, marked by centralism, state control and isolation from international economic processes, was finally signalled by such moves as Hungary's membership of the International Monetary Fund in 1982 and the equivalent initiatives undertaken by Poland in the search for a way out of its protracted economic crisis.

NOTES AND REFERENCES

1. Zeman, *The Making and Breaking*, p. 237.
2. Kaser, *Economic History*, p. 19.
3. Rupnik, *The Other Europe*, p. 171.
4. Marer, 'The political economy', p. 156.
5. Ferge, *Society in the Making*, p. 189.
6. Heinrich, *Hungary*, p. 116.
7. Brown, *Eastern Europe*, p. 497.
8. Batt, *Economic Reform and Political Change*, p. 59.
9. Teichova, *The Czechoslovak Economy 1918–1980*, p. 119.
10. Jeffries and Melzer, *The East German Economy*, p. 237.
11. Alton, 'Comparison of overall economic performance', p. 37.
12. Schöpflin, 'Stalinist experience in Eastern Europe', p. 146.
13. Griffith, 'Central and Eastern Europe', p. 2.
14. Stent, 'Technology transfer to Eastern Europe', p. 97.
15. Marer, 'Economies and trade of Eastern Europe', pp. 47–48.
16. Landau and Tomaszewski, *The Polish Economy*.
17. Dennis, *German Democratic Republic*, p. 74.
18. Scharf, *Politics and Change in East Germany*, p. 120.
19. Berend and Ranki, *The Hungarian Economy*, p. 223.
20. Kaser, *op. cit.*, pp. 160–63.
21. Dawisha, *Eastern Europe*, p. 135.
22. Lewis, 'Soviet and East European relations', p. 335.

CHAPTER SIX

Social Change and the Nature of Communist Society

THE EFFECTS OF STRUCTURAL CHANGE

The countries of Central Europe after the Second World War were more developed socially and economically than the Balkans and the areas that made up the Soviet Union, and were the most advanced societies to have the experience of communist rule imposed on them. Many areas, nevertheless, remained impoverished, backward and dominated by unproductive peasant agriculture. There was, as we have just seen, considerable scope for the policy of socialist industrialization adopted soon after the war, and major consequences were anticipated from the accelerated economic development and social change that formed part of the socialist vision. This was conceived of as one possessing an advanced industrial economy in which the urban working class played a dominant part – numerically, socially and politically. The bourgeoisie and capitalist property-owning classes were expropriated and virtually eliminated from the social scene – in many cases, initially by the war and German occupation, later by Soviet occupation forces and the economic reparations they administered and, finally, by growing socialization and the strengthening of state control under communist auspices. The peasantry were also soon affected by the accelerating pace of industrialization and implementation of the collectivization policy in the countryside.

These changes did not bring the working class to power in the ways envisaged by some idealistic thinkers or claimed by cynical politicians. Nor were they sufficient to abolish social divisions or enhance social equality as much as was often suggested in ideological pronouncements. Official statistics tended to betray the uncertainty of communist leaders about the level of their achievement. Hungarian statistics, for example, lumped together agricultural and industrial workers in the apparent attempt to give the impression of a stronger working class and a more dynamic process of socialist construction. After 1963, similarly, GDR statistics stopped separating workers from non-manual employees, which provided them with the conclusion in 1985, for example, that 85 per cent of the total of employed people belonged to the working class. Nevertheless, there can be little doubt that the policies implemented in the early years of communist power in Central Europe did bring about major changes in social structure and created new forms of social order there.

As a result of post-war change and the implementation of socialist policies, the rural base of the Central European societies rapidly shrank as opportunities for industrial employment and (less frequently) urban residence opened up. Major portions of the labour force moved out of agriculture into industry and other sectors of employment (Table 6.1). To a large extent this provided an effective solution to the rural underemployment that had been such a serious problem in the pre-war society and the catastrophic poverty that had accompanied it. However, it did not necessarily lead to the development in socio-economic terms of the agricultural sector or to an increase in the attractiveness of the agricultural way of life. This was partly because of the relative lack of overall development but also because of declining possibilities for private or genuinely co-operative agricultural development in the face of growing state domination. The post-war years thus saw persistently high levels of rural emigration and a sharp fall in the proportion of the work-force employed in agriculture (if not always much of a decline in their absolute number). Countries like Poland and

Table 6.1 Percentage of the labour force employed in agriculture

	1950	*1960*	*1970*	*1978/80*	*1987/88*
Czechoslovakia	38	26	19	13	12
GDR	24	18	13	11	11
Hungary	49	37	25	21	21
Poland	56	47	39	30	28
UK	6	2	2	1.6	

Source Morris, *Eastern Europe Since 1945*, p. 115; GUS, *Rocznik Statystyczny 1990*, p. 531

Hungary lost their strongly peasant character, becoming less agricultural and increasingly urban in character. This was by no means wholly attributable to communist policy. The part played by farmers and agricultural labourers in the French work-force fell from 27 to 16 per cent between 1954 and 1967 alone.[1] Between 1949 and 1965–66 in the FRG 1.56 million full-time workers also left farms less than 10 hectares in size, and 109,000 quit farms of between 10 to 20 hectares.[2]

The processes of structural change did not always run in clear-cut fashion. At the end of the war, for example, many Hungarian workers left for the countryside to take advantage of the land reform, bringing about an immediate decline in the proportion of the existing blue-collar group from its 1941 figure of 54 per cent to 38 per cent. The long-term tendency, however, was towards industrial employment and higher levels of urban residence (Table 6.2). This had significant consequences for the nature of the societies and for patterns of stratification. Much of the attraction for those leaving the countryside lay in better living standards and benefits for urban immigrants in terms of employment, access to public goods and overall changes in life-style. Provision for education and health, recreation and cultural pursuits, and the advantages of a more developed infrastructure were all relevant here.

Table 6.2 Percentage of the population classified as urban

	1949–51	*1960–64*	*1970*	*1980*	*1988*
Czechoslovakia	51	48	62	73	76
GDR	71	73	74	76	77
Hungary	37	40	50	57	60
Poland	39	48	52	58	61
UK	80	78	77	76	

Source Morris, *Eastern Europe Since 1945*, p. 116; GUS, *Rocznik Statystyczny* 1987, p. 537; *Rocznik* 1990, p. 520

The rural influx, however, put great pressure on urban development and post-war recovery, and the goods and improvements sought were by no means always to be found in the towns. Real wages, as we have seen (Table 5.6), fell in most countries in the early 1950s, and living standards were hit by the cuts in consumer-good production and outlays on social facilities as the rate of investment in heavy industry and armaments accelerated. There was also a strong belief in some quarters that with the consolidation of the revolution and the strengthening of communist power, the authorities no longer needed to pay attention to such matters and that social policy as a whole could be abandoned. With the establishment of 'socialized' (or state) ownership of production facilities and the achievement of high rates of economic growth on that basis, the spread of socialism was in some senses believed to be an automatic process.[3] Communism did not, therefore, turn out to be synonymous with the development of social planning.

Accommodation and housing provision was a major factor governing the growth of the urban population. Shortages in this area were a major characteristic of social change and critical in influencing the developing patterns of stratification. Even with the more egalitarian distribution of such goods and a smaller allocation for each urban household in the early socialist period (and, indeed, subsequently), there was far from enough to go round. This was reflected in the contrast between the pace of urbanization and the rate of decline in the proportion of the labour force employed in agriculture (Tables 6.1 and 6.2). The proportion of those working in agriculture fell more rapidly than the urban population rose. In the early period the decline was just as high in a relatively developed country like Czechoslovakia, although over the twenty-year period between 1950 and 1970 the agricultural portion of the population also fell by nearly half in Hungary. In Poland the proportion in agricultural employment fell by 16 per cent between 1950 and 1960 and 30 per cent in the twenty-year period following 1950. This was a lower *rate* of decline than seen in the other countries, though one which had considerable national impact because of the greater numbers of those originally employed in agriculture (over half the work force in 1950) and in the light of the very high birth rate in Poland (Table 3.1).

Between 1950 and 1960 urban growth was therefore considerably higher in Poland – at 23 per cent – than elsewhere, which reflected the extensive shift in population that had occurred and its overall expansion. In both Poland and Hungary the urban population grew by around a third in the twenty years following 1950. Housing resources were under considerable strain and further suffered from the reappraisal of policy priorities during the industrialization drive. During the Hungarian five-year plan of 1950–54 the construction of flats fell far below target and fewer than half those planned were completed. In the mid-1960s, 4 people lived in the average Polish dwelling, compared with 3.4 in Hungary, 3.6 in Czechoslovakia, 2.8 in France and Sweden and 2.9 in the GDR.[4] Comparison with Western society showed the bleakness of the housing situation in Central Europe. While provision in the GDR did not look at all bad in comparison with Central European neighbours, its performance fell way behind that of the Federal Republic. During the 1960s the amount of dwelling space in West Germany was increasing at three times the rate it was in the East.[5] The housing problem in the GDR was still being targeted as a priority problem for solution in the five-year plan adopted for the late 1980s.[6] The high rate of emigration and the declining population in the GDR (which fell by 10 per cent between 1958 and 1970) nevertheless meant that housing provision was considerably better than in neighbouring Central European countries which had a higher rate of demographic growth.

During the early 1960s, Poland and Czechoslovakia had the highest density of inhabitants per room – indeed, Poland probably had the worst housing record overall in Central Europe. Even so, many of those who abandoned agricultural work for off-farm employment did not live near their new place of work and either stayed in rudimentary workers' hostels during the week or travelled to work on a daily basis. Many continued to do so throughout the communist period and the partial nature of the urbanization process in Poland and Hungary continued to place additional burdens on many working-class households and remained a source of considerable hardship. This hidden demand for urban accommodation and facilities, combined with the dire situation inherited from the early industrialization period, meant that there was no easing of the pressure on resources and that the housing shortage remained critical. It also gave rise to a sizeable group of worker-peasants (or peasant-workers, insofar as agricultural work continued to provide the major source of income) who combined industrial work with rural residence. Although this situation was forced on some, others concerned regarded it more positively. Some families saw the dual status as a way of keeping a foothold in the country, thus retaining a portion of land and providing the means to produce some of the household's food requirements.

Peasant-workers clearly constituted a variegated group whose character probably changed considerably in the post-war period. It was certainly not just a product of the early phase of socialist industrialization and was more than a transitional group in the formation of a modern social structure. Membership also reflected a new form of social differentiation, whereby access to urban facilities and urban residence (particularly subject to political control under communist rule) represented a major value within the new social order, and developed as a significant factor in the new pattern of social stratification. The peasant-workers' status as a group that fell between the category of town and country should not be exaggerated, for those living on small-holdings could well be employed as workers (or, indeed, white-collar staff) in plants or institutions located in the countryside or in quite small towns. To this extent, they carried some possibility of overcoming the town/country distinction highlighted by the early theorists of socialism, although for most dual-occupation households this condition imposed great material hardship and punishing transport schedules.

OCCUPATIONAL MOBILITY AND SOCIAL EQUALITY

The conditions experienced by the new working class, peasant-workers, and other social groups were, nevertheless, more tolerable than might otherwise have been the case because they were largely new groups in terms of composition. Living standards for the urban population were lower during the early 1950s than before the war, while both white-collar workers and the working class had less purchasing power than they had in 1938. This was not necessarily a source of dissatisfaction, however, because many of the members of the latter groups compared their situation not with pre-war predecessors but with previous experience in, respectively, the working class and peasantry. The communist parties had targeted the working class for the rapid growth in membership after 1945 and working-class origin, particularly in association with party membership, was a definite advantage when appointments to the increasingly numerous governmental, administrative and managerial positions were made. Growth in the state administration, proliferation of bureaucratic employment and the rapid growth of state-run industry meant that there were plenty of such posts to fill. Similarly, the expansion of the industrial working class that followed the pursuit of policies of rapid economic development sucked in many members of peasant families. The high post-war levels of social mobility, associated also with emigration and war-time losses of population as well as post-war policies of socio-economic change, went a long way to compensate for the rigours and shortages of the early years of communist power. The novelty of newly-acquired status and hopes of future social development outweighed the problems of the contemporary period.

Table 6.3 Intergenerational social mobility – the percentage of those born into one socio-occupational group who had moved into another group, responses from 1967 to 1973

	Manual to non-manual	*Worker to non-manual*	*Peasant to non-manual*	*Peasant to worker*
Czechoslovakia	29.0	35.9	20.6	50.3
Hungary	17.2	27.5	10.7	48.8
Poland	16.9	27.6	10.3	33.7

Source Connor, *Socialism's Dilemmas*, p. 144

The level of social mobility that had occurred by the 1960s was indeed a high one, as Table 6.3 indicates. The rate of mobility, interestingly enough, was highest in Czechoslovakia, where economic development had already been at a high level (no data, unfortunately, were available for the GDR). More than a third of the working class moved into non-manual occupations, and large numbers of peasants moved into the working class to take their place (while large numbers of peasants also moved into non-manual occupations). Rates of mobility for Hungary and Poland were surprisingly similar, reflecting the comparable levels of economic development in the two countries. A smaller proportion of the Polish peasantry, though, moved into industrial employment – reflecting the larger size of the agricultural population in Poland, although even here one in three peasants moved into the working class. Bearing in mind the size of the peasant population soon after the war, with one half (or more) of the labour force employed in agriculture in Hungary and Poland and less than 40 per cent of the population living in towns, the movement out of the peasantry was truly enormous and must be identified as the most striking social change to have occurred during the early post-war period.

In combination with changes in the situation of other groups, this injected considerable fluidity into the social structure of Central Europe and gave it the *appearance* of greater equality, even if the resulting patterns of stratification did not provide quite the kind of social equality that socialist ideology suggested was likely to be the case. This movement was, however, clearly associated with the nature of the facilities provided in the towns and the growing social demand on resources, which intensified well before the losses and damage incurred through war-time destruction had been made good. Neither was it just a question of the number of people involved, large though this was. Families divided and households split more than would have been the case without policies of accelerated social and economic change, producing more individual social units with their particular needs. The associated social dislocation also caused problems in relation to care of the young, sick and old.

In the context of such extensive social change, issues of social equality and questions of stratification were particularly complex. According to orthodox Marxist-Leninist theory, it was full communism that would overcome all social contradictions and major conflicts: only its onset would usher in conditions of true social equality. The transitional period of post-capitalist socialism was, nevertheless, also held to be capable of establishing new dimensions of social equality and enhancing social justice in terms of establishing equity between an individual's contribution to society and the remuneration and benefits derived from it. While, for Marx, equality would not in itself be an attribute of socialist society, nor was it a major aspect of his definition of socialist and communist societies, social equality was understood to be a self-evident precondition for the kind of developments envisaged by his followers. This was only partly achieved in Central Europe, insofar as the socialist order created after 1945 restricted existing forms of social inequality but also established new ones. Meanwhile, the dynamic of socialist industrialization also began to run out and hopes of rapid overall economic advance soon proved to be illusory. The degree to which the new social order embodied principles of equality thus proved to be particularly important as gains from the socialist revolution in terms of political democracy also turned out, by the early 1950s, to be particularly limited and continued to be disappointingly meagre in the post-Stalin period. Guarantees of a basic material level of existence and broad equality of hardship, therefore, proved to be a significant source of consolation.

Income inequalities, nevertheless, continued to exist under socialism, as indeed was to be expected from a system whose principles paid attention to the specific social role and contribution made by different socio-occupational groups. In general, inequalities of consumption in communist Central Europe followed the occupational hierarchy, and distinctive life-styles associated with these differentials could also be identified. But the impact of such inequalities was qualified by various factors. The range of income inequalities was narrower than in Western countries. The inequality of income distribution in Hungary was radically reduced in comparison with the pre-war situation: in the early 1980s 5 per cent of the economically active population earned ten times the monthly average, and 28 per cent of the population were estimated to have an income below the established minimum. Nevertheless, income differentials in Hungary still appeared to be in the process of levelling out.[7]

Other factors also had an important influence on the character of social development in Central Europe: the high rate of female employment, in the absence of significant levels of unemployment, affected family and household income, and the significance of the number of dependents, levels of transfer payments and the availability of social benefits also had to be taken into account. The East German system of family support was, for example, judged to be among the most comprehensive in the world.[8] Income distribution was clustered more tightly around the average figure than in the Federal Republic, but was in essence probably not very different: top employees within the communist system enjoyed a range of additional amenities in kind while taxation in the FRG was more progressive. Pensions in the GDR were also quite low, and considerable income was derived from self-employment. East German society was generally judged to be more egalitarian than the West because of differences in the distribution of wealth rather than because of contrasts in income structure.

All in all, five sources of inequality in Central Europe could be distinguished in the 1980s: those arising from and perpetuated by property relations (most widespread in Poland due to the persistence of private agriculture but also becoming more important with the resurgence of private enterprise); the influence of the system of political power and the differential distribution of power between groups; influence of the division of labour relating to the distribution of different talents and skills common to all industrialized societies; the role of the family as an agency of social reproduction and structure of power in its own right; the historical transmission of regional and ethnic differentials.[9] Some observers have, nevertheless, claimed that there was a relatively more rigorous pursuit of social equality in the period of immediate post-war development and the years of Stalinism. This tendency was attenuated once the needs of economic reform were recognized and new possibilities opened up by the implementation of policies that took a more permissive attitude to issues of social differentiation. To that extent, economic reform could be seen as the motor of the new inequality in Central Europe.

In this, most forms of inequality in Central Europe had a relatively traditional character, or at least one shared with comparable Western societies, a feature that was strengthened as market forces were increasingly tolerated and encouraged. The most differentiated outcomes could be seen where policies of reform or accelerated economic growth were pursued which permitted high wage increases in some parts of the economy (as in Poland during the seventies), enhanced income inequality, and stimulated widespread hopes for rapid improvement – but then fell far short of the economic objectives pursued.[10] Nevertheless, the communist period saw the development of specific forms of inequality in Central Europe and there were few signs of official eagerness to abandon them. Leninist rule also placed great emphasis on principles of hierarchy, although strong expectations of equality arose during the period of early communist development.[11] An important part was played in this by the role of the party-state leadership in setting priorities and determining great areas of social policy and outcomes; it retained overall control of economic institutions and the vast majority of prices and incomes; and it had powers of appointment in many areas of political, economic, social and cultural life. To this extent, social inequality had a significantly political character and was frequently inextricably linked with bureaucratic position.

MODERNIZATION, CULTURE AND SOCIAL CHANGE

The extent of structural change, including the formation of such patterns of inequality, was associated with the emergence of the forms of a modern society. Overall contours of the population in the countries concerned and shifts in the birth and death rates were one clear sign of this. The relatively low trend in population growth characteristic of modern societies was detectable in most countries of the area, and has been noted in an earlier chapter (Table 3.1). The consequences of the Second World War, with their impact on the demographic structure of the population of the region, and the political context (with high rates of emigration from the GDR in the early period to the Federal Republic) exerted a significant influence on developments in Central Europe in this respect. But the situation was differentiated in this, as in other, respects. Birth rates were low from the outset in the GDR and soon declined in Czechoslovakia and Hungary. In Poland, they were particularly high initially and fell only later to a somewhat lower level (Table 6.4).

Table 6.4 Birth and death rates per 1,000 inhabitants

	Czechoslovakia	*GDR*	*Hungary*	*Poland*
1948: birth	23.4	12.1	21.0	29.4
death	11.5	15.2	11.6	11.2
1958: birth	17.4	15.6	16.0	26.2
death	9.3	12.7	9.9	8.4
1968: birth	14.9	14.3	15.0	16.2
death	10.7	14.2	11.2	7.5
1978: birth	18.4	13.9	15.7	19.0
death	11.5	13.9	13.1	9.3
1988: birth	13.8	12.9	11.7	15.2
death	11.4	12.8	13.1	9.8

Source United Nations Statistical Yearbooks; GUS, Rocznik Statystyczny 1990, p. 528

Modernization and rising levels of social development found an even sharper reflection in rising standards of medical provision and standards of health care. These could be clearly seen in terms of post-war changes in features such as access to doctors and rates of infant mortality, which are generally taken to provide a good indication of overall health care, (Table 6.5). They also suggest the differentiated nature of the modernization process in post-war Europe. While, for example, the modernization drive seemed to follow a more intensive course in West rather than East Germany, it was the GDR that showed the greater improvement in medical and health indicators.

The acceleration of processes of socio-economic development could also be seen in increasing public access to education, higher levels of domestic equipment and the wider distribution of consumer durables. Examples of the growth of public access to such goods in Central Europe are shown in Table 6.6. While social

Table 6.5 Indices of social development in terms of health care – infant mortality per 1,000 live births, doctors per 10,000 inhabitants

	Czechoslovakia	GDR	Hungary	Poland	UK
Mortality:					
1948	83.5	94.0	94.1	110.7	36.0
1958	29.5	44.2	58.1	72.7	23.3
1968	22.2	20.2	35.8	33.4	18.6
1977	19.6	13.1	26.1	24.5	14.0
1988	11.9	8.1	15.8	16.1	9.0
Doctors:					
1948	9.0		10.0	3.5	
1960	17.5	12.2	15.3	12.7	
1970	20.0	16.8	19.2	15.2	
1977	25.3	18.9	23.0	16.5	
1987	31.1	23.5	29.1	20.1	

Source United Nations Statistical Yearbooks

mobility and the transformation of social structure was most intense in the early post-war period, the advent of a consumer society, broader exposure to the mass media and access to central agencies of modern culture like television sets came a little later. Modernization in this sense was slower in Hungary and Poland than in Czechoslovakia and the GDR, in keeping with relative levels of socio-economic development. This can further be seen in the growing ownership of television sets, with all Central European countries lagging behind Western Europe, as exemplified by Britain. In broad terms, the television revolution took hold of Central Europe in the 1960s – rather than the 1950s, as in Britain, or the late 1940s, as in the United States – and it was only during the 1970s that fuller coverage was achieved. Even then, the level of saturation was less intense than in the west.

A similar pattern of diffusion could be identified in the case of telephone and car ownership, although levels here were lower than for television sets, especially in a rather more backward country like Poland. Access to some major services still tended to be restricted to a relatively limited group and could be regarded as a valid guide to major lines of social division. In Hungary, for example, at the end of the 1970s, the possession of a telephone was identified as a significant distinguishing factor between different groups. Only 6 per cent of unskilled and semi-skilled workers had a phone in

Table 6.6 Indices of social development in terms of education access and consumption – number of students in higher education institutions; ownership of television sets, motor cars, telephones, washing machines, all per 1,000 population

	Czechoslovakia	*GDR*	*Hungary*	*Poland*	*UK*
Students:					
1949/50	4.4		2.7	4.6	2.0
1960	6.9	13.2	4.5	5.6	2.5
1970	9.1	17.8	7.8	10.1	3.8
1980	12.9	24.0	9.4	16.6	
1987	11.0	26.4	9.4	12.2	
Television:					
1960	58	60	10	14	211
1970	215	264	171	129	294
1977	259	325	240	206	317
1987	285	374	276	261	347
Cars:					
1960	18	17	3	4	108
1970	58	68	23	15	215
1977	121	133	70	44	261
1988	171 (1984)	225	156	120	349
Telephones:					
1960	74	75		30	157
1970	138	123	80	57	268
1980	206	189	118	95	477
1988	246	233	152	122	524
Washing machines:					
1970	276	205	179	185	
1975	363	277	228	217	
1980	411	328	300	253	

Source United Nations Yearbooks; Morris, Eastern Europe Since 1945, p. 155; Rocznik Statystyczny 1990, pp. 585, 588, 596, 599

contrast to 40 per cent of professionals. Post-1945 Central Europe saw, therefore, not just a fundamental transformation of social structure and the demise of the peasant society that had dominated in many areas before the Second World War. This was succeeded by the structures characteristic of modern industrial society, which were accompanied by the arrival of many of the features of consumer society associated with developed capitalism and the emergence of new forms of mass culture.

Despite numerous similarities to post-war developments in other parts of Europe and the West, the socialist society that emerged in Central Europe after 1945 and the culture it developed had distinctive features both in form and content. One of its most obvious characteristics was that it was state-funded and -organized, virtually insulated from the pressures of the economy and consumer choice and planned (or at least administered) by the methods applied to all sectors of political and economic life. Central European culture had a distinguished past and its representatives had made contributions of great international significance and value in many areas. Before 1939, however, access to such cultural traditions had been quite limited (though less so in German areas and the Czech lands) and had reflected the bottom-heavy social structure of the region. Large numbers of impoverished peasants (and a relatively small number of industrial workers) supported a restricted group which had the education, time and resources to participate and benefit from the national cultural heritage. It was in response to such limitations and elitist traditions that the communist governments undertook to broaden channels of access and democratize national culture.

In association with this commitment, great emphasis was placed on the development of an extensive mass education system. The recently adopted UN Declaration of Human Rights stipulated the provision of universal primary education and availability of secondary education on the basis of merit. Similar guarantees were written into the constitutions of the new Central European regimes, with that of the GDR promising also free general polytechnic and higher education.[12] The school network was greatly extended and care taken to ensure compulsory attendance. School-leaving ages were raised. By the 1960s basic schooling lasted for eight years in Hungary (where it was soon raised to ten years) and Poland, but nine years in Czechoslovakia and already ten in the GDR. Different forms of technical, vocational or extended secondary schools then offered further training for entry into the work-force or preparation for higher education.

Technical and vocational provision was particularly stressed as a way of breaking down the traditional dichotomy between intellectual training and manual instruction. For example, the number of technical school students quadrupled in Poland between 1954 and 1964. This tendency followed Nikita Khrushchev's emphasis on such developments in the Soviet education system, although even there it was the object of considerable public controversy. It was greeted with more enthusiasm in some countries than others, with the GDR maintaining its commitment but Poland re-evaluating this emphasis later in the 1960s.[13] Higher education, though expanded, remained restricted and very selective in terms of intake procedures, particularly in university and more elite institutions. This was partly because of direct economic constraints but also because of a continuing high demand for labour and shortages of skilled workers. By no means all the costs of higher education were met by the state. 48 per cent of Hungarian students lived in hostels in the late 1960s and little more than half of all participating in higher education received any form of direct financial aid. Financial constraints were still for many a formidable barrier to entry into higher education. The development of a more comprehensive and accessible basic education system was, nevertheless, a major factor, in the promotion of a mass socialist culture and the 'nationalization' of what had hitherto been largely the prerogative of the better-off and privileged classes.

Reference to the range of activities and new facilities open to the working masses was a major *leitmotiv* in government publicity in Central Europe and the communist propaganda that proclaimed the virtues of the new regimes. Elevation of his cultural standards and the refinement of artistic taste was an important characteristic of the 'new socialist man' (rather less was heard of the new socialist woman, although there were undoubtedly elements of social emancipation there, too). And, indeed, the communist authorities had much to be proud of in this area. Books were published in large editions and widely distributed at low prices. While there might well have been too many political tracts and propagandist fiction of dubious quality and interest, many people did welcome the availability of literary classics and learnt much of value about national cultural traditions from them. What pre-war communist radicals might well have dismissed as 'bourgeois culture' often received particular emphasis as this was precisely the preserve of former elites that now needed to be opened to a mass public. Thus there was an 'unprecedented growth in theatrical activity and attendance everywhere and the establishment of theatres in many areas where none existed before'. Poland had over 80 theatres, Hungary 40 and Czechoslovakia 65 (in which 103 different companies played). East Germany had 51 drama companies – amongst them the renowned Berliner Ensemble founded by Bertolt Brecht in 1949 – and 45 opera groups and 41 ballet troupes, too.[14]

Numerous dramatists, directors and theatrical innovators were well known in the West. Amongst them were prominent Poles like

Jerzy Grotowski, Andrzej Wajda and Ida Kamińska who headed, until 1968, the Warsaw Jewish State Theatre. Václav Havel, whose theatrical career was abruptly curtailed in 1968 by the invasion of Czechslovakia, came into greater prominence with his election as first post-communist president of the country in 1989. Some found it easier to pursue their careers in the West; others, for political and artistic reasons, had no other option. Polish theatre-writer Sławomir Mrożek had little choice but to live abroad after 1968, while the most prominent Hungarian dramatist, Gyula Háy, was imprisoned for his part in the 1956 uprising and later took up residence in Switzerland. For many in the West, though, it was the cinema that demonstrated the cultural achievements of post-war Central Europe most clearly. There could be fewer starker contrasts between East and West in terms of funding, organization and style than that between Hollywood and the Central European cinema. (Many directors, however, found it quite possible, as they had since the early days of the industry, to move successfully from one world to the other – generally westward.)

Not surprisingly, the production of films of intrinsic international interest began only after the death of Stalin. The first was perhaps Wajda's *A Generation*, made in Poland during 1954. *Kanal* and *Ashes and Diamonds* followed soon after, extending the theme of Poland's fate during the late war years and the ambiguities of liberation. Major films were also made by Andrzej Munk, Jerzy Kawalerowicz and Wojciech Has, but particularly interesting were those of younger directors like Roman Polański (*A Knife in the Water*) and Jerzy Skolimowski (*Walkover, Barrier*) who then pursued their careers in the West. Even more than theatre and literature (for obvious organizational and economic reasons), film production was particularly susceptible to the political climate. Thus a small-scale, but striking, presage of the Prague Spring was Milos Forman's *A Blonde in Love*. A number of remarkable films followed in Czechovslovakia, some of which were surrealistic and politically pointed (Němec: *The Party and the Guests*, Chytilová: *Daisies*), while others were more personal and quietly witty – but none the less political for that (Menzel: *Closely Observed Trains*, Passer: *Intimate Lighting*).[15] The extinction of the Czechoslovak experiment was, appropriately enough, marked by Forman's *The Firemen's Ball*, after which he left for the United States and continued his reflections on the condition of Central Europe (it might well be argued) in an examination of conditions in a lunatic asylum in *One Flew Over the Cuckoo's Nest*.

A renaissance in the Hungarian cinema could also be seen soon after the relaxation of cultural policy in the early 1960s, most prominent in the films of that period being those of Miklós Jancsó (*My Way Home, The Round-Up*). His films concentrated on themes from Hungarian history and made imaginative use of the country's landscape, notably its central plain, or Puszta. Unlike Czechoslovakia, whose film production was critically weakened after 1968, Hungary maintained a steady flow of diverse and interesting films in the following years, while Poles also produced some major films, particularly during the late 1970s. Little to compare with this came out of the GDR.

From this brief overview it is not difficult to see that, though opportunities were provided for cultural and educational democratization – predominantly in the sense of mass access to the products and services they offered – they were accompanied by significant restrictions in terms of content and the subjects the relevant media and institutions were able to deal with. Established traditions of culture and political behaviour exerted an important influence on this. Culture and those involved in its production and dissemination throughout Central Europe – intellectuals and particularly writers – had long played a more important part in the political life of Central Europe than in other societies.[16] This was, indeed, one reason why cultural initiatives were given such prominence in the newly established communist regimes. But it was also a reason why the authorities devoted so much detailed attention to the development of cultural activities and exercised strict control over the content of education and what might generally be termed as cultural artefacts. Intellectuals and writers were to the fore of events in a way that they were not in the West. It was the Hungarian Petőfi Circle (a debating circle of the young intelligentsia named after the great writer of the 19th century) that spearheaded the movement of 1956; the trigger for the student demonstrations of March 1968 in Warsaw was the closure of a particular production of Mickiewicz's 'Forefathers' Eve', while in the same year the Writers' Union of Czechoslovakia was at the forefront of the reform movement.

Thus, while culture in communist Central Europe was, broadly speaking, extended and democratized, it was simultaneously politicized and thereby restricted. This was most clearly expressed in the model of 'socialist realism' that was developed in its most refined form by A. Zhdanov and imposed throughout the Soviet bloc after 1946. Intellectuals, writers and artists were supposed to depict society truthfully (and thus 'realistically') while expressing socialist conviction and conveying what was known (following Lenin) as 'party spirit'. For Central European intellectuals, who had worked in a tradition that gave particular value to sentiments of national affiliation, authentic social attachment and political commitment, this produced major problems. The demands of socialist realism clearly required a denial of contemporary reality, as realistic portrayals of society and personal lives were often unlikely to promote socialist values. This was particularly likely to be true of intellectuals themselves, whose origin was often bourgois and inclination generally libertarian. The situation would have appealed most to those committed to surrealism, which had a strong base in Central Europe – but this, too, was regarded as a bourgeois deviation and at odds with socialist culture.

For this, as well as other reasons, sport came to occupy a special place in the social and political policies pursued in communist Central Europe. Like art and culture, which were supposed to project the achievements of socialist society, it could demonstrate superiority over capitalism – in, however, a more symbolic and intangible form. For young athletes and players, on the other hand, it offered a chance to excel and demonstrate individual achieve-ment while remaining within a framework of identification with the collective. Sport was, indeed, dignified by the appellation 'physical culture' and recognized to be a constituent part of the new socialist civilization. It also fulfilled a number of more practical functions. In domestic terms it offered the chance of individual advancement and substantial remuneration for successful performers; inter-nationally, sport was an arena for non-military competition and a potentially cost-effective way of demonstrating socialist superiority. It could also be a major vehicle for health promotion and the improvement of living standards. Unfortunately, the former functions tended to predominate. Drug-taking to enhance per-formance became commonplace and sport was inextricably linked with the central institutions of the communist establishment. The military was prominent in supporting sports activities, while clubs called 'Dynamo' were always associated with security police organizations. As with so many other social activities, sport became highly politicized and its achievements identified with state interests.

CONSUMERISM, SOCIALISM AND SOCIAL VALUES

The way in which Central European societies developed after 1945 raises a number of questions about the extent to which socialism was established there in any broader sense – beyond the establishment of extensive state control over the economy and social processes, the dominance of communist party organizations over public life and the expenditure of much effort on demonstrating the symbolic primacy of Marxist-Leninist ideology over other modes of thought. The question of how far the communist period saw the development of a new form of society, different in structure, values and processes from that which had emerged in Western Europe, leads to consideration of more fundamental processes of change. In terms of social values and the behaviour of much of their population, Central European societies often seemed little different in kind (if not degree) from the more developed countries of the West, many of whose socio-economic patterns and cultural forms they appeared to have emulated. Materialism has been a strong theme in most developed countries and accords only in a limited sense with the concept of economic determinism characteristic of the Marxist approach and the balance between social contribution and material benefit that was supposed to have been sought during the socialist phase.

The self-interest and individualism with which materialism was associated also contradicted the collectivist ethic and official emphasis placed on community values within the communist ideological framework. While socialist values often received a general endorsement by the population for much of the post-war period (although the degree and form of their implementation were strongly criticized), even this level of commitment had fallen away in many groups by the mid-1980s. Survey data showed widespread doubts amongst young Polish people about the nature and even possibility of any socialist future. This cannot have been a surprise for the authorities. There had long been criticism of the effectiveness of youth groups in fostering loyalty to the regime among young people and of the poor results achieved by ideological indoctrination programmes. The growing signs of nationalism were deplored and there appeared to be a widening gulf between the between the communist authorities and young people in terms of attitudes and values.[17] Aspects of international youth culture fostered a strong awareness of Western trends in music and fashion and were often a stronger socializing force than any domestic ideological agency.

Religious commitment, too, showed no signs of having weakened in most parts of the region and remained a particularly significant force in Poland, as well being a major influence in areas like Slovakia and the GDR.[18] This was probably in large part the result of unpopular governments crudely pursuing policies of indoctrination and attitude change. While the consequences of Stalinism in the public arena may have been the imposition of Soviet-style uniformity, rejection of national traditions and promulgation of the communist ethic, the influence on individuals and their private life may well have been quite the reverse. The reaction of younger people was likely to have been even stronger. More prone to identify hypocrisy and inconsistency, they turned angrily against the ideology and the system that promoted it.[19]

The reduction of opportunities for social mobility that followed from the slowing down of structural change was also making it increasingly clear that the operation of the socialist system was falling far short of its formal ideals and proclaimed goals. This was true, firstly, in the sense that the movement of large groups out of lower social strata into higher ones came to a halt and the contours of a different social structure had become established – one that was considerably more urbanized and tied to industrial or white-collar employment than had been the case before the war. Reduced social mobility meant that individuals had fewer opportunities for social advancement and social ambitions and aspirations had less chance of satisfaction. While it was clear that individual life-chances were not distributed equally among the different social and occupational groups, there was now less chance of such differences being overcome. To the extent that these differences were perceived to be more closely linked with obstacles to social advance, inequality appeared to be more firmly entrenched and social discrimination that much more prominent. Economic growth rates were slowing down largely due to the exhaustion of the short-term benefits gained from the mobilization of people and resources into the growing industrial sector as well as to general problems of inefficiency and lack of competitiveness, and this produced slower income growth and poorer material prospects for working people.

At the same time, the new groups formed during the processes of post-war social and economic change developed settled patterns of behaviour and became accustomed to the new frames of reference. These factors fostered more critical views of the system amongst the less advantaged groups and, to the extent that the slower rate of change and the lack of further channels of advancement made it more difficult to defuse dissatisfaction, provided grounds for the emergence of overt opposition. Early signs of such developments could be seen in the actions of youth and, particularly, student groups in Poland, Yugoslavia and Czechoslovakia in 1968.[20] The impact of 'second-generation socialism' was analysed in more detail by Zygmunt Bauman soon after that date. He saw the rise of a new party elite which made its bid for power some 25 years after the original communist power-seekers had begun to consolidate and extend their position after the Second World War.[21] The first signs of stabilization among the new socialist elite in Hungary could be detected in developments during the early 1960s, with 57 per cent of children from that group moving into their parents' positions between 1962–64 compared to 48 per cent in 1949. The 'self-reproduction of the intelligentsia' was also observed in the GDR during the 1970s. Amongst those aged 35–54, 73 per cent had fathers from the working class or farming population; 54 per cent of those under 35 had fathers from these groups.[22]

There had, of course, been sporadic outbursts of worker unrest in Central Europe since 1953, but the slowing down of economic growth and reduced social mobility seemed to have produced conditions that favoured the emergence of more wide-ranging criticism on the part of workers and the formation of more integrated movements of opposition. To the extent that such sentiments can be charted, indications are that such an awareness developed among the working class only after the Czechoslovak reform movement and its demise following the Soviet invasion of 1968. The developments that took place in Poland towards the end of the 1970s and the emergence of Solidarity in 1980 certainly provided clearer signs of this awareness.

One indicator of relevant background conditions from countries like Poland and Yugoslavia was the increasing difficulties experienced by young people with working-class backgrounds in gaining entry to higher education, and thus securing access to the major channel of social advance. Problems in this area were compounded by the high Polish birth rate, 42 per cent of workers in Poland by the mid-1980s being under 30 years of age and continuing, moreover, to maintain a strong commitment to a Catholic church which did little to encourage loyalty to official regime institutions. However, the reduction in the intensity of central direction and control in the 1980s, and the increased scope for individual initiative in Hungary as well as Poland may have served to modify some of these strains and open up alternative sources of gratification and personal advance. In this situation much will have depended on geographic and social location. In Poland, 45 per cent of industrial workers and engineering staff took additional employment to generate supplementary income, and individual access to additional sources of income had become an important new dimension of stratification.[23]

SOCIALISM AND THE NEW CLASS

Throughout the post-war decades of communist rule it thus became clear that social dissatisfaction, while frequently contained militarily or politically for lengthy periods, had gradually spread through many sectors of Central European society. It had proved able to activate and mobilize increasingly large numbers of people, and tended more and more to bring into question some of the basic principles of the communist system. Declining possibilities for social advancement and material improvement doubtless played their part in this, but it was not just the degree to which the societies fell short of socialist principles and the ideas of social equality and economic advance associated with them that underlay the resentment and opposition. Official ideological preference was expressed for the interests of the working class and socially underprivileged groups, and government policy was supposedly formulated to favour them. It became increasingly clear, however, that this was not the case. Popular alienation and opposition were also, and perhaps predominantly, responses to the new forms of social inequality that had emerged and reaction against manifestations of communist elite privilege. Much of the social dissatisfaction directed against ruling and elite groups thus derived from sentiments that contained strong elements of a class nature.

At issue, of course, were not the privileges of the former ruling groups or the inequalities of capitalism identified by Marx and Lenin. What this concerned was the rise under socialism of a 'new class', a formation identified and discussed in the well-known book by the former Yugoslav communist leader Milovan Djilas. This class, he proposed, 'may be said to be made up of those who have special privileges and economic preference because of the administrative monopoly they hold'.[24] It thus derived its power from bureaucratic position, and sustained it by maintaining a combined monopoly of political and economic power and denying organizational resources and the capacity to use them to alternative forces. This position could be partly explained by the recent history of Central Europe, like that of the Soviet Union, having progressed very rapidly from a condition of social backwardness and having inherited a traditional and non-democratic culture. Such views were frequently heard from the communist establishment and were not uncommon elsewhere.[25] But it was – certainly in the eyes of most of those concerned – due to rather more than this. The lack of democracy and prevalence of inequality also had roots in the recently imposed culture and organizational forms of Soviet communism. Under conditions of continuing material scarcity these factors provided a favourable situation for the development of forms of inequality different from those of pre-war capitalism but no less real and oppressive in many of their effects.

Even where conditions of social backwardness, material scarcity and poverty were less onerous, aspects of inequality and elite privilege were present. This was particularly true in the case of Czechoslovakia, which contained some of the most developed regions of Central Europe and could hardly be described as socially backward. By 1967 Czechoslovakia had completed the most effective process of social levelling found anywhere in the European communist bloc, and had achieved a high degree of harmonization between the life-styles of different social groups.[26] A major exception to this generalization, however, was sexual equality and the position of women, which had significantly worsened since 1948 (time budgets, for example, showed that higher participation in full-time employment gave them considerably heavier work commitments). Sexual inequality, however, was certainly not worse than elsewhere in Central Europe. Czechoslovakia's relatively sound economy in 1945 and socio-cultural factors made significant contributions to this development, as did, probably, the rapid exhaustion of the labour reserve which reflected the smaller proportion of the work force initially committed to agriculture.

The situation, however, was somewhat different when ideology and political inequalities were taken into account. Czech communism undoubtedly had some of the strongest popular roots in Central Europe and working-class values and habits were closely adhered to by the party elite, taking a particular form of workerism.[27] Stratification was here combined with an understanding of the prevailing ideology that interpreted the idea of proletarian dictatorship as a distinct form of rule and guide to social behaviour. Thus, the wife of a Czech minister (herself middle-class and Jewish) noted the '*nouveau-riche* snobbery' that thrived among the very people who made the most of their working class origins and proletarian principles, and who ruled in the name of workers and farmers.[28] She herself was castigated for wearing too simple a gown to a reception given by the Soviet ambassador, an event which demanded full formal attire and due external recognition of the honour bestowed on those who represented the workers and peasants of Czechoslovakia.

Ideology and the ethos of the communist elite by no means, therefore, implied condemnation of all aspects of inequality (the situation under full communism in the distant future would, of course, be another thing). Like the inequalities characteristic of the capitalist order, those which attended the formation of the new class in Central Europe did not necessarily cause disquiet on the part of the privileged or clash with their understanding of the morality that could be derived from Marxist-Leninist principles. Policy shifts towards greater egalitarianism did occur, though, particularly after the death of Stalin and in response to developing political tensions. The mid- to late 1950s thus saw the emergence of a greater concern for income equality. The economic slowdown was threatening to increase social dissatisfaction and thoroughgoing economic reform remained an unpalatable option for the elite, so a greater emphasis on equality and the adoption of measures to ameliorate its effects provided a more attractive way of defusing potential opposition.

There were, consequently, major increases in the budgetary allocations for social consumption in Czechoslovakia between 1955 and 1957 and in Hungary during 1957 and 1958. While the 1956–59 period appears to have been a time of some equalization in economic well-being throughout the Soviet bloc, the trend was most pronounced in Central Europe and, particularly, in Poland and Czechoslovakia where growth was sluggish and productivity low. Policies designed to enhance income equality thus became associated with low levels of efficiency, being most intensively pursued in Czechoslovakia where economic and political reforms were most assiduously avoided.[29]

Elite resistance to egalitarianism was only overome, then, in order to avoid the adoption of more threatening reform measures – which would have weakened the principles on which its power rested and meant a more direct qualification of elite privilege. Not surprisingly, such forms of egalitarianism and any success the policy had was short-lived. While helping to modify some of the problems posed by a weakening economy, the strategy failed to provide an appropriate basis for the formulation of policies for stronger economic growth and the effective management of processes of social change. The reduction of class inequalities under socialism thus remained a major formal aim, but one which clashed with other policy objectives and competed with them for scarce resources.[30] As critical dimensions of social change and development, issues of social inequality and economic reform retained a close relationship under socialism. Although, in the early post-Stalin period, egalitarianism was pursued as an alternative to facing the need for reform, later (and more consistent) attempts to improve the economic mechanism and promote more effective reform also had the effect of generating new forms of social inequality.[31]

Hungary took the lead in this, following the introduction of the New Economic Mechanism in 1968 and the pursuit of the most consistent reform initiative seen in Central Europe. But others moved in the same direction and even Czechoslovakia, previously marked by a strong egalitarianism, developed greater inequalities during the 1970s. Growing inequality was not just associated with reform initiatives for which some degree of success could be argued. The persistent failure of such measures in Poland prompted growing recognition that economic and social crisis was not just a passing phenomenon and led to the emergence of a variety of strategies for group and individual survival. On that basis arose new forms of social division, which formed a complex and fragmented pattern of social inequality. Interpretations of such trends were by no means unanimous, however. Eminent Hungarian social theorists argued, for example, that accounts of growing inequality in that country were in fact misleading. While these were based on relative views of the living standards of the working class, what was really at issue, they argued, was the levelling up of the income and life-style of the communist technocracy to the standards enjoyed since the early post-war years by the politically-based ruling elite.[32] But perceptions of the working class were, in any case, also a significant part of the equation, and about its relative position in the social order that emerged during the communist period there was little real doubt.

NOTES AND REFERENCES

1. Blondel, *Contemporary France*, p. 11.
2. Franklin, *Rural Societies*, p. 19.
3. Ferge, *Society in the Making*, p. 63.
4. GUS, *Rocznik Statystyczny* 1967, p. 691.
5. Krejci, *Social Structure*, pp. 43, 47.
6. Childs, *The GDR*, p. 331.
7. Heinrich, *Hungary*, p. 113.
8. Scharf, *Politics and Change in East Germany*, p. 105.
9. Lovenduski and Woodall, *Politics*, pp. 164–68.
10. Bielasiak, 'Inequalities and politicization', p. 228.
11. Nelson, 'Leninism and political inequalities', p. 35.
12. Holmes, 'Education in Eastern Europe', p. 442.
13. Heath, 'Education', p. 226.
14. Trilling, 'Theatre', pp. 507–17.
15. Taylor, 'Cinema', p. 523.
16. Gömöri. 'The political and social setting', p. 495.
17. Heath, *op. cit.*, p. 252.
18. Krejci, *Social Change and Stratification*, p. 38.
19. Brown, *Eastern Europe*, p. 400.
20. Connor, *Socialism's Dilemmas*, p. 153.
21. Bauman, 'Twenty years after'.
22. Dennis, *German Democratic Republic*, p. 53.
23. Kolankiewicz and Lewis, *Poland*, pp. 43, 47.
24. Djilas, *The New Class*, p. 49.
25. Lane, *The End of Social Inequality?*, p. 160.
26. Teichova, *The Czechoslovak Economy*, pp. 110–11.
27. Wright, 'Ideology and power', pp. 130–33.
28. Kovaly, *Prague Farewell*, p. 99.
29. Bunce, 'Neither equality nor efficiency', p. 19.
30. Mason, 'Policy dilemmas', pp. 397–98.
31. Brown, *op. cit.*, p. 409.
32. Konrád and Szelényi, *Intellectuals*, pp. 207–8.

CHAPTER SEVEN
De-Stalinization and Political Instability

MODIFICATIONS IN THE STALINIST MODEL

While Stalin's death on 5 March 1953 in some ways marked the end of a dramatic and often painful phase of Central European history, in others it represented the start of a transition from a founding period whose consequences and typical processes still had several decades in which to elaborate their characteristic nature. Some changes did flow directly from the death of the Soviet dictator and the subsequent modifications in the nature and composition of the Kremlin elite and its *modus operandi*. The inclination to stage show-trials and conduct full-blooded hunts for conspiracies and well-placed traitors passed as it became clear that all members of a collective leadership were equally at risk, although little immediate change was apparent in Czechoslovakia where Husák and fellow 'bourgeois nationalists' (as well as others) were put on trial in 1954. In general, however, the role of the security organs and the secret police was reduced and political processes increasingly flowed in and around the formal institutions of rule – the government, ministries, state administration and, in pride of place, the communist party and its organization. The cult of personality and the intensity of individualized arbitrary dictatorship thus declined. The rigorous economic discipline imposed on the populace was also relaxed. This was reflected in the reduced pace of economic change, an easing off of the collectivization drive and less emphasis on heavy industrial development, all of which helped to provide a greater opportunity to develop consumer industries and increase supplies of agricultural produce.

In other ways the changes were less pronounced. The balance

between personalized and bureaucratic rule shifted, but average citizens did not find their rights more firmly established or easier to implement. Democratic choice was little enhanced; for the most part, the outcome of elections was still firmly controlled and opportunities to exercise real political choice were very rare. Decision-making and political rule remained firmly within the domain of the party-dominated bureaucratic complex, while little modification was made in the structures that sustained the system and ensured its operation. Although the intensity of the indust-rialization drive diminished and the emphases within economic policy were changed, the economy remained very much an administered one, subject to centralized bureaucratic direction. On occasion, economic reform was seriously considered and steps taken to implement a variety of changes. Yet none was fully successful, and the conventions of central planning and economic adminis-tration consistently held back qualitative development and increasingly perpetuated relative economic backwardness. The changes in the relations between the Soviet Union and Central Europe were also mixed in their consequences. Some possibilities for taking a national road to communism were opened up but proved, in the different cases of Hungary and Poland, not to mark out a very different route or point the way to a more desirable goal. The basic forms of Soviet control over Central Europe established in the immediate post-war years were, therefore, little changed.

Stalinism, in one conception, was understood to contain three core elements as a structure of regional control and pattern of international relations. It imposed, firstly, a single political model derived from that developed over the preceding two decades in the Soviet Union. A structure of international relations was established which subordinated the satellite countries to Soviet control and in practice denied the independent, sovereign and equal status of the Central European states. Secondly then, relations within the communist bloc took on the form of an extension of Soviet *domestic* politics. Soviet relations with bloc countries were, thirdly, conducted on a bilateral rather than multilateral basis. Relations of communi-cation and exchange were established by Moscow with each communist state according to the principle of democratic centralism rather than permitting a system of regional integration to develop, such as those mooted by Tito and Dimitrov in connection with a Balkan Union, or floated in Polish and Czech ideas about regional association.[1]

Although alternative forms of influence and control gained

greater prominence after 1953, these features were qualified rather than abandoned after Stalin's death. More room for manoeuvre was permitted in terms of implementing the communist model – but, as the experiences of Hungary in 1956, Czechoslovakia in 1968, and Poland in 1981 were to show, the margin of variation and national interpretation remained a narrow one. Such cases demonstrated the limitations placed on the sovereignty and independence of the Central European states as Soviet leaders continued to exercise the rights of a paterfamilias over the family of communist nations. Elements of national autarchy and bilateral relationship with the Soviet Union persisted, though policies of greater integration on the economic and military plane were pursued with greater vigour.

Soviet control and influence over Central Europe after the death of Stalin was, then, far from eliminated. It did become less direct, however, and was exercised more in terms of the compliance and self-imposed restraint of the national communist leaders. It also operated through institutionalized political channels rather than the direct influence and power of Soviet plenipotentiaries or representatives and greater emphasis was placed on the Marxist-Leninist conventions that governed its operation. These may also be summarized in the three key principles of: socialist internationalism (best known later, after the invasion of Czechoslovakia in 1968, in the form of the Brezhnev Doctrine, which gave the Soviet Union the right to involve itself in the internal affairs of its allies to defend the achievements of socialism); democratic centralism, which derived from Lenin's early insistence on organizational discipline and dominance of the party centre; and the leading role of the communist party in relation to other organizations.

In accordance with these principles, three mechanisms can be identified which underwrote the system of party control. There was, firstly, a parallelism between the party organization and the hierarchical structures of government and state which placed party officials at all levels in positions to supervise the workings of other institutions. Secondly, the *nomenklatura* system continued to develop, and party control over all major (and often minor) appointments was judged to be of fundamental significance.[2] Party authority over appointments was distributed throughout the hierarchy, according to the level of importance of the posts under consideration. Finally, 'local' party committees existed in all ministries, government offices and public associations as they did in most places of work. Occupants of posts of any importance were invariably party members, and thus subject to general party discipline as well as being under the specific authority of the local party secretary.[3] Party supervision was therefore exercised from a variety of angles – from the side, so to speak, from above and from within. Over this complex structure the Soviet party authorities exercised a general leadership based on the principles applied in each of the countries subject to communist party rule. The occupants of major party positions in the Central European states were thus placed in consultation with the leading Soviet party organs, while detailed CPSU control and surveillance over 'local' Central European parties was maintained by the Soviet Central Committee apparatus.[4]

The post-Stalin changes thus brought about some relaxation of direct Soviet control over Central Europe and qualification of the rigidity with which the orthodox model was imposed. Soviet influence, however, was not so much reduced as refined and institutionalized within more strictly political channels and codified according to Leninist principles for the conduct of communist party life. This greater degree of flexibility and complexity in Soviet control meant that, on occasion, national communist leaders could establish more freedom of manoeuvre for themselves. The Poles succeeded in doing so in 1956 – but the terms on which it was achieved were so restricted that what appeared to be a novel solution to the problems of establishing communist authority in Central Europe brought little divergence from the more orthodox path followed elsewhere. The refinement of processes of control and the institutionalization of communist power thus affected the mechanisms rather than the bases of political rule. As outlined in Chapter five, the restrictions they placed on the development of increasingly complex modern economies made the maintenance of economic growth and the improvement of living standards increasingly difficult. Neither did they fit well with the effects of social change described in Chapter six and the emergence of a more urbanized, educated population with continuing expectations of improved living conditions. The growth of these contradictions caused increasing problems for the exercise of communist power and its ultimate survival in Central Europe.

EARLY POST-STALIN TURBULENCE

The successive political crises of the post-Stalin period that engulfed Central Europe demonstrated with increasing clarity the limitations of even this more sophisticated version of communist rule. There can be little doubt that the system of government and political regulation became subject to greater strain with the passage of time as the popular mood changed and dissatisfaction with the communist order grew. Memories of the traumas and deprivations suffered during the hostilities and the immediate post-war period faded and the mood of fatalism surrounding the Soviet-imposed system weakened. The post-war modernization of Central Europe created urbanized societies with more ambitious populations who became less willing to tolerate the continuing restrictions on social autonomy and political participation. At the same time, material improvement was patchy and irregular, providing ample grounds for discontent and increasing political dissatisfaction. As social mobility slowed down after the initial changes in socio-economic structure brought about by intensive industrialization, these failings and defects became more keenly felt. It was a development that coincided with growing awareness of the new forms of inequality that had emerged under communist rule and the patterns of privilege that had developed as a component of 'actually existing socialism'. Nevertheless, it was initial reductions in the tyranny exercised by security organs and the secret police, and a slackening in the pressure exerted by Soviet dictatorship after the death of Stalin, that provided the conditions for a climate of greater confidence and hope.

Some turbulence became evident soon after the death of Stalin, although its causes were associated rather with the problems surrounding the economic policies pursued in the early 1950s than with issues arising from a changed political situation. It was not without significance that the earliest cases of public unrest occurred in the more developed parts of Central Europe, where imposition of the Soviet model of rapid industrialization had brought least benefits and often ran counter to the interests of an already developed working class. In Czechoslovakia the decline of consumer industries and falling agricultural production had been accompanied by rising inflation. This prompted the leadership to plan a monetary reform which was duly announced on 30 May 1953 and put into operation the next day, drastically curtailing the purchasing power of those with savings, particularly if these had not been placed in the state bank. The shock was all the greater because further cutbacks and more austerity had not been expected under the apparently improving conditions of the new situation. The day after the announcement protests were made in the mines and steel works at Ostrava, a Prague machine factory, and the Lenin (Skoda) works at Pilsen, where 5,000 workers occupied the town hall and demanded free elections.[5] Soviet flags were destroyed and portraits of Gottwald and Stalin trampled on. Local militia fraternized with the workers and a full mobilization of party and trade union forces was needed to restore discipline. The vigorous reimposition of control and promises of wage increases helped to calm the situation, though major disagreements developed within the Czechoslovak leadership over economic policy and doubts about the efficacy of forced collectivization were expressed by President Zapotocký in August 1953.

Around the same time related problems developed in East Germany. In 1952 measures had been taken to accelerate the construction of socialism and extend collectivization, which caused many peasants to leave the countryside and was responsible, by the spring of 1953, for growing food shortages. A request for Soviet aid was refused in April 1953 and it was suggested that the East German leadership should modify its policy and relax the pressure, advice that Walter Ulbricht was not inclined to take. On the contrary, he resolved to take measures to step up production and raise industrial output, publishing a decree to this effect on 28 May 1953. His actions at this time seemed to confirm his reputation as a died-in-the-wool Stalinist.[6] (Having begun his career as a socialist, he had joined the German Communist Party (KPD) before the Second World War. He became a member of the Reichstag in 1928 but, when Hitler gained power, sought refuge first in Paris and then in Moscow. In the Soviet Union he helped found the National Committee for a Free Germany in 1943 and was active in the formation of the SED, becoming its general secretary in July 1950.) On 5 June a new Soviet commissar, V. Semionov, arrived in East Berlin and secured the agreement of Ulbricht to amend this policy. On 11 June *Neues Deutschland* stated that the government would correct past mistakes and raise living standards, and that compulsory deliveries of agricultural produce would be reduced as 'erroneous attitudes' had been taken towards some sectors of the peasantry. Nevertheless, the decree of 28 May remained in force and was due to come into operation on 16 June.

On the morning of that day workers on the Stalin Allee construction project, discontented with demands for increased output and a decrease in real wages, stopped work and went on to the streets. It was then that Ulbricht's talent for reading public opinion let him down. 'It's raining', he was reported to have said, 'and people will go home'.[7] But demonstrations spread throughout the city and police cordons were soon breached. Political demands were now made to accompany the original protests on economic and social grounds. The resignation of the government and free elections were soon placed on the agenda. Ulbricht finally announced that the demand for increased output was withdrawn, although he did not judge the situation to be particularly serious. But on 17 June most of East Berlin came out on strike and mass demonstrations took place, with several thousand people attempting to occupy government offices. At midday the commandant of the Soviet sector of Berlin declared a state of siege and committed two Soviet divisions to the restoration of order. Some rebels were seized, summarily tried and executed before the end of the day. The disturbances spread throughout East Germany, with strikes and occupations of government buildings in Leipzig and demonstrations occurring in many other cities. In Leipzig workers occupied the headquarters of the youth movement and the prison, burning all official portraits save that of Karl Marx. Workers were once more spearheading opposition to a state that supposedly ruled in their name. The situation was worryingly similar to that which had developed in Kronstadt, outside Leningrad, in 1921. Order was swiftly restored by the Soviet occupation forces and 25,000 people were arrested, with 42 being executed. The East German uprising was more violent and extensive than the demonstrations in Czechoslovakia and reflected the deep unpopularity of the Ulbricht regime. The events were used by the German leader, though, to strengthen his position and remove his opponents. This process was facilitated by the expulsion of secret police chief Lavrenty Beria from the Soviet leadership for, amongst other things, supposedly having pursued a policy of capitulation in East Germany.[8]

By implication this attack on Beria supported Ulbricht's leadership, despite the domestic vulnerability of the East German regime and the impolitic obstinacy he had shown during the events which led up to the revolt. It certainly provided him with the opportunity to rid himself of colleagues who had urged greater moderation. Justice minister Fechner, who had decided not to declare strikes illegal, was dismissed in July and the first secretary of the Berlin SED organization replaced. Major opponents Rudolf Herrenstadt (editor of party newspaper *Neues Deutschland*) and Wilhelm Zaisser (minister of state security) were removed from their posts and expelled from the party at a Central Committee meeting in January 1954. A full-scale purge was carried out in the national party organization, with 62 per cent of members of the regional (*Bezirk*) committees being replaced by 1954 and a similar fate befalling 71 per cent of senior secretaries of lower-level (*Kreis*) committees.[9] This was accompanied by the provision of Soviet financial aid to support workers' living standards and the decision of the Soviet Union not to take any further reparations.

The repercussions of the uprising were, therefore, significant both in domestic and international terms. Having initially under-estimated the threat of popular opposition, Ulbricht adroitly made use of the events to consolidate his position and remove political opponents. The Soviet leadership, in a state of confusion and some fear after Stalin's death, responded decisively by using military force to quell the opposition. It also drew lessons in terms of the future treatment of Central Europe and took measures to lighten the hefty economic burden placed on the region. The uprising was in these senses something of a turning-point in the history of communist Central Europe. Occurring so soon after the demise of the Soviet dictator, it assumed symbolic dimensions and pointed both to the intensity of opposition to communist rule and the tenacity with which Soviet leaders were likely to defend their recently acquired gains.

Soviet leaders tended to favour those who were ready to maintain stability and they supported the foundations of the status quo in Czechoslovakia, too. After Zapotocký's measured criticism of the collectivization policy, peasants immediately began leaving the farms and redistributing land. Antonín Novotný, first secretary of the party and fellow-member of the collective leadership (the form it took after the death of Gottwald on 14 March 1953) mobilized party forces to prevent further dissolution and criticized Zapotocký for his views. This response found favour with Soviet leaders and, at a joint session with the Czechoslovak leadership in April 1954, they expressed their support for Novotný, who henceforth exercised clear leadership over the party and overall power within Czecho-slovakia.

POLAND: CONTROLLED CHANGE

The aftermath of the events in East Germany and Czechoslovakia foreshadowed future emphases in the pattern of post-Stalin rule. Party purges and firmer organizational discipline were combined with remedial measures to maintain living standards, while the Soviet endorsement of Novotný reflected the primacy of the communist party as an agency of rule. Economic difficulties were the major factors underlying these disruptions, although political aspects were also clearly to the fore. Public life in Poland and Hungary over this period was more calm, but over the longer term more serious political conflicts were developing. No significant political response was made in Poland to the ending of the Stalin dictatorship, but measures were taken to improve the economic situation and halt the decline in living standards. The fall of Beria and his subsequent execution in December 1953, however, made a significant impact on the Polish security organization. Colonel Światło, one of its leading officials, defected to the West, where he agreed to make known his experiences in radio programmes transmitted back to Poland. Beginning in September 1954, they had an enormous impact both on public opinion and on the morale of the elite, prompting criticism of party leaders from various quarters.[10]

Formal Polish responses to the adoption of the post-Stalin New Course in Moscow had been more restrained. At the II PZPR Congress in March 1954 Bierut acknowledged the prevailing convention of collective leadership and, retaining his position at the head of the party, resigned as premier and passed the post on to Józef Cyrankiewicz. Press activity and literary life quietly unbuttoned themselves and took on some of their former vigour and autonomy. A major impact on the central institutions of rule was only felt in the wake of the Światło revelations, though. The party leadership under Bierut was suddenly faced with the fact of its severe political isolation and large numbers of political prisoners, including former resistance leaders and anti-communist politicians, were released. Gomułka left detention in December 1954. Criticism of the security police became widespread and Radkiewicz, its head throughout the post-war period, was demoted and removed from the Politburo. The effect on the party was, however, limited and conservative currents again began to flow more strongly after the removal of Malenkov from the Soviet premiership in February 1955, although the Politburo took up a more reformist position again at the end of the year.

The shifting emphases in Polish political life were clearly linked with changes in the Soviet Union. This took on particular importance as it became increasingly apparent that the XX CPSU Congress, finally held in February 1956, would express criticism of

Stalin and his practices and reaffirm the continuation of the New Course taken after the death of the dictator. Khrushchev's denunciation of Stalin's crimes, in a supposedly secret speech whose contents were soon made known to leading circles in the Central European parties (and, in Poland, to all party members – and even many outside it), fully satisfied these expectations and probably contributed to the failure of Bierut's health. He died of a heart attack in Moscow on 11 March 1956 and Edward Ochab took over the Polish leadership.

Although he was reported not to have been the favoured choice of Khrushchev he was at least more acceptable to the Soviet leader than Roman Zambrowski, proposed by the PZPR elite but rejected by Khrushchev for being Jewish. Ochab proved to be an astute and rather subtle leader. He completed the release of Poland's political prisoners, promoted some industrial decentralization and took further measures to improve living standards. More security chiefs and officials formerly responsible for implementing 'socialist legality' were removed and some sent for trial. Public discussion became more open and often heated, while few restrictions remained on press freedom. Many of these changes, however, were largely restricted to the nation's capital and were of greatest interest to the cultural elite.

Other groups became more involved following developments in the industrial city of Poznań during June. There a grievance over wages and tax allowances in the ZISPO (Cegielski) works, at that time the largest in Poland (producing railway equipment but also tanks and armaments), had dragged on since 1955. As the affair continued, wage-levels continued to be a source of dissatisfaction. Shortly before the situation erupted, the first secretary of the provincial party committee reported to party headquarters that there now threatened something similar to the developments which had taken place in Berlin three years earlier.[11] As the overall political atmosphere within the country appeared to change workers took to the streets on 28 June 1956 and demonstrated as the annual International Trade Fair was being held. After some time had passed violent outbreaks occurred and the army was eventually called out to restore order, in the course of which 53 people were officially recorded as being killed and 300 wounded.[12] Initial PZPR leadership response blamed the events on foreign provocation. The Soviet authorities were also clearly shaken by a development which seemed to flow from the stand taken at the XX CPSU Congress earlier in the year and now threatened serious political instability.[13]

As the Soviet leadership began to draw back from its joint commitment to the stand taken by Khrushchev against Stalinism, though, the Poles changed tack and on 1 July began to allude to the workers' 'legitimate grievances' and the failings of party and state officials. A significant step towards national political independence had been taken and commitment to further democratization was affirmed at the VII Central Committee Plenum which met on July 18.[14] The trials of those involved in the Poznań events opened in September and were conducted with all due propriety, relatively light sentences being awarded to those judged guilty. At the same time, a workers' council was set up in Warsaw at the Żeran motor factory and further councils were set up elsewhere in the capital. The reform movement was gaining a significant national dimension and moving considerably beyond the confines of the party and the cultural intelligentsia.

The PZPR leadership, however, was now seriously divided. One group, named after the village of Natolin near Warsaw where they met, was against significant democratization and the apparently liberal tendencies of much of the former political establishment. Its position hardened as alarm grew amongst CPSU leaders about developments in Poland and the threat of Soviet military intervention became an increasingly serious one. In October Soviet troops based in Poland were ordered out of their bases and moved towards Warsaw. Workers and party activists in the capital were mobilized in defiance of this threat and prepared to act in defence of the PZPR leadership, which met at its VIII Plenum on 19 October 1956 with the participation of Gomułka and former leadership colleagues. At the same time, Khrushchev and other members of the Soviet leadership suddenly arrived in Warsaw and confronted the Poles with their fears about the future of communism in Poland. The PZPR leadership, in the company of Gomułka, succeeded in reassuring them about the security of future developments and impressed on them the dangers of forcible intervention. Polish determination prevailed and Ochab stood down to permit the election of Gomułka as leader.

THE HUNGARIAN REVOLUTION

Developments in Poland moved slowly after the death of Stalin but built up to a significant stand in support of political change and greater national autonomy. The situation in Hungary also took several years to develop and culminated in a major political crisis at around the same time – indeed, the Polish example exerted an important influence on Hungarian conflicts. Stalinism in Poland had been *relatively* mildly implemented – or, in an alternative view, had been implemented more consistently over a longer period, beginning with the Soviet seizure of the eastern part of pre-war Poland in 1939. In Hungary it gathered momentum at a relatively late date (Rajk was arrested in June 1949 and executed in October) but took on a savage intensity, leading to the deaths of 2,000 communist cadres and the imprisonment of 150,000 or more. It also included the rigorous repression of both Catholic and Calvinist Churches.[15] Considerably earlier than was the case in Poland, the Hungarian communist leader Rákosi responded to the introduction of a collective leadership in the Soviet Union on 4 July 1953 by handing over control of the government to Imre Nagy, a post-war minister of agriculture and later minister of the interior.

Nagy himself came from a family of poor peasants (according to one version of his biography, though other accounts differ) and joined the Hungarian Section of the Russian communist party in 1918, having been taken prisoner in Russia during the First World War.[16] After fighting in the civil war he returned to Hungary in 1921, by which time Béla Kun's communist government had already been defeated, and he became an activist of the Socialist Workers' Party, a front for sympathizers of the banned communist party. This finally led to a prison sentence, after which he took refuge in Vienna and then in the Soviet Union, where he developed interests in agriculture and economics. In 1937 he became director of a Siberian collective farm. During the war he worked there on Hungarian language broadcasts and developed a close relationship with Georgi Malenkov, who was later to formulate and implement the New Course that was followed after Stalin's death. Nagy's treatment of Hungarian agriculture, tailored to the climate of the immediate post-war period, had accordingly been appropriately moderate and stood in considerable contrast to the later collectivization campaign pursued under Rákosi, during which period Nagy was suspended from his party functions. He was expelled from the Politburo in August 1949, following criticism of the collectivization policy, and then worked in academic life.

Nagy's appointment in 1953 had been imposed on Rákosi by Soviet leaders, and the policy pursued by the new Hungarian prime minister represented the most radical revision of Stalinist policies

157

seen by that stage in Central Europe. Peasants were permitted to leave collective farms, measures taken to raise living standards by increasing wages and consumption, and reforms to promote decentralization and greater participation were adopted. The contrast between Rákosi's harsh Stalinism and Nagy's New Course orientations soon developed as a political fissure, however, rather than as a diverse but collective leadership reflecting a coherent new policy orientation. This, further, gained institutional expression in the division between party and government hierarchies. Nagy's policy ran into difficulties in early 1955 due to shortages of raw materials and capital, and his position was further undermined by the removal of Malenkov from the Soviet premiership in February 1955. Nagy was expelled from power in April and Rákosi enforced on him a series of demotions and expulsions, including those from the Academy of Sciences and the party itself, in November 1955. Under the new conditions prevailing in the Soviet bloc, however, there could be no question of any return to Stalinism and Rákosi was unable to devise or implement policies appropriate to contemporary needs. Literary and intellectual circles were also strongly resistant to any attempt to turn the clock back to the beginning of the decade. Further reformist gestures made after Khrushchev's secret speech, moreover, only served to antagonize the political establishment, isolate Rákosi politically and weaken his position.

He made an attempt to extricate himself from this situation in July 1956 by proposing a crack-down on literary circles and cultural activities, and even the arrest of Imre Nagy. Although political sensibilities in the Kremlin were again hardening after the Poznań revolt, Rákosi's initiative was quite unacceptable and he was pressed to resign the party leadership to Ernő Gerő – another war-time Muscovite and long-standing colleague of the Hungarian leader. Nagy remained excluded from the leadership (he was only readmitted to the party on 13 October) and Gerő's administration did nothing to stabilize the political situation. The Hungarian public, however, was greatly impressed by Soviet acceptance of Gomułka's return to the Polish leadership, and many seemed to assume that it had established a general principle in terms of a significant diminution of Soviet claims over Central Europe. On 23 October this led students in Budapest to organize a demonstration at the foot of the statue of Józef Bem, a Polish general who had led Hungarian insurrectionary forces in 1848. They called for extensive reforms, free elections, Nagy's return to power and the withdrawal of Soviet troops. Clashes with the security police occurred and some of them were shot as they attempted to defend the communist regime. Gerő called for Soviet support and their troops moved out of barracks on 24 October. But their intervention did not progress far and was halted, initially in the provinces and then in the capital, once it was discovered that workers and the population as a whole shared many of the views and demands of the students. Soviet representatives now envisaged a political solution, with the replacement of Gerő by János Kádár as party leader and endorsement of the proposal that Nagy return as premier.

Unlike Rákosi and Gerő, but like Rajk and Gomułka, Kádár was more of a 'domestic' communist and had not spent the 1930s and war-time years in the Soviet Union. He initially worked as a mechanic and joined the illegal Hungarian Communist Party in 1931 at the age of nineteen. He was also active in the Young Communist League and became a member of its secretariat. A two-year prison sentence was awarded for this activity and, on being released in 1937, Kádár then joined the legal Social Democratic Party. During the war he helped set up an underground communist movement and worked closely with László Rajk. He was arrested after the German occupation of Hungary in the course of an unsuccessful attempt to flee the country and join Tito's forces in Yugoslavia. After the liberation he was elected to the Politburo of the reformed communist party and placed in charge of the party organization of greater Budapest, combining this with the post of deputy chief of police. Kádár's close association with Rajk led to his implication in the conspiracy that the latter was charged with having organized and for which Rajk was executed. He was reported to have been sent by Rákosi to persuade Rajk to confess to the charges, for which the latter's life would supposedly be spared and he would be able to retire into exile in the Soviet Union. This, of course, was not the way the Rajk affair ended. Kádár was then himself arrested in 1951 and imprisoned until 1954, when he was released, rehabilitated and restored to his former post in the Budapest party organization.

By the time he had been placed in charge of the party leadership in late October 1956, the situation was virtually beyond political control. Nagy's views, it seemed, had also changed in recent years. He now thought it impossible for Hungarian interests to be realized and a national brand of socialism constructed within the area of Soviet influence, and concluded that both blocs should be dissolved. Soviet hesitancy over intervention had also been misinterpreted, and popular demands were expressed for Hungary's departure from the Warsaw Pact (which for some time seemed feasible in view of the nature of Soviet actions), and the holding of multi-party elections. Nagy and Kádár nevertheless set out to restore order by attempting both to satisfy these demands and fulfil Soviet expectations. Moves were taken to form a coalition government, but former social democrats only agreed to join if their old party was reinstated. This Nagy agreed to on 30 October, although Kádár and the Soviets deemed it inadmissible. Some, rather ambiguous, conciliatory statements were made by the Soviet leadership at this stage but they had no effect on what had now become a much stronger social movement for change in Hungary. Nagy now moved closer to the revolutionary forces, repudiating Gerő's original request for Soviet intervention and reconstituting the multiparty government coalition as it had existed in 1945.

After new contingents of Soviet troops began to invade the country early on 1 November 1956, Nagy formally withdrew Hungary from the Warsaw Pact, proclaimed its neutrality and requested protection from the United Nations. This move was, however, particularly ill-timed in view of the dramatic actions initiated by leading Western powers in the Middle East and the severe disagreement that broke out between Britain and France, on the one hand, and the United States on the other. Following an Israeli attack against Egypt, British and French aircraft had attacked Egyptian bases on 31 October to increase the pressure on the country in response to its nationalization of the Suez Canal Company in July 1956. As the Hungarian crisis escalated, so did that in the Suez area and Anglo-French forces staged an airborne invasion of Port Said on 5 November. The time could hardly have been worse to appeal to the West for assistance against great-power interference in the affairs of a smaller nation, especially as divisions between the Western powers were also prominent and the United States expressed strong opposition to the Anglo-French action. Western response to the Warsaw Pact invasion of Czechoslovakia in 1968 suggests, however, that its action might not have been any different even if the Suez conflict had not erupted at this time.

By way of response to Nagy's pronouncements, meanwhile, the Soviet army moved into action in Hungary on 4 November. That morning Kádár, who had formally dissolved the old workers' party some days earlier and formed instead a Hungarian Socialist Workers' Party (HSWP), now announced from a location in eastern Hungary both the formation of a new government and the fact that it had called for Soviet assistance. The fighting was fierce and had mostly ended by 10–11 November. During the conflict 3,000 people were officially recorded to have died and 13,000 were wounded.[17] Nagy took refuge in the Yugoslav Embassy which he left on 22 November with a guarantee of safe conduct from Kádár. He was, however, seized by Soviet troops and taken to Romania. He was tried with other leaders of the uprising and executed in June 1958. But it took more than a few days to crush the revolution, and the Central Workers' Council of Greater Budapest remained a major force in the political situation. During the early stages, Kádár conferred frequently with its representatives and continued to express his support for the October uprising while denouncing the later counter-revolution and insisting on the coincidence of Hungarian interests with overall Soviet influence.[18] This mid-way position had little viability in the aftermath of the invasion and the overall balance of power now lay with the Soviet forces, who moved to strengthen their control in early December. The remaining revolutionary committees and the Central Workers' Council were banned, and activists and dissident journalists arrested. In January 1957 a new law was introduced to provide for special courts with accelerated proceedings, and 2,000 Hungarians were later executed. The revolution was steadily crushed and communist power reimposed, a process which, in terms of its human and political costs, went far beyond the overthrow of the Nagy government by Soviet forces.

The Hungarian events marked the end of the first phase of post-Stalin developments and contributed to a clarification of the principles of communist rule that had emerged in Central Europe. The Soviet leadership certainly showed greater flexibility than had Stalin and was willing to permit a measure of domestic autonomy and some degree of policy variation (as shown in the tolerance of the Church and a private farming sector in Poland). But no retreat from communist political rule was envisaged, a point on which Gomułka soon showed himself to be in full agreement with his Soviet comrades, and the military integration of the communist bloc also emerged as a major priority. The sequence of events in Hungary seemed to suggest that it was Nagy's willingness to return to the immediate post-1945 form of coalition and abandon overall communist party leadership and control that triggered the return of the Soviet military in force to Hungary on 1 November.[19] Both Gomułka and Kádár, having fallen into disfavour under Stalin, understood the implications of subsequent Soviet actions and took care to apply the lessons they had learnt.

CZECHOSLOVAKIA AND THE PROBLEMS OF MODULATED REFORM

The apparent mutual comprehension of the rules of the political game, reinforced by grim memories of the Hungarian experience, was reflected in a period of relative stability in Central Europe during the late 1950s and early 1960s. The immediate post-Stalin years had also seen a revision of economic policy and reassessment of priorities which contributed to a rise in popular living standards – measures which further assisted the process of relative stabilization. The changes that had taken place in 1956 had an important influence on subsequent political developments. The Hungarian revolution and its suppression constituted, not surprisingly, a traumatic episode in the development of Hungarian society and the life of Central Europe as a whole. The Polish drama was regarded as a major turning point which, if disappointing in its political and economic consequences, was nevertheless understood to have brought some gains and probably to have achieved in practical terms as much as was possible in Central Europe under the conditions that prevailed in the immediate post-Stalin period. Following the consolidation of Novotný's position in April 1954, though, Czechoslovakia saw little in the way of any attempts at political change but rather a continuation under supposedly post-Stalin conditions of the traditions established by the former Soviet leader. The circumstances of the post-Gottwald leadership adjustments (which were very different from those apparent in the reformist tendencies evident in Hungary at the same time) and the relatively high levels of economic development and living standards played a part in this, as did the greater strength of the pre-war national communist movement combined with an historical sympathy with the Soviet Union.

Following the XXII CPSU Congress in October 1961, which saw a renewed attack by Khrushchev on Stalinism, this situation began to change and a new phase of de-Stalinization began. Novotný had long resisted attempts to investigate and reappraise the purges, trials and wave of executions that had taken place between 1949 and 1954 (a process which had at least gained some momentum in Poland and Hungary during 1956) but eventually acceded to Soviet pressure, with a review body being appointed in 1962. At the same time the Czechoslovak economy was encountering serious problems, gaining the distinction in 1963 of being the first European communist country officially to record a decline in national income. In this area, too, Soviet influence was exercised and Khrushchev urged measures of economic reform on the local leadership. A third source of pressure on the Prague elite emanated from Slovakia, where the long-established centralization of the Czechoslovak political and economic system (a feature dating back to pre-war years) had given rise to growing dissatisfaction. Prompted by this, Slovak party organizations took advantage of Novotný's weakening position to publish critical materials which were increasingly divergent from the orthodoxy characterizing Czech publications. One boost to their growing autonomy was the election of Alexander Dubček as first secretary of the Slovak section of the party in April 1963. The Slovaks proceeded briskly to rehabilitate victims of the Stalinist purges and restore some of the local institutional autonomy steadily reduced since 1946.

Born in 1921, Dubček had spent 13 years in the Soviet Union, beginning in 1925. He joined the communist party in his own country during 1939 and worked in a Skoda plant from 1941 to 1945, taking part in the Slovak uprising of 1944. After the war he advanced through the party hierarchy and was sent in 1953 to attend the Moscow Party High School where he spent the next five years. Following Dubček's promotion, Novotný remained far from sympathetic to the process of economic reform that had got under way and progress was slow, a further braking influence being exerted by the attitudes of workers who felt threatened by proposals for more labour discipline and greater economic stringency. Something of a turning point was reached in late 1967 when it was recognized that, if they were to have any effect at all, more force had to be put behind the reforms. Openly challenged and hoping to gain some support from the disgruntled workers, Novotný attempted to put a stop to further reform by staging a coup with the participation of some military units. This, however, was blocked by security agencies and the Main Political Directorate of the army (under the leadership of Václav Prchlík).[20]

The action of the army's Political Directorate foreshadowed in an interesting way the critical role an analagous organization was to play in instituting the future State of War in Poland during December 1981. The failure of this initiative, further, spelt the end of Novotný's tenure as party leader, with Alexander Dubček replacing him in that post on 5 January 1968. On March 30 retired general Ludvík Svoboda also succeeded him as president of the republic. The general, although not a party member in the 1940s, had facilitated the communist takeover and had the confidence of the Kremlin, his appointment therefore being intended to reassure the Soviet leadership. Dubček, too, although he had played a major part in the downfall of an established communist leader who had long enjoyed stable relations with the Soviet authorities, had spent a considerable length of time in the Soviet Union and undergone party training there. Neither showed any signs of anti-Soviet feelings or, even less, opposition to communist rule.

The pace of change accelerated rapidly. Many restrictions on public debate were lifted and censorship was effectively abandoned in early March. There was extensive turnover of government personnel and party reformists took over many key posts. None of this was intended to endanger communist rule or undermine the leading position of the communist party. Nevertheless, at the end of April, growing doubts and reservations began to surface in Moscow and various conferences, visits and military manoeuvres exerted growing pressure on the Czechoslovak leadership. There was strong Soviet disquiet over the 'Two Thousand Words' statement issued by intellectual representatives on 27 June 1968, which achieved great popularity and called for more extensive reform but was criticized by Dubček for its provocative tone. On 11 July *Pravda* drew a comparison between Czechoslovak developments and Hungary in October 1956, while on 15 July Warsaw Pact members (with the exception of Romania) called for the return of censorship (formally abolished in June), restrictions on intellectual activities and reversal of the liberalization of the country's institutions. The draft of new party statutes, due to be presented to an Extraordinary Party Congress opening on 9 September, was published on 10 August and this may well have decided the Soviet leadership on its final course of action.

The draft proposed federalization of the communist party by establishing a separate Czech organization. It also provided for the election of party officials by secret ballot and permitted minority groups to maintain and defend their own position. This clearly threatened established principles of democratic centralism and the major instruments of its implementation, which included central control over party appointments, the monopoly of party leaders over policy making and strict subordination of lower party organs to those higher up. The Soviet leadership also estimated that the remaining conservatives on the Czechoslovak Central Committee – not much less than one half of its membership – could be mobilized to block these changes and prevent further deterioration of the situation before the Congress (at which they were likely to lose their seats in any case), opened in September. It was probably on the basis of such calculations that the Soviet Union, in the company of small contingents from the other Warsaw Pact members (excluding Romania), invaded Czechoslovakia in the small hours of 21 August. The intervention was met with enormous popular, mostly non-violent, resistance and with far less sympathy than had apparently been anticipated among some of the higher echelons of the Czechoslovak party organization. No alternative conservative leadership sprang into existence to fill the power vacuum created by the Soviet action and there was general resistance, amply recorded by Z. Mlynář from the side of the leadership, to the usurpation of the authority of the unusually popular Czechoslovak communist leadership.[21] Dubček and other leaders were therefore abducted and taken to Moscow, where further pressure was exerted on them.

They had little alternative but to accept the Soviet judgment on the Czechoslovak experiment, and Dubček only remained party leader until 17 April 1969 as Soviet representatives and domestic allies began the slow and methodical process of 'normalization'. He was replaced by Gustáv Husák, perhaps in the hope of repeating the relative success of the Hungarian counter-revolution under Kádár, which had then been followed by an encouraging degree of economic recovery and political stability. Husák had been born in 1913 and was thus somewhat older than Dubček. He read law at the University of Bratislava and practised as a lawyer from 1938 to 1942. Husák had joined the Slovak communist party in 1934 and played a leading part in it during the Second World War, emerging as a key figure in the uprising of August 1944. Having spent a period in the Soviet Union he became head of the Slovak Office for Church Affairs. In 1951 he was arrested and, continuing to plead his innocence, was sentenced in 1954 to life imprisonment for 'bourgeois nationalism'. Released in 1960, he was a construction worker until 1963, only returning to political life in March 1968, initially as a deputy prime minister and then (from August) as first secretary of the Slovakian Communist Party. His participation in the reform movement had ceased with the intervention of the Soviet forces.

The stability imposed in Czechoslovakia lasted for 20 years, with the assistance throughout the period of large numbers of active security agents. However, the 'normality' achieved had only a partial success and was rather different from developments in Hungary. It was not marked by the combination of control and relaxation seen in Hungary, which provided its citizens with some scope for autonomous activity and, perhaps to a greater extent, impressed Western observers with its relative openness. Neither were any adventurous economic initiatives undertaken although, despite a sluggish pace of growth in comparison with Western neighbours, Czechoslovakia maintained steady rate of growth which kept its population in a relatively comfortable situation and avoided the unstable pattern of development seen in Hungary and Poland.

A firm regime of political control, softened by a generous level of economic provision, was therefore maintained, against which only the relatively small group of Charter 77 activists showed any degree of public opposition. Czechs and Slovaks increasingly concerned themselves with private affairs and became largely alienated from the sphere of public activity. One reason for this was the conformity and rigidity of the regime imposed after the Soviet invasion which had, after all, taken place in order to remove a leadership already firmly committed to the maintenance of communist rule, Czechoslovak membership of the Council for Mutual Economic Assistance, and allegiance to the principles of the Warsaw Pact as the institutional expressions of Soviet regional supremacy. Even this, it now appeared, was not enough to satisfy Soviet requirements of regional uniformity. No variety of reform could be countenanced, it seemed, which qualified the underpinnings of communist rule according to principles of democratic centralism, accepted any measure of social spontaneity, or showed any likelihood of tolerating the loosening of controls over social organizations.

NOTES AND REFERENCES

1. Dawisha, *Eastern Europe*, pp. 70–72.
2. For an outline of the original model see Harasymiw, 'Nomenklatura: the Soviet communist party's recruitment'.
3. Dawisha, *op. cit.*, pp. 76–79.
4. See Frank, 'The CPSU local apparat', p. 167.
5. Fejtö, *History*, p. 43.
6. Narkiewicz, *Petrification and Progress*, p. 63.
7. Fejtö, *op. cit.*, p. 36.
8. Baras, 'Beria's fall and Ulbricht's survival', p. 392.
9. Childs, *The GDR*, p. 39.
10. Lewis, 'Legitimation and political crises', p. 20.
11. *Polityka* (Warsaw), 1981, 24.
12. Makowski, *Wydarzenia czerwcowe w Poznaniu*.

13. Leslie, *History of Poland*, p. 351.
14. See Zinner, 'National Communism', pp. 145–186.
15. Rothschild, *Return to Diversity*, p. 137.
16. White, *Political and Economic Encyclopaedia*, p. 169.
17. Hoensch, *History of Modern Hungary*, p. 219.
18. Lomax, 'Hungary', pp. 78–79.
19. Jones, 'Soviet hegemony in Eastern Europe', pp. 216, 241.
20. Rothschild, *op. cit.*, p. 169.
21. Mlynář, *Night Frost in Prague.*

CHAPTER EIGHT

The Politics of Mature Communism

THE GDR: DE-STALINIZATION SURVIVED

The conditions of Soviet control over Central Europe thus proved to be even more stringent than initially thought in the aftermath of the Hungarian invasion. The resistance to change and innovation they reflected in the long run brought, though, not just a degree of political stasis that made the processes of communist rule decreasingly effective but also reinforced a systemic aversion to economic reform that threatened the material survival of the regimes themselves. The countries that had begun the post-war period with a stronger economic base were, nevertheless, in a better position to survive these pressures. This characteristic could be traced through to the closing phase of communist rule in 1989, as Czechoslovakia and the GDR continued to hold fast against the tide of opposition and popular dissatisfaction that was breaking around them. Having weathered the turbulence of the 1953 revolt, soon after Stalin's death, the GDR indeed survived the rest of the communist period under conditions of relative stability, despite political problems associated both with the attractions of West Germany to its people and the changing policy of the Soviet Union towards the Federal Republic. Although it encountered most of the problems in sustaining growth experienced elsewhere during the post-Stalin period, these pressures were less keenly felt in the GDR and, in the absence of large-scale popular opposition, its leadership was not pushed towards major economic reform or liberal experimentation. The unique international position of the GDR and high level of international sensitivity experienced over the German question (including the status of West Berlin) in combination with the strength of the Ulbricht leadership, continued to support tendencies towards greater stability.

Ulbricht's apparent misjudgement over the events that led up to the Berlin uprising and the lack of support for the communist regime it demonstrated did not lead him to moderate his attitude or change the regime's character in any fundamental way. The GDR under Ulbricht rode the backwash of de-Stalinization that caused such unrest elsewhere and saw little major change in the institutions or processes of communist rule. The IV Congress of the SED, which opened on 30 March 1954, thus followed the CPSU Statute adopted in 1952 under Stalin in announcing a general claim to party leadership over all sectors of social life. More consumer goods were promised, but priority was still given to the development of heavy industry and food rationing was retained. The pre-eminence of Ulbricht's political position was evident and, although the post of SED chairman (previously occupied by Pieck and Grotewohl) was abolished, Ulbricht's title changed from general to first secretary, in keeping with current Soviet practice.

As international deliberations over the future of Germany and the possibility of reunification continued at the four-power Geneva conference in July 1955, the survival of the GDR did not appear to come under any serious doubt. A further obstacle to reunification was introduced by the formation of the Warsaw Pact, with the GDR locked into the organization as a founding member, in response to the admission of the Federal Republic to NATO in May 1955. The dissatisfaction of the East German population with this situation was nevertheless evident from the continuing emigration to the west which ran at a level of 184,198 in 1954, somewhat higher than in 1952 but below the record 331,390 recorded during the year of the uprising in 1953. The growing regimentation of East German society and official concentration on the enforced socialization of the younger generation meant that they accounted for a large number of those leaving, the proportion of under-25s amongst the emigrants reaching the level of 52 per cent in 1955. Not surprisingly, though, after the events of 1953 the response in the GDR to developments in Poland and Hungary was very muted.

There was a moderate reaction within the SED to Khrushchev's denunciation of Stalin at the XX CPSU Congress and the release of political prisoners in 1956. However, as revolutionary forces gained momentum in Hungary, and Gomułka moved quickly after the consolidation of his leadership to curb the more committed reformist groups, Ulbricht also acted against the threat of revisionism. Leading intellectual and reform theorist Wolfgang Harich was sentenced to ten years' imprisonment in March 1957 for having founded an anti-state group. Economists who advocated reform, like Friedrich Behrens and Arne Benary, had to withdraw their proposals while other independent thinkers also left for the West.[1] As Khrushchev routed the anti-party group in the CPSU Central Committee during June 1957 so Ulbricht, too, took measures to eliminate critics and potential rivals, and confirmed his dominance at a Central Committee meeting held in 1958. While Khrushchev was aiming to reduce party bureaucracy and bring in economic reform, though, those ousted by Ulbricht included a number of economic experts and precisely those who had argued for more realism and flexibility in economic planning. Nevertheless, this purge of the party leadership secured Ulbricht's political position for over a decade. Further confirmation of his position came following the death of President Pieck in September 1960. It was decided to replace the office of president with a collective head of state in the form of a Council of State (based on the Presidium of the Supreme Soviet), and of this body Ulbricht became chairman. An important National Defence Council with extensive powers was established, and Ulbricht became chairman of this group as well.

Consolidation of communist power occurred in other spheres and state policy towards the churches hardened in the late 1950s. A renewed drive to extend the area of collectivized agriculture was launched in 1958 and most of the land was brought into collective ownership before the end of 1960. Growing pressure was exerted on small businesses and individual craft workers. A significant celebration of Stalin's birthday was carried by *Neues Deutschland* on 21 December 1959. Economically and in material terms, however, 1959 was not at all a bad year domestically and the relatively small number of 143,917 people decided to leave the country, the fewest since 1950. However, food shortages became more widespread towards the end of the year, to which the agrarian policy had certainly made some contribution, while other shortages also persisted. The election of President Kennedy in the United States in the autumn of 1960, brought no improvement in superpower relations, and no progress was evident either on the question of Berlin.

Khrushchev had precipitated one major crisis over Berlin in 1958 when he attacked the West for having violated the Potsdam accords and threatened to terminate Berlin's occupied status and transform it into a 'free', demilitarized city. He declared that, if the West did not co-operate, he was prepared to carry out this change unilaterally in association just with the GDR. It represented, therefore, a threat to place the whole of Berlin under communist rule. Khrushchev soon backed down but launched, in June 1961, further demands for a peace treaty to be signed by all those holding responsibility for Germany's contemporary status. If this did not happen he was prepared, once more, to conclude a separate treaty with the GDR. But Khrushchev was now in a weaker position than he had been three years earlier, and it was after consideration of this situation that the decision to erect a wall through the heart of Berlin was taken on 13 August 1961.[2] That year 155,402 people had already left the country and registered at western reception centres and, from 1949 to that date, a total of 2.7 million refugees had been recorded. Just before the construction of the wall emigration was averaging more than 20,000 a month.[3]

One immediate consequence of the building of the Wall was a shortage of construction workers, many of whom had already left for the West while others now became committed to the 'improvement' and reinforcement of the barrier.[4] This had an influence on the cutback of the housing programme reported to the VI SED Congress in 1963. At the same time, though, a New Economic Programme was adopted which involved some decentralization and greater use of economic incentives. These measures, in combination with the ending of the flood of labour to the West, brought considerable economic gains. By 1965 industrial production was reported to be 43 per cent above the 1958 level and the conditions of life were easier for East Germans in many ways. But controls began to tighten again after the fall of Khrushchev. A new trade agreement was prepared with the Soviet Union which carried little advantage for the GDR (so much so that the chairman of the planning commission, Erich Apel, shot himself the day the treaty was due for signature). Greater emphasis was also placed on ideological controls and the maintenance of orthodoxy, a leading part in this campaign being played by Ulbricht's close collaborator, Erich Honecker. Much disquiet was caused to the SED leadership by developments in neighbouring Czechoslovakia during 1968, and Ulbricht was thought to have exerted some influence over the decision to invade.

The Soviet Union, however, was becoming increasingly interested in the establishment of better relations with the Federal Republic, a process to which Ulbricht was implacably opposed. His attitude reflected the traditional fear of the SED that its position would be fatally weakened in any situation that held out hope of reunification and a return to democracy in the East. Soviet pressure was stepped up and Willi Stoph, chairman of the Council of Ministers (or prime minister), met with West German Chancellor Willy Brandt during March 1970 in the East German town of Erfurt. The enthusiastic welcome accorded the Western leader gave Ulbricht serious grounds for concern and reinforced his fears about the fragility of the East German regime.[5] A treaty renouncing the use of force was nevertheless signed between the FRG and the Soviet Union in August, and the GDR Council of Ministers had little option but to endorse the treaty on 14 August 1970. As international relations with the Federal Republic became more cordial, Soviet awareness of the negative position taken by Ulbricht grew keener and he resigned his party position in May 1971 before the VIII Congress. He was allowed to retain some honorific posts and had a reasonably dignified retirement before his death at the age of 80 in August 1973.

Ulbricht was succeeded by Honecker who had, at an early stage, shown some sensitivity to the interests of the Brezhnev leadership. Aged 58 at the time of his instatement, he was raised by a mining family in the Saar. Having joined the German communist party in 1929 at the age of 17, he was jailed by the Nazis in 1935 and released only with the liberation of the country by the Soviet army. (Much later, after another form of liberation – that which occurred throughout Eastern Europe between 1989 and 1991 – he would be committed to the same prison in 1992 in anticipation of trial for having given orders for refugees to be shot.[6]) From 1946 he had been a member of the party's Central Committee and had sat in the Politburo since 1950. After political training in Moscow he exercised CC authority over security affairs from 1956. This period was, indeed, one of extensive leadership change in Central Europe. Between the changes that took place after the invasion of Czechoslovakia and that in the GDR one more occurred, as the Polish leader's political career also came to an end in circumstances very different from those under which it had undergone such a spectacular recovery in 1956.

POLAND: NATIONAL CREDIT EXHAUSTED

The return of Władysław Gomułka to the leadership of the PZPR had clearly been a popular move domestically, and the approach taken with respect to the Soviet leadership received great support. While never hinting at any relaxation of the essentials of communist party rule, he did introduce or permit a number of changes that countered some of the worst abuses of Stalinism and improved the conditions of life for most Poles. The decollectivization carried out spontaneously by many peasants was accepted and the campaign to socialize agriculture never resumed in the countryside; relations with the Church were regularized and religious instruction permitted in state schools; Soviet military decision-makers and supervisors were sent home and the Polish armed forces 'nationalized'; greater freedom was permitted in the Polish Diet (*Sejm*) and in elections to it; police abuses were curbed and political arrests ended. The rate of economic growth and living standards also rose, largely due to the changes in economic policy made as a result of the New Course and reduction in the powers of the central economic administration.

Nevertheless, Gomułka had no intention of reducing party control over public life or qualifying the practice of democratic centralism within the party. He moved quickly to tighten up discipline within the organization and restore authority over regional and local party organs.[7] A campaign against ideological revisionism was swiftly launched (while due condemnation was also made of 'dogmatism') and press freedom was steadily reduced. The role of the workers' councils, which had sprung up in 1956 and played an important part in Warsaw in creating the conditions that made Gomułka's return to power possible, was reduced and by 1958 they had been neutralized.[8]

While following a national road to socialism, a condition he had persistently argued for in the 1940s, the route was clearly marked out according to Marxist-Leninist ideology and the motor force provided by the communist party (PZPR). It was also clear, Gomułka was reported to have stated, that in Poland the party was too weak to rule democratically.[9] In holding this opinion and acting accordingly he appeared to satisfy Soviet requirements. His pursuit of communist orthodoxy and clear desire to fall in with most Soviet demands, moreover, removed any threat posed by conservatives formerly associated with the Natolin group, while his rigorous treatment of revisionist (and, increasingly, any reform-minded) forces forestalled challenges to his political position from that quarter.[10] Nevertheless, such political threats could not be avoided for ever. In the 1960s growing dissatisfaction with the restrictiveness of Gomułka's rule, and the increasing problems encountered in maintaining economic growth and securing any improvement in living standards came to be associated with the position taken by a group which had formed around Mieczysław Moczar, minister of the interior since 1964. He was well placed to mobilize support for his political ambitions among the police, security forces and party apparatus. Such supporters were known as the Partisans, in reference to a claimed war-time resistance record (Moczar had served in the communist People's Army), and appeals were made to patriotic attitudes and sentiments fed by anti-intellectualism, illiberalism, xenophobia and, eventually, anti-semitism.

The last factor came to the fore in the wake of the Arab-Israeli War of June 1967. Polish opinion was emphatically in favour of the Israelis because the Arabs were seen as Soviet clients. By way of response to this unsympathetic climate of opinion, official condemnation of the Israeli action and of the 'Zionism' associated with it soon developed into attacks on Jewish intellectuals and, by association, various liberals and intellectuals in general. The mobilization of support for Gomułka's endorsement of Soviet policy developed into an apparent threat to his position, however, and a critical situation developed in March 1968, when student demonstrations were brutally dispersed and leading Jewish professors excluded from Warsaw University. There was no direct challenge to his leadership, but Gomułka's position was weakened. In another area, though, the changing Soviet attitude to West Germany bore fruit in 1970 from the Polish point of view with the formal recognition by the FRG of Poland's western border along the Oder-Neisse Line, an agreement being signed to this effect on 7 December.

This achievement was quite overshadowed, however, by measures taken to implement policies adopted in response to Poland's persistent economic stagnation and the looming threat posed by continuing low living standards. The increase in Polish wage levels throughout the 1960s had been the lowest throughout Central and Eastern Europe. In preparation for later reform, prices were drastically increased by a decree of 13 December and wage scales simultaneously revised. This immediately gave rise to workers' strikes and demonstrations which took a particularly intense form in northern Poland, notably in the towns of Gdańsk, Gdynia and Szczecin. The response of the authorities was especially violent, and was perhaps purposely contrived to be so by some individuals in order to destabilize the Gomułka leadership.[11] Under the pressure of events, Gomułka suffered a stroke on December 18 and was taken to hospital where he was informed two days later that he had been replaced as party leader by Edward Gierek. Gierek had been favoured to some extent by Gomułka in order to provide some political counterbalance to Moczar's Partisan faction, although he had also been prominent during the events of March 1968 and had undoubtedly used them to strengthen his position.

Gierek had been a major regional leader throughout the 1960s and gained a reputation for effective administration and management. His record was viewed positively by the Polish public who were eager for something different from the old-fashioned puritanism exemplified by Gomułka and the stringent living conditions with which it had been associated. The new leader also carried some hope of a more general reorientation and the adoption of more Western practices.[12] Gierek's family had migrated to Western Europe and he had worked for a considerable length of time in the mines of France and Belgium, joining the French Communist Party (PCF) and taking part in the war-time resistance movement there. He had, then, extensive international experience (in the West rather than the East, moreover) and his outlook and political views were understood to be significantly different from those of former communist leaders. Workers' strikes and dissatisfaction, nevertheless, subsided only slowly under the new leadership, and something more than vague promises was demanded. Leadership change, the Poles were now realizing, was no substitute for the identification and effective implementation of appropriate policies.

THE KADARIST COMPROMISE

If leadership change was no substitute for policy innovation, leadership continuity at least seemed to provide better conditions for the development of more coherent policies. The situation in Hungary was quite different in this respect from that in Poland. Kádár's leadership of the party in Hungary had begun under conditions radically different from those experienced by Gomułka. His rule had been imposed on a society in violent opposition to communist dictatorship and, in stark contrast to Gomułka, the party and Kádár's leadership would have lacked any political substance had it not been for the force of Soviet arms. But, as Gomułka's rule moved steadily and quite quickly to take on the forms of Soviet orthodoxy, thereby losing its basis of popular support, Kádár sought to formulate policies that could overcome social resistance and help the leadership put down roots among the population. This, however, was only contemplated once all traces of opposition were overcome.

It also required further encouragement from the Soviet authorities, who were instrumental in changing Kádár's view of Nagy's pattern of behaviour as flawed by political weakness to one characterized by outright treachery. They thus influenced him to take firmer measures against the legacy of counter-revolution.[13] What could equally well be termed the communist counter-revolution that was then launched was finally completed at the cost of some 2,000 lives and the imprisonment of tens of thousands (200,000 had also fled to the West at the time of the revolution and its suppression). In 1959 Kádár also moved to reimpose collectivization and completed this process in three years. Having reassembled the main elements of the communist system, Kádár turned to establish more positive inducements for Hungarians to acquiesce in communist rule, a change of emphasis both facilitated and encouraged by Khrushchev's resumption of the anti-Stalinist drive at the XXII CPSU Congress in October 1961.

The altered mood in the Kremlin thus helped him remove ideological conservatives like Kiss and Marosán from their party posts in 1962. At Central Committee meetings in March and August, the responsibility of Hungarian party leaders for the crimes of the Stalinist period was admitted (while clemency was shown at the same time to those Stalinist security chiefs imprisoned until then). Growing numbers of political prisoners were released and, increasingly, Kádár's policy became governed by the statement made in January 1962 that 'He who is not against us is with us'. The centre-piece of this policy was the carefully planned New Economic Mechanism, which was put into operation on 1 January 1968 and which had been prepared while reform forces in Czechoslovakia were struggling to exert some influence. The NEM represented, particularly for its time and location, a significant and coherent programme of economic reform, but it was not permitted to involve any measure of direct political change or form part of an overall reform movement which might threaten the major political parameters of communist rule. Hungarian forces participated, with apparent reluctance, in the invasion of Czechoslovakia but did not allow this traumatic setback to the cause of reform in Central Europe to interfere with the implementation of the NEM. It permitted the self-management of collective farms with regard to production and marketing, and encouraged cultivation of private plots; monopolies were broken up and subsidies curtailed; and, small-scale private economic activity was legalized and encouraged in particular areas. Elements of market forces and productivity incentives were introduced into the socialist sector as enterprises achieved a greater freedom to arrange their own supplies and organize their markets, import raw materials and production equip-ment, and set production levels without outside interference.[14] In consequence of this, real wages between 1966 and 1975 increased at twice the rate they had during the 1961–65 period.

The course of economic development, however, did not run at all smoothly and, while imbalances arose in the process of reform, the Hungarian trade deficit with the West rose, peformance fell short of planned targets and living standards stagnated. As Hungary was very considerably dependent on Soviet raw materials, displeasure in the Kremlin at the political implications of the reform and at some of Hungary's foreign initiatives also had major economic implications. Such areas of major economic weakness led Kádár to reaffirm Hungary's political links with the Soviet Union and secure the benefits of continuing dependence on the Soviet economy. This was followed by extension of the powers of the central planning authority and the establishment of a new State Planning Committee in June 1973.[15] Even more significant was the decision of the Central Committee in March 1974 to remove from their CC posts the economics secretary Rezső Nyers and the liberal culture and ideology secretary György Aczél, and to retire the deputy prime minister and agriculture expert Lajos Fehér. Credits from the West were also taken in some quantity in the hope of curbing the economic slowdown, a dubious solution similar to that adopted by Poland around the same time. The results, too, were similar to those experienced there, without being quite so severe in economic terms or as destabilizing as they were in Poland. The operating principles of the NEM were also reaffirmed and strengthened in 1979, although domestic problems and prevailing world economic conditions meant that no simple economic remedy was available. Some improvement in the rate of growth was achieved in 1982, but it was followed by further decline. At the XIII Party Congress in March 1985 Kádár admitted that austerity measures had reduced both the standard of living and real wages, and the assembly was characterized by an unusual degree of candour and public criticism.[16]

While not wholly unsuccessful in steering Hungary out of the disastrous situation associated with the 1956 Soviet invasion and in maintaining both national stability and his own political position, Kádár's overall strategy produced few positive results. His attempt to separate economic reform from political change and satisfy both national aspirations and Soviet demands proved to be impracticable, particularly under the more stringent world economic conditions of the 1980s. In somewhat less dramatic fashion than elsewhere, the New Economic Mechanism demonstrated once more the fundamental barriers to reform that were imposed within the communist system. Dissatisfaction with Kádár's limited achievements and overall leadership also became more intense in the party itself, and he was forced out of the leading post in May 1988 at the age of 76. He was given the honorary post of party chairman and replaced as party leader by Karoly Grősz. Kádár had headed his party for 32 years, longer even than the other great Central European survivor Walter Ulbricht. In July 1989 Kádár died and, although removed from power primarily for political reasons, was accorded considerable respect for his attempts to build a national consensus after 1956.

CONSUMER-BASED CONSERVATISM

Kádár was not the only leader to enjoy a long period of tenure which lasted until the closing phase of communist rule. Leaders who had been installed somewhat later, in the wake of the invasion of Czechoslovakia and in the early stages of the Pax Sovietica devised by Brezhnev, also proved to be relatively secure in their positions during this final phase. The stability and increasing stagnation of the Soviet Union under Brezhnev was most closely reflected within Central Europe in the conditions imposed on Czechoslovakia under the policy of normalization. Like the invasion itself it lacked the violence of the Hungarian developments, while the reimposition of communist orthodoxy was achieved largely through the steady application of due bureaucratic process and a carefully conducted purge of all public organizations. The sheer pressure of official propaganda over a sustained period, according to Milan Šimečka's elegant account, eventually caused many people simply to doubt the truth of their own experience of the reform period.[17] Whereas the effect of the Hungarian counter-revolution, had been traumatic this process tended gradually to numb social and political processes and was made more tolerable by Soviet economic support in the form of subsidized oil deliveries. After the mid-1970s, though, levels of productivity, wages and consumption fell and, while the export potential of Czechoslovakia's once thriving industrial sector waned, few ideas of reform or alternative strategies to cope with the decline were considered seriously by the leadership. (Some new policies were, however, proposed in the late 1970s and early 1980s.)

In comparison with Poland and even the unsteady course of development in Hungary, however, Czechs and Slovaks were generally able to lead a life cushioned by basic material comforts and, in many cases, to accommodate themselves to relatively tolerable conditions of authoritarian repression. Some exceptions slowly emerged. The group Charter 77 took its name from the year of its foundation and directed its activities to the observance of human rights and evaluation of the effectiveness of the Czecho-slovak leadership's implementation of the UN Covenant on Human Rights signed by Czechoslovakia in 1968 and the Helsinki Final Act of 1975. The Committee for the Defence of the Unjustly Persecuted (VONS) was founded in 1978 and pursued similar, though more closely defined, aims. Great care and substantial official manpower was devoted to the surveillance of the relatively small numbers involved in these activities, and the leadership was generally successful in isolating them from the mass of the population. By late 1987, after ten years of activity on the part of Charter 77, only 2,500 people had signed.[18] But signs of popular dissatisfaction and the beginnings of more general opposition could be detected. Demonstrations against the deployment of nuclear missiles occurred in 1983 and the younger generation, in particular, showed a greater inclination to mark anniversaries associated with national independence.

Nevertheless, no major signs of political strain preceded the retirement of the 74–year-old Husák on 17 December 1987. It followed a visit to Czechoslovakia by Mikhail Gorbachev earlier in the year, and could be interpreted as a change in accordance with the prevailing tide of *perestroika* which had, by that stage, gained some momentum within the Soviet Union but had little visible effect so far on Soviet-Central European relations. Certainly, some statements about the desirability of reform were made by Miloš Jakeš, Husák's successor, but no major signs of action in this direction were evident and the credentials of Jakeš hardly seemed to suit him for an active role in this area. 65 at the time of his appointment, one of his major achievements had been the purge of one-third of the party's membership in the period following the 1968 invasion. Conservatism and observance of the political principles imposed by the Brezhnev leadership of the late 1960s and early 1970s had characterized Czechoslovak politics since the invasion, and Jakeš seemed little inclined to diverge from this course. It had, after all, not been notably less successful than the more independent and adventurous policies pursued in Hungary and Poland.

Political life was similarly stable in the GDR under Honecker, although social and economic conditions were somewhat less stagnant. His orthodoxy was demonstrated at an early stage when he moved in April 1972 to nationalize the remaining private enterprises, which still employed about two million workers (compared with 6.7 million in the socialist sector) and produced over 14 per cent of the national income. Honecker was also concerned to consolidate his own position and had replaced 17 of the 19 Politburo members by the time the next party Congress was held in May 1976. Relations with the Federal Republic and the outside world continued to improve, a Basic Treaty being signed with the former on 21 December 1972 which recognized the separate existence of the GDR and its equality with the FRG. While this gave the Honecker leadership considerable cause for satisfaction, the rapprochement carried certain dangers in terms of encouraging and facilitating comparison of the two Germanies and had long been resisted by hard-line elements in the SED. The situation became, in these terms, both better and worse with the growing success of the West German Social Democratic Party (SPD) and the increasing popularity of its *Ostpolitik* amongst the electors of the Federal Republic.

The development of these normalized relations, enabling family and other kinds of social ties to be maintained or extended, was well received by the East German population and clearly carried political benefits for the GDR leadership. SED leaders remained committed to the maintenance of a separate GDR identity, however, and this was no easy matter as political tensions continued to decline. After the developments of 1970 they pursued this attempt through an ideological drive to promote a delimitation (*Abgrenzung*) between the two societies. The class-based cultural and historical divisions within German society were emphasized and an idea of two Germanies embodying different traditions in this sense was articulated.[19] While intra-German relations strengthened, then, they were also the object of extensive surveillance and suspicion, which varied according to the nature and prominence of the group concerned. Equivalent care was often taken with respect to relations developed between East German partners and members of the Soviet bloc, particularly Poland, whose practice was also thought to diverge from orthodox principles and pose some threat to East German ideological purity.

The growth of economic links between the two Germanies tended, nevertheless, to take precedence over any ideological and political misgivings on the part of the GDR leadership. By the mid-1980s trade with the Federal Republic accounted for more than half that conducted by the GDR with developed Western economies and about 10 per cent of its total external trade. Trade, however, was only one aspect of the economic relationship and it brought many other sources of income: West German banks granted 1 billion *Deutschmark* in credit during 1983 and only slightly less the following year; large sums were derived from West German visitors and transport and communication charges; payment was made for the release of political prisoners and to assist family reunifications; and individual institutions such as churches helped support their counterparts in the GDR. Taken together, these inputs constituted a major source of support for an economy which, while apparently less afflicted than its communist neighbours, was clearly flagging in a broader perspective. West German subventions made an important contribution to the maintenance of social and political stability in the GDR and, as in the case of Czechoslovakia, sympathetic external relations and material assistance were an important component of successful consumer-based conservatism in this part of the Soviet bloc. The growth of the intra-German relationship was finally marked in September 1987 by Honecker's much discussed and previously postponed visit to Bonn and other parts of the Federal Republic, the first such visit by a top East German leader.

Under these conditions, it was hardly surprising that the GDR leadership remained highly resistant to the pressures for change which were emerging with increasing strength from the Soviet Union. In a marked departure from earlier practice, it was now denied that the Soviet Union represented a model in terms of technological progress and socio-economic development (in more homely terms, it was argued that it was hardly necessary to change the wall-paper just because your neighbour redecorates his house).

Moreover, despite the pro-reform forces gathering momentum in other parts of the region (particularly Poland and Hungary), there were still few signs of political pressure in the GDR. Expressions of protest did become more prominent in 1988 and 1989, though. The limitations of *Abgrenzung* also became evident in 1989 as growing numbers of East German summer tourists took advantage of relaxations on travel, first in Hungary but then in Poland and Czechoslovakia, to gain transit to the Federal Republic. The problems did not arise from changing relations within Central Europe, but were rather associated with growing signs of the permeability of the Iron Curtain. GDR citizens had previously been free to visit other parts of the communist world on the assumption that the fraternal regimes would not permit unrestricted access to the non-communist world. It was the system on which these assumptions were based that began to break down during the late spring and summer of 1989 in Hungary. But it was ironic that it was Gorbachev's presence at the celebrations held in October 1989 to mark the fortieth anniversary of the foundation of the GDR, and the extensive demonstrations which broke out soon afterwards, that played a major part in forcing Honecker's resignation, at the age of 77. Like Husák at the time of his resignation, Honecker had led his party for 18 years.

POLAND'S PERMANENT CRISIS

Political life and patterns of party leadership in Poland showed considerable differences from the situation produced by the lengthy tenure of Kádár in Hungary or even the less prolonged rule of Husák and Honecker. The instabilities of Polish politics were the occasion for the rise and fall of a larger number of leaders and greater diversity of policy approach. The tendency to seek new solutions to Poland's problems was certainly apparent during Gierek's leadership. Taking office after the conservative and rather puritanical Gomułka, Edward Gierek was more inclined to follow the inventive, flexible line taken by Kádár rather than the cautious dogmatism shown by Ulbricht. Gierek made great play of his more modern political style and ability to communicate, suggesting that significant reform and decentralization were likely to be the order of the day. In his first weeks, several factory visits were made (with Gierek making personal approaches for assistance from the work-force) and appeals for the workers to return to normal production practices publicized, but employees remained unimpressed by the leadership reshuffle and pressed for tangible improvements. On 15 February 1971, in the face of a strike by angry women mill-workers, the December price rises were withdrawn. Gierek also moved swiftly and effectively to consolidate his political position and strengthen his hold over the party organization. From the point of view of his standing in the country as a whole and the national position of the party leadership, though, the question of economic development and improved living standards was paramount.

In connection with this, issues that had surfaced earlier in communist Central Europe concerning the relative emphasis to be placed on reform and macro-economic policy change re-emerged. After the early period, less and less was heard of reform and institutional change and, in keeping with his international perspectives, Gierek paid increasing attention to the use of foreign credits. Large Soviet credits to help stabilize the new leadership and the growing influx of foreign capital resulted in a sharp rise in output indices and the income of the work-force.[20] Production topped plan targets in 1971 and 1972, while even faster growth took place the following year when national income rose faster than at any time between 1950 and 1972. As food prices remained pegged at the same level, real wages rose by 11 per cent during that year alone. The strategy carried considerable dangers, though. Imports were considerably higher than exports in 1972 and growth was achieved with the considerable assistance of machinery brought in from the West, the value of which rose from roughly $100 million a year in the late 1960s to $1,900 million in 1974. The balance of payments deficit rose accordingly, from a minimal $60 million in 1970 to $2,050 million in 1975. By the end of that year total foreign debt had risen to $6,352 million (or over 6 billion dollars).

Political stability and the quiescence of the work-force were therefore literally bought at a high cost, while the rapid growth initially achieved soon began to tail off. According to official figures, annual growth of national income fell from over 10 per cent in 1973 to 6.8 per cent in 1976. Increases in real wages earned in the socialized sector slumped from over 8 per cent in 1973 and 1975 to 3.9 per cent in 1976.[21] The effective value of higher incomes had in fact begun falling earlier, as the supply of consumer goods and resources rapidly fell behind the greatly increased demand. The need to rein back demand, stimulate production and move towards market equilibrium again became pressing and a major increase in food prices was announced once again on 24 June 1976. Consultation and any form of public discussion were conspicuously lacking, while worker response was swift and determined. Strikes broke out and demonstrations took a dramatic form in Radom and the Ursus plant outside Warsaw. The price rises were immediately rescinded but police repression was determined and often brutal. Many workers were beaten, arrested and later sentenced.

Gierek's promised reforms were now abandoned and the political climate was worsened by an escalating economic crisis. A new element in the subsequent period, however, was that this round of worker protest and violent repression was followed by the formation of a Workers' Defence Committee (KOR) composed of leading intellectuals and political activists. It had considerable success in defending the rights and restoring the position of individual workers, but also took on a broader role within the tendencies of opposition. This was facilitated by the fact that the authorities found it difficult to curb the committee's activities when the Polish government was so dependent on the West for the sensitive management of its economic situation and the international climate was imbued with the spirit of the 1975 Helsinki Agreement. The Committee was remarkable for providing a symbolic and social core around which, for the first time since the Stalinist period, worker and intellectual opposition could be co-ordinated and developed in some organizational form.[22]

As the inability of the party leadership to master the economic situation was becoming increasingly evident, the capacity of Polish society for integration in the face of the increasingly unpopular Gierek regime was greatly enhanced by the election of Cardinal Wojtyła, archbishop of Cracow, as Pope John Paul II on 16 October 1978. This became particularly evident from the response to the first visit he paid as Pope to his homeland in the summer of 1979. When a further poorly handled attempt to impose price rises was made on 1 July 1980 the popular response was, therefore, more decided, widespread and better organized than on previous occasions. The strike wave rolled on for weeks, gaining intensity in different parts of the country, and only ended when agreements (at Szczecin and the Silesian mining town of Jastrzębie as well as in Gdańsk) were signed between representatives of the increasingly organized and integrated workers' movement and government representatives. The agreement signed by Lech Wałęsa in Gdańsk on 31 August 1980 provided not only for economic concessions by the authorities but also the legal right of workers to strike and organize independent trade unions.

Wałęsa had been born in 1943 in a peasant family. His father died in 1945 soon after release from a German prison camp. At the age of sixteen he took a course in agricultural mechanics and started work in a State Machinery Centre as an electrician. After national service he settled in Gdańsk and took employment in the shipyard. He was elected to the chair of a workshop strike committee in 1970 and was dismissed from his job after speaking out in 1976. After further interrupted employment, his work in the free trade union movement became more systematic during 1978 and he was again arrested at the end of 1979 for celebrating the ninth anniversary of the 1970 strikes.[23] When a further strike broke out at the Lenin shipyard in August 1980, Wałęsa climbed over the fence and co-ordinated the strike movement into a workers' organization capable of shaking the foundations of the communist regime in Poland. There were divisions within the party leadership about the appropriate response to this evident crisis of communist rule and matters were clearly moving way beyond Gierek's capacity to cope. He resigned, pleading ill health, on September 6 and was replaced by Stanisław Kania, a Central Committee secretary who had taken over responsibility for security matters after Moczar's removal in June 1971 and later also that for church-state relations. The Gierek inner circle was eliminated at this stage and Józef Pińkowski appointed prime minister.

A new attitude of humility was announced on behalf of the party but, while the party leadership of Kania and the governments of Pińkowski and (from 9 February 1981) General Wojciech Jaruzelski expressed their commitment to political and economic reform, progress in both these areas was painfully slow. There were clearly many at all levels of the political establishment and administration who were opposed both to recognition of the rights embodied in the Gdańsk agreement and to Solidarity's further demands, some of which in any case could not be met under contemporary conditions. Relations were complicated by the background of continuing economic crisis, declining production and falling living standards. Strikes organized in pursuit of Solidarity's demands were often blamed for this, but the roots of economic weakness extended much further back. As forces within Solidarity were beginning to show greater impatience and a desire to exert greater pressure on the authorities, the multi-million, functionally diffuse union became increasingly difficult to control and hold together. Kania also showed signs of a decreasing ability to cope with this situation as forces associated with the party apparatus sought to enhance their position after the Extraordinary Party Congress of July 1981.[24] He lost a vote of confidence in the Central Committee on 18 October 1981 and was replaced as PZPR first secretary by Jaruzelski, still prime minister and also minister of defence since 1968.

In spite of this remarkable collection of posts (which might, however, have reflected a less impressive accumulation of power than their sheer number suggested) Jaruzelski gave the appearance of being a modest and relatively retiring man, his rather enigmatic character hidden behind the dark glasses he invariably wore. He was born in 1923 into a family of landed gentry and attended a Jesuit boarding school. During the war he was in the Soviet Union in circumstances which have remained somewhat obscure (although it is recorded that his father died there during this period). Until 1943 at least he was employed as a labourer before entering the Ryazan military academy and joining the Polish army raised in the USSR by General Berling. Having fought with it throughout the campaign of liberation, Jaruzelski joined the communist party (PPR) in 1947. In 1956 he became the youngest general in the Polish army, in 1960 he was appointed head of the Main Political Administration of the armed forces and then, two years later, vice-minister of defence. He became Chief of General Staff in 1965.

From his more elevated political position in October 1981 he espoused a relatively conciliatory policy and called for an accommodation between the conflicting social forces, a process which showed little sign of achieving any success. Although there was a growing public awareness that some new arrangement or political approach was likely to be needed, Jaruzelski's declaration on 13 December 1981 of martial law (a 'State of War' according to the constitutional formulation) to safeguard national security was, nevertheless, a considerable shock. Officially undertaken to forestall an internal threat to state power and, by implication, a threatened Soviet invasion, there were also well-founded suspicions that martial law was forced on Jaruzelski by the conservative obduracy of much of the party apparatus and communist political establishment. According to Colonel Kukliński, a member of Polish General Staff who later turned out to have been passing information to the US military, Jaruzelski was fully convinced of the need to impose a military solution by June 1981, while Kania was becoming increasingly doubtful of the wisdom of such a move.[25]

In the event the introduction of martial law was efficiently carried out and effective in its immediate objective. Most of Solidarity's leadership and activists were swiftly rounded up and placed in internment camps. The activities of trade unions and most social organizations were suspended, and those which had taken an anti-regime stance dissolved. The party was also purged of reformist and some hard-line elements. The circumstances of martial law were used by the authorities to put through major price rises but no coherent programme for economic recovery was implemented. The State of War was suspended and finally lifted in July 1983, and an increasingly conciliatory stance adopted by the authorities towards Polish society – although the return of Solidarity in anything like its original form was repeatedly ruled out.

While the process of economic decline was halted, recovery was half-hearted and no real dynamic for growth or further development was set in motion. A 'second stage' of reform was formulated and introduced in 1987 but had little impact on the economy – unlike the further wave of strikes which broke out in 1988. These brought the authorities into discussion with strike leaders and, after protracted negotiations, led to the agreement that permitted the relegalization of Solidarity and the organization of semi-free elections in June 1989. In Poland, more than elsewhere, the politics of mature, post-Stalinist communism had turned out to be ultimately self-defeating and incapable of sustaining the rule of the Workers' Party. The absence of any threat from the Soviet Union on this occasion was, of course, also a decisive factor, but the weakness of communist rule had long been apparent in the recurrent phases of political instability and the successive leadership crises seen in Poland.

NOTES AND REFERENCES

1. Dennis, *German Democratic Republic*, p. 27.
2. McAdams, *East Germany and Detente*, p. 26.
3. Scharf, *Politics and Change in East Germany*, p. 183.
4. Childs, *The GDR*, p. 68.
5. Schulz, 'Recent changes', p. 56.
6. *The Guardian* (London), 16 January 1993.
7. Lewis, 'Anatomy of ruling parties', p. 13.
8. Kolankiewicz, 'The working class'.
9. Korybutowicz, *Grudzień 1970*, p. 35.

10. Brzezinski, *The Soviet Bloc*, pp. 255–64.
11. Tarniewski, *Płonie komitet*, pp. 73–78.
12. Bromke, 'Poland under Gierek', pp. 6–7.
13. Lomax, 'Hungary – the quest for legitimacy', p. 80.
14. Richet, *The Hungarian Model*, p. 3.
15. Hoensch, *History of Modern Hungary*, p. 244.
16. Heinrich, *Hungary*, p. 48.
17. Simecka *The Restoration of Order*, p. 15.
18. Wolchik, *Czechoslovakia in Transition*, pp. 38–39.
19. McCauley, 'Legitimation in the GDR', pp. 47–48.
20. Brus, 'Aims, methods and political determinents', p. 103.
21. Landau and Tomaszewski, *The Polish Economy*, p. 297.
22. Lipski, *KOR: A History of the Defense Committee*, p. 43.
23. Wałęsa, *A Path of Hope*, p. 100.
24. Lewis, *Political Authority*, pp. 160–61.
25. Kukliński, 'Wojna z narodem', pp. 4–47.

CHAPTER NINE

The Military Basis of the Communist Order

SOVIET MILITARY POWER AND CENTRAL EUROPE

Among the major political crises in Central Europe prior to 1989 only the last one, in Poland during 1980–81, did not see the use of Soviet military force. Even then, though, the supposed threat of its use was a major factor justifying Jaruzelski's imposition of martial law and deployment of national security forces. The Soviet military had clearly played a major part in establishing communist power in Central Europe after 1945 and in maintaining it in the face of successive uprisings against Soviet-backed dictatorship – and even of attempts to reform the mechanisms of communist rule from above. The role of the Red Army in establishing communist power had been decisive in Poland and Hungary, but significant more as a background condition and part of a critical international context for Czechoslovakia. Soviet force was later decisive in crushing opposition to communist rule and ensuring its survival in orthodox form in Hungary in 1956 and in Czechoslovakia in 1968. It was of determinant significance throughout in East Germany, where around 400,000 Soviet troops were instrumental in maintaining the communist regime – having also overseen the formation of the German Democratic Republic and underwritten its survival as a separate state. When, indeed, the withdrawal of Soviet troops from German soil later came on to the agenda it was reported that as much as 10 per cent of GDR territory had been under the direct control of Soviet military authorities.

For much of this period, the Soviet military presence in Central Europe was associated primarily with the institutions formed on the conclusion of the Warsaw Pact, which were also jointly known as the

Warsaw Treaty Organization (WTO). The Soviet invasion of Hungary was linked (after the event) with the responsibilities assumed by the signatories of the Pact for the defence of socialism, while the intervention made in Czechoslovakia during 1968 was explicitly organized within its framework. But communist power was imposed and maintained in the immediate post-war years mainly by Soviet forces under direct Moscow command – indeed, the Warsaw Pact itself was not concluded until 1955. Certain questions arise at the outset, then, about the role of the Warsaw Treaty Organization and the reasons for its creation ten years after the end of the Second World War and in the light of the proven adequacy of Soviet forces in securing Kremlin objectives within Central Europe. Why, for example, was the refinement of the military framework of Central European order initiated and pursued only after 1953? By that time the culmination of the Stalinist dictatorship was past, a greater degree of national variation was already permitted, and more care was being taken to fit the political forms of communist rule to the conditions of the individual Central European countries.

Tight military links, the co-ordination of security activities and firm subordination of Central European forces to Soviet interests and command centres had, not surprisingly under the conditions described in earlier chapters, been established at an early stage. Occupation forces in newly liberated countries provided a solid base from which Soviet influence could be exercised. Bilateral friendship, political and co-operation treaties were also soon signed by individual countries with the Soviet Union (before the end of the war in the case of Czechoslovakia and Poland). These already had the effect of creating defence alliances between the signatories and barred them from participation in coalitions opposed to the interests of those concerned.[1] By the early 1950s Central European military establishments had been fully Stalinized: command positions were filled with communist cadres or sympathizers with communist military training; organization and doctrine was tailored to the Soviet pattern; multiple channels of party control were established. Soviet military intelligence (GRU) agents remained active throughout the region. Direct Soviet control was then enhanced (particularly in Poland) by placing Soviet officers of non-Russian origin in allies' armies and endowing them with the appropriate citizenship; large numbers of Soviet advisers were also placed in Central European armies to constitute a separate chain of command.[2] This extreme degree of submission to Soviet control was, however, relaxed after the death of Stalin.

The formation of the WTO was, nevertheless, hardly a response to any perceived lack of regional co-ordination, let alone absence of Soviet control. Its origins most probably lay outside the area of Soviet influence, the direct signal for the agreement being the accession of the Federal Republic of Germany to the North Atlantic Treaty Organization (NATO) on 5 May 1955, nine days before the signature of the Warsaw Treaty. While the formation of NATO itself in 1949 had not prompted any such reaction in the East, the integration of West Germany within the Western alliance was clearly another matter and one which elicited a direct Soviet response. NATO was, moreover, one in a series of US-sponsored alliances formed around this time, which included Anzus (1951, made with Australia and New Zealand); the South-East Asia Treaty Organization (1954); and the Baghdad Pact (or Central Treaty Organization, 1955). The formation of the WTO was, then, also a response to the developing bipolar global system and a measure taken by the Soviet Union within the context of an international tendency to form regional alliance systems.

There were, of course, other factors involved. Some have seen the Treaty reflecting a new vision of military relations appropriate to the situation created by the changes that occurred after the death of Stalin – although meaningful consequences in terms of the nature of these relations could only be identified after the passage of some years. These involved a reduction in the emphasis placed on the sheer weight of military numbers and limitation of the sphere of direct Soviet control. The WTO also provided a legal basis for the presence of Soviet troops in Hungary and Romania, which should otherwise have been withdrawn following the signature of the Austrian State Treaty and agreement on the removal of occupation forces from that country. It may well have reflected different tendencies in the Soviet foreign policy of the time. On the one hand, it served to enhance military security according to the perceptions of foreign minister Molotov. On the other, it provided party leader Khrushchev with a more solid and formally unified regional base from which to explore more adventurous policies and contemplate the establishment of a post-Stalinist détente. It could even be interpreted as a new Soviet gain now available as a bargaining chip in a changing international situation.

AIMS AND ORGANIZATION OF THE WTO

Whatever the reasons that underlay the formation of the Warsaw Treaty Organization, the body created had a number of clear-cut aims and principles. It committed its signatories to the settlement of international disputes by peaceful means; to work towards the prohibition of weapons of mass destruction; to assist other members in the case of armed attack in Europe on any one of them; to establish a joint military command; to further relations of economic and cultural co-operation without interfering in other countries' internal affairs; and to seek a more general European treaty of collective security whose establishment would replace the existing pact. It did not involve any formal commitment to the communist order but left open the possibility of other members joining without regard to the nature of their social or state system. The treaty was initially to remain in force for a period of twenty years with a provision for an automatic ten-year renewal for those who had not previously renounced their membership. It was further renewed in May 1985 on the initiative of Mikhail Gorbachev (after only two months as leader of the USSR) for a period of twenty years with little apparent resistance or major discussion.[3]

In addition to Czechoslovakia, Hungary, Poland and the German Democratic Republic, other signatories to the Treaty on 14 May 1955 were Albania, Bulgaria, and Romania in association, of course, with the Soviet Union. With the intensification of Soviet-Chinese conflict over de-Stalinization, the USSR severed diplomatic relations with Albania in late 1961 and it stopped participating in the activities of WTO bodies, although it was only after the invasion of Czechoslovakia in 1968 that Albania finally withdrew from the Organization. Soviet relations with Romania also worsened over questions of national autonomy and Ceauşescu refused to participate in the 1968 intervention. Nevertheless, a basic level of military collaboration was maintained and some accommodation on contentious issues was reached in 1967, although Romania continued to refuse permission for the transit of foreign troops and maintained its participation in many WTO activities at a low level. Military and political threads were thus interwoven in the development of the WTO, and the dual focus evident from its inception in 1955 was perpetuated in the relations that developed between member countries as well as in the structure of the organization itself.

As specified in the text of the Treaty, the main body of the organization established in 1955 was the Political Consultative Committee (PCC). At the same time a Joint Command was set up. The formation of the Joint Armed Forces of member countries, placed under the command of the Soviet Marshal Konev, was announced and a central staff headquarters, with representatives of member states, established in Moscow. Additional bodies, whose composition and duties remained somewhat unclear, were soon formed. A Permanent Commission and Joint Secretariat, for example, were set up at the first meeting of the PCC in January 1956. The PCC, as the WTO's leading body and formally responsible for appointing its commander-in-chief, chief of staff and general secretary, was initially supposed to meet at least twice a year, although this frequency soon turned out to be unrealistic. PCC meetings were, in practice, held less frequently than once a year and, on occasion, more than two years elapsed between meetings. The formal structure of the WTO did not provide much guidance to the real nature or significance of the Organization.

The forms of regional organization, and particularly the nature of the control exerted by national leaderships, both under normal conditions and in the event of hostilities, were also a matter of considerable uncertainty. The modification of direct Soviet military control over Eastern Europe after the death of Stalin with the subsequent reduction in the numbers of military personnel, the modernization of the armed forces, and the professionalization of East European military forces all played a part in this situation. The changes in status and number of the national armed forces injected a further element, and this situation varied significantly with the rise and fall of the diverse challenges to Soviet power throughout the post-Stalin period. The Hungarian armed forces were numerically the smallest in the WTO and had been virtually disbanded after the confrontation of 1956. In 1969 their number remained limited to half that of 1956 and army numbers were further reduced from that date to 84,000 in 1987–88 (not much larger than the level of the Soviet forces stationed there which stood at 65,000).

Czechoslovak forces also experienced a significant reduction after the 1968 invasion and their numbers fell from 225,000 in 1967–68 to 168,000 as a result of mass resignations from the officer force and purges of those who remained. They rose again to 201,000 in the late 1980s – although this did not involve an increase in the size of the army itself. Czechoslovak forces were considerably larger than those of the Soviet Union stationed there, which amounted to 80,000. These had been introduced to stabilize the situation after the 1968 invasion, but developed as a permanent garrison force. Despite having a slightly larger population than Czechoslovakia, East German forces (which had existed only in embryonic form in 1955) were smaller in the late 1980s than those of their southern neighbour and stood at a level of 176,000. The Soviet force stationed there, at 380,000, was a considerably larger one, though. The armed forces of Poland, commensurate with its larger population, were the most numerous in the area at 380,000 while those of the Soviet contingent, following the agreement of late 1956, were restricted and remained at a level of 40,000.[4] Overall, the national forces represented a substantial military contribution and made up nearly half the WTO's conventional strength in Central Europe.[5]

The combined forces of the Warsaw Pact countries offered the West an image of considerable military power deployed in strength on sensitive NATO borders. Their sheer number and proximity to the leading West European countries, and indeed the veritable siege conditions they threatened to impose on West Berlin on more than one occasion, were certainly considered to be a major threat by NATO strategists, particularly in the light of known Soviet sympathy for the principle of offensive defence. However, as long as the West outpaced the Soviet Union in the development of nuclear weapons and (even more important) the means for their delivery, the size and level of equipment of WTO forces in conventional terms was not regarded with excessive anxiety. This situation began to change in 1970s as the Soviet Union showed signs of catching up in terms of nuclear weapons technology. It also appeared to be placing considerably greater emphasis on the co-ordination of WTO forces with the holding of joint exercises in the late 1960s and early 1970s. US strength also looked less assured, with the Vietnam debacle, the political weaknesses of its leadership exposed during the Watergate scandal, and the signs of a growing economic vulnerability that contributed to cutbacks in military expenditure.

By the late 1970s, then, NATO 'was perhaps weaker in comparison to the Warsaw Pact than at any time in the past'.[6] The access to Central European territory that Soviet forces gained from the military organization and the sheer number of forces they deployed there (31 divisions with nuclear-capable tactical missiles, modern fighter aircraft, extensive stocks of tanks, artillery and other equipment) clearly gave the Kremlin 'a forward staging area from which to launch an offensive campaign against Western Europe'.[7]

Soviet transport capabilities made great advances: in 1972 they were able to move 25,000 soldiers from one side of Eastern Europe to the other in 40 days; by 1976 they transferred 100,000 in less than 10 days. Analysts known for their critical views of the NATO were not reluctant to acknowledge that Warsaw Pact forces were greatly superior in their supply of tanks. NATO had 17,000 main battle tanks in Europe, in contrast to 26,000 WTO tanks in Eastern Europe and a further 19,200 in the western parts of the USSR.[8] By 1980, then, it was possible to acknowledge that 'Soviet plans for rapid rates of advance, if successful, would overwhelm NATO's forces more quickly than they could be reinforced'.[9]

The economic burden of this powerful military force fell largely on the Soviet Union (not surprisingly, perhaps, in view of the degree to which it served Soviet strategic interests), which was thought to bear 80 per cent of the costs of the alliance. In 1979, the USSR was estimated to spend 11–13 per cent of GNP on defence, although ten years later more realistic estimates would put it at between 20–30 per cent. By way of comparison, the US allocated (out of a larger budget) 6.5 per cent of GNP in the late 1980s and the average West European country 3.5 per cent. Regardless of absolute levels of military expenditure, though, it was clear that the burden of military expenditure for the Central European countries was considerably less than it was for the Soviet Union. Even if the 1979 Soviet estimates were unrealistically low, those for Central Europe were considerably lower. Hungary spent only 2.1 per cent of GNP, and Poland and Czechoslovakia 2.4 and 2.8 per cent respectively. Only the GDR was thought to spend as much as 6.3 per cent.[10] If the military organization of the forces of the Warsaw Pact countries was geared primarily to the service of Soviet interests, it was also the Soviet Union that footed most of the bill.

MILITARY INTEGRATION AND WTO OPERATIONS

In the sphere of military organization in Central Europe, as in other areas, the Soviet leadership had taken pains to build up the machinery of strict control and, despite certain changes in approach and style after 1953, seemed strongly committed to the maintenance of this prerogative. According to one interpretation, any independent national military forces in Central Europe were unreliable from the Soviet point of view.[11] In the event of major international hostilities it was considered possible that WTO forces would have just been absorbed by the Soviet military machine and become subject to direct Soviet command.[12] Despite its formal existence as a military organization and the extensive authority over regional military forces exercised by its commander-in-chief, it appeared that the powers of the WTO commander would be considerably curtailed in wartime and that control over all major forces of the alliance would be taken over by a direct representative of Soviet domestic interests.

While the *raison d'être* of a military organization and its leadership must ultimately be the capacity to wage war it was, paradoxically, precisely this right that seemed to be denied the Warsaw Treaty Organization and its commander-in-chief (whose principal role under such conditions would then be to transfer major war-making powers to the Soviet command). The WTO was, therefore, essentially a peace-time organization, geared to the requirements of marshalling, controlling and managing the armed forces as a potential resource rather than to those of actual warfare.[13] It provided an appropriate base for the development of the Warsaw Pact forces and their organization for potential use but had few clear implications for their actual military deployment. The issue was not one of the military importance of the region, quite the contrary. The Soviet problem was rather that the region was recognized to be of considerable military importance and remained so throughout successive phases of Soviet military thinking, but that WTO allies were not seen as either strong or reliable enough to ensure Soviet security interests independently of a Soviet-dominated defence organization.

Major developments did take place within the WTO after 1956, but these fell far short of transforming the alliance into a fully integrated military machine, or one formally empowered to intervene in the internal affairs of member states. Until 1961 any changes made concerned the co-ordination of military activities rather than any process of integration.[14] Before that, in military terms, the WTO was little more than a paper organization.[15] During the 1960s a programme of multinational exercises between Soviet and East European forces was developed, principles of coalition warfare reinforced, and joint training procedures and collaboration in military education strengthened. All of these probably strengthened the internal structures of the WTO, but they fell far short of establishing a basic capacity for integrated action, either externally or internally, in terms of direct intervention in the affairs of member countries during situations of internal crisis. Nor was it even clear that they were capable of counteracting the strengthening centrifugal tendencies of member states in relation to military affairs. Nevertheless, the processes set in train during the 1960s culminated in the high point of integration during the late 1970s, when the WTO took on the form more of a concrete multi-national force, with more authentic multi-national institutions and exercises.[16] Even this did not achieve the degree of integration that Soviet decision-makers thought appropriate, though, and more direct forms of Soviet control were later sought.

Basic Soviet military perceptions of the role and importance of Central Europe thus changed little in the years that followed the death of Stalin and the signature of the Warsaw Treaty two years later. In this view, the establishment of the WTO further affirms suggestions already made that it was primarily a political response to the condition of post-Stalin Europe. The origins of the Warsaw Treaty Organization, as well as its formal stucture and the course taken by its institutional development (whatever particular inter-pretation is placed on this process), all point to the fact that its primary significance was as a political entity. Despite the impli-cations of ideological neutrality contained in the text of the Warsaw Treaty, subsequent definition of its role, as well as the nature of its activity and major interventions in the domestic affairs of individual countries with which it was associated, suggests a different status for the military organization. Allusions to its responsibility for defending the gains of socialism were frequent and the Treaty was already referred to in justification of the Soviet invasion of Hungary in 1956, although no PCC meeting appears to have been called to discuss the crisis.

Considerable stress was later placed on the WTO membership of the invading forces during the Czechoslovak crisis of 1968, but even here there was little validity to the claim that the intervention in Czechoslovakia was actually organized within the framework of the Organization.[17] The Treaty did not sanction military intervention in the internal affairs of member states and the major meetings held to discuss the crisis – in Warsaw during July and in Bratislava during August – involved leaders of the WTO countries (although not all of them) but were not WTO meetings themselves. As in 1956, the invasion of Czechoslovakia was essentially an initiative of the Soviet armed forces rather than one undertaken within the framework of the WTO. Subsequent references to the Brezhnev doctrine of limited sovereignty as its underlying principle, and to the primacy of the views of the Soviet leadership were by no means inappropriate. Similar references could also have been made in relation to the action in Hungary where subsequent justification had equally been sought in the Warsaw Treaty, but it was only in 1968 that the Organization really began to claim its function of guarantor of the Soviet Union's socialist conquests.[18]

POLITICAL FUNCTIONS OF MILITARY CO-ORDINATION

The Warsaw Treaty Organization was, then, set up at a time when Soviet military supremacy within Central Europe was fully established and a variety of arrangements were already in place to guarantee its security. The reasons for its establishment derived more from global developments and international relations than from regional considerations. While steps were taken to develop the organization as a basis for integrated military activity, they never progressed far enough to satisfy the rigorous demands of the Soviet Union for effective control and, while the Soviet military presence was dominant within the WTO, the Soviet military command also maintained its powers of control over the Organization. As tendencies to instability continued within the Soviet bloc, though, the political role of the alliance grew. The critical processes which supported Soviet supremacy and maintained bloc integration increasingly rested on the military alliance. The steps taken in its name to check the course of reform in Czechoslovakia were its most visible action, but that was only one consequence of the political functions it performed.

The nature of these functions has been understood in different ways. One argument has been that the developments seen within the WTO were essentially bilateral rather than multilateral in nature, and served to reinforce the regional position of the Soviet Union rather than developing the WTO as a supranational body. By integrating national military forces within a broader framework, the dangers of political autonomy taking on a military dimension were correspondingly reduced.[19] The position of Central Europe within the Soviet bloc was thus more firmly established by reducing the threat that tendencies towards the assertion of national independence might take more concrete and effective form. An alternative view of regional relations expressed earlier was that the course of WTO development reflected less the strengthening of bilateral relations between the USSR and the WTO allies and a desire to inhibit tendencies towards greater national autonomy through enhanced surveillance procedures, than a higher level of Soviet sensitivity to the needs of consultation and conflict containment. At least the early years of the post-Khrushchev period, particularly in the handling of Romanian independent-mindedness, seemed to show some respect for divergent national interests and attempts to establish a bargaining relationship within the organization.[20] This tendency, however, diminished in the wake of the Prague Spring and West Germany's development of an *Ostpolitik* that also sought to make use of the differing national orientations emerging in Central Europe.

Whatever the implications of the developments within the WTO that gathered pace during the 1960s, though, it was nevertheless clear that their success in curbing tendencies towards national autonomy was at best partial, and that effectiveness in reconciling the conflicting interests within the regional military and political complex was less than complete. The problems faced in containing successive crises and preventing their escalation into bids for national independence led to the proliferation of the WTO's organizational structure, and the continuing search for more effective forms of co-ordination that could give more solid guarantees of Soviet dominance. Nevertheless, greater success was achieved in containing the crises that broke out after the bloody conflicts of the Hungarian revolution.

The Polish emergency of 1981 and the period of military rule begun in December of that year provided some instructive pointers in this respect. It was, firstly, significant that it was Poland's military and political rulers (groups whose membership had increasingly merged during 1981) who acted against Solidarity and reform groups, rather than Soviet forces or those of WTO member countries. There were various suggestions as to the precise motives of party leader and military chief Jaruzelski in staging the coup of 13 December 1981. It was argued that he was acting either to forestall Soviet military action on the lines of earlier invasions or to pre-empt a coup of a more hard-line character. While considerable emphasis has been placed on the threat of Soviet invasion, the extent to which the Polish authorities were really acting under Soviet duress or just making use of the external threat to justify their repressive actions has remained controversial.

There is, however, little evidence to support the view that

Jaruzelski was in any way acting against Soviet interests or preferences. There were a number of WTO meetings in the days preceding the coup (although it was not reported what happened at them) and WTO commander-in-chief Kulikov was actually in Warsaw when it was staged. Polish developments seem to indicate, then, that the forces that repressed Solidarity and acted to strengthen the components of orthodox communist dictatorship did so in accordance with Soviet preferences. In this view, Jaruzelski's group basically acted as a Soviet proxy and demonstrated a firm commitment to Soviet interests – either from motives of loyalty or from more detached calculations of *force majeure* and Polish *raison d'état.*

A second significant feature of the Polish developments was that it was leading echelons within the military and select party figures in association with security forces and the political administration of the army that actually carried out the coup. Standard military units played little direct part in the action, although they were certainly placed in a state of heightened readiness and given some peripheral tasks to perform. While the coup was relatively successful in technical and even political terms, the way in which the crisis was resolved does suggest that the doubts concerning the morale and loyalty of the Polish army evident in the 1970s had not been dissipated and that great care had to be taken both in defusing the Polish conflict and in safeguarding the place of the military in it.[21] Whatever the form taken by WTO structures and the degree of military integration, there were still major doubts about the adequacy of national armies themselves for eventual action. More than providing any direct evidence about the specific place of Polish forces within the WTO and their reliability as instruments of Soviet policy, though, the events of December 1981 demonstrated the complex integration of military, political and security agencies both nationally and regionally, and the capacity at least of critical parts of this machine to ensure the achievement of key political objectives and the satisfaction of core Soviet interests.

DIVERSITY AND CHANGE IN SECURITY CONCEPTIONS

The tendency towards closer military integration within the WTO and the care taken to ensure Soviet supremacy did not, however, rule out the emergence of further political conflict and disagreement within the alliance. The military implications of Soviet security imperatives had also changed radically since the mid-1950s. Developments within the WTO became less determined by Soviet regional interests and perceptions and more by the course of superpower competition and the growing dominance of the nuclear balance in Soviet military policy. This had direct implications for relations within the WTO and the military status of Central European countries. Indeed, the installation of intermediate nuclear missiles in the 1980s and the growing importance of negotiations leading to European security agreements, had direct political consequences in Central Europe. Diversity in views on these matters had not been lacking within the Soviet bloc in relatively early days, however.

One example of this had been the Rapacki plan, launched in 1957 and named after the Polish foreign minister of the time. It proposed the elimination of nuclear weapons from Poland, Czechoslovakia and the two Germanies. It is by no means clear that it was proposed in accordance with Soviet wishes or that it enjoyed the whole-hearted support of the Soviet leadership. In any case, it met with little success or much response from the Western powers. A later initiative in this area was made in 1987 by General Jaruzelski, who proposed not just the progressive elimination of tactical and battlefield nuclear weapons from Central Europe but also possible reductions in conventional weapons.[22] This, too, met with little success – not surprisingly in view of the overwhelming dominance of the superpower dialogue and the advancing process of large-scale mutual force reduction. Rapacki, on the other hand, could claim some measure of eventual success with a proposal made in 1964 for an all-European security conference, which eventually led to the Helsinki conference and final agreement of 1975.

The progress of the Conference on Security and Co-operation in Europe (CSCE), or the Helsinki process, was from 1973 of particular significance for Central Europe and other countries in the shadow of the superpowers. The lengthy proceedings of the Conference were a diverse and multi-faceted affair, which were subject to differing interpretations by the participants. According to the WTO PCC, the Conference confirmed the 'territorial and political realities' of the post-war European order and endorsed détente within the framework of the contemporary status quo. But the agreement also included a 'Basket III', which carried a general affirmation of human rights and was viewed critically by the WTO for threatening interference in the internal affairs of the Soviet bloc. Such a transgression was, of course, strictly forbidden by the Warsaw Treaty itself – although it can hardly be claimed that its terms in this area were scrupulously observed in Central Europe. This feature of the agreement proved to be of growing significance and soon became the object of attention from small but significant groups (like Charter 77 in Czechoslovakia). They served to create a focus of independent opposition whose importance persisted and grew through the period of worsening superpower relations and progressive erosion of the foundations of communist power throughout the 1980s.

Analagous views on regional security issues to those expressed in Poland also emerged during the 1960s in Czechoslovakia. A tendency developed there towards the establishment of closer relations with West Germany (which had not yet developed its *Ostpolitik*, whose principles would eventually be accepted by the Soviet Union). Some discontent was expressed with Soviet domination of WTO strategy and its institutional machinery. This followed earlier criticism and refusal to participate in joint man-oeuvres by the Romanian leadership. The Czechoslovak criticisms took published form in 1968 and were partly incorporated in the Action Programme drawn up in April of that year, a fact that can have hardly failed to fuel Soviet concern about the course of events in Czechoslovakia. The possibility of Soviet deployment of nuclear missiles in Central Europe also contributed to Czechoslovak anxieties, although little further transpired in this area for some years. It was, however, firmly placed on the agenda with the announcement of NATO's 'dual-track' decision in December 1979, which linked the continuing Soviet deployment of its intermediate-range forces (notably the SS-20s) to the introduction of new missiles by the West.[23]

Whatever the logic of the Soviet position within the framework of the global superpower contest, it was clear that Central Europeans did not share Soviet perceptions of the need to deploy medium-range nuclear missiles on their territory. The Central European countries had invariably fared better during periods of international détente and were disquietened by the onset of a new cold war; the prospect of installing additional Soviet weapons on their territory at the same time as Western powers were building up an intermediate-range capability (i.e. one with Central and East European targets) added to their anxieties. WTO statements during this period were markedly circumspect and appeared to disguise significant doubts on the part of Central European countries about the spread of nuclear weapons to the area. While it is not clearly established whether Hungary and Poland actually refused to accept additional deployments in response to the Western measures, it was the case that the only ones made were those by Czechoslovakia and the GDR – both of which moves evoked clear signs of leadership disquiet and the emergence of small, though significant, signs of popular opposition.

Political tensions were partly relieved when much of this build-up was reversed following the signature of the INF treaty in December 1987, but by then the renewal of superpower tension had played its own part in exacerbating the internal problems of Central Europe. Other aspects of shifting superpower relations and the complex mixture of détente, military competition and arms agreement that was involved in the Helsinki process had already made a significant contribution to Central European political life. But although the weakness of the Soviet-inspired processes of political control was becoming increasingly evident with the progressive reduction of Soviet power and the diminution of the system's capacities that had set in under Brezhnev, the WTO was still regarded by Gorbachev as a relatively attractive and viable model with which to develop intra-bloc relations and as a secure basis on which to promote the articulation of his 'new thinking'.[24] The timing of the renewal of the original Treaty, which lapsed in May 1985 (two months after the accession of Gorbachev to the top leadership), must also have presented it to the new leader as a convenient starting-point for the launch of central features of his new strategy.

But processes of military integration and the payment of close attention to the continuing capacity to exercise enormous military power – whether Soviet or that controlled by the leaders of Central European countries – were far from sufficient to secure the region's stability or fully appropriate as a solution to the recurring political crises and the increasingly critical state of the region. Neither national military forces nor those of the Soviet Union were in a position to sustain the existing system or the power structure on which it was based, let alone provide the framework for its economic rejuvenation and appropriate conditions for the development of its social order. The normalization imposed on Czechoslovakia following the Soviet-led invasion of 1968 had sustained the communist order but latterly showed signs of running completely out of steam. In Poland, the maintenance of some form of Soviet-style orthodoxy had only been achieved through police action and the operations of the security forces, while Polish military forces themselves had been largely kept on the sidelines.

As the 1980s progressed the overall condition of the economic and political order grew even worse. At the same time, the major responsibility for the integration of the Soviet bloc had increasingly devolved on the WTO and this political function had become central to the way its institutions and activities developed. The installation of the communist order may well have been secured primarily by Soviet military might, but the main pillar of communist domination soon became that of political power. However, political processes alone were inadequate to secure regional integration and their functions became more and more prominent within the WTO itself.

This characteristic was reflected in the speed with which the WTO melted away once the political climate underwent a radical change, political reform accelerated in the Soviet Union, and the Central European countries broke free of the communist framework. No resistance was offered by the Gorbachev leadership to requests for the withdrawal of Soviet troops, first from Czechoslovakia and Hungary. By the end of February 1990 Moscow had agreed to remove a substantial portion of its forces from Czechoslovakia before the June elections in that country (while the rest were hoped to follow by the end of the year). A similar agreement had been virtually concluded with Hungary. The last Soviet troops left these countries in June 1991. Talks on withdrawal of the smaller number of Soviet troops from Poland (which had qualms about the consequences of the rapid movement to German unification) started somewhat later.

There were clearly doubts within the Soviet political and military establishment about these actions, but Gorbachev's initiatives in these areas proceeded apace. It was not originally proposed to dismantle the WTO entirely, Moscow agreeing in June 1990 rather to transform the Pact into a treaty between sovereign states with equal rights, 'formed on a democratic basis'.[25] However, the pace and scope of the fundamental, wide-ranging changes under way in Central Europe left little place for the WTO in any form, and it was wound up as a military alliance at the end of March 1991, its residual political functions being brought to an end in Prague three months later on July 1. Its end was foretold by an ultimate failure to perform its prime functions: to enhance the military security of the Soviet Union by maintaining a solid cordon sanitaire on its western and southern borders, and to secure the political integration of the

Soviet bloc. Final lack of success in this area was reflected in growing political tensions within the bloc (although these alone would not have been sufficient to bring about the dissolution of the bloc), the progressive collapse of its economy, and the policy changes introduced by the Gorbachev leadership itself.

NOTES AND REFERENCES

1. Brzezinski, *The Soviet Bloc*, pp. 108–10.
2. Johnson, 'The Warsaw Pact: Soviet military policy', pp. 258–59.
3. Hutchings, *Soviet-East European Relations*, p. xxii.
4. Holden, *The Warsaw Pact*, pp. 47–49.
5. Herspring, 'The Soviets', p. 130.
6. Urwin, *Western Europe Since 1945*, p. 294.
7. Herspring, 'The Warsaw Pact at 25', p. 11.
8. Halliday, *The Making of the Second Cold War*, pp. 60–61.
9. Ulam, 'Europe in Soviet eyes', p. 25.
10. White, *Political and Economic Encyclopaedia*, p. 288.
11. Jones, 'Agencies of the alliance', p. 164.
12. Holden, *op. cit.*, pp. 52–53.
13. Carnovale, 'The Warsaw Pact at thirty', p. 165.
14. ibid., p. 158.
15. Johnson, '*op. cit*', p. 260.
16. Volgyes, 'The Warsaw Pact', pp. 552.
17. Holden, *op. cit.*, p. 22.
18. Carrère d'Encausse, *Big Brother*, pp. 276–77.
19. Jones, *Soviet Influence in Eastern Europe*, p. ix.
20. Remington, *The Warsaw Pact*.
21. Herspring, 'The Soviets', pp. 140–41.
22. *Polityka* (Warsaw), 6 June 1987.
23. Talbot, *Deadly Gambits*, p. 38.
24. Jones, 'Gorbachev and the Warsaw Pact', pp. 217, 230.
25. Mason, *Revolution in East-Central Europe*, p. 100.

CHAPTER TEN

The Regional Economic Framework

THE ESTABLISHMENT OF COMECON

Political and military ties formed, as we have seen, a highly institutionalized framework for the Soviet control of Central Europe and provided a dense network of processes through which the supremacy of Soviet interests could be assured. They were the main means through which Soviet regional dominance and the specific forms of communist party rule were secured. Alongside the multiple structures of political linkage and military co-ordination, however, were those of the Committee for Mutual Economic Assistance (COMECON, also known as CMEA). Established in 1949, several years before the Warsaw Treaty Organization, COMECON was the counterpart of the regional military institution in more ways than one. As we have already seen, in the case of the military organization the issue of regional integration was somewhat ambiguous, priority being assigned to the assurance of Soviet control rather than to the development of relations of complex interdependence. Like the WTO in the military sphere, COMECON served primarily to demarcate the Central European economies from those of the capitalist West, and its record in furthering the integration of the individual communist-governed economies was not a strong one. Considerable doubts have, in any case, been expressed about whether the idea of integration has much applicability to economies organized on the basis of bureacratic administration and central planning.

Allusions to and loose comparisons with the West European Common Market during the period of communist rule were, therefore, rather wide of the mark. If integration refers to a process by which parts are combined into a greater whole which tends to develop its own processes and methods of operation, then that idea does not seem to have had much relevance to economic processes within the Soviet bloc. If, on the other hand, integration is understood rather to concern movement towards a common institutional framework, then stronger arguments can be mounted for the growth of economic integration on the basis of the COMECON framework. In this conception it is more the common implementation of selected economic policies and the attempt to level up differences in terms of the distribution and relative scarcities of goods that are involved than changes in the operating principles of the system as a whole. Only in this more limited sense did COMECON provide a basis for regional economic integration.

The early record of the organization was not just a skimpy one in terms of movement towards the co-ordination of economic activities; it seemed to be devoid of any activity whatsoever. The very date and manner of its founding even remained something of a mystery. It was, however, certainly established in January 1949 as a direct response to the announcement of the Marshall Plan (and possibly, following the defection of Yugoslavia, to reaffirm the unity of the Soviet bloc as the foundation of the Cominform in 1947 had also previously attempted to do). The Committee for Mutual Economic Assistance was originally composed of the Soviet Union and Bulgaria, Czechoslovakia, Hungary, Poland and Romania. The membership of Albania was registered soon afterwards (although it stopped participating in its activities in 1961) and the German Democratic Republic joined in 1950. Mongolia, Cuba and Vietnam were also later accepted as full members (although the activities of non-European members were never responsible for more than 5 per cent of intra-COMECON trade).

As divisions within Europe grew during the early years of the Cold War, it was the countries of Central Europe that were most affected by the reorientation of economic relations this involved. It was the more developed, Western-oriented countries of Czechoslovakia, Poland and Hungary who had initially showed greatest interest in the Marshall Plan, and the foundation of COMECON compounded for them the political effects of the post-war division of the continent. The inability of Central Europe to take advantage of the opportunities embodied in the Marshall Plan was not the only source of economic loss. In the period up to 1955, through imposed trade agreements, war reparations and specially low export prices, the Soviet Union extracted from Eastern Europe roughly the same amount as the US contributed to Western Europe.[1] The economic setback for the Central European countries was soon worsened by the United States' imposition of a licensing system on all exports to Europe (the forerunner of COCOM, the economic arm of the North Atlantic Treaty Organization). This restricted the access of COMECON countries to high technology and products with defence significance, an embargo which generally had more serious economic consequences for the Western-oriented Central European countries than it did for the Soviet Union. Meanwhile, activity within COMECON itself remained very limited and, during Stalin's lifetime, consisted mostly of bureaucratic surveillance and the collection of statistics.

It is not clear whether there were originally other plans underlying the formation of COMECON which might later have been abandoned. It is possible that there were intentions to create a more active sphere of East European co-operation that were undermined by political conflicts centring on the fall from power of Soviet State Planning Commission chairman Vosnesensky and his execution in March 1949.[2] On economic grounds there might indeed have been arguments for contemplating co-operation between the smaller countries in isolation from the Soviet Union. The early post-war period had seen significant initiatives in this area, not least from local communist leaders in Czechoslovakia, Hungary and Poland.

Any remaining designs for more active co-operation (and certainly for more independent Central European activity) were disrupted by the rising tensions within the bloc which followed the outbreak of the Korean War, and the strengthened emphasis on direct Soviet control and regional co-ordination that became evident in the Kremlin.[3] This had direct military and economic consequences. By 1955 the total strength of the Soviet armed forces had risen to 5.763 million from 2.874 million in 1948, the bulk of the increase having occurred before 1952. Military budgets also rose considerably over this period.[4] All this imposed further burdens on the Central European economies and subjected them to additional Soviet pressure. Rearmament led to a considerable increase in demand for steel products and the further redirection of investment and production resources to heavy industry, changes that were by no means beneficial to the relatively advanced economies of Central Europe. The sequence of meetings that had followed the formation of COMECON was also abruptly altered with the outbreak of the war and the activities of the Council's Bureau restricted to relatively minor regional matters, all of which suggests that the outbreak of hostilities had considerable practical impact on the development of economic relations within the Soviet bloc.

Whatever the doubts concerning its role in the early period, the establishment of COMECON clearly formed part of the pattern of tightening Soviet control over Central Europe and the move towards homogenization that had been evident since 1947. There were certainly grounds for paying some attention to the economic disparities that existed between the countries of the region. Poland, like eastern parts of Germany (portions of whose pre-war territory were now within the frontiers of Poland), had been devastated by the war and was far from having recovered by 1949. Czechoslovakia, on the other hand, not only experienced minimal damage but had, in some ways, advanced economically during the same period. Some countries, further, paid heavy reparations to the Soviet Union while others benefited substantially from United Nations relief.[5] Early Soviet demands for war reparations had already been scaled down before the foundation of COMECON, however, those made of Hungary being halved in 1947 to counteract the attractiveness of America's initial European Recovery Programme. Wartime experience, moreover, overlaid the existing differences that had been evident in the region. Bulgaria and Romania derived over half their net product from agriculture in 1950 in contrast to 20 per cent for East Germany and 34 per cent for Czechoslovakia (Hungary and Poland occupied a midway position in this respect, at levels of 38 per cent and 43 per cent respectively).

The establishment of COMECON made little, if any, difference to this situation in practical terms due to its low level of activity. In the five years that followed its foundation the COMECON Council, the organization's governing body, met on only three occasions – and two of these were in 1949. Post-war recovery, the imposition of the Soviet model of rapid industrialization, and development of a collectivized model of agriculture were all pursued without regard to the regional organization, and it played no part in the collection of its war-reparations by the USSR or the punitive terms of trade imposed by the Soviets on their economic partners. During the early years Soviet control in this area, as in others, tended to be exerted through personal channels as frequently as possible and was subject as a process to the judgments and predilections of Stalin himself. The founding agreement of the organization, it has been suggested, might provide a reasonable guide to the structure of its activity in 1949 and 1950 if the statements referring to the

COMECON Secretariat General and Council were simply replaced by others naming the Soviet Politburo and Gosplan (Moscow's central planning agency).[6]

Direct Soviet control over Eastern Europe was further strengthened with the persistence of the Cold War and intensification of the Korean conflict. The dominance of bilateral agreements channelled through the Soviet foreign trade ministry and its embassy-based system of liaising with national leaderships led to the further marginalization of the recently established economic organization. In the light of this experience, the establishment of the COMECON in 1949 had more the appearance of a symbolic gesture of strengthening Stalinist control than a planned organizational initiative.

INSTITUTIONAL DEVELOPMENT AFTER STALIN

As in other areas, the situation changed significantly after the death of Stalin in 1953. Soviet economic advisers (together with those in the defence, security and political areas) began to be withdrawn and the unequal (i.e. enforced) trade treaties were renegotiated. Most of the joint-stock companies set up to impose Soviet control over East European resources and specialist production areas were abolished, thus opening the way to their more effective integration within the national economies. After the consolidation of Khrushchev's power, there was greater institutional activity in the COMECON framework established several years earlier. From 1955 its governing Council began meeting as often as twice a year and started to concern itself more actively with such basic tasks as plan co-ordination, production specialization and the development of regional trade links. The fact that the COMECON organizational framework was only described in any detail in a Charter published in 1960 lent credence to the idea that it had earlier existed only in rudimentary form and had been of little practical significance. The publication of the Charter was a sign that COMECON activities were growing in importance, this being confirmed by the rounding out in 1962 of the organization's structure – which then retained broadly the same form for nearly 30 years. An Executive Committee composed of six permanent delegates with the rank of deputy prime minister from the relevant countries was thus established in June 1962, this body then taking on primary responsibility for policy implementation.

This line of development, it appeared, was strongly encouraged by Polish leader Władysław Gomułka, who was impressed with the progress made on the basis of growing West European integration under the executive authority of a more coherent supranational body. Detailed executive and secretarial work remained the responsibility of a Secretariat, which was really the only permanent COMECON body and was always headed by an experienced Soviet official with an office located in Moscow. Specialist work on policy formulation was carried out by Standing Commissions composed of experts drawn from the member states. The first 12 commissions were formed in 1956, and by 1988, 21 were in existence. In broad terms, however, this institutional development did not have much of an impact on the operation of the individual Central European economies.

Moves towards effective action in substantive policy areas were made and initial attempts at the systematic co-ordination of national economic plans began in May 1956, but the influence of the process remained restricted to regulating the volume of trade and exchange between the member states. These were in any case generally supplied from surplus or 'above-plan' production and left the basic processes of industrial production essentially untouched. Autarchic economic development continued and little conception of complementarity was shown in patterns of national economic planning across the region. Gomułka's espousal of integration in 1962 thus had little effect beyond contributing to the institutional proliferation of the organization and the establishment of its Executive Committee in 1962. Member-states and their leaders harboured deep suspicions of one another and were more inclined to compete in order to maximize relative advantage than to co-operate with one another. Greater co-ordination of economic plans implied a higher level of dependence on economic partners, and this was perceived as a threat rather than a development carrying the promise of potential specialization.

The notion of all-round economic development solidly rooted in a heavy industrial base continued to be very influential and pervaded national elite conceptions of overall social development, contributing to the persistence of the orthodox Soviet model of comprehensive industrial growth. But it remained clear that prospects for effective economic development on a national basis were limited and Gomułka's idea did receive the support of Soviet leader Khrushchev, taking more concrete form with the latter's proposal of an all-COMECON planning agency. This, however, soon encountered opposition from those jealous of infringements on national sovereignty and the more reasoned economic doubts of those who thought the project required prior reform of the communist economies if any rational calculation and allocation of resources was to be arrived at.[7]

Analagous moves towards the enhancement of production specialization, were made in 1956 and received a further boost in 1962, but they encountered objections similar to those arising in the case of plan co-ordination. The early specialization agreements drawn up in the immediate post-Stalin period were shelved in the wake of the political instabilities that became evident soon afterwards, although further (if modified) emphasis on a rapid industrialization policy emerged around the same time. The strongest resistance to this initiative was mounted by Romania, where the leadership objected to a division of labour that threatened to perpetuate existing levels of economic development and expressed vehement opposition to the country's implied relegation to the status of agricultural backwater. Similar doubts were harboured by other COMECON members, as consistent specialization would mean the imposition of relations of dependence on suppliers over whom no effective sanctions could be brought to bear. Czechoslovakia, Hungary and Poland, in particular, saw little advantage in replicating the problems of rigid planning and the disadvantages of the administrative economy at the regional level.

Enterprises within the individual communist economies already had, with good reason, little confidence in national suppliers of their necessary inputs and sought to enhance their autonomy by retaining control of as much of the production process as possible. There were few incentives to acquiesce in a process that would be likely to duplicate these problems at regional level. Specialization in a particular line of production meant the assumption of a certain level of risk by the producer, the commitment of resources above the level to satisfy national requirements, and some danger that the producer might be left with unsold stock – Czechoslovakia, for example, was left with a surplus of machine tools on its hands.[8] Medium-term commitment might also carry dangers for the purchaser, whose investment might not be returned on time or who might find himself bound to accept outdated or poor-quality products. While some specialization was inevitable due to natural advantage and resource endowment, the process did not go very far. Some products did, however, establish themselves throughout the region and the movement was carried forward (metaphorically and literally) by such vehicles as Czech trams and Hungarian buses, while the GDR developed a line in diesel motors.

The expansion of intra-COMECON trade was viewed as a third area of policy innovation, emerging as a further aspect of regional development and a necessary condition for the advancement of the two processes already discussed. As in those cases, progress in terms of trade was limited. In view of the fact that trade was conducted primarily as an administered process and carried out through barter, with prices acting as a unit of account rather than regulator of supply and demand (and then only loosely based on world trade prices), it did not have the capacity to exert much influence over the national structures of production. Since, for obvious reasons, COMECON member-countries showed broadly similar system priorities, they tended to produce roughly the same range of goods which carried the same level of attractiveness in the different national markets. Economic growth throughout the 1960s, moreover, tended to be of the 'extensive' rather than the desired 'intensive' variety. All countries favoured production of the same new commodities which were thought to be 'progressive' – cars, trucks, tractors, metal-working machines, textile and chemical equipment, power generators, railway engines. The principles of specialization and co-ordination were pushed to the margin when actual production decisions were taken.[9] Shortage goods and those which were more readily available tended to be the same in the different countries and regional trading opportunities were correspondingly limited. Attractive goods from one country were traded against similar products from another, and stock that was hard to shift in one country was off-loaded against similar produce of a different national origin.

Table 10.1 Part played by European COMECON members in West European trade

	Exports %	Imports %
1937	20	16
1987	5	4

Source Tygodnik Solidarności (Warsaw), 22 September 1989

Such tendencies also had their roots in pre-war relations. Before the war the Central European countries had traded more with Western Europe than between themselves, and there was more competition than complementarity in their manufactured exports and outflows of resources. The defeat and physical devastation of Nazi Germany, formerly the overwhelmingly dominant economic power in the region, obviously had a major effect on this situation, although the Western orientation of Czechoslovak, Hungarian and Polish trade flows soon began to reassert themselves after 1945. By 1947–8, the Soviet share of their trade had already fallen to nearly 30 per cent and even tended to decline further for a short period as trade with the West resumed and gathered pace.[10] From the Western perspective, however, trade with Eastern Europe had never been very prominent and soon after the creation of COMECON it became even more limited (Table 10.1).

Table 10.2 Distribution of European COMECON trade

	Intra-bloc %	Developed market economies %	Rest of world %
1938	10	73	17
1948	44	40	16
1958	61	19	20
1968	64	21	15
1977	55	29	16

Source Botsas, 'Patterns of trade', p. 87

After the Second World War, in more general terms, trade between European COMECON members clearly prevailed over links with developed market-based countries and those with the rest of the world (Table 10.2).

The reorientation of trade patterns itself, however, reflected one form of regional specialization. The Soviet Union itself purchased about half the total exports of machines and manufactured equipment of the other COMECON countries. In the period 1966–70 this accounted for 85 per cent of ships, boats and marine equipment, 60 per cent of railway equipment and 60 per cent of equipment for chemical and food industries.[11] However, since the USSR was by far the largest member in the COMECON group in terms of population, this could hardly be considered either surprising or the reflection of any developed pattern of production and trade specialization. National specialization remained quite limited. Some progress was made, as noted, in transport equipment and joint energy programmes were fundamental to the region's economy.[12]

International contributions were made between 1959 and 1963 to the construction of the *druzhba* pipeline, which then led to the distribution of Soviet oil between Czechoslovakia, the GDR, Hungary and Poland. The construction of a gas pipeline agreed on a similar basis in 1974 linked Orenburg with the Central European countries. A shared electricity network was developed in the early 1960s. Production specialization was most developed in the area of mechanical engineering.[13] Components for Soviet cars were produced in Hungary and Poland, as well as in other COMECON countries, and were paid for by the supply of finished cars. Most effective forms of co-operation, however, were bilateral in nature and linked Poland and the GDR, East Germany and the Soviet Union, and Hungary and Poland.

Nevertheless, as COMECON developed as an organization, inherent obstacles to the pursuit of joint goals and effective regional integration continued to make themselves strongly felt. Payment, in the absence of an appropriate market or proper prices, was a further obstacle to the growth of trade, and only some of the existing problems were mitigated by the establishment of a COMECON International Bank of Economic Co-operation which began operating in January 1964. Questions of national sovereignty also became more important as post-Stalinist leaders emerged in Hungary and Poland, and Khrushchev sought to employ somewhat more diplomatic means to maintain the stability of the Soviet bloc. The interests of countries at different levels of socio-economic development, and which showed contrasting degrees of enthusiasm for economic reform, contributed to the conflicts of interest and orientation that emerged within COMECON. They reinforced the tendencies that helped keep it to a rather conservative path of co-ordination and concerted growth, and left it to operate within a framework of regional control rather than one fostering a more dynamic system of integration and mutual development.

The more developed countries, notably Czechoslovakia and East Germany (sometimes in the company of Hungary and Poland), tended to coalesce on some issues against Bulgaria and Romania (particularly with respect to the issue of specialization which was placed on the agenda in 1964). On the questions of rationalizing COMECON structure and reducing the barriers to integration, however, Czechoslovakia and Hungary had a similar perspective due to a shared interest in economic reform throughout most of the 1960s. They eventually signed an agreement to permit limited commodity convertibility, whereby Czech enterprises would be able to purchase supplies in Hungary for Czech currency and vice versa. Poland also showed interest in this venture. The provision only came into operation in early 1968, though, and the experiment came to an end after the invasion later that year. Resistance to the more effective development of COMECON persisted. Ideas of supranationalism remained anathema and tendencies that might have led in that direction continued to be rejected. However, agreement on this principle could itself provide some common basis for co-operation with regard to the direction that relations took within the organization of COMECON.

FURTHER MOVES TOWARDS INTEGRATION

In the wake of the Czechoslovak crisis (which originated, it should be remembered, in attempts to counteract economic decline and stagnation), the Brezhnev leadership launched in 1971 a 'Comprehensive Programme for the Further Intensification and Improvement of Collaboration and the Development of Socialist Economic Integration'. This was intended to establish a framework that would halt the spread of economic reforms in the region; continue the pursuit of established objectives of plan co-ordination; promote former ideas of economic integration through inter-governmental co-operation, and provide a basis for the Soviet Union to review what it regarded as the artificially low prices it was receiving for raw materials and energy supplies. On the other hand (in order not to discourage more recalcitrant members like Romania), participation was not meant to be coerced. Expectations of the integration programme and its relation to the different strategies of national economic development were clearly quite different, then, and had a marked effect on the form and degree to which its principles would subsequently be implemented.

Despite the publicity and high level of formal activity which now surrounded COMECON, few significant consequences emerged from this further programme and little new developed in the Committee's activities. Several factors were responsible for this. Soviet leader Leonid Brezhnev's preoccupation with the maintenance of political control over the region after the invasion of Czechoslovakia was significantly modified by the climate of growing détente, while his fears for East European stability were largely allayed by the performance of politically experienced and apparently loyal leaders in the bloc countries. National leaders, however, particularly in the more developed countries of Central Europe like Czechoslovakia, Hungary and (later) Poland, were themselves becoming increasingly exercised by poor economic performance and growing signs of stagnation. They were drawn to pay more serious attention to questions of reform and the implications of the need for change. These pointed to the need to develop processes of decentralization and marketization and made them even less sympathetic to the goals of regional co-ordination and conventionally conceived integration, particularly as these still involved conceptions of bureaucratic control and rigid planning rather than ideas of combined development and the encouragement of more complex forms of interdependence.

Growing involvement with the world economy and Western partners (particularly in Europe) also helped direct their attention away from Moscow and the conservative (and fundamentally unpromising) views of economic development still articulated within COMECON. These provided some hope of alternative forms of economic partnership and other, more promising, paths of development. But they, too, fell considerably short of fulfilling their promise and left several East European countries in a state of indebtedness, which grew considerably during the 1970s and rose again in the mid-1980s (Table 10.3). This further contributed to the economic troubles of the region, which were now also shaped by the successive energy-price shocks, the general problems of international recession, and the escalating challenges of technological innovation which were far beyond the capacity of COMECON members to meet. While Brezhnev's programme of COMECON development and integration was never disavowed, then, it seemed to be quietly sidelined and was largely ignored under the changing conditions and with the new problems of the 1970s.

Table 10.3 Gross hard currency debt, 1971–86, US $ billion

	1971	1980	1982	1984	1986
Czechoslovakia	0.5	4.9	4.0	3.6	4.4
GDR	1.4	14.1	13.0	12.2	15.3
Hungary	1.1	9.1	7.7	8.8	15.1
Poland	1.1	25.0	24.8	26.8	33.5

Source Prybyla, 'The great malaise', p. 77

The successive waves of COMECON 'co-operation', 'co-ordination' and 'integration' had achieved virtually nothing of the sort. Nevertheless, trade processes within the region took place predominantly between COMECON members. A higher proportion of Central European international trade was transacted within COMECON in 1980 than in 1970 – with the exception of Poland, which had developed a singular (and by no means advantageous) pattern of relations with the West during the 1970s (Table 10.4). Following the major political and economic crisis that had erupted by the late 1970s and the measures taken to cope with it, though, that situation had again changed by the mid-1980s. COMECON links in the case of Czechoslovakia and Hungary were also stronger in the mid-1980s, a point that should be noted in the light of changing terms of trade with the Soviet Union (in favour of the dominant power) and its higher volume of East European imports. Only with the GDR was this tendency not apparent – and here the effect of West Germany's *Ostpolitik* and the GDR's privileged access to the West European markets played a major part.

Table 10.4 COMECON exchanges as percentage of national trade, estimate of real trade values

	1970	1975	1980	1985
Czechoslovakia				
Exports	71	73	73	75
Imports	69	74	72	75
GDR				
Exports	74	79	77	66
Imports	69	73	69	62
Hungary				
Exports	66	73	72	75
Imports	65	70	67	67
Poland				
Exports	64	66	62	71
Import	69	53	61	72

Source van Brabant, *Economic Integration*, p. 353

A significant aspect of the economic situation in which Central Europe (in common with other COMECON members) found itself was the relative isolation of each national economy, and its low level of economic integration in terms of regional as well as global trade patterns. The four countries of Central Europe were, of course, both considerably less populous as well as less advanced economically than the four largest EC partners. Not surprisingly, then, the latter accounted for 26.8 per cent of world exports in 1989 (24 per cent in 1985), compared with a share of only 2.3 per cent taken by Central Europe (3.2 per cent in 1985). Nevertheless, even on a per capita basis, Central European exports were worth only $1,031 per annum in 1989, compared with $3,503 in the case of the West European powers ($940 and $2,013 respectively in 1985), which meant that EC economies produced more than three times the value of exports than did even the relatively developed Central European representatives of the Soviet bloc.[14]

RELATIVE DISADVANTAGES OF THE EASTERN ECONOMIES

The root problem associated with this economic situation was that the maintenance of the sphere of Soviet control and the continued application throughout the region of principles derived from the Soviet model kept it blocked off from alternative economic influences and more productive forms of interaction. In general terms COMECON developed in line with key Soviet preferences and satisfied their fundamental demands.[15] Unlike the rising East Asian economies, therefore, the COMECON countries failed to participate in the international specialization of production that took on particular importance in the 1970s and 1980s, becoming increasingly disadvantaged and badly placed to participate in the processes of accelerating international economic competition.[16] The failure of these particular phases of COMECON development was later recognized in Soviet sources. In 1987 it was finally observed that 'The old forms of co-operation took shape when there was a tendency to maintain the pace of development of "extensive" methods . . . By the late 1960s, however, many of these resources had been exhausted. But the task of all-round intensification had not yet been formulated'.[17]

The relative backwardness of the Soviet economy, in combination with the rigidly enforced dominance of the development model it had evolved, exerted an especially negative influence on the more developed Central European economies as well as affecting intra-bloc relations more generally. The overall performance of European COMECON partners, as can be seen from Table 10.5, was not much lower than that of the United States or the EEC, although all lagged behind the performance of Japan. Within the COMECON group, however, it was the less developed countries, including the Soviet Union, which achieved higher growth rates, while those already better off to start with showed distinctly less impressive results. This was the case with Czechoslovakia, which failed also to reap the same benefits as the GDR from West German *Ostpolitik* and did not have the same preferential access to EC economic benefits.[18] According to one estimate, Czechoslovakia fell from tenth position in the world to around fortieth in these terms.[19]

Economic development within the COMECON framework can in this sense be understood to have enhanced regional equality – but by imposing barriers to the further development of already advanced members and imposing considerable costs on the region as a whole, rather than just accelerating the development of the more backward to catch up with the leading economic regions. But even for the less developed countries, the value of COMECON membership in sustaining economic growth policies may have been somewhat dubious. Romania had the highest rate of domestic consumption of machinery products for investment purposes of all COMECON members in the 1960s (reaching its highest level in 1965 and halving by the mid-1980s). A similar tendency could be observed in the case of Bulgaria.[20] Even in these cases, then, the specialization of trade processes that was possible within COMECON and might have made some contribution to their economic development did not appear to have had any positive influence. The substantial degree of autonomy in domestic policy-making remained one of the most surprising features of the centrally planned economies.

It can be argued, however, that Central Europe, like other COMECON members, derived other benefits from the regional association and that its effects were by no means all negative. With the exception of Poland and Romania, Eastern Europe had few raw materials and the establishment of a close and regular relationship with the Soviet Union could be seen as advantageous in securing a steady supply from the dominant COMECON partner. COMECON markets and the shortage economies of communist Eastern Europe provided dependable opportunities for the sale of otherwise unattractive goods that would have been unlikely to have found buyers elsewhere. The relative advantages of COMECON member-

Table 10.5   Estimated real GNP, billion US $

	1960	1984	Increase (%)	Per capita GNP($, 1984)
Japan	237.9	1,233.5	418	10.3 th.
USA	1,647.2	3,662.8	122	15.5
EEC	1,030	2,200	114	8.7
Eastern Europe (excluding USSR)	363	771	112	6.9
Romania	39.4	117.6	198	5.2
Bulgaria	22.7	56.4	148	6.3
(USSR)	821.7	1,957.6	138	7.1
Poland	104.8	228.5	118	6.3
Hungary	40.2	77	92	7.2
GDR	85.8	163.7	91	9.8
Czechoslovakia	69.9	127.9	83	8.3

Note   Non-communist data is from OECD sources. Estimates of Soviet GNP are expressed in 'geometric mean dollars' based on an average of US- and Soviet-weighted purchasing power parity ratios. East European figures are derived from recalculation of official data on a dollar basis.

Source Dawisha, *Eastern Europe*, pp. 138–39

ship should not be exaggerated; as we have seen, the costs of the association were also considerable. It was clearly, for example, the isolation of the COMECON economies from the world economy and the more dynamic pressures of technological and economic development that led to their relative weakening and the degree of mutual dependence that did exist between them.

While, too, there may have been some strength behind the argument that the Soviet Union had been providing some degree of subsidy for Central Europe after the oil shocks of the 1970s and during the years when the Brezhnev leadership was willing to preserve political stability in Eastern Europe at some domestic cost, this was certainly not a permanent feature of the regional relationship. There was no doubt that the early years of COMECON membership saw the significant disadvantaging of the East European economies in the way relations with the Soviet Union were structured (although this was a function of relations with the USSR rather than a consequence of the operation of COMECON as an institution). A clear negative symmetry existed between the COMECON relationship and that which developed between the

United States and Western Europe during the years of the Marshall Plan. This was due to rigorous reparations demands and high Soviet-determined prices.

This situation changed after 1956 as the rigours of the Stalinist domination of Eastern Europe were mitigated following the death of its originator, and Khrushchev sought to place Soviet-East European relations on a new footing. Opinions about the nature of the later relationship differ, and simple estimates of the balance of economic relations are difficult to arrive at in the absence of anything like conventional market prices.[21] By the 1970s, however, the economic balance had clearly shifted.[22] One estimate was that the Soviet subsidy of Eastern Europe during the 1970s was equivalent to the amount taken out between 1945 and 1953.[23] But while the effect of higher world energy prices in Eastern Europe was buffered by the maintenance of existing agreements with the Soviet Union and the latter's agreement to phase higher prices in over a longer period, this also meant that the terms of trade steadily shifted to the advantage of the Soviet Union. Its improved bargaining position then allowed the USSR to insist on better quality products from East European suppliers.[24]

By 1985 the level of Soviet imports from Eastern Europe by volume (if not by price) had risen by 30 per cent over the 1980 level, and experienced analysts concluded that Soviet subsidization of its partners had come to an end by the mid-1980s.[25] This tendency was confirmed and strengthened following Gorbachev's assumption of the Soviet leadership.[26] The level of subsidization also varied considerably, with more conservative leaderships like those in Czechoslovakia and the GDR receiving the highest sums and more troublesome (and more populous) allies like the Poles receiving less in absolute (let alone per capita) terms.[27]

Further change in Soviet policy towards COMECON and the adoption of a more rigorous structure for regional economic development could be dated from 1984. In that year a major Council summit was held in Moscow, the first in fifteen years. Emphasis was placed by the Soviet leadership on the development of joint enterprises as a means of introducing a stronger dynamic into the sluggish pattern of regional economic development and enhancing the 'socialist division of labour'. Joint ventures had already been developed with Poland on a bilateral basis to help cope with some of the effects of persistent economic crisis, more recently overlaid with the problems of indebtedness and Western sanctions imposed in the wake of martial law. The provision of

Soviet inputs in exchange for a supply of finished products was a model already partly developed in some other countries. Although occurring on a bilateral basis rather than within the COMECON framework, this seemed for a time to promise more effective regional integration than the activities pursued with the existing – and supposedly already well-developed – supranational organization.

PERESTROIKA: THE FINAL PHASE

But, once more, this further attempt at a conservative form of *perestroika* (which slightly predated Gorbachev's pursuit of the principle in more liberal terms) had only limited results as implementation of the agreements proved to be difficult to carry out. Gorbachev placed continuing emphasis on COMECON reform in this vein at the 27th CPSU Congress in 1986, when he argued that the future status of socialism depended on a qualitative improvement in economic performance, and movement away from the mediocre levels of production recently achieved. This was likely to make considerable demands on the Central European partners. COMECON production potential, it was stated in 1987, should be doubled by the year 2000 and an annual growth rate of 4–5 per cent was to be achieved, more than half as much again as had been reached in recent years. A further broad plan was drawn up and presented as the Comprehensive Programme for Scientific and Technological Progress for COMECON member countries (COMPSTEP) which, it was officially noted, was likely to make special demands on the COMECON integration efforts.

Gorbachev seemed to be aware of the considerable problems this would involve yet, while he clearly differed in vision and approach from his Kremlin predecessors, he continued to lay stress on what appeared to be sharply conflicting principles. Although favouring economic as well as political reform he was also, at this early stage of his leadership, emphatic in his interest in strengthening co-ordination and Soviet control over COMECON – as well as over the WTO and other dimensions of the regional complex.[28] This met with open resistance from the outset – particularly from the more developed Central European countries. At the 1984 Council Summit, representatives from the GDR and Czechoslovakia had been at one with more reform-minded Hungary in their opposition to the Soviet promotion of joint enterprises and the proposed use of energy price formulas. Central European leaders, in particular, favoured the increase of market processes in intra-COMECON links rather than the more administration-led conception of joint enterprises.

Both Nyers, the reformist Hungarian economist, and Czech Prime Minister Adamec complained of COMECON's obsolescence. Like its predecessors, then, the COMPSTEP plan, signed in 1985, proved to be ineffective in the face of such opposition and remained largely a paper initiative. As *perestroika* and Gorbachev's domestic reform programme gathered pace (accompanied by the growing signs that the Soviet grip over Eastern Europe was not just being released but might well disappear altogether), the plan started looking increasingly irrelevant to the course that events were taking and the path that any viable programme for the economic development of the Soviet bloc might take. In recognition of this a new document on the 'International Socialist Division of Labour in the Period 1991–2005' was drawn up which did not, however, require the establishment of any mechanism for co-operation and integration before 1990 or the taking of any concrete steps before 1991.

A Council meeting held in Prague during July 1988 indicated that the creation of a common market on the lines of the West European model was envisaged, along with moves towards a properly convertible currency. Although this received the support of Hungary and Poland, it was less warmly welcomed by the more conservative COMECON members and an agreed programme of action did not appear to be any closer. The increasing departure of the Soviet Union from its former dictatorial habits and position of regional dominance, on the other hand, gave it even less opportunity to enforce its views on the organization as a whole. The rapid breakup of the Soviet bloc in 1989 removed any remaining prospects for regional integration and eliminated most of the factors that had supported its continued existence. In January 1991 the COMECON Executive Committee declared that it would hence-forth act on a different basis as an organization for 'economic co-operation', but its complete dismemberment was announced the following month.

NOTES AND REFERENCES

1. Marer, 'The political economy', p. 156.
2. Kaser, *Comecon*, pp. 33–35.
3. White, *Political and Economic Encyclopaedia*, p. 67. See also Chapter 5.
4. Nove, *An Economic History of the U.S.S.R.*, p. 312.
5. Korbonski, 'Cmea, economic integration', p. 50.
6. van Brabant, *Economic Integration*, p. 22.
7. Korbonski, *op. cit.*, pp. 54–55.
8. Lavigne, *The Socialist Economies*, p. 310.
9. Fallenbuchl, 'Comecon integration', p. 31.
10. van Brabant, *op. cit.*, p. 14.
11. Fallenbuchl, *op. cit.*, p. 33.
12. White, *op. cit.*, p. 69.
13. Lavigne, *op. cit.*, p. 323.
14. GUS, *Rocznik Statystyczny 1990*, p. 590.
15. Marrese, 'CMEA: Effective political economy', p. 287.
16. Prybyla, 'The great malaise', p. 62.
17. Ladygin, *CMEA*, pp. 4, 9.
18. Pick, 'Quo vadis ?', p. 106.
19. Glenny, *The Rebirth of History*, p. 31.
20. van Brabant, *op. cit.*, pp. 363–72.
21. Lewis, 'Soviet and East European relations', pp. 321–22.
22. Bunce, 'The empire strikes back', pp. 1–46.
23. Dawisha, *Eastern Europe*, p. 9.
24. Hutchings, *Soviet-East European Relations*, p. xvii.
25. Marer, 'The economies and trade', pp. 54–55.
26. Lynch, 'Changing contours', p. 429.
27. Crane, 'Soviet economic policy', p. 119.
28. Brown, 'The East European setting', p. 38.

CHAPTER ELEVEN

The End of Communist Rule

STABILITY AND CONFLICT IN CENTRAL EUROPE

At the end of the 1980s the network of regional links (political, military and economic) that had been developed to hold Central Europe firm within the Soviet bloc, where it had been anchored since the end of the Second World War, suddenly loosened and crumbled away. It became apparent to the national leaderships that the regimes of Central Europe could no longer count on the determination of the Soviet leadership to support the forms of communist rule over which presided, and they soon proved incapable of maintaining the structures of orthodox communism on their own account. There were even suggestions that Gorbachev and the Soviet leadership lent extra weight to help shift the more conservative regimes and open the way to a more enlightened path of political development in Central Europe. The domestic roots of communist collapse ran deep, however, and the failure of the Soviet-established systems to sustain themselves in political, economic and social terms had causes that were associated with the whole history and operation of the post-war communist systems in Central Europe.

Political instabilities had developed at an early stage and, once the rigours of Stalinist rule had passed, each country of Central Europe saw the development of situations which required military intervention to preserve the order imposed in the immediate post-war years. Command economies had been installed and developed which soon showed themselves unable to satisfy the needs of the societies they were supposed to serve. Regional patterns of economic integration were weak and Soviet-style policies of heavy industrial development tended to be replicated in each country – leading to similar problems of inefficiency, waste and consumer shortage. The isolation of COMECON countries from the world economy and the technological developments occurring elsewhere exacerbated these problems. Although the exposure of some COMECON members to international financial processes provided a short-term respite from current pressures, it led to longer-term problems of indebtedness, which continued to provide a major headache in the post-communist period.

The inability of the communist systems to generate political support and failure to maintain levels of economic growth or provide a general level of consumer satisfaction combined to feed growing social discontent. Such sentiments grew as early processes of social mobility petered out and the beneficiaries of communist development consolidated their position in the social order. The consequences of progressive economic failure and the poor capacity of communist systems to develop political processes and structures capable of successfully involving their members and securing their allegiance, left a large portion of the population without a secure stake in the new order. On the positive side, however, there was virtually no unemployment, a form of public order was generally maintained and, although there were signs of discontent, no major social groups were fully alienated from the postwar system. But there was little evidence of positive support nor could there be much hope that such sentiments would develop to any great extent in the future. These negative tendencies were particularly marked among the young.

Eventually, the communist systems showed a complete inability to sustain the trajectory of development on which they had embarked, and a growing failure to respond to the pressure of contemporary demands. In short, they were unable to secure the conditions for their social reproduction.[1] The problem of economic reform, which if successfully implemented might well have helped overcome this deficiency, was therefore fundamental to the breakdown of communist rule in Central Europe.[2] The leaders of Hungary and Poland were critically aware of the reform issue and tried on numerous occasions to encourage the reform processes in the attempt to maintain their power. But their efforts were half-hearted, particularly so in Poland, and the consequences of partial reform were themselves negative for political stability and harmful to prospects of economic development. The post-1968 leadership in Czechoslovakia was also well aware of these issues and set its face resolutely against change – but ultimately found that stability could not be maintained by a policy of consistent reaction, either.

Signs of this complex of problems were seen early on. Political problems surfaced immediately following Stalin's death and the tensions associated with economic disequilibrium and unbalanced development could be detected not long after that. Reform measures, of significantly different natures and having radically different consequences, were taken in Czechoslovakia and Hungary while Poland, during the strikes and demonstrations of 1970, showed some of the problems of failing to confront the tensions arising from the weakening course of communist economic development. All these features of uneven and inadequate development made themselves known well before the collapse of the systems at the end of the 1980s. However, it was the Solidarity period in Poland, during 1980–81, and the recourse to martial law in response to the challenges to continuing communist rule, that provided the most graphic evidence of the bankruptcy of the communist system and the difficulties it faced in continuing its progress down the path it had taken since 1945. Less dramatic but also telling were developments in Hungary, where outdated production structures survived the initial reform initiative, budget deficits rose and hard-currency debts reached unmanageable levels – leading to comparable signs of political system breakdown.

Yet even at this stage the decrepit Brezhnev leadership and his successors, Yuri Andropov and Konstantin Chernenko, struggled to keep the Soviet Union on the same course and restrain Central Europe within most of the limits that had been set in the late 1940s. This did not even seem to be too difficult in the case of Czechoslovakia and the GDR, which were successful in keeping up the appearance of political stability and were able to base their continued power on relatively affluent and well-supplied economies. (Here the GDR benefited from the close relationship it had developed with West Germany and the special terms established with the EC.) These countries were able to keep their citizens in some comfort and material ease. The task was more onerous for Hungary and Poland, however, both of which had high levels of foreign debt and whose long-established attempts at economic reform were becoming distinctly threadbare. (In Poland, indeed, economic reform had never displayed many signs of taking off or being effectively implemented.)

Successive crises, political instability and economic failure were, in any case hardly new phenomena in post-war Central Europe.

Crisis of some sort had been endemic since 1953 and the status quo had only been maintained with the use of military force. The situation, Central Europeans were apt to say over the years, was critical but not necessarily serious. This meant that crises might well develop within one country but that, given the preponderance of Soviet military might and its regional dominance (supported in other ways also by the framework of superpower relations and the global division of political influence), the overall stability of the area was unlikely to be threatened. Temporary political breakdown and outbreaks of national conflict were, therefore, very unlikely to undermine the greater equilibrium. Even in Poland it was by no means obvious that the situation was not containable or that the forces of opposition, influential and established as they were, had the capacity to promote and sustain change on their own account, far less to threaten the stability of the regional order.

According to some accounts, even Solidarity was close to being written off as a political force after several years of militarized rule and the reimposition of a form of communist order that was unusual and notably unideological, but essentially effective in keeping political opposition under control.[3] While Solidarity might have appeared close to being neutralized politically in 1986 and 1987, events were soon to show that it retained a basic political strength and continuing relevance to Polish developments. This was particularly true in view of the lack of vision or any alternative prospects offered by the Jaruzelski *équipe*, which was essentially engaged in a holding operation and had little capacity for effective leadership and the realization of any new vision of national development. In this his regime reflected the fundamental crisis that had emerged in the Soviet Union as well as the problems – more evident at that stage in Hungary than in Czechoslovakia and the GDR – of the rest of Central Europe. While the situation clearly developed differently and took specific national forms in the countries of the Soviet bloc, the underlying reasons were the same and the broad dimensions of a general crisis could be seen throughout the region.

THE GORBACHEV INFLUENCE

It was a crisis the leaders of Brezhnev's generation either did not appear fully to recognize or were content to ignore (responses that could be detected to some extent in the leadership career of Gorbachev himself during its early stages). After all, even if no action were taken, the final form and consequences of the crisis would not be fully seen during the lifetime of the older leaders. That could not be said of Mikhail Gorbachev, whose response both to the Central European situation and the contemporary problems of the Soviet Union turned out to be significantly different. His behaviour on accession to the leadership in March 1985, however, gave no indication that he was likely to acquiesce in the break-up of the Soviet bloc, the departure of Central Europe from the communist world – and even less the reunification of Germany. During the first phase of his tenure, for the rest of 1985 and (roughly speaking) the following year, his approach towards Central Europe was similar to that taken towards the domestic situation.

The approach was characterized by activism and a style quite different from that of his predecessors – but Gorbachev displayed a reformist stance that aimed less to change the nature of the system than to improve the method of its operation. His avowed commitment to modernization and the pursuit of greater efficiency within the communist system initially had implications that were quite different from the later consequences of his actions – i.e. greater co-ordination and a tighter integration of regional activities. This was clearly a priority in Gorbachev's view of relations within the framework of the Warsaw Pact, where there had been some dissension and conflict in the early 1980s following the intensification of nuclear rivalry between the superpowers and the growth in relations between Central and Western European states. A similar emphasis could be detected within COMECON and in the sphere of economic relations. Both organizations, however, were becoming riven with greater conflicts and tensions which were not susceptible to the general solutions and proposals made previously – and even these had shown scant signs of success.

The economic interests of COMECON members were becoming increasingly divergent, and it soon became clear that the roots of COMECON backwardness lay far deeper than the structure and form of the organization itself. If there was to be any scientific and technological revolution within the Soviet bloc it could not occur exclusively, and probably not at all, within the COMECON framework but depended far more on relations with the West. Gorbachev's initial views on Central Europe, like those on the domestic situation of the Soviet Union, soon underwent considerable change not so much because he chose to adopt different policies and solutions but due more to growing awareness of the intractability of the problems faced by the region. Indeed, for the first two years after his accession to the Soviet leadership little was said explicitly about the Central European countries. Increasingly, however, Gorbachev's policy with regard to the former satellites showed itself to be one largely of *laissez-faire*.

The Soviet Union reduced its former insistence on orthodoxy and indicated that it would hold back from imposing solutions on COMECON partners and Warsaw Pact allies. The main decision seems to have been taken in the second half of 1986 and was transmitted to Central European leaders in Warsaw Pact meetings with top alliance officials in the autumn of that year. Some, however, have suggested that Soviet policy towards Eastern Europe was fundamentally turned around in 1985 as soon as Gorbachev took over the leadership, while others have indicated a later date for the change of approach, spring 1988 being one of the later dates put forward.[4] It is not possible to give a wholly unqualified account of this reorientation or to present an uncontested date for its occurrence. Perhaps there was a sequence of changes – or even advances and retrenchments in Gorbachev's view on these matters. Sheer lack of certainty during a critical period of change should not be discounted, either. In response to the question of whether the removal of Soviet decision-making powers over Central Europe was really intended Henry Trofimenko, who was chief analyst at the Soviet Institute of the US and Canada, stated that to answer it truthfully 'neither Gorbachev nor anyone else in the Soviet leadership really anticipated the extent of the radical change' that was taking place in the Soviet Union's western neighbours.[5]

Gorbachev's first eighteen months at the pinnacle of the Soviet leadership had clearly exerted a great influence on his view of Central Europe, and his approach to major aspects of Soviet bloc relations changed accordingly. This was a factor further encouraging policy differentiation between the Central European countries and one which, effectively, set the seal on aspirations towards further integration within the established regional organization. Poland and Hungary developed further reform plans, while Czechoslovakia and the GDR became more resolute in setting their face against political change and contemplated only more restricted notions of economic reform. This sort of variety seemed to be quite acceptable to Gorbachev, but there is nothing to suggest that he foresaw or encouraged anything like the regional fragmentation or revolutionary change that was to get under way in the middle of 1989. His conception of change and the basis of a new economic and political dynamic were to be found within the socialist system – although by no means the one then embodied by the Soviet Union.

Gorbachev's education process and the evident shift that had occurred in his views in 1985 and 1986 were significant and quite dramatic in comparison with the outlook of his immediate predecessors. Nevertheless, they were not quite broad enough to offer radically new perspectives or encompass the kind of change that such adjustments and strategic reconceptualizations might eventually unleash. He remained over-optimistic about the capacity for change inherent in the communist system as it had developed in the Soviet Union, and underestimated the resentment and mistrust that the imposition of Soviet-style socialism in Central Europe had engendered. In his extended promotion of the *perestroika* concept, prepared in the summer of 1987, there was still considerable complacency in the treatment of this area. Surveying the achievements of world socialism in the mid-1980s, he argued, that 'we can safely state that the socialist system has firmly established itself in a large group of nations, that the socialist countries' economic potential has been steadily increasing, and that its cultural and spiritual values are profoundly moral and that they ennoble people.' It was, in Gorbachev's opinion, chiefly 'miscalculations by the ruling parties' that had been responsible for political instability in Central Europe rather than any more deeply rooted fault within the socialist order.[6]

Gorbachev's review of international affairs on the broader plane and of Soviet capacities at this level was certainly more radical. It was at this stage that he decided on the need for a Soviet retreat from Afghanistan and by April 1988 a series of agreements on the conditions of Soviet withdrawal were ready for signature.[7] It has been argued that it was precisely through this inititiative that new thinking eventually came to shake the established order closer to home: 'Afghanistan showed the limitations of military power very clearly and convincingly . . . it would be fair, if a little surprising to Europeans, to say that it was not so much thinkers in the corridors of the Kremlin as the *mujahadin* in the hills of Afghanistan who were the real liberators of Eastern Europe'.[8] It was certainly not part of any plan of Gorbachev's that Soviet influence over Central Europe would diminish so radically and so rapidly. In short, it may be concluded with one eminent analyst that, in relations with Central Europe, he made a huge miscalculation with whose consequences he had no option but to live.[9] Quite different views have also been expressed, though, and some have denied that Gorbachev was taken by surprise by the turn of events in Central Europe.[10]

Amidst this uncertainty there was still a distinct feeling in Central Europe even in mid-1989, after the Polish elections and during the process in which the Solidarity-led government was being formed in August and September, that not all the limits had been removed and that serious attention had to be paid to continuing Soviet interests in the area. Thus, as well as the agreement to accept General Jaruzelski as president, care was taken in Poland during 1989 to ensure that the apparently sensitive posts of defence and interior ministers were given to communists and that an accurate balance was maintained between communist and Solidarity-sponsored members of the Mazowiecki cabinet. Three elements could thus be identified as a putative 'Gorbachev doctrine' to replace the clearly outdated Brezhnev doctrine, which had determined the limits of Central Europe's sovereignty in the late 1960s and the succeeding years. As well as the reservation of 'sensitive' ministries for communist personnel, this was assumed to include the provision that existing bilateral and multilateral obligations (notably COMECON and – especially – the guarantees contained in the Warsaw Pact) should be respected and that the state should retain a basic 'socialist content' (although there was little precise meaning attached to this).[11] But while many clearly believed these limits had some meaning in the summer of 1989, they too were soon shown to have little substance and it became clear that the only doctrine that had any validity was that named after a well-known American singer. In the happy formulation of Soviet spokesman Gennady Gerasimov (whose witty formulations were soon to prove too much even for the new-style Soviet leader) it was the Sinatra doctrine that now prevailed, as each player did it 'My Way'.

Doubts certainly remained for some years after 1986 about whether the Brezhnev doctrine really had lost all relevance to the signatories of the Warsaw Pact. Signals and assurances might have been given, but the stakes were high if they were subject to misinterpretation – Dubček, indeed, had believed in 1968 until the military invasion that he had been acting in accordance with Soviet precepts and not against the perceived interests of the USSR. The lessons of 1956 and 1968 were that estimations of Soviet response and the limits to change imposed involved a substantial element of risk and were a considerable political gamble. Both leaders and people were uncertain as to whether Soviet military forces might not once more intervene – and while some fear of this persisted, it represented a powerful force for stability and maintenance of the status quo in Central Europe. The emphasis on 'socialist unity' and restrictions on the freedom of action of the Central European leaders nevertheless clearly lessened between 1986 and 1989 as a different rhetoric took over. According to one account, as far as Moscow was concerned, the Brezhnev doctrine was dead by the autumn of 1988 when the conservatives were defeated at the September Central Committee meeting (after which important organizational changes in the foreign policy apparatus were also made).[12]

There was, however, no explicit rejection of the doctrine of limited sovereignty and Gorbachev's recurring endorsements of the supremacy and potentialities of socialist development left doubts that the old conception had fully disappeared. Thus it is quite possible to date the abandonment of the Brezhnev doctrine and the public incorporation of the principle of non-interference in Soviet policy as late as June 1989.[13] Its full elimination from the political life of Central Europe could, indeed, be set as late as November 1989, with the disappearance of its original raison d'être, the orthodox communist regime in Czechoslovakia. The putative Gorbachev doctrine, moreover, did not seem to last much longer than the more solidly established and slow dying Brezhnev variant, and for practical purposes it evaporated with the collapse of communist power in the German Democratic Republic, the most critical Soviet bastion in Eastern Europe. Much changed in the short period after the elections held in Poland during June 1989 – and even more since the signs of a renewed reform movement first became evident in Central Europe, during 1986 in Poland.

THE POLISH ROAD TO POST-COMMUNISM

Martial law in Poland had finally been lifted in 1983. Repression was now more selective and judiciously applied than in many conventionally conceived communist dictatorships, but the communist party remained a marginal participant in public life. Membership had grown in the front organizations carefully nurtured by Jaruzelski, although the population was far from showing any enthusiasm for the leaders who had swept Solidarity aside in the attempt to re-establish the 'normal' procedures of a communist society. Meanwhile, economic recovery was sluggish, despite several years of freedom from any significant level of industrial disruption resulting from free trade union activity. Party membership had continued to decline until 1985, initially because of purges and mass resignations but then because of public anatagonism and apathy in the face of an organization that was not just discredited but now also largely irrelevant. It was in this situation that the X Congress of the Polish United Workers' Party opened in June 1986 and continued its proceedings in the presence of Mikhail Gorbachev.

Its proceedings were dull and formalized, marked by further retreat from the gestures towards inner-party democracy made at the previous congress held at the height of the Solidarity period in July 1981. Jaruzelski announced another attempt to launch a variant of economic reform based on principles of centralism and firm administrative control. Gorbachev made little direct contribution to the pallid proceedings of the party congress but appeared to have expressed strong personal support for Jaruzelski, who two months later ushered in a further period of political decompression by announcing a total amnesty of political prisoners. This had several favourable consequences. It made a direct impact on public opinion; it was well received by the Church authorities (paving the way for Pope John Paul II's reception of Jaruzelski in January 1987); and it was seen as a positive move by the West (contributing to the decision of the United States in February 1987 to lift the economic sanctions imposed five years earlier).

The amnesty made a significant difference to the tenor of political life in Poland for, while there had been some partial amnesties, the period preceding the X Party Congress had also seen the imposition of a more repressive climate, with continuing detention of opposition activists and several reports of deaths in mysterious circumstances (following the well-known example of that of Father Jerzy Popiełuszko in November 1984). It also prepared the ground for further bridge-building to influential groups in Polish society, with the establishment at the end of the year of a social-consultative council composed of notable authorities endowed with the capacity to advise the president. A further development was the preparation of a further round of reform measures, the so-called 'second stage', which – significantly – accompanied the development of Gorbachev's Soviet reform offensive in 1987. A novel feature of this reform initiative, at least in terms of the established modus operandi of communist dictatorships, was the fact that it was preceded in November 1987 by a public referendum on the acceptability of the new economic proposals.

Voters were given the chance of expressing their views on two issues, presumably in the hope of enhancing their commitment to processes of economic and political change rather than just of eliciting their opinions on the matter. They were asked to endorse a model for the democratization of political life and a programme for economic recovery – but also to accept further austerity during the latter process. It was not possible for the Polish population to reaffirm acceptance of an objective to which it had clearly expressed its commitment – if only by creating and sustaining the Solidarity movement – without also taking on board the costs of an economic programme a demonstrably bankrupt regime decided it should further bear. Despite the elements of participation the referendum embodied and a promise of yet another reform initiative, it smacked very much of political gimmickry. The proposals were cast, moreover, in tortuous wording and a cumbersome voting procedure was involved.

However, while two-thirds of voters endorsed the proposals, a third of the electorate did not participate in the referendum at all. This meant that the government initiative was defeated, as two-thirds of those eligible to vote were required to give a positive response for the proposals to go through. There were suggestions that those opposed to reform had encouraged these clumsy formulations and procedures in order to obstruct the government's plans, and even that the leadership had purposely dug this pit for itself in order to demonstrate that the Polish populace was not really committed either to democratization or to economic reform. The truth probably was that the operation was simply bungled as the leadership had a hazy understanding both of democratic procedures and of the true inclinations of the people – misjudgments the same ruling group was to repeat less than two years later in the elections of June 1989.

The outcome of the referendum did not seem to make any great difference either to Jaruzelski's intentions or his policies, but it was reported to have modified the speed with which they were carried out. Major price rises, which were intended to help stabilize the market and prepare the ground for economic reform, were nevertheless introduced early in 1988 and this set the scene for the greatest industrial unrest since the beginning of the decade and the most effective threat to political stability since the imposition of martial law. Coming after years of economic stagnation and the failure of Jaruzelski's recovery programme, the price rises sparked off strikes for higher wages and the restoration of Solidarity's legal status. They petered out in early May without apparently having achieved very much, but returned again during the summer – eight years after the emergence of the wave on which Solidarity had so rapidly risen to prominence. In 1988, though, the movement was staffed by younger workers, most of whom had not lived through the years of conflict and disappointment and had played little part in the original Solidarity experience.

This was in some ways an advantage, as they had personally suffered less from the defeats of martial law and had less experience of the disintegration of the movement. It was also important for the growing significance of the new strike movement that Solidarity had retained a residual organizational presence as well as its irrepressible leader, Lech Wałęsa – and that its traditions and ideas still carried considerable attraction for much of Polish society. As the wave of strikes continued during August 1988, the ruling group came up with a rather more radical proposal to end the industrial unrest and reduce the major tensions that had been evident in Polish society, in either open or repressed form, since the early gloss had worn off the Gierek leadership. It was probably also a sign that the views of Gorbachev, who had again visited Poland in July 1988, had undergone further evolution and policy advanced a further stage in the Kremlin. (It may be noted in this connection that just three months earlier, for the first time since the takeover of Central Europe, Soviet leaders had not intervened to promote a preferred candidate in the choice of a new Hungarian party leader to replace the ailing János Kádár.)

In Poland the Jaruzelski leadership now felt able to propose negotiations with Solidarity, open the prospect of its relegalization and tackle questions of trade union pluralism. Hints of a changing regional context and Soviet reappraisal of critical bloc relationships were strengthened by the role played in this initiative by General Czesław Kiszczak, a leading member of the Jaruzelski leadership and government minister since August 1981, with a lengthy prior record in military intelligence and the counter-intelligence organs. The offer of negotiations represented a major evolution in the political strategy both of the Soviet Union and the Polish leadership. It had immediate repercussions in the latter with the resignation of prime minister Zbigniew Messner and his replacement by Mieczysław

Rakowski. Rakowski had long been identified with the liberal, reform-oriented wing of the PUWP, but was no favourite of Solidarity, with whom he had developed a stormy relationship following his appointment in February 1981 under Jaruzelski as deputy prime minister with responsibility for trade union affairs.

Major changes within the party leadership were also necessary, taking place over two Central Committee meetings held over December and January, before the round-table talks (as the negotiations came to be called) were eventually able to open in February 1989. Preparations for the negotiations were protracted as there were objections to the participation of Solidarity's key advisers (such as Jacek Kuroń and Adam Michnik), but these problems were finally overcome with the Central Committee changes initiated at the end of the year. The latter, however, only occurred under a threat of resignation from leading reformist figures and the top leaders. The Central Committee changes altered the balance of party opinion on questions of political change, reduced the power of long-established hardliners and opened the way to better relations with non-communist forces. On 17 April 1989, as a result of agreements reached at the round-table talks over a range of issues, Solidarity was again registered and given legal status by the Warsaw judiciary.

Equally important were commitments to electoral and institutional change. Elections to the *Sejm* (or Polish parliament) were advanced to the coming June with a striking feature being introduced in terms of their possible outcome – 35 per cent of the seats were not reserved for candidates representing any particular political constituency but remained open to general electoral contestation. A second chamber, the Senate, with limited though significant legislative powers, was established. Voting to this body was also open and no seats at all were reserved for establishment parties. The final results of the elections held on this basis on 4 June 1989 were a considerable shock to all concerned. Solidarity-sponsored candidates took 160 of the 161 seats in the *Sejm* which had not been reserved for the governing coalition and 92 of the 100 Senate places. 35 of the *Sejm* seats were not open to competition but 33 of them were not filled either. Rather as in the case of the 1987 referendum, these candidates failed to gain election not because of electoral competition but by virtue of the electoral regulations, 50 per cent of the electorate taking the care to delete their names from the national list of candidates.

These seats were only filled as a result of a somewhat humiliating constitutional fudge in which new candidates were allowed to present themselves. Although the conditions of the round-table agreement were observed, the results of the elections, in which the ruling establishment appeared to emerge with a solid legislative majority, were still a shock for all concerned. It is, again, slightly surprising why this should be so, as there were no reasons for believing that the communist regime (in its reformist guise or otherwise) had much support from Polish society or that any opportunity to vote against it would be refused. The reason for this overwhelming electoral victory was, it appeared, the mobilization of the political centre which had previously shown greater inconsistency and uncertainty in its choices.[14] Polish political life was, in any case, cast into considerable confusion by the electoral process (completed only after a two-week gap by a second round on 18 June). When the result of the second round of elections was known, Solidarity-sponsored candidates held in the *Sejm* all the 161 seats which had been open to competition, and 99 of the 100 seats in the Senate.[15] Despite the formal establishment majority, which materialized as arranged, it did not prove easy to form a government.

Those successfully elected on the party list during the second round had often received Solidarity support and the established auxiliary parties (the Democratic Party and the United Peasant Party) were now also reconsidering their position. They suddenly realized that their future in the shadow of the communist party establishment was by no means assured and that a more independent approach would have to be contemplated. The positions both of president and prime minister were also filled after some hesitation and delay. General Jaruzelski first proposed Kiszczak for the newly strengthened presidency, which did not prove to be a popular idea, and then agreed to stand himself. His nomination was accepted with the barest of majorities (one vote), and this was only achieved due to a number of deputies absenting themselves from the chamber or spoiling their papers with the intention of securing what seemed at the time to be the only viable political solution. In accordance with this development, Jaruzelski resigned the party leadership on 29 July 1989, his place being taken by Mieczysław Rakowski, the outgoing prime minister.

The nomination of a prime minister proved to be equally problematic. Kiszczak was further proposed as prime minister, but this was also received without enthusiasm and soon showed itself to be an option which had little possibility of receiving overall parliamentary approbation. Ideas of different combinations of political parties which included Solidarity representatives were floated, a process in which Lech Wałęsa came to play an increasingly important part. A significant step in this process was the proposal from Adam Michnik, opposition activist, editor of the recently established Solidarity daily paper and now *Sejm* deputy, that there might be a division between communist establishment interests and Solidarity – popular – preferences along the lines of 'your president, our prime minister'. This, indeed, was the solution that was finally arrived at with Jaruzelski's proposal on 19 August to Tadeusz Mazowiecki, a noted Catholic intellectual and then editor of the Solidarity weekly newspaper, that he should become prime minister, a proposal that was further endorsed by parliament on 24 August. In September agreement was reached on a new government headed by Mazowiecki, which had the distinction of being the first non-communist controlled administration in Central Europe since the immediate post-war period. Poland was thus the first country to see the effective abandonment by a ruling communist party of its leading role (although the extent and finality of the communist defeat was not immediately apparent in the summer of 1989).

Mazowiecki, the new prime minister, was born in 1927 and had been an early activist of the official Catholic organization PAX and the editor of a Catholic weekly in Wroclaw. He was, however, excluded from PAX in 1955 after a confrontation with Bolesław Piasecki, its politically dubious leader who had been known for his fascist affiliations before the war. In 1956 Mazowiecki founded the Warsaw branch of the Club of the Catholic Intelligentsia and represented the independent Catholic group *Znak* in parliament from 1961 to 1972. His early parliamentary career ended at this stage after an attempt to organize a commission to investigate the authorities' response to the workers' demonstrations of 1970. He was associated with the Workers' Defence Committee and acted as its spokesman in 1977 during a hunger strike.

Led by a Solidarity nominee, Poland's first post-communist government also included deputy premiers from Solidarity as well as the Polish United Workers', United Peasant and Democratic Parties. The new government provided for a further 11 posts for Solidarity; 3 for the PZPR (PUWP, or communist party); 3 for the ZSL (UPP: United Peasant Party); and 2 for the SD (DP: Democratic Party). It was a carefully balanced cabinet which reflected the end of communist rule while providing for the satisfaction of what appeared to be continuing Soviet strategic interests by assuring communist occupation of the presidency and of the ministries of defence and the interior. It soon, however, became less a predominantly non-communist government than a post-communist one, despite the predominance of PZPR-nominated deputies in its legislative chamber. In January 1990, following further developments in the Soviet bloc, the PZPR dissolved itself and was succeeded by a party called The Social Democracy of the Polish Republic (SdRP) as well as a smaller organization (The Polish Social-Democratic Union: PUS).[16] While the formation of Mazowiecki's government had signalled the effective end of communist rule in Poland, the disappearance of the PZPR further confirmed the elimination of the communist movement as an organized political force.

PARALLEL BUT DIFFERENT: THE HUNGARIAN PATH

Despite the different strategy adopted by the Kádár leadership in Hungary with regard to economic and political change and the contrasting sequence of developments in that country, crisis tendencies emerged at approximately the same time as in Poland and increasingly pointed to the same conclusion. Although the economic and political collapse that took place in Poland at the end of the 1970s was not replicated in such a dramatic form in Hungary, the 'second industrialization' without effective reform that occurred during that decade had brought the country to a highly critical state. The beginning of the end of communism in Hungary can be traced to a series of meetings of the party's Central Committee in late 1977 and 1978, when the failure of economic policies earlier in the decade and the deleterious effects of the reversal of economic reform were recognized. In the summer of 1979, however, as Poland moved into open crisis, a stabilization programme was introduced and measures taken to relaunch the essentials of the Hungarian NEM, whose principles had first been implemented in 1968.

Compared with Polish experience of the time, as the conflicts and disruption of 1980–81 were succeeded by a period of martial law, creating conditions which were far from ideal for the implementation of economic reform proposals, Hungarian economic developments did not appear too bad. (Indeed, they continued to provide something of a model for the emulation and envy of the Polish leadership.) The liquidity problems evident at the beginning of the decade were coped with and there were signs of economic recovery during 1983–4 within the framework of the relaunched Hungarian programme. But there were also doubts about whether the return to principles first applied in the late 1960s was really likely to provide a full solution to the problems of the 1980s, and whether, in any case, the reforms were being pursued with the same level of commitment as had first appeared. The continuing weakness of the Hungarian economy became further evident as attempts were made to accelerate the pace of economic development and the country's external debt doubled between 1985 and 1987 from $8.8 to $17.7 billion.

Hungary had avoided the outright conflict that had erupted in Poland and the harsh measures subsequently imposed under the guise of martial law, both conditions that did nothing to ameliorate Poland's economic crisis or provide a solid basis for the steps that were needed to tackle it. Hungary's political situation was far from favourable, either, though. Central power over the economy had weakened and corruption had become firmly rooted and extensive in its reach. In this sense, Hungarian developments reflected the situation that had emerged in the Soviet Union during the late Brezhnev period and the succeeding years. Hungarian problems were also similar to those elsewhere in the Soviet bloc, in that the insistence on central control and orthodoxy lying at the heart of Brezhnevism weakened the capacity to apply effective reform measures and undermined the foundations on which any recovery could be based. The growing economic fragility apparent among COMECON members and increasing formalism evident in the practice and structures of orthodox political life further reduced central political authority and reinforced the feelings of aimlessness and ideological barrenness widespread in the Soviet Union and Central Europe during the early 1980s.

In Hungary, as in the Soviet Union, the problems of an aging leadership also entered into the equation. Kádár's centrist position, which had played a significant role in bridging the gulf that had opened up in 1956 between the insurgent nation and his Soviet-supported communist leadership, became increasingly untenable as economic solutions ran out of steam and his political views grew more rigid. The running-down of the reform process during the 1970s (against the views of economic experts) culminated in further conflict during the subsequent decade, when it became evident that the resumption of economic reform had not been thorough enough. Serious crisis tendencies began to resurface. Following the Congress of the Hungarian Socialist Workers' Party in 1985, at which some of these problems were publicly acknowledged, major Hungarian economic experts became increasingly disenchanted and gravitated away from the party authorities towards opposition forces and vehement criticism of leadership behaviour.

Kádár's position had now become one of outright conservatism and his career, like that of Brezhnev and his entourage, took on the clear appearance of having run its course. As in the case of the Soviet leaders, however, this was more evident to those outside the leadership circle than to those in positions of power. With Gorbachev's accession to power, the changes in the Kremlin highlighted the contrast between Hungary and a more dynamically changing Soviet Union. Regional changes strengthened the reform tendencies in Hungary and weakened the continuing resistance to it. Thus, in contrast to his influence on the top leadership in Poland, in Hungary Gorbachev helped to break Kádár's grip on power. Kádár nevertheless continued to take measures to weaken the position of competitors and delay the political reckoning. Karoly Grősz, for example, was moved in 1987 from his position at the head of the Budapest party organization to the apparently elevated, but generally uninfluential, post of prime minister. This, however, was used by Grősz as a platform to reach out to groups outside the party and forge links with technocrats and groups of experts, providing him with the means in September 1987 to present parliament with a programme for tackling the economic situation. Imre Pozsgay, the major reformist figure within the party, had been moved in 1982 from the HSWP organization to the more marginal Patriotic People's Front from which he, also, was able to organize more fruitful public debate.

As in Poland, though for rather different reasons, the party was moving away from the centre of the political stage and displaying with increasing clarity its lack of ability to control and lead social processes. It was soon presented with the opportunity to deal with the immediate problems of Kádár's leadership, however, and in May 1988 at a Party Conference he was removed from the leadership and the Politburo purged of his supporters. The sweeping rejection of the former leadership was an important sign of the gathering pace of change in Central Europe (at least in the two countries in the vanguard of the movement) and the removal of former Soviet limits placed on it. The replacement of Kádár was also, according to leading officials, the first occasion in communist Hungary when the Soviets did not make their preference for the political succession known. The Hungarian party leadership appeared to relinquish its own *nomenklatura* powers over appointments early the next year, when a new government was formed without Politburo approval being secured. Reformist groups gained strength within the party organization. As in the case of other groups with a new perspective on the future, attention was also paid to past events – in particular to 1956 and the major turning-point in the history of communist Hungary.

Criticism of Kádár's conservatism and his failed economic record thus extended to embrace the role of the HSWP as a whole and prompted deeper examination of the developments that had been the cause of the Soviet invasion in 1956, and had provided at the same time a basis for Kádár's subsequent leadership career. An historical commission charged with this broad remit concluded that 1956 had seen a popular uprising rather than a counter-revolution. This undermined the justification for Kádár's actions taken in response to the Soviet intervention. It destroyed what legitimacy remained to the communist order which had been installed on the basis of the coercive means used to cope with the crisis. The acceptance in February 1989 of this judgment by the party's Central Committee thus signalled a fundamental breach in the structure of communist power and a departure from the order that prevailed for much of the communist period in Hungary. It also confirmed the defeat of the conservative faction associated with Kádár in the leadership.

Later in the year, in June, the new public interpretation of 1956 and the Kádár years was sealed with the rehabilitation and reburial of the executed leader of the early period, Imre Nagy. It was understandable, then, that the CC meeting that accepted the new historical interpretation of 1956 also opened up prospects for the establishment of a multi-party system and a rapprochement (as in Poland) with the increasingly numerous and influential opposition groups that now existed. The ground had been prepared for this with the attempts that had gathered force during 1988 to constitutionalize public life, and with the intensification of the work undertaken by regime reformers to change some of the country's basic laws. This presented something of a contrast with Poland, where most activity focused on the legalization of the opposition itself and the enhancement of its access to the power centre by opening the path to freer elections.

As in Poland, though, there was some hesitancy and resistance on the part of opposition groups to responding to initiatives from reform-oriented groups within the party leadership. The opposition had based its identity and strategy precisely on remaining distinct from the party-state establishment and evolving values and forms of action that ran counter to its influence. It was best summed up in the writings of George Konrád in terms of 'greater independence with respect to redistributive centralism; a brisk circulation of freely associating and self-governing intellectual groups in the market-place of ideas; alternative enterprises dedicated not to maximum profit but to intellectual activity for its own sake . . . in short, an amalgam of the second economy and the second culture'.[17] This view, however, was more strongly held in Hungary by the Free Democrats than amongst the activists of a parallel group, the Democratic Forum – as later conflicts and the tussle over the presidential elections were to show. In Poland, Solidarity forces and the opposition had, naturally enough, been seriously affected by martial law and the years of repression; much of the population had become accustomed to the post-martial law Jaruzelski leadership and had slowly come to tolerate its existence, if not accept its legitimacy. The Hungarian democratic opposition had always been a more restricted group in terms of its membership and social appeal, and had remained relatively isolated. The process of organizational development had only really begun in 1987.[18] Groups in both countries, then, had some reason to fear incorporation by the party – even if it was increasingly weak and more open to the influence of reformist groups. The right of individual (and often largely self-selected) opposition repre-sentatives to negotiate with the authorities was also contested, and many felt uncomfortable about taking on such a role.

The threat of economic collapse, social crisis and the unpredictable response of the Soviet Union was a powerful motivating force for co-operation in Poland, however, while the experience of 1956 provided most reformist groups in Hungary with equally strong incentives to join forces in order to accelerate and control processes of change. Nevertheless, the internal differ-entiation of the opposition took different forms in the two countries. In Poland, a major line of division ran between the Solidarity establishment and the younger generation of activists, who now joined those who had criticized Wałęsa and his intellectual advisers for the relative moderation of their approach during 1981. In Hungary, the question of collaboration with party forces in 1989 divided the Democratic Forum (a moderate opposition with significant establishment links) from the Alliance of Free Democrats, a more radical and liberal group which incorporated the existing Democratic Opposition and reflected more urban traditions. Negotiations between opposition and establishment forces finally began during June 1989 in Hungary – shortly after the shock of the Polish elections, whose outcome and problematic consequences for the process of government formation provided valuable lessons for Hungarian sympathizers.

The electoral agreement reached in Poland and the perspectives that even partially free elections now opened up for political change in Central Europe cast a new light over the whole situation. The contemporary extent of Soviet tolerance was becoming clearer and, in the light of Polish experiences, the Hungarian party moved increasingly on to the defensive. Echoes of the sovereignty proclaimed by Nagy in 1956 were evident in the decision taken during September to open Hungarian borders with Austria to permit the exit of East German tourists en route for West Germany. This, however, followed a decision already taken in May 1989 to begin removing the barbed wire that formed that part of the Iron Curtain. The 1969 treaty with the GDR not to permit the transit of citizens to other countries without authorization was declared suspended, because it was now deemed incompatible with adherence to United Nations conventions.

As the dynamic of political change accelerated and the existing regional framework crumbled, the institutional context of domestic change was also transformed. Rather than the opposition being permitted a limited voice in decision-making and some partici- pation in the exercise of power, it was now the future political status of the communist party that was coming increasingly into question in both countries. This was not just recognized as a threatening fact by some within the establishment and leading ranks of the Hungarian party, but it was a development seized on and made as much use of as possible by the reformist wing associated with Pozsgay, which now took an increasingly radical stance. By such means they hoped to retain the initiative and not look as though they had received a traumatic shock, as had been case with their closest equivalents in Poland.

This was reflected in the establishment of a new leadership within the HSWP, which included both Pozsgay and reformist Prime Minister Németh, as well as Party First Secretary Grősz and Rezső Nyers (who became Party Chairman). This realignment was accompanied by the formation of a round table, which also included Democratic Forum, the Free Democrats, the Fidesz youth movement, representatives of new parties and independent trade unions. The terms of discussion also changed as it became clear that the prospect of wholly free elections was not only a realizable objective but the only realistic basis for discussion. Agreement was reached relatively swiftly on a new electoral law but conflict continued about the timing of elections to the newly defined presidency. Regime forces argued for an early election to fill that post and assure some political stability before parliamentary elections could be held around the turn of the year. This, however, was seen as likely to assure the rapid transition to that post of Imre Pozsgay – and thus maximize the political opportunities open to the HSWP.

Arguments for this proposal came from the Democratic Forum, but more radical groups in the opposition succeeded in gaining support for a referendum on the issue, which was held on 26 November and resulted in a small majority for the radicals' position. Further setbacks for the party had by then occurred at a specially convened HSWP Congress held in October, when the old party was dissolved and a new Hungarian Socialist Party (HSP), conceived along the lines of the democratic socialist parties in Western Europe, was set up to replace it. Of the existing 720,000 members of the HSWP, however, only 50,000 had joined the new party by the end of 1989 while conservative forces joined forces to reform a rump HSWP. The rapid erosion of the old communist party as a leading political force was further hastened by the decision of the existing National Assembly (divested of their former party responsibilities and allegiance before their Polish counterparts) to ban party organizations from workplaces; to disband the Workers' Guard formerly controlled by the HSWP; and to undertake an investigation into the property and finances of the former party. During the same session a new Hungarian Republic (no longer 'socialist') was proclaimed, to take effect from 23 October 1989, thus bringing the communist period in post-war Hungary to a formal end.

MOVEMENT IN THE GERMAN GLACIER

The crumbling of the communist order in both Poland and Hungary can be dated in its origins to the late 1970s or – in more immediate terms – to 1987 at the very latest. It took place as the German Democratic Republic retained a position of strict political orthodoxy and showed, at least in outward terms, signs of the continuing viability of the communist order. The German position was maintained through the round-table negotiations in Poland and the official acceptance of the revisionist view of the 1956 events in Hungary. It clearly lasted in public form until the German municipal elections in May 1989. Held according to the rules established under Stalinism and thoroughly rigged, they produced results reassuring to the communist old guard and recorded an official 98.55 per cent level of support for the SED. Signs of a changing mood were, nevertheless, also appearing in the GDR. While travel between the two Germanies had become notably freer by the mid-1980s and seemed to have eased many of the earlier frustrations, in 1987 the level of applications for emigration from the GDR seemed to show a notable rise once more. By the end of 1988 the public mood was reported to have become more obviously hostile. While the leadership could guard and police the territorial boundaries of the state it could not isolate the population from all means of communication. Radio and, increasingly, television transmissions from across the border were important in presenting the image of an alternative Germany and a way of life that could be easily compared with the conditions prevailing in the GDR.

Even by the late 1980s, however, little change was evident in official political processes. Despite promptings to the contrary from Moscow and growing signs that the SED was finally losing control of the situation, the 1989 municipal elections were still held in single-candidate form and perpetuated the established traditions of single-party dictatorship. They demonstrated East Germany's continuing determination to withstand both the strengthening tide of change in Hungary and Poland and the apparent acquiescence of the Kremlin in that stance. There was, in fact, little real choice. If a sharp distinction in terms of identity and system-operation between the two Germanies were not maintained, there would be precious little reason to argue for any difference between them. Such differences underlay the whole *raison d'être* of the GDR's separate existence and, in the absence of a separate national identity or clear superiority in terms of systemic operation, constituted the only source of its legitimacy. As late as the summer of 1989, the president of the Academy of the Social Sciences was reported to have reiterated that the GDR could only exist as an 'anti-fascist state' and that if it adopted a Hungarian type of reform which introduced capitalist elements 'there would be no reason for a capitalist GDR to exist'.[19] In resisting the reformist tide flowing from the Kremlin, moreover, the GDR was only following another of Gorbachev's precepts: that of identifying and implementing national solutions to suit national conditions. Despite relatively good results in the early 1980s, the economic picture was less impressive during the second half of the decade – but it was markedly less gloomy than the situation in Poland. The GDR had also escaped the recurring hiatus that periodically threatened the Hungarian economy and had been responsible for Hungary's acceptance of the accelerating process of economic and political reform in that country.

During the summer of 1989 party leader Honecker returned from a standard comradely visit to the Soviet Union with what seemed to be a serious illness. While Honecker was undergoing hospital treatment, the East German regime also began showing signs of a significant loss of capacity and progressive political paralysis. Increasing numbers of GDR citizens crossed from Hungary to the West; others took refuge in the West German embassies in Prague and Warsaw. Honecker's response on 3 October was to ban all unregulated travel to neighbouring states. Before this, however, relatively low-key peace meetings and demonstrations had been held since 1987 in a church in Leipzig, developing and perpetuating the official dissatisfaction that had earlier been expressed by the GDR leadership against NATO and deployment by the Warsaw Pact countries of short- and medium-range missiles in the early 1980s. The Evangelical Church had shown increasing sympathy for Gorbachev as his commitment to change deepened, and its relations with the GDR leadership had been growing more fraught from late 1987. The demonstrations and popular dissatisfaction changed tack in the late summer of 1989, involving more participants and attracting more repressive action from the police. On 2 October 1989, 20,000 people demonstrated in Leipzig in the largest demonstration seen in the GDR since 1953.

Under these unpropitious conditions, preparations for the fortieth anniversary of the GDR on 7 October 1949 continued and President Gorbachev arrived from the Soviet Union to take part in them. His view was clearly more focused on contemporary problems than on celebrating the longevity of the communist regime in East Germany, while Honecker and the GDR leadership were now preoccupied with political damage limitation and resisting

Gorbachev's encouragement for them to change their ways. Gorbachev's judgment was reportedly delivered to Honecker as a private statement that 'Those who delay are punished by life itself', while Honecker's response was summed up in the strange and broadly inaccurate pronouncement that 'Those who are declared dead usually live a long time'.[20] Events on Gorbachev's departure seemed to bear out his analysis rather than that of the German leader. Further demonstrations, some attracting severe police retaliation, broke out in East Berlin and other cities as well as Leipzig, where on 9 October 70,000 marched and on 16 October as many as 100,000 – the latter finally meriting a report in the still closely vetted official media.

On 16 October the party's Politburo also met and finally received Honecker's resignation after other members impressed on him their conviction that a national uprising might occur if matters developed further along the same course. They repeated the message delivered by Gorbachev that the GDR leadership could no longer count on the intervention of Soviet troops to maintain them in power.[21] But Honecker's resignation did not yet mean the end of communist rule in East Germany. In his place was elected Egon Krenz, who at 52 was the youngest member of the Politburo but who proved to be an even shorter-lived party leader than either Jakeš in Czechoslovakia or Grősz in Hungary. Like Honecker and several other national leaders, Krenz had been responsible for domestic security matters (including the formidable secret police, or *Stasi*) within the party leadership, a sign that some central conventions of communist rule were observed in the GDR until the very end. Although taking care to smile a lot in public, his features nevertheless strongly reminded people of the long-fanged wolf rather than Red Riding Hood's grandmother whose benevolence he was trying to convey. Apparently more open to change, Krenz nevertheless showed little inclination to modify the leading rule of the party or to extend 'dialogue' in any meaningful sense to give the admittedly weak organized opposition any voice in government. After a visit to Moscow in early November, though, his actions became more energetic.

The head of the union organization, Harry Tisch, was sacked and on 7 November the government resigned, followed within the day by the whole Politburo. The decision to solve the crisis by peaceful means, however, may well have been a narrow one and it was later reported that on 7 November the Politburo had rejected a proposal to put the army on the streets by just one vote.[22] The former prime minister, Willi Stoph (who had first held the post in 1964), was now replaced by Hans Modrow, a reform-minded economist who had supposedly been disliked by Honecker and was kept at arm's length as head of the party organization in Dresden. Demonstrations against the SED leadership, however, continued. Particular opposition was reserved for Krenz's support of the massacre of student protesters in Tiananmen Square which had been ordered by Chinese leaders some five months earlier. This appeared to reflect the position he might personally have favoured taking towards demonstrators in his own country. He had, indeed, conferred with Chinese leaders only three weeks before his election as party leader. Large numbers of GDR citizens continued to head for the West through Hungary and Czechoslovakia and, by the time of the opening of the Berlin Wall late on 9 November, as many as 225,000 had left the country in 1989 alone – most of them between the ages of 20 and 40. The Wall was therefore opened for reasons similar to those for its erection: to encourage East Germans to stay in their reserved portion of the country.

Whatever the moral and political judgment passed on its construction in 1961, the construction of the Wall was at least more successful in keeping people in than its demolition. The weekend after it was opened, two million East Germans visited the West. At the crossing-point at Helmstedt the line of traffic waiting to pass through the exit stretched for 30 miles, and it took East Germans a whole day to reach the border. Krenz's promises of reform became somewhat less cautious and, on 18 November, Modrow presented a government in which 11 of the 18 seats were occupied by non-communists. He proceeded to unveil plans for a sovereign East German state with a market-oriented economy, guarantees of civil liberties supported by a constitutional court, and closer relations with the European Community. The attention of the parliament, however, as well as that of much of the East German public, was increasingly taken up with investigation and revelation of the former elite's corruption and the luxury that had quietly been built up behind the stability and public austerity of the communist regime.

Apart from the plush homes and sanatoria there were more colourful stories like those about the £72 million derived by the secretary of state in the economics ministry from trade deals (much of it from arms sales to the Third World); items from state museums sold in the West; the possible involvement of Honecker in the cocaine trade; and even football matches which were rigged so that security chief Mielke did not have to see Dynamo Berlin, his favourite team, suffer the ignominy of defeat. Such stories fed waves of resentment and bitterness hidden for decades behind the stolidity of 'actually existing socialism' – and tendencies to seek direct retribution against employees or sympathizers of the former regime. A particular focus of anger were members of the *Stasi*, short for *Staatssicherheit*, or state security agency, and a wholesale popular assault on their East Berlin headquarters was mounted on 15 January 1990. 7,000 angry citizens were reported to have stormed the *Stasi* complex, partly due to long bottled-up frustration and ambitions to expose the extent and nature of its agents' activities, but also in some cases to examine personal files and take possession of incriminating evidence.[23] The degree of surveillance and level of penetration of East German society had been truly enormous. Official records admitted to 85,000 full-time operatives and 109,000 paid informers, although West German estimates went as high as 600,000 full- and part-time informers. Files were kept on 6 million East Germans, a third of the whole population, and the *Stasi* had 1.3 per cent of the state budget at its disposal.

The *Stasi*'s activities had not been scaled down during the 1980s. Indeed, they had been intensified to cope with the threat of growing dissidence, and even with the consequences of what might be regarded as the dangerously lax practices in this area which were becoming apparent in Gorbachev's Soviet Union. While, then, security activities had been prominent throughout Central Europe and the area remained one of general controversy and particular sensitivity during the post-communist period, the issue became especially prominent in the GDR and was immediately placed on the public agenda. Nor did its effects die away as further information on *Stasi* activities gradually became available and it became clear how they had involved even prominent intellectuals like Heiner Muller and Christa Wolf, the latter known particularly for her critical stance and moral rectitude.[24] Krenz's leadership had no capacity to cope with the repressed discontent such conditions had created and the recently installed Politburo resigned on 3 December, two days after parliament had ended the party's monopoly of power and eliminated its leading role from the constitution. This was the event that had dispelled all illusions about the future viability of the GDR. It was crucial not just for Krenz and the GDR but also for Germany and the whole of Europe.

Direction of the party now passed temporarily to a working committee headed by a young lawyer earlier involved in human

rights cases, Gregor Gysi. The resignation of the Politburo meanwhile prompted a general and rapid collapse of the established
political system. After all these years, however, there were no
organized forces capable of filling the vacuum. There were
spontaneous attacks on former security officials, party functionaries,
or just those who looked as though they had enjoyed material
privilege. The loosely organized opposition and leading groups like
the independent social movement New Forum called for calm and
restraint, and continued to talk in terms of a separate East German
identity for what already appeared to be the former GDR. In this,
they betrayed the weakness of their links with the newly
emancipated East German masses and failed to provide adequate
expression for their recently released frustration and grievances. At
an emergency party congress in December Gysi was elected in the
place of Krenz, and the latter was expelled from the party in the
company of other leading former officials. However, none of this
now made much difference to the future of either the SED or of
the GDR.

Modrow promised all manner of change and reform within East
Germany, but rejected notions of German unity, which had soon
become the main item on the political agenda. Federal Chancellor
Helmut Kohl had put forward proposals for a German confederation as early as 28 November and he showed little restraint in
promoting unification. Apart from concentrating on an enormously
popular political issue and building up momentum for forthcoming
West German elections, this focus was also designed to reassure East
Germans about their future and diminish the attractiveness of
joining the headlong dash for the West that had gained strength in
the GDR. Free elections were promised for May 1990, but fears of a
continuing communist stranglehold over the political process
persisted. Anxiety about the lack of real progress towards democratic political development prompted New Forum to threaten to
organize a general strike and the Christian Democrats to withdraw
from Modrow's government. Elections were brought forward to 18
March and the opposition was now invited to participate in a
government of 'national responsibility'. In February Modrow, too,
was forced to produce a unification plan and the inevitable now
became part of the formal East German agenda, with the apparent
acquiescence of Moscow, consulted just before the announcement
of the volte-face. In this process, however, the East German political
parties did not so much enter into agreements or pacts with West
German counterparts as suffer a direct takeover and they, like the

rest of the communist system, were absorbed by their powerful Western partners. At its first national congress New Forum fell into internal dissension, with those favouring unification now emerging ascendent. The growing influence of the Federal Republic and the multiplication of links anchoring the East into the West were irresistible. The end of communist rule had effectively come with the fall of Egon Krenz and the resignation of his Politburo. The no-man's-land until the final unification in October 1990 only remained to be traversed as a territory which had effectively fallen to the West some time before.

THE CZECHOSLOVAK SUITE

The longest defence against the accelerating slide to Europe and the West was in fact mounted by Czechoslovakia, East Germany's southern neighbour and undoubtedly the most Western of the Slav countries. A critical demonstration took place on 17 November 1989 and political tension mounted during the following days. As late as 21 November (three days after the new East German prime minister, Hans Modrow, had presented a cabinet containing 11 non-communist members) matters still hung in the balance in Czechoslovakia. At that stage, as the Czechoslovak primate, Cardinal Tomášek, noted at one of the increasingly numerous gatherings held in Prague's Wenceslas Square, the country was surrounded by those who had already broken the back of totalitarianism but itself remained in the neo-Stalinist camp of political laggards such as Romania and Albania. Like the GDR (and Bulgaria), Czecho-slovakia could look back to an indigenous communist tradition and claim significant domestic sources of support for the post-war regime. This may well have played a part in maintaining the country's relative stability and preventing the emergence of any opposition with extensive roots in Czechoslovak society (although a certain tradition of passivity was probably also relevant). Charter 77 was a major focus of political opposition – but remained a fairly select organization and never had many signatories. While there was some dissent from intellectuals, the younger generation, and religious groups there were – as in Hungary – no signs of dissatisfaction or political action from the working class.

Unlike Hungary, however, Czechoslovakia saw no development of an alliance between disenchanted intellectuals and regime groups sympathetic towards reform proposals. As in the GDR, opposition forces remained relatively isolated and were far from developing any critical political mass – a situation helped immeasurably by the tolerable material circumstances of much of the Czechoslovak population and the relative strength of the country's economy. Living standards were maintained and, in fact, rose during the 1970s, even in the face of longer-term economic disproportions. By 1980 Czechoslovakia was paying nearly five times as much for Soviet oil as it had in 1970 – and it was importing twice as much. In what looked like a recapitulation of the economic slowdown and looming crisis of the early 1960s, the economy shrank in both 1981 and 1982. Steps towards economic reform were taken in the following years which, although not particularly striking in comparison with Hungarian and Polish measures, were by no means insignificant in terms of the Czechoslovak context.

Yet when Husák retired from the leadership in December 1987, he was not succeeded by Lubomir Štrougal, the prime minister who had been associated with reformist circles for some years, but by the more conservative Miloš Jakeš, who seemed to have little inclination either for political change or economic reform. Public opinion in Czechoslovakia, though, while restrained by the application of relatively effective measures during the normalization process applied after 1968, and kept quiescent by continuing success in avoiding the socio-economic fate of Poland (or even the problems of Hungary), had slowly begun to change. Charter 77 and VONS (the Committee for the Defence of the Unjustly Persecuted) had been established in the 1970s, but public opinion began to stir later with the political impact of the growing strength of religious faith throughout Central Europe. In Czechoslovakia this became evident with the celebrations in 1985 of the 1100th anniversary of the death of St. Methodius, early apostle to the Slavs.

This movement underwrote demands for greater independence of the Church from the state and was accompanied in the second half of the 1980s by a proliferation of independent social groupings. The twentieth anniversary of the Soviet-led invasion was marked by a major demonstration, while in January 1989 large crowds emerged to commemorate the death of Jan Palach who set fire to himself to demonstrate opposition to the crushing of the reform movement. It was at one such meeting that Václav Havel was again arrested and sentenced to nine months' detention. During 1989 feelings became more intense and were fed by the public re-emergence of Alexander Dubček who, amongst other things, gave a major interview to Hungarian radio which evoked a sharp response from the Czechoslovak authorities. Opposition contacts with Hungarian and Polish dissidents, before whom there was now the imminent prospect of transition into government posts, became stronger and more public. The twenty-first anniversary of the invasion by Warsaw Pact forces was the occasion for an unusually strong demonstration in August 1989, and on 28 October, the anniversary of the founding of the Czechoslovak republic, the largest demonstration since 1948 was held as 10,000 people gathered in Prague. As change had accelerated in Poland and Hungary, some members of the elite (particularly those associated with Prime Minister Štrougal) had been inclined to go along with the tide of reform. Most, though, remained committed to the existing state of affairs (which was certainly not, on the face of it, worse than the situation in Poland and Hungary) and drew comfort from the continuing conservatism of the GDR leadership and the lack of opposition from most of Czechoslovakia's industrial and farming population.

For the bulk of the elite the situation was not in fact a matter of policy but one of survival. However, the slowly surfacing signs of popular dissatisfaction and growing political uncertainty were increasingly having an effect on intra-elite relations. Rumours spread in the spring of 1988 concerning the complete retirement of Husák from the leadership and the removal of the thoroughgoing conservative Bilak – but little of significance happened at that stage. It was, paradoxically, after alterations with contrasting implications in the Soviet leadership during October 1988 that significant changes in the Czechoslovak elite were seen. In the Soviet Union it was Gorbachev's position that was strengthened following Gromyko's removal from the presidency, the demotion of Ligachev, and Chebrikov's removal as head of the KGB. In Czechoslovakia, however, it was the more reform-oriented Štrougal who was removed from the premiership after a period of 18 years. He was replaced by Ladislav Adamec, a technocratic economic administrator who was more of a centrist and relatively moderate in his approach to social issues.

Adamec's economic policies reflected ideas of reorganization rather than principles of reform, and his actions carried little hope for those anticipating more radical ideas of economic improvement. As in Hungary some time before, many economists now joined dissidents in developing a commitment to extensive political reform. Discontent was slowing spreading, though it remained far more restrained than was already the case in Poland and Hungary.

The growing signs of collapse in the GDR represented a further step towards political change in the region, however. As part of the growing flight from the GDR, thousands of the East Germans took up temporary residence in the Prague embassy of the Federal Republic during September and October 1989, after the GDR government had banned its citizens from travelling to Hungary. Popular dissatisfaction in Czechoslovakia also grew, and the brutal police response to a demonstration held on 17 November was a watershed in the process of political change. There appeared to be some evidence that this action was organized in collaboration with Czech and Soviet security agents to produce further changes in the political leadership.[25] Later accounts, however, suggested that Soviet representatives took care to establish that their position was a neutral one and offered unambiguous advice against the use of force.[26] Following the police response on 17 November, demonstrators took to the streets, not just in Prague but also in Bratislava and other centres, in a constant stream of restrained but determined opposition that was soon dubbed a 'velvet revolution'.

On 19 November 1989 Civic Forum was founded as a broad social movement combining existing opposition activists with large numbers of informally organized supporters seeking the end of communist rule in Czechoslovakia.[27] A major demonstration involving three-quarters of a million people was held on 25 November, while a further political blow to the regime was the general strike called by Civic Forum for 27 November. This finally involved a significant response from the workers, who had begun to express more open scepticism about the political leadership. The Jakeš party leadership had finally resigned on 24 November 1989 and a new group under Karel Urbánek was installed. Adamec formed a new federal cabinet on 3 December, but this also proved to be unacceptable to Civic Forum and the Public Against Violence, its counterpart in Slovakia, and Adamec also resigned on 4 December. A government was then formed on 10 December under the Slovak, Marián Čalfa, which offered a rough balance between communists and non-party members. Čalfa, still a communist at the time, soon left the party, while former leader Gustav Husák resigned from the presidency immediately after the formation of the Čalfa government. With these acts the end of communist rule in Czechoslovakia, too, was also made public, and dissident writer Václav Havel was installed as president in time to make the address for New Year 1990. He had been prominent in the early 1960s and was the leading playwright of the Theatre on the Balustrade, where his political satires were produced. He had played an important role in the situation that developed during 1968 and argued for the necessity of a multi-party system to prevent further abuses of power.

From 1969 Havel's work was banned in Czechoslovakia and he was one of the initial signatories of Charter 77, frequently acting as its spokesman. Havel was also closely involved in VONS (the Committee for the Defence of the Unjustly Persecuted) and made important contributions to *samizdat* political literature, receiving prison terms on several occasions. He had been a leading figure in the demonstrations of 1988 and 1989, emerging as a natural representative of the opposition when its views could be made known in public. He also led negotiations with the communist government on behalf of Civic Forum which, had been founded after the demonstration of 17 November 1989. Even while accepting the post of president, Havel remained suspicious of power, political life and politicians themselves. His concept of politics was one based on morality and, while acknowledging the pressing need for free elections, he argued that the campaign should not 'besmirch the clean face of our gentle revolution' and that the country should not get caught up 'in a flurry of skirmishes for power'.[28] Although Havel might have become rather more intimately involved in the complexities of political life than he initially intended, his presence certainly made a distinctive contribution to post-communist Czechoslovakia and gave it a particular ethical dimension.

NOTES AND REFERENCES

1. Schöpflin, 'The end of communism in Eastern Europe'.
2. Batt, *East Central Europe*, p. 4.
3. Staniszkis, 'The obsolescence of Solidarity'.
4. Kramer, 'Beyond the Brezhnev doctrine', p. 35.
5. Trofimenko, 'Soviet policy', pp. 12–13.
6. Gorbachev, *Perestroika*, pp. 163–64.
7. White, *Gorbachev and After*, p. 205.
8. Piontkowsky, 'The Russian sphinx', pp. 168–69.
9. Brown, *Surge to Freedom*, p. 60.
10. Hough, *Russia and the West*, p. 233.
11. Brown, *op. cit.*, p. 61.
12. Batt, *East Central Europe*, p. 25.
13. de Nevers, 'The Soviet Union and Eastern Europe', p. 23.
14. Jasiewicz and Żukowski, 'Elections of 1984–89', p. 113.
15. Lewis, 'Non-competitive elections', pp. 97–100.

16. Lewis, 'The long goodbye', p. 48.
17. Konrád, *Antipolitics*, p. 175.
18. Hawkes, *Tearing Down the Curtain*, p. 42.
19. Ito, 'Eastern Europe: achieving legitimacy', p. 296.
20. Hawkes, *op. cit.*, p. 68.
21. Piontkowsky, *op. cit.*, pp. 169–70.
22. Smith, *Berlin*, p. 92.
23. *ibid.*, p. 196.
24. *Libération* (Paris), 8 February 1993.
25. Urban, 'Czechoslovakia', pp. 116–17.
26. Draper, 'A new history of the velvet revolution', p. 16.
27. Glenny, *The Rebirth of History*, pp. 46–47.
28. *East European Reporter* (London), Winter 1989/90.

CHAPTER TWELVE

Post-Communism and the Transition to Democracy

CONFLICTING FACTORS IN POST-COMMUNIST POLITICS

While the collapse of communist dictatorship in Eastern Europe was rapid (or at least had the appearance of being so), democratization, economic modernization and the restoration of market relations, and the emergence of parliamentary systems were clearly going to be more protracted processes. In the pre-1939 period only Czechoslovakia had anything like a functioning democratic system, and even in that country there was dissatisfaction about the absence of self-government for the Slovak population. While the democratic traditions of Eastern Europe were not particularly weak in comparison with democratizing countries in Africa, Asia, Latin America, or even Southern Europe, the historical background was certainly different from that of Western Europe during earlier phases of democratic development. The divergent experiences of authoritarian rule, Nazi tyranny and communist dictatorship meant that the post-communist countries of Central Europe were not generally able to hark back to previously established patterns of representative government and political participation. While extensive and fundamental in their implications, moreover, the events of 1989 differed from the classic revolutions of 1789 in France or 1917 in Russia in that they did not sweep the ground clear of the institutions and personalities of the old order but left much of the former system to be coped with and only eventually, it was hoped, to be built over and transformed into something quite different.[1]

International conditions also had mixed implications for ongoing processes – the attractions of democratic values within contemporary global society and the growing influence of the European Community certainly contributed to the strength of democratic currents in the post-communist situation. But the concurrent requirements of capitalist development coming after the economic problems of the late communist period produced forces which fitted uneasily with the progress of democratization. Attempts to switch to a capitalistic, market-based economy and encourage industrial modernization resulted in recession, inflationary pressures (particularly acute in the case of Poland), rising unemployment and growing social inequalities. They all exerted pressure on newly established political processes, on occasion producing sentiments which were difficult to accommodate within the partially formed institutions of democratic government. All these factors exerted a significant influence on the development of democracy, the growth of responsible government and the emergence of multi-party systems.[2]

The processes that gained momentum during the growth of opposition to communist rule and the forces that came into prominence during the critical transition phase also played a significant role here. They shaped the specific social and political forms that emerged during the retreat of the Soviet-sponsored authorities and then occupied an important position in the early stages of post-communist development in Central Europe. The role of the social movement – Solidarity in Poland (which was, above all, the regional model for institutionalized opposition to the visibly crumbling communist power in Eastern Europe and its political successors), *Neues Forum* in the German Democratic Republic and Civic Forum in Czechoslovakia – was identified with a specific kind of political force and perceived to act as a characteristic basis for the early stages of post-communist rule. This was less evident in Hungary where popular energies had been presented with greater opportunities for self-expression in terms of economic enterprise and private activity. The political opposition also developed closer relations with communist authorities and the political establishment there. In general, however, such groupings – which could easily be identified with the new social movements to which attention had recently been paid in the West – were regarded as a major feature of East European democratization processes and often perceived as a characteristic component of its specific path of political development.

Such social movements met the needs of the moment in a number of ways. Developing outside and in opposition to the bureaucratized power structures which spread through and across the different levels and facets of the communist system, the movements provided a focus for the resentments and aspirations of society in relation to the agencies of the state, which were clearly subject to the dictates of the party and its specialized apparatus of power. They served to integrate those who shared the widespread disillusion and antipathy against communist authority, and provided a distinctive vehicle for the expression of political opposition whose form as well as content was quite different from that of the political establishment and incumbent power-holders. They were effective in conveying the distaste increasingly felt for the objectives and methods employed in the exercise of communist power, and carried the spirit of 'anti-politics' that encapsulated the revulsion felt against the Soviet-backed dictatorship. Its ethic was expressed in the writings of a number of Central Europeans.[3] A typical instance of this was the decision of the Citizens' Committees set up in Poland to contest the 1989 election not to extend their reach beyond the Solidarity organization to include the relatively small political groups and proto-parties already in existence. Disagreement with this attitude was the reason for Tadeusz Mazowiecki not standing as a candidate in the elections, although it did not prevent him from later taking on the role of prime minister.

It should also be recognized that, in various ways, the form and ethic of the social movements also reflected some of the characteristics of the power-structures their activity and spirit were so set against. These were not wholly conducive to processes of democratization or the development of multi-party systems. They rested, to varying degrees, on relatively undifferentiated forms of organization and represented an inclusive form of alternative political authority. Solidarity, in particular, was criticized for its monolithic form and tendency to express a near-universal opposition to communist authority that mirrored the general Marxist-Leninist claims to overall leadership. Their attachment to anti-politics, embodying different elements of religious, ethical, and national sentiment, was also in practice not so far removed from the opposition of communist officials and the resistance of Marxist-Leninism to pluralism, a reluctance to engage with the institutionalized expression of social conflict and characteristic features of the operation of democratic politics.

Blanket opposition to communist state authority and those who exercised it was a general characteristic of the social movements that emerged in the 1980s. It could also be argued, though, that the dictatorship of the communist party was as much one over the state – in its legal, constitutional form – as over society and the groups that made it up.[4] Western democracy has, in fact, been dependent on the continuing existence of stable state structures and the performance of their functions by the proper agents of the state – in short, on the existence of a reasonably strong but constitutional and legally constituted state order. The implicit values underlying Central European movements in terms of their rejection of formal politics and doubts about the nature of state authority flowed, however, from the ready identification of communist power with that of the state in general. These values were at the outset rarely contrasted with the normative underpinnings of Western pluralism and the conditions that sustained the modern democratic forms they also sought to establish.

The tensions soon became evident and exerted a significant influence on the institutional development of the post-communist systems. It was not one that was generally favourable to the growth of pluralism, expressions of social diversity or the development of civil societies.[5] The tendency of the movements to adopt a general form and develop an inclusive mode of organization was also linked with their aspiration, and often effective capacity, to express the hopes and feelings of society as a whole against communist party-state power. This impressive aim and, on occasion, achievement of representing society as a whole against communist power reflected as much as a process of transcending the concrete forms of society, its actual structures and lines of division, as of articulating its specific interests and of pursuing the achievement of concrete objectives. It was often more a form of symbolic expression of national and religious sentiment (most notably in the archetypal emergence of Solidarity in 1980) than a process of representation in any way related to the expression and pursuit of social interests observed in developed Western democracies.

Yet representation may be regarded as the critical innovation of the modern age that has made democracy a practicable form of rule and effective as a basis for government under contemporary conditions. Its emergence in symbolic form within the framework of the social movement rather than as a pragmatic articulation of group interest was a further factor distancing the Central European oppositions from the practice of Western democracy. The very forces that contributed to their success and to the collapse of communist power were marked by features, then, that were highly problematic for democratization and carried implications that were less than positive for the emergence of competitive party politics. The current of anti-politics; the tendency of the new social movements to mirror the inclusive, monolithic communist party organization; their antagonism to state authority; their inclinations to strive in political action for broadly conceived symbolic expression rather than group representation all seemed in some ways to point as much back to the practices and structures of traditional Soviet-style communism as forward to the processes of modern democracy and structures of Western pluralism.

The initial stages of the transition to democracy also served to strengthen this association in terms of the central role played by elites in the process. While broad social movements seemed to be the characteristic mode in Central Europe for the mobilization and expression of discontent and the articulation of opposition, the critical junctures of regime transition and the mechanisms of power transfer remained very much within the domain of elite politics.[6] It has often been argued that democratization is invariably an elite-based process – but it does carry some threat of reinforcing tendencies that can conflict with more general principles of mass democracy.[7] In these respects Hungary stood very close to Poland in its experience of elite conflict followed by negotiation and accommodation as the initial phase of political democratization. It was the small group which had made up the Democratic Opposition since the 1970s, and became the basis for the Alliance of Free Democrats (AFD: founded in November 1988), and significant forces within the reformist wing of the Hungarian Socialist Workers' Party (HSWP: disbanded in October 1989) which led the way to elite accommodation and joint commitment to reform in September 1989. Other groups also entered the process, pre-eminent among them the Hungarian Democratic Forum (MDF), whose organization had been founded in September 1987 and which drew on the established traditions of Hungarian populism. But it was only prior to the historic free elections of March 1990 that, as Glenny puts it, 'the slumbering bear of Hungarian populism awoke from its hibernation and the MDF conquered all in sight'.[8]

The initial transition to democracy, however, had been very much a matter of elite negotiation. In distinction to Hungary, Poland had seen the emergence of a highly significant mass movement in the form of Solidarity during the summer of 1980. But by the time prospects for effective democratization began to emerge in 1988, Solidarity had for some years lost the capacity to act as a social movement, following the repression of the union during the period of martial law and the official suspension of its activities. When the opportunity for negotiation again presented itself, its representatives acted in combination with leading figures from reformist circles in the communist party as members of a relatively restricted opposition elite rather than presenting themselves as leaders of a multimillion-member movement. Nevertheless, once the negotiations bore fruit and the opportunity to participate in elections with even a limited scope for democratic choice emerged, Solidarity again gathered massive support and received the active allegiance of the great majority of the population.

In contrast to Poland, Czechoslovakia saw a mass popular movement well up in November 1989 and the collapse of communist rule soon after. Here, too, the beginning of the transition to democracy was the result of a process of elite negotiation, but one carried out in a context very different from that of Czechoslovakia's neighbours. The opposition had long roots which led back to the previous decade and the formation of the human rights group, Charter 77, which provided a focus for political opposition during the lengthy period of Soviet-inspired normalization. It remained, however, a very small body and neither it nor any of the other independent initiatives that emerged during the 1980s could offer any significant threat to the solidly-based communist establishment. Leading members of the opposition founded Civic Forum as part of a broader movement only on 19 November 1989, two days after the mass demonstration and brutal police retaliation it attracted, which proved to be the beginning of the final phase of communist power in Czechoslovakia.

That demonstration further underlined the political significance for Central Europe of an indigenous new social movement similar to those seen in the West. After round-table negotiations in early December between Civic Forum in company with its Slovak counterpart, Public Against Violence, and surviving members of the establishment grouped around Prime Minister Adamec, the balance of power rapidly shifted towards the popular movements to the extent that Alexander Dubček had been elected Federal Assembly chairman and Václav Havel the country's president before the end of the month. However, the tasks they were now faced with, in terms of guiding the processes of formal democratization and preparing the way for parliamentary elections, were not those generally thought to be appropriate to new social movements. Civic

Forum stood out against its transformation into a political party, and retained much of its original character for a surprisingly long time, at least until the internal changes carried out in October 1990. This was associated with the strong commitment to a broadly-based movement, antipathy towards traditional party structures, and the decided views on this matter held by the inner circle of Havel and a handful of experienced activists who occupied a particularly strong position within the movement. Major components of this ethic were perpetuated within the Civic Movement, one of the groups that emerged with the break-up of the Civic Forum in February 1991.

The processes and organizations which played a leading role in the early stages of Central Europe's transition to democracy were, then, by no means always ones that might be expected, or those that seemed most likely to foster the development of a Western-style liberal democracy. They did, however, influence the conditions under which the processes of post-communist development were to take place. Amongst the already diverse experiences of post-communist democratization the greatest contrasts could be seen in Poland, the scene of the first and most influential movement to emerge in Central Europe and also the first example of a negotiated political settlement between opposition representatives and the communist establishment. The outcome of this complex situation had been a qualified solution in the form of the partially free elections of June 1989, which turned out to be the trigger for the whole process of decommunization and system change in Central Europe.

THE ELECTORAL OPENING TO POST-COMMUNISM

Following the elections in June 1989 a devastatingly low level of support for the communist-led ruling coalition suddenly became evident in Poland. It was the first of a series of elections in the region that marked the beginning of the transition from communism and the opening to a new political order. The limited participation of opposition forces in communist-dominated elections thus paved the way to the creation of a *de facto* competitive party system – one in which, however, the challenging force showed no desire to present itself as a political party or formal opposition.

Solidarity had entered the election with the intention of acting as a stabilizing presence endowed with a capacity for exercising political influence, rather than of mounting a direct challenge to the communist power structure. Neither were there many signs pointing to the emergence of a competitive party system in the following months. The advantages of a popular, mass movement sustaining the authority of a government which felt itself constrained to take potentially unpopular economic measures were self-evident and proved their value for a lengthy period. The political climate remained remarkably mild during the months which followed the implementation of finance minister Balcerowicz's tightly structured programme of economic stabilization and recovery in January 1990, despite its severe consequences for Polish industry and the living standards of much of the population.

There were certainly few major signs of the development of alternative political forces, new parties or the institutionalization of a political opposition. Local elections were held in May 1990 and, although more than a hundred organizations and political groupings were reported to have taken part in the campaign, final results tended to confirm the existing constellation of political forces. Candidates proposed by Solidarity and its civic committees took 4 per cent of the 51,987 seats (48 per cent if the now autonomous Rural Solidarity was included) and a further 38 per cent were occupied by candidates who were independent or not affiliated to any particular party. In practice, therefore, it seemed that it was the form of the social movement that continued to appeal to the Polish public rather than that of the formally constituted political party. Only the Polish Peasant Party (PSL) won as many as 6.5 per cent of the seats in the local elections, while all other parties received a far smaller proportion. Social Democracy, (SdRP) the reformed rump of the communist party (PZPR) gained 0.2 per cent, while right-wing groups and the Confederation of Independent Poland (KPN) each took 0.1 per cent of the available seats. Solidarity and its representatives continued, then, to dominate the political arena during the first year of non-communist rule in Poland.

While Poland had in many senses led the way in laying the foundations for democracy in Central Europe and hastening movement away from the Soviet model – particularly in the organization of at least partly free elections and the installation of a non-communist led government – other countries were not far behind. If we measure the progress of Western-style democracy by the holding of free elections and the development of competitive political parties, others soon began to outpace Polish developments. Round-table negotiations in Hungary opened in June 1989, just after the Polish elections, and it was already clear that free elections rather than just a non-communist share in power were now a main issue. While disagreement continued about the procedures for filling the office of president and the appropriate sequence for the early stages of the transition to democracy, accommodation was soon reached about the electoral law that should be adopted and the advisability of arranging a general election with all due dispatch. The date for the holding of general elections was finally set for March 1990.

The overall situation in Central Europe had already changed considerably within just a few months. In Poland, the limited political influence open to non-communist forces after the round-table agreement and then the carefully balanced government put together by Mazowiecki in the summer of 1989 gave way to the virtually unqualified rule of Solidarity representatives for a number of months. Hungary, however, faced the prospect of free elections with several contending political forces already in place and with the tensions and conflicts characteristic of Western liberal democracy being given free rein. The implications of this for post-communist developments in Hungary were mixed. The undoubted authority of the Solidarity government during late 1989 had given it the capacity to confront the catastrophic state of the Polish economy and move quickly to take remedial action in the form of the Balcerowicz programme of economic stabilization and recovery. In Hungary during late 1989, however, the communist government of Miklós Németh remained in place without any democratic legitimacy and with little ability to take the unpopular measures that were required by the IMF and seemed to be unavoidable if the looming collapse of the Hungarian economy was to be warded off.[9] It also promised to be, as noted Hungarian academic Elemer Hankiss pointed out, more difficult to transform a country quickly when it had a multi-party democratic parliament than when it was led by a single charismatic leader or the 'revolutionary aristocracy' than had taken charge in Czechoslovakia.[10]

On the other hand, the situation in Hungary was not an unfavourable one for the free play and development of contending political forces. While the election campaign was marked by some ill-tempered conflict and political exchanges, the situation remained quite positive for the emergence of a Western-style party-system and the development of political pluralism. Democratic Forum and the Alliance of Free Democrats were, it soon emerged, the leading political contenders, smaller political parties and groupings being discouraged by the 4 per cent vote threshold prescribed by the election law, one element in a framework described as the most complex electoral system in Europe.[11] In the two-round elections held in March and April 1990 Democratic Forum won 165 of the 386 parliamentary seats and was able to form a centre-right government with the support of the Independent Smallholders' Party's 44 seats and the Christian Democrats' 21. The election not only produced the nucleus of a stable government but also the promise of an effective opposition, with the Free Democrats occupying 91 seats and the Young Democrats a further 21. The recently formed Hungarian Socialist Party gained 33 seats, although the rump conservative force of the HSWP fell victim to the 4 per cent rule and did not survive to contest the second ballot. The result of the election could, then, be judged relatively successful in setting Hungary on a steady course towards parliamentary democracy.

One source of disappointment to the Hungarians concerning the elections was that the East German government had been forced to bring its general election forward to 18 March 1990. This denied Hungary – an undeniable leader in terms of the retreat from communism and all-round advance to parliamentary democracy – the distinction of being the first to hold free, competitive elections in post-communist Central Europe. By the time the elections were held in the German Democratic Republic, however, there remained little of importance to be decided by political means and scant sense of a newly liberated society determining its own future. As attempts were made to keep pace with the rapidly changing situation, each decision seemed to be further outpaced by new domestic and international developments. Prime Minister Modrow announced in February 1990, two days after his return from talks with Gorbachev, that unification now formed part of his official programme, thus affirming that the Soviet leader also now recognized the inevitability of unification.

Not much more than three months after the opening of the Berlin Wall, West and East Germans now seemed to share a general conception of the German future and an agreed framework for the course of coming developments. The final attempt to maintain some elements of a vision deriving from the position and experience of the GDR was made with Modrow's claim that a united Germany should also be a neutral one. The suggestion received short shrift from West Germany and the NATO authorities (and was, indeed, highly reminiscent of the equally ill-received proposal made by Stalin in 1952). By March, then, there was little left for the East German elections to decide apart from the electoral base that West German Christian Democrats, Social Democrats and other political parties could build for themselves in the East. There was already little political space left for New Forum, the movement that had only recently pointed the way to a new East Germany – and had also seen it retaining an identity distinct and separate from that of the capitalist Federal Republic.

Most of the electorate were primarily concerned with securing higher wages and approaching the standard of living enjoyed in the West. The only major issue that remained, according to one of the new politicians in the East, was to negotiate the terms of surrender.[12] The new *Volkskammer* (East German legislature) that was elected on 8 March 1990 accordingly saw a striking victory for the Christian Democratic Union (CDU), a party which had formed part of the SED-dominated National Front throughout the GDR's history, but which had over the past months come under the strong influence of its considerably more powerful West German counterpart. Gaining 40.8 per cent of the votes (on a 93.4 per cent turnout) the CDU ended up with nearly twice the number of seats of its nearest rival, the socialist SPD.[13] While this brought CDU leader Lothar de Maizière into the post of prime minister, it was really the influence of West German leader (and head of its CDU) Helmut Kohl over remaining developments in the GDR that was most enhanced. The only other party to receive more than 10 per cent of the vote in the March election was the PDS (or reformed communist party) which was not, however, brought into the broad coalition government formed by de Maizière.

Matters also moved swiftly in Czechoslovakia, where, despite few signs of mass opposition being evident throughout the 1980s, communist power also rapidly crumbled during December 1989. The Czechoslovak communists were not slow in drawing appropriate conclusions from developments in the neighbouring countries, and its leaders instructed members who were deputies to the Federal Assembly to accept the Government of National Understanding with its majority of non-communist ministers. This first post-communist government was sworn in on 10 December, with communist members following the directive of the party leadership to vote for the removal from the Constitution of the clause on the leading role of the party. Co-operation was extended to recalling the majority of the party's deputies from the Assembly, and the co-option in January 1990 of substitutes for them along the lines of the agreement reached with Civic Forum and other independent groupings at the Czechoslovak round table. Husák himself had remained in post as president to swear in the new government on 10 December and then also resigned, leaving the path clear for Václav Havel.

The way was now open for the organization of free elections and these were set for 8 and 9 June 1990, only two months after those held in Hungary which had been the conclusion of a lengthy period of communist reform and progressive political demo-cratization. Unlike Poland and Hungary, too, the Czechoslovak electorate responded to the recently unveiled prospect of democratic participation by recording a high turnout of 96 per cent. This produced a clear majority for Civic Forum and its Slovakian counterpart, Public Against Violence, in both Houses of the Federal Assembly. Civic Forum also predominated in the National Council of the Czech Republic. Following the elections, Marián Čalfa (who had subsequently joined Public Against Violence) was again confirmed as prime minister and head of a wholly non-communist government in charge of a coalition of CF and PAV representatives in association with the Christian Democratic Movement of Slovakia. On 5 July 1990 the reconstituted Federal Assembly also re-elected Havel as president.

VAGARIES OF THE POLISH COURSE

Throughout the region, the task of creating the conditions for stable democracy and parliamentary government now had to be faced and the foundations of an effective market economy and modern capitalist development laid. Czechoslovakia, as noted above, was in some important ways fortunate in being able to deal rapidly and effectively with the initial tasks of democratic construction before turning to the problems of economic reform and develop-ment. Hungary was also relatively advanced in terms of the development of political pluralism and democratic government before the full impact of the need for a reorientation of economic policy was faced. The transition to democracy in terms of the holding of free parliamentary elections contested by a range of independent parties was only the first step in the move away from communist rule in Central Europe. It was one which, at the end of 1990, still had to be faced by Poland, where the half-way house of the round-table agreement had been sufficient to sustain the first stages of the move towards liberal democracy and stabilization of Poland's economy.

The situation in Poland was rather different in several ways. Conditions for economic development and recovery were no better in the 1980s than they had been during the previous decade, when Gierek's dash for growth had left the country with enormous debts and the economy in a state of major imbalance. Poland thus entered the post-communist period soon after the round of strikes in 1988 in a state of considerable economic debility, with large debts, public services disorganized and impoverished, and the country now suffering major ecological damage. The total cost of environmental damage there was estimated to be equivalent to 10–15 per cent of GDP. It was, indeed, very much a regional problem, being centred in the heavily industrialized south-west of the country, affecting the adjacent areas of East Germany and northern Bohemia which were dependent on high levels of use of brown coal.[14]

The decline in national income had been halted and some stabilization achieved in 1983, but even that level of recovery was not sustained during the succeeding years. In 1988 per capita national income was still some way below the level that had prevailed 10 years earlier, while 1989 saw further intensification of the economic crisis and the arrival of galloping inflation. From May 1989 production in the state sector went into decline and, during the first nine months of the year, production was 1.6 per cent lower than in the same period of 1988; exports were down by 1.8 per cent and imports up by 3 per cent. Average pay over the nine-month period was, however, up by 177 per cent on the previous year, with retail prices for goods and services higher by 120 per cent.

The political vigour and optimism that accompanied the establishment of Solidarity in 1980 had, moreover, been dispersed amidst the rigours of martial law. The formation of a non-communist government in 1989 was greeted with restrained enthusiasm and little hope of immediate improvement. A shift of gear in the rate of increase in prices and wages occurred from the beginning of August 1989 as the incumbent Rakowski government decided to set prices more in line with available supplies, with the declared intention of creating a more balanced market. Few, however, had envisaged the severe consequences that would follow from the adoption of finance minister Balcerowicz's stabilization policy and its implementation from the beginning of 1990. Balcerowicz's strategy involved the use of economic shock therapy and was heavily influenced by Harvard economist Jeffrey Sachs, who had organized the application of similar measures to even worse problems in Bolivia. It was a two-stage programme that involved, first, the ending of market shortages and control of inflation and then, from 1 January 1990, the rapid transition to a market economy through deregulation and privatization.

From the beginning of the month the Polish złoty was made convertible with other currencies (at approximately the rate previously prevailing in the black market). This allowed domestic enterprises to purchase foreign currency and import goods and permitted exporters to convert their foreign earnings into złotys. Many trade barriers were lifted, the free flow of imports was facilitated, and measures were taken to encourage Polish exports. Most government price controls were lifted and prices allowed to respond to supply and demand in the attempt to achieve a market equilibrium. Many state subsidies were eliminated, with the intention of forcing enterprises to become profitable or go out of production. The monetary screw was tightened by anti-inflationary restrictions on wage increases, reduction in money supply and increases in interest rates. Inflation thus fell dramatically in 1990 – but industrial output also declined by 30 per cent, wage levels fell by 40 per cent and unemployment rose to over 0.5 million by mid-year and to 1.089 million by the end of November 1990. The cost of food purchases rose to account for more than 55 per cent of household expenditure, the highest level for over 30 years. Not surprisingly, discontent grew and popular disillusion became more widespread.

Dissatisfaction with the Solidarity-sponsored government and its economic policies spread during the spring and early summer of 1990. At the same time, relations within the Solidarity elite worsened and Lech Wałęsa, leader of the now politically marginalized trade union, who occupied no position in either parliament or the government, launched a campaign to accelerate the pace of political and economic change. Thus began the 'war at the top' which fragmented the Solidarity movement, hastened processes of political division, and put the idea of party formation firmly on the political agenda. While political groupings and specialized parties had proliferated, few had much of a following and there was little sign of popular enthusiasm for the formation of political parties or the breakup of the existing Solidarity movement. Initially, indeed, it was not with the development of parties and their parliamentary representation that the conflicts within the elite were concerned.

Other areas of the political system were at issue. By early 1990 the political situation in Central Europe looked quite different from that of the summer of 1989, when Mazowiecki's Solidarity-led government had emerged slowly and cautiously and careful attention had been paid to the satisfaction of what were seen as continuing Soviet interests. By the spring of 1990 Poland was just one among several post-communist countries, the PZPR was no longer in existence and what was left of the communist elite had only a minimal organizational presence in Polish public life. In concrete terms, the occupation of the presidential office by General Jaruzelski – not just a relic of the communist establishment but also a stark reminder of martial law and the military underpinnings of communist rule in Poland – already appeared highly anachronistic. As Wałęsa's role became increasingly marginal, both as leader of the Solidarity union during a period of Solidarity government, and as head of only one of a number of union organizations (the old regime-sponsored confederation of unions, OPZZ, had twice as many members as Solidarity at the end of 1989), it was hardly surprising that his attention was drawn to the question of the presidency.

Significantly, though, it soon became evident that this interest met with little sympathy from the Warsaw intellectuals who had increasingly dominated Poland's political establishment since the installation of the Mazowiecki government and the melting away of communist power. For Wałęsa, very much the worker rather than intellectual and at home in Gdańsk rather than Warsaw in more ways than one, this response only strengthened the conviction that the process of political change needed to be not just faster but also more thoroughgoing. Influences from the longstanding divisions of Polish society and significant personal antagonisms thus also played a part in the decomposition of the Solidarity movement and the acceleration of existing processes of party formation. Both contribute to an explanation of the bitterness of the conflict sur-rounding the subsequent presidential elections and the prominent role played by personality in the development of Poland's party system.

These features became more prominent with Wałęsa's dismissal of the respected Solidarity parliamentary club chairman, Henryk

Wujec, from his post on 1 June 1990. Support was also withdrawn from Adam Michnik as editor of the daily *Election Gazette* (*Gazeta Wyborcza*), established in 1989 to inform and mobilize support for Solidarity candidates. The growing tensions took on more organized form with the establishment of a 'Centre Coalition' in Gdańsk by Senator Jaroslaw Kaczyński, a close associate of Wałęsa. In Cracow a 'Citizens' Accord' was formed during June to provide an infrastructure to channel public support for the government, soon providing a basis for the emergence of a Centre Alliance. In July, a Citizens' Movement for Democratic Action was founded (ROAD, following its Polish initials) with a view to encouraging the holding of new elections as soon as possible and mobilizing support for them. It denied any left- or right-wing affiliation but took a stand against Wałęsa's pronouncements and expressed broad support for the Mazowiecki government. It was, according to its leaders, situated rather to the 'West of Centre' – referring here to the political group with which it was in competition.[15] Divisions grew within the Citizens' Parliamentary Club (OKP) which was formed of the deputies elected in 1989 under the banner of Solidarity by the network of Citizens' Committees. This brought about the dissolution of its Presidium in October, although the final split in the group did not occur until January 1991.

The movement for a more decisive confrontation between the different political currents was clearly growing stronger, and the occasion finally arrived with Jaruzelski's decision in September 1990 to resign the presidency. The conflict between Wałęsa and Mazowiecki and their respective supporters understandably emerged as the immediate focus of the presidential campaign, but in the first electoral round Mazowiecki (with 18 per cent of the votes) was defeated both by Wałęsa (gaining 40 per cent) and a somewhat mysterious Polish émigré, Stanisław Tymiński (23 per cent). Tymiński had emigrated from Poland some twenty years earlier and made a considerable fortune in Canada. He appeared to have some support from security forces and former communist activists but his career also held considerable attractions for hard-up Poles. Turnout for the first round of the election was 61 per cent, higher than that for the local elections (when it reached only 43 per cent) and slightly below that of June 1989 (62 per cent). These figures were markedly lower than in Czechoslovakia or the GDR but were not greatly different from those recorded in Hungary (63 per cent in the first round of the general election of March 1990 and 40 per cent in local elections held the following September).

In the light of such experience it should not be surprising that relatively high levels of anomie (around 70 per cent of the Polish population identified in one study) were reported to have been found in Poland, and that such levels of personal dislocation and confusion were rising in the wake of recent social changes. Tymiński voters were found to show higher levels of anomie than supporters of the other five candidates and Poles who had decided not to vote.[16] In December 1990, though, Lech Wałęsa was finally elected to the presidency by a decisive majority, gaining 74 per cent of votes cast against Tymiński's 26 per cent. The relatively low turnout in successive elections, apparent instability of electoral behaviour and evidence of the electorate's confusion and psychological disorientation all suggested that the emergence of a stable multi-party system in Poland would be an arduous process. But while Mazowiecki had resigned after his poor performance in the presidential election, Solidarity forces remained strong in parliament and the influence of the Mazowiecki government persisted in relatively undiluted form.

Wałęsa's election to the presidency thus changed little in terms of government policy, and the focus of political conflict now switched to questions surrounding the timing of the coming parliamentary elections and the nature of the electoral law to be adopted as the basis for them. The president's hope that they would be held within a matter of months was not fulfilled and they were eventually planned for the end of October 1991 as disagreement continued over the electoral framework within which they would be held. An initial proposal from the Solidarity camp for a simple majority system had been rejected by the *Sejm* as far back as June 1990, largely because of fear on the part of representatives of the former establishment (who still, of course, held 65 per cent of parliamentary seats) that a single political force might sweep all before it. That would have meant that the former communists would be deprived of all representation and influence. Nor were all within Solidarity convinced that the achievement of stable, party-based government should be a prime objective of the electoral system – resistance to the idea of party persisted and significant numbers felt that the idea of the political party itself belonged to the past.

The outcome of a proportional or mixed majority-proportional electoral system became virtually inevitable. Further conflict and disagreements within the parliament (as well as others between it and the president) meant that the process was a protracted one, and many felt dissatisfied with the complicated nature of the voting system decided on. Political groupings and associations had, of course, begun surfacing and often pursued a reasonably auto-nomous public existence even before the demise of the communist system. By April 1989 over 1,200 associations of a general character had been registered in Warsaw and around 2,000 of them were estimated to be operating at a national level. New legislation which permitted the formal registration of political parties only took effect in August 1990, though, and under its guidelines 42 organizations had been registered by the end of January 1991.[17] By the time preparations for the October elections were complete, voting lists to the *Sejm* were presented by 112 different organizations – although representatives of the different groupings did not stand in each of the 37 constituencies.

In Warsaw, for example, 35 lists were presented, each containing from 3 to as many as 17 candidates – leaving the voter to opt for any one of the lists. A preference could also be expressed for any one of the candidates, which would have the effect of moving the candidate up the list and enhancing personal chances of election.) With a low turnout of 43 per cent, it appeared that the anomic condition of the Polish electorate identified the previous year had taken firmer hold. Now, however, it appeared to be further exacerbated by the complicated voting mechanism, the extended wrangle that had attended its preparation, increasing disillusion with the course and tenor of national political life, and (by no means least) the continuing burdens of everyday existence in post-communist Poland. The low turnout favoured parties with firmer support and stronger organization. It also helped to explain the success of the ex-communist Union of the Democratic Left (SLD), which gained 60 parliamentary seats, only 2 behind the Democratic Union (UD), which had been formed on the basis of the support group organized to promote Mazowiecki's campaign for the presidency.

Five other groups, including the post-communist Peasant Party (PSL), Catholic Election Action (WAK), the nationalist Confederation of Independent Poland (KPN) and the Congress of Liberal Democrats (KLD), each obtained 37 or more seats in the 460–place parliament. The proportional emphasis in the electoral system finally adopted had indeed borne out predictions of a fragmented parliament – but this also reflected the nature of an increasingly diverse society and its fragmented political culture. An artificially contrived majority might have made the process of government formation easier – but it would also have reduced the *Sejm's* capacity to establish its legitimacy as a representative body, created further problems in the sphere of government powers and weakened its authority in terms of policy implementation. As many as 10 groups gained significant parliamentary representation (12 seats or more) and accounted for 78.1 per cent of total votes cast. A further 18 parties received lower levels of representation.

It was not clear how a single-party majority or one constructed by a small number of parties could have been realistically achieved (at any rate, through a single ballot), as it already took five parties to form a simple majority in the 460–seat parliament. Apart from the difference in post-communist electoral systems within East-Central Europe, then, it was unlikely that a reasonably clear-cut parliamentary majority could in any case have been achieved in Poland.[18] Six parties took 375 (97.2 per cent) of the 386 seats in the Hungarian parliament, while Civic Forum gained around half the votes for the two houses of the Federal Assembly and the National Council of the Czech Republic (rather more in terms of the proportion of seats). Public Against Violence was somewhat less successful, but received around a third of votes cast in Slovakia. It was difficult to see how such forms of representation and majorities were available in Poland without doing considerable violence to the principle of democratic representation and leaving large parts of Polish society feeling as though their vote did not count.

After several weeks a group of five parties, with 205 parliamentary seats, emerged with the proposal of Jan Olszewksi of the Centre Accord (PC) as prime minister. He was not the candidate favoured by President Wałęsa, but his candidature was eventually accepted and a government assembled under his leadership and supported by his own party, the Christian National Union and Peasant Accord was endorsed by the *Sejm* just before Christmas 1991. That act, however, did not put an end to the political and governmental uncertainties surrounding Poland's first freely elected post-war parliament. Issues of economic policy and budgetary proposals were particularly contentious, and Finance Minister Lutkowski had already resigned before the government's budgetary guidelines were rejected by parliament in March 1992. Attempts to construct a more secure parliamentary base for the government were not successful, and conflict with the president persisted over a range of issues. Following a maladroit, and largely illegitimate, attempt by the interior minister to bolster the government's position in May 1992 by releasing details of leading politicians' supposed security affiliations, Olszewski was voted out of office and the nomination of Waldemar Pawlak, leader of the Peasant Party (PSL), as prime minister received parliamentary endorsement on 5 June.

This initiative turned out to be a short-lived one as Pawlak proved unable to form a government that was capable of securing parliamentary support. (This was, perhaps, not surprising as he led a party which only three years earlier had formed part of the communist-led coalition.) It did serve to strengthen President Wałęsa's position, though, and underline his ability to produce novel solutions to difficult political problems. Pawlak's mission was followed by that of Hanna Suchocka who succeeded in forming a seven-party coalition in July 1992 and leading a government that saw Poland through to the year's end. Suchocka was a member of the Democratic Union but managed also to secure the support of the Christian National Union, particularly because of her willing ness to carry on with the preparation of legislation for a bill out-lawing abortion. This was passed by the *Sejm* at the end of 1992 with the addition of some provisions that were not to the liking of the Christian Union, and relations within the coalition became increasingly unstable.

Poland's economic problems remained particularly difficult, although by the end of the year the shock therapy seemed to be paying off and the national product had (unlike that in other countries of Central Europe) stopped falling. However, unemploy-ment continued to grow throughout 1992, the value of earnings fell by 6 per cent and an unusually strong wave of strikes spread through-out the country during the summer. Parliamentary agreement on the measures needed to keep the nation's budgetary deficit within limits was again only achieved with some difficulty, but this con-dition of government survival was finally secured in February 1993. Difficulties with public sector workers and treatment of the agricul-tural sector persisted, though, and a peasant party left the govern-ment coalition, making its parliamentary base even more tenuous. The inevitable soon happened and the Solidarity group of deputies tabled a motion of no-confidence in the government. Nevertheless, its outcome was by no means a foregone conclusion. Several opposition groupings saw little possibility of forming any new coalition but were not yet prepared to face further parliamentary elections which, in their view, the electorate was hardly likely to welcome. On 28 May 1993, though, the vote of no-confidence in the Suchocka government was passed – by just one vote. (It was two members of the Christian National Union, actually part of the governing coalition, who failed to vote – one of whom had only recently been sacked from his ministerial post by Prime Minister Suchocka). The president had the choice either of dismissing the government or of dissolving parliament, and it was the latter course he chose. New elections were therefore called for 19 September. This time an electoral threshold of 5 per cent was imposed (or 8 per cent in the case of coalitions) and the results were dramatically different. The post-communist Union of the Democratic Left (SLD) and Polish Peasant Party (PSL) gained a clear majority and formed a government under the leadership of W. Pawlak. No unequivocally right-wing parties received parliamentary representation, while Polish dissatisfaction with the consequences of post-communist liberal reform was also evident.

PATTERNS OF CHANGE IN GERMANY AND HUNGARY

The consequences of several years of post-communist rule and, particularly, the economic effects of the Balcerowicz plan clearly had a great influence on the electorate and the way in which the future prospects of economic and political development were viewed in Poland. Indeed, the timing of elections throughout Central Europe had a major effect on their outcomes, and it was clear that the sequence and pace of events were a significant factor in the different outcomes and patterns of national development detectable in the region. The rapid rate of change in East Germany was particularly striking, and post-communist leaders in the GDR were soon struggling to maintain any semblance of control over the situation. As the German Democratic Republic moved swiftly towards, firstly, currency union with the Federal Republic and then direct political union, the effects of direct exposure to Western economic forces became dramatically evident. Currency union was achieved on 1 July 1990, converting GDR salaries and pensions (and the first 4,000 ostmarks of savings) into Western Deutschmarks on a 1/1 basis (additional savings were exchanged at a 1/2 rate). The *Treuhand* agency was also set up to administer a privatization programme.

Disagreement over the timetable for political union continued, however, and tensions persisted in the post-communist governing coalition of East Germany as the different parties attempted to maximize their chances in the coming all-German elections. The Liberals and Social Democrats (SPD), for example, argued for union before the elections due to be held on 2 December. This would mean that the 5 per cent electoral threshold would also apply in the east and lessen the threat of a split in votes for the left and centre parties. The accelerating rate of change could not expunge recent memories of the unsavoury methods of communist rule and the degree to which they had involved those who were now caught up in the headlong dash for the West. First SPD leader Ibrahim Böhme and then Wolfgang Schnur, head of Democratic Awakening, were charged with *Stasi* links and thus forced to resign.[19] Free Democrat minister Axel Viehweger was similarly charged in September 1990 as was, in December 1990, Lothar de Maizière (by that stage minister in the all-German government and CDU deputy chairman). De Maizière was cleared but allegations persisted and he resigned his parliamentary seat in September 1991. These were just the most prominent figures involved: in summer 1990 a list was published which claimed that 68 government members and parliamentarians had *Stasi* connections.

Following currency union it was the progressive collapse of the East German economy that attracted most public attention. By early August a state of virtually total ruin was admitted by de Maizière, and his earlier determination to argue for the postponement of political union and the holding of all-German elections was reversed. Estimates of the East German budget deficit grew higher and higher, and analysts began predicting that two-thirds of East German firms might be forced to close by the end of the year. The contrast between the quality and productivity of the two German economies was far greater than many had anticipated and mass unemployment had become an immediate prospect for much of the East. A matter of weeks after economic unification, Eastern premier Lothar de Maizière proposed, with the agreement of Western Chancellor and fellow Christian Democrat Helmut Kohl, to advance the voting timetable and hold all-German elections on 14 October (although the implications of this for the timing of political union were becoming increasingly unclear). The extent of the East German economic problems uncovered in the process of economic union convinced both leaders that their prospects in terms of party politics were better if the electoral timetable was advanced and the electorate not allowed to experience further economic disappointment before the vote was registered.

As the catastrophic economic situation in the East revealed itself (with the unemployment rate doubling during the month of July alone) de Maizière was therefore content, in the interests of social and political stability, to accept a date for political union as early as 14 October, with all-German elections being held somewhat later. On the last day of August 1990 the treaty of unity was signed, at the insistence of the GDR leader, in East Berlin's Crown Prince Palace – a final, if minor, political success. Political union was again brought forward and finally occurred over 2/3 October. When elections were finally held during mid-October to restore parliamentary authority in the former East German *Länder*, or states, the Christian Democrats confirmed their political supremacy by gaining 45 per cent of the vote in contrast to the 25 per cent taken by the Social Democrats. Full national elections within the unified country were held in December 1990 and these both underlined the success of Kohl's policy of accelerated change and set the seal on the formal political integration of the former East within Germany as a whole.

Political and economic developments were, therefore, closely linked, with the growing evidence of East German economic weakness having a strong influence on the pace of political change and the range of political options available to the post-communist leadership. In the event, both East Germany and its leaders virtually collapsed into the arms of the West. In distinction to the Poles and East Germans, the Hungarians moved swiftly towards general elections and the installation of new political structures, but showed a greater degree of caution with regard to economic change and the dismantling of the existing system. The process of forming a government coalition was itself a lengthy one and the inclusion of the Independent Smallholders' Party had significant implications for economic policy. Having insisted, not surprisingly, on taking the agricultural portfolio, it also held to its electoral commitment to return all agricultural land to those who had owned it in 1947. Many had doubts about the wisdom and practicality of this objective, and tensions arising from the issue fed into other uncertainties surrounding the activity of the new government.

In other respects, political order was more smoothly established. Democratic Forum (HDF) won the agreement of the Free Democrats (AFD) to modify the original requirement of a two-thirds parliamentary majority for the passage of major legislation and itself adopted proposals from the Free Democrats concerning the election of the president and agreed to support their candidate for the post, the writer Árpád Göncz. As in the case of dealings with the Independent Smallholders, however, relations within the party were the source of numerous problems. A further weakness of the Democratic Forum was a lack of economic experts, and the lead in proposing legislation in the area of economics was in fact taken by the Free Democrats. Prime Minister Ántáll had made public his reservations about the shock therapy applied to the Polish economy and argued for a less radical policy. The government had requested, and received, parliamentary agreement on a period of grace to consider the options for economic policy, but it was by no means clear that it was approaching a firm decision on the appropriate strategy to be adopted.

No effective counter-inflationary policy had been applied and new price rises (in a reflection of pre-Balcerowicz Polish policy) added to inflationary pressures; the government appeared unable to contain the budget deficit and satisfy the conditions for IMF support. Prospects for the critical process of privatization also seemed to be undermined by the absence of any clear conception of ownership. The emphasis in this area switched from workers's councils to the enhancement of the power of small private owners; plans for an influx of foreign investment were contrasted with others favouring protection from the involvement of foreign capital. The lack of a definite policy, however, only tended to focus attention on the idea of reprivatization and the contentious objective of returning farmland to its 1947 owners.[20] Economic developments in the closing phase of communist rule had, moreover, been rather different in both Hungary and Poland from other countries of the Soviet bloc in terms of the involvement of the communist *nomenklatura* in different forms of privatization of state property, and this also showed signs of influencing developments and future policy in this area.

The low turnout (46 per cent) in the second round of the Hungarian general election had already shown that popular support for the new government was likely to be quite weak, and this became even more evident in some areas during the local elections held in September. In urban areas only 33 per cent of the electorate went to the polls, and the 40 per cent minimum required for a valid election was therefore not met. Following the experience of the previous months, too, support for the parties of the governing coalition fell and both Free Democrats and FIDESZ performed better than they had in the spring election. The failure to evolve an effective economic policy and to come up with a realistic alternative to the Polish measures certainly played a part in the growth of popular disappointment with the government. The government's economic programme was finally published in September 1990 and met with immediate opposition. The legislative process was already behind schedule and the atmosphere of confusion seemed set to continue.

Relations within the government coalition, particularly those concerning the Independent Smallholders, did not improve and confidence in the National Assembly continued to plummet. On top of this, on 25 October 1990 the government announced a two-thirds rise in oil prices – following a drop in deliveries from the Soviet Union and the increase in world prices after the Iraqi invasion of Kuwait. Budapest taxi drivers immediately came out on strike and were soon followed by freight carriers, bringing the whole country to a virtual standstill. The government's response to this crisis was also ill-judged (its activity not being helped by the poor health of the prime minister at the time), and the situation was only retrieved by the statesmanlike action of President Göncz who adopted a relatively even-handed approach. Various trade unions and representative organizations were involved in negotiations with the government. A key point made (and accepted) was that the drivers felt penalized by the influence of forces beyond their control, and that they were also victims of the government's failure to control the budget deficit by other means.

The affair thus uncovered both the weakness of a government that had initially seemed to cope with the early political demands of post-communist development and build on its initial phases rather successfully, and the dangers of an initial gradualism in economic policy which had sought to avoid the harsh effects of the Polish strategy. Government authority and that of the recently established parties had not fared well, although the president's actions and effectiveness of the new interest groups and representative institutions received more public approval. In this situation earlier conceptions were revived and calls for a grand coalition of the HDF and AFD and a further review of the Hungarian post-communist order were strengthened once more. Prime Minister Ántáll, however, held to his view expressed immediately after the election in early 1990 that such a coalition would be counter-productive to the development of democracy in Hungary, and that the free development of relations between independent parties was a critical aspect of post-communist evolution.

Ántáll's refusal to be stampeded into any major change in the pattern of party relations largely paid off. The period that followed the taxi-drivers' strike was not without its political conflicts and economic progress remained disappointingly slow and inadequate in its results for many. But overall, and particularly in comparison with some of the tensions developing in its Central European neighbours, the situation was not a negative one. In a survey compiled at the end of 1991, it was possible to conclude that Hungary had a functioning government, parliament and legal system, and could be considered the most successful among the former communist bloc countries in setting up a market economy.[21] Relations between the ruling Democratic Forum and the country's second largest party, the Free Democrats, who constituted the major opposition, deteriorated and numerous points of contention arising from fundamental areas of political conflict emerged. But even in a comprehensive summary of criticisms compiled by Tamas Bauer, a member of the AFD's National Council, the conclusion was hardly devastating. The Ántáll government could not really be judged any better than the communist administration than had preceded it – but it was not any worse either: the economy had not collapsed, there had been no violent social upheavals, and no open conflicts with Hungary's neighbours had broken out. In Poland – still struggling to emerge from major economic recession and finding it increasingly difficult to sustain the processes of parliamentary government, or in Czechoslovakia – faced with the challenge of the Slovak independence movement after the elections of June 1992, criticism from a comparable source would hardly have been so mild.

There was no lack of major political problems, however. Hungary had seen the most fundamental constitutional revision within Central Europe, and the shift away from communist rule towards liberal democracy was achieved in that country far more than elsewhere through processes of constitutional change. Nevertheless, political tensions between the HDF and AFD developed during 1991 into conflict between Prime Minister Ántáll and President Göncz (who belonged, respectively, to each of the two major parties) over their powers and the authority inherent in the offices they occupied. This arose over interpretations of their respective rights and duties in matters of foreign policy, command over the armed forces and appointments in the mass media. A ruling of the Constitutional Court was made in September 1991, but the president maintained his resistance to rubber-stamping what he regarded as politically tendentious appointments in the television organization.

The alienation of much of the population from the political process continued, and there were no signs that the strong tendencies towards apathy had been overcome. Several by-elections had to be declared invalid because only 10–15 per cent of the electorate turned out to vote. Membership of most political parties stagnated or declined, and the Free Democrats saw the departure of as many as one-third of their members during 1991. Under these discouraging conditions their chairman, Janos Kis, resigned and was replaced by Peter Tolgyessy, whose advent caused much disquiet amongst other sections of the leadership, and who was himself replaced by Ivan Peto at the Alliance's next conference in November 1992. This development seemed to point to the possibility that closer relations with the socialist party might be established. Only FIDESZ, the Alliance of Young Democrats, showed signs of successful development and polls taken at the end of 1991 suggested that they had the support of 34 per cent of the electorate, although in the 1990 elections they had attracted only 5.7 per cent of voters.

Economic progress, while not striking, was by no means negligible. Unemployment continued to rise and involved 7.3 per cent of the workforce by the end of 1991. Industrial production also declined and contributed to a fall in GDP of 7 to 8 per cent over the year. Like other countries of Central Europe, Hungarian exports and its economy in general were shaken by the conversion of the Soviet Union to trade in convertible currency and the disappearance of much of the Eastern market. In stark contrast to the situation only a few years earlier, 70 per cent of Hungary's foreign trade during 1991 was conducted with developed Western countries. This, however, was more a sign of the collapsing Soviet market than of success in redirecting trade flows; only about 20 per cent of Hungary's trade within the COMECON, it appeared, was of a kind and quality capable of being transferred to Western markets. Nevertheless, prospects for future development were certainly not unfavourable. More than $3 billion dollars of foreign investment had flowed into Hungary by the spring of 1992 and it had succeeded in attracting more than half of all the investment that had been directed into Eastern Europe.

While the speed and effectiveness of privatization had received considerable domestic criticism, against a comparative background the record looked rather different and quite rapid progress could be recorded. Measures to centralize and accelerate the process had been taken with the establishment of the State Property Agency in March 1990, although they by no means satisfied all critics.[22] Agreements with US and Japanese car manufacturers began to bear fruit as the advantages of Hungary's location and national resources became evident (Hungarian labour costs were only one-tenth of those in Germany). Thus it was in Hungary during March 1992 that the first passenger car produced in Central Europe by a Western company (an Opel Astra) left the factory. This had particular significance in historical and regional terms, as it was virtually the first car produced in the country since the 1930s. Ironically enough, one of the limited achievements of COMECON in terms of regional integration and production specialization had been to hold back the re-establishment of the Hungarian car manufacturing industry after the war and direct capacity to the production of buses, and it was this admittedly modest success that was now superseded by the beginnings of Hungary's integration with the broader world economy.

While Hungarian Gross Domestic Product continued to decline during 1992 (by around 6 per cent) and the progress of privatization was somewhat sluggish, the picture, then, was certainly not a wholly negative one (particularly in comparison with some other post-communist countries). Hungary, in particular, remained the recipient of considerable inflows of foreign investment, to the tune of some $1 billion in the first three quarters of the year. By the end of 1992 the cumulative total of foreign investment attracted to Hungary had reached $8.7 billion, more than twice as much as directed to the Czech Republic and way above the $2.6 billion invested in Poland.[23]

Hungarian stability was not without its darker side, however. Popular – and populist – opposition was becoming more vociferous and fed racial and ethnic tensions. Attacks on gypsies received some publicity and conflict grew between the liberal and populist wings of the HDF. István Csurka, one of the party's vice presidents, criticized its leadership and government representatives along lines not unlike those heard in Poland for failing to press ahead with more radical changes, tolerating the continuing influence of the former *nomenklatura* and giving in to the demands of the opposition. Particularly controversial was the anti-semitic cast of some of his statements and it was this that particularly threatened to disrupt the unity of the Democratic Forum. At its national congress in January 1993, Ántáll was nevertheless re-elected party chairman and secured the party's support for his centrist policy. Representatives of the radical orientation were elected to the praesidium, though, and it was clear that internal party divisions had not been eliminated. In June the party's national committee finally voted to expel Csurka and three of his supporters from the party, following which he proceeded to establish a separate parliamentary grouping called

Hungarian Justice and Life. It did not, however, take up a position of outright opposition either to the government or to the HDF, and a cautious approach continued to prevail on both sides.

THE BRIEF LIFE OF POST-COMMUNIST CZECHOSLOVAKIA

Somewhat like the experience of Hungary, Czechoslovak developments in the immediate post-communist period were characterized by a relatively smooth process of political transition and movement towards parliamentary government accompanied by growing controversy about the scope and pace of economic change. Certain elements of continuity were involved in this. At the beginning of 1990 the key economic posts were for some time occupied by former members of the Institute of Prognostics, which had produced the main currents of reformist economic thought during the 1980s. Its head, Valtr Komárek, now first deputy prime minister, argued for a moderate pace of market development and the pursuit of structural reforms rather than the rapid liberalization of prices and foreign trade. The new Minister of Finance, Václav Klaus, however, was in favour of more rapid movement towards the market.

While the economic situation in Poland and, to a lesser extent, Hungary had supported arguments for a more radical strategy and a fast rate of liberalization, conditions in Czechoslovakia did not seem to indicate any urgency to introduce such a crash programme. There was no large foreign debt to encourage the adoption of IMF-favoured solutions and signs of serious internal disequilibrium, in terms of consumer shortages and inflationary pressure, were relatively few. The lengthy period of stability seen in post-invasion Czechoslovakia and the absence of marked socio-economic disproportions presented a somewhat misleading image of structural soundness and economic resilience, though, while the foreign currency account looked less promising once the realities of third world debt were taken into account. Klaus and Vladimír Dlouhý, minister responsible for economic affairs, took a more critical view therefore, and held that a policy of gradual change would not be sufficient to transform the Czechoslovak economy to meet modern needs and satisfy the demands of international integration.

Political considerations also entered into the situation in Czechoslovakia as Komárek, who had been involved in the reform movement of 1968, spoke from a social democratic position and did not feel that the government was as yet empowered to take more radical measures, while Klaus was identified with neo-liberalism and a stronger market orientation. These divisions became more apparent in the spring of 1990 and intensified during the election campaign. Major elements of economic legislation were passed in April but had no immediate success, and little radical change appeared to be in train. Financial measures taken by Klaus in January seemed to benefit tourists more than the domestic economy, and conditions for the development of private enterprise were not very favourable. Following the June 1990 elections and the formation of a government in which members of Civic Forum and the Slovak Public Against Violence predominated, however, economic policy took a more radical turn.

Václav Klaus retained his post as minister for finance and Dlouhý was reappointed as minister for the economy, while Komárek now left the government. This provided conditions for the more rigorous pursuit of a liberal economic policy and a greater emphasis on the market. Ethnic considerations were also important in the new coalition, with a government balance of 10 Czechs and 6 Slovaks, while the Slovak Čalfa remained prime minister in tandem with Czech President Havel. This factor, indeed, seemed for a time to take precedence over more strictly economic matters and nationalist sentiment was clearly on the rise in Slovakia during the spring and summer, the Slovak National Party winning 9 of the 75 places reserved for Slovakia in the 150–seat House of Nations (12 per cent) as well as 22 of the 150 seats in the Slovak National Council (nearly 15 per cent). The ethnic issue was, not surprisingly, closely bound up with questions of the redistribution of budgetary resources and national decision-making. This also impinged on the federal commitment to a unified economic policy and the growing preference for a swifter and more rigorously pursued programme of economic transformation.

Slovakia had previously been favoured in terms of heavy industrial development and investment in armaments production, both now sectors of the economy that were ripe for overhaul and reform. However, firmer insistence on federal policy would further worsen ethnic tensions and threaten to compound the problems of growing government weakness that were becoming critically evident throughout Central Europe during 1990. A full solution to the national problem could only be expected when new constitutions (both federal and republican) had been prepared – and these were unlikely to be drawn up before 1992. For a time it seemed that less

289

attention could safely be paid to the issue, as the Slovak National Party gained only 3.2 per cent of the seats during the local elections of November 1990. The Christian Democrats gained most, with 27 per cent of seats, whilst Public Against Violence now trailed them with 20 per cent. Support in the Czech areas for Civic Forum also declined, as they now held less than a third of the seats.

Meanwhile, a 'Scenario for Economic Reform' had been drawn up by the government after the elections to identify key tasks and prepare a parliamentary timetable. On this basis negotiations opened in August between federal and national governments (including that of the Czech lands) in the attempt to seek a practical solution. On 12 December, an agreement was reached in terms of amendments to the 1968 federal constitution which also provided for the adoption of a coherent economic programme to be implemented in the new year. This included elements of price liberalization, internal convertibility of the currency, and some measure of privatization. The programme appeared to take care to avoid the pitfalls of Polish shock therapy and, despite the strengthened position of Klaus and the liberal wing of the economic establishment, not to cause excessive disruption to the relative stability of the Czechoslovak economy. Some part in this outcome appears to have been played by President Havel, whose views on economic change helped to balance those of Klaus. In both Czechoslovakia and Hungary, then, presidential performance had some influence at times of decisive change, although in both cases there were either questions of uncertainty about the presidential prerogatives involved, or problems of political weakness. Both examples, nevertheless, stood in some contrast with the unresolved issues surrounding the occupancy of the Polish presidency, where they remained liable to erupt at a critical time of economic change. Rather than helping to defuse the situation, such aspects of uncompleted transformation in Poland had served to enrich the already combustible political mixture in that country.

Factors with a capacity to disrupt the relative political calm that had prevailed in Czechoslovakia during the initial phase of post-communist transition soon came into greater prominence. Despite Havel's cautious approach to questions of economic reform issue after the election, his views of the prospects for further development in this area had clearly become less positive. His 1991 New Year address began with the observation that the past twelve months had brought a number of unpleasant surprises, not the least of which was the discovery that the Czechoslovakia inherited from the communists was physically run down, in a poor state of physical repair and in need of major reconstruction: 'We have found that what we saw a year ago as a neglected house is basically a ruin'.[24]

It was with this observation that the concerted programme of economic reform prepared over the preceding months now got under way and that the effects of recession really began to take hold. GDP fell by 14 per cent and personal consumption by an estimated 28 per cent during the year as a whole. Industrial production fell by 23 per cent, with between 40 and 50 per cent of this decline being attributable to the collapse of COMECON markets. Exports to the OECD area as a whole rose by a relatively modest 5 per cent, and those to the EC by 9 per cent. Against this background the unemployment rate rose overall to 6.6 per cent. Slovakia, however, was considerably harder hit. Unemployment there rose to 11.8 per cent, compared with 4.1 per cent in the Czech lands. Inflation, at 58 per cent over the year as a whole, was also 5 per cent higher in Slovakia. The flow of foreign investment (86 per cent of which came from Germany) into Slovakia was also minimal, its share being limited to 4 per cent. Public reaction to this economic shock was nevertheless restrained. No major protests or strikes were organized and the changes were accepted with a large degree of equanimity. Nevertheless, the dispiriting economic situation provided the foundation for a major realignment of political organizations and forces during 1991.

An overall assessment of the nature of the economic changes and their implications for the future course of development and economic recovery also seemed to be difficult to reach. There was a strong feeling at the beginning of 1992 that much of the more difficult work had yet to be undertaken. In the spring an imaginative voucher privatization scheme was launched, whereby the 8.5 million citizens who had bought investment vouchers were able to exchange them for shares in state-owned companies. By the end of 1992 nearly all the companies targeted for privatization in the first round of the scheme had been sold in this way, although most of the shares were then purchased by the numerous investment funds which had sprung up to take advantage of the new economic opportunities opened up by these developments. Precisely what this would mean in terms of management and the actual operation of the economy remained somewhat uncertain, however.

If there was little overt political response to these changes it could not be said, however, that the political situation was static. By mid-1991 the number of parties in the parliament had risen from the total of 8 represented in parliament as a result of the 1990 elections to 15. In February 1991 Civic Forum, which had spearheaded the revolution of 1989 in the Czech lands, divided into a Civic Democratic Party (led by Václav Klaus) and a Civic Movement (led by foreign minister Jiří Dienstbier). Issues relating to the programme for economic transition lay at the heart of the split, and Dienstbier's group held a position favouring more gradual change for which Havel also had considerable sympathy. A third group also emerged from the split, while some parliamentary deputies formerly associated with Civic Forum became members of the Social Democrat Party which occupied, however, a relatively marginal political position.

In Slovakia soon afterwards the Public Against Violence also disintegrated, largely over issues of nationalism and the status of the federation. Slovak Prime Minister Vladimír Mečiar distanced himself from other PAV government members (notably the deputy prime minister in charge of economic affairs in Slovakia) and split the group to form a Movement for a Democratic Slovakia, which immediately became the most popular party in the republic. This provoked a Slovakian governmental crisis which was further deepened by accusations of misbehaviour and the removal of Mečiar from his post by the presidium of the republic's National Council in April 1991. It was alleged, among other things, that he met secretly with Soviet generals around the time that the Slovakian Movement was established.[25] It is difficult to avoid the conclusion that personal ambition also played a large part in the actions of the former prime minister, Mečiar. He was replaced as prime minister by Ján Čarnogurský, leader of the Christian Democratic Movement (which with the split became the largest party in the Slovak National Council), who was supported by what remained of PAV.

These changes also had the effect of severing cross-republic party alliances and enhancing the importance of political forces based firmly in Slovakia or the Czech lands. The residue of PAV was close only to the Czech Civic Movement (while also maintaining good relations with Klaus's CDP) but was much less strong itself in political terms, a relationship that was hardly capable of forming the basis for a significant alliance. Relations between the surviving elements of the communist organization and their inheritors throughout Czechoslovakia also became more distant. The Slovak Communist Party transformed itself into the Party of the Democratic Left and gained extensive support among the local population (around 11 per cent of the electorate prior to the 1992 elections) prompting, indeed, the formation of two small, more traditionally left-wing parties in opposition to its markedly social-democratic orientation. The Czech Communist Party of Bohemia and Moravia (the last significant group in Central Europe to retain the name) was also, with 380,000 members (of whom two-thirds were nevertheless pensioners), a powerful force and seemed to have good prospects of emerging as the single largest opposition party in the new parliament.[26] The attention paid to various issues became increasingly differentiated in regional terms, as nationalist forces came to predominate in Slovakia while Czech politics grew more secular and progressively concerned with economic issues.

The question of the constitutional status of the Czechoslovak federation thus came increasingly to dominate political life and achieved a virtual monopoly within it throughout the second half of 1991. Havel had organized talks since the beginning of the year in the attempt to reach a constitutional solution – and with the ultimate hope of saving the union. He also argued consistently for a referendum to be held on the national issue, but federal assembly deputies were again unable to decide on a viable format in which it could be put to the electorate. The fact that Havel was unable to achieve virtually any of his major political goals in 1991 despite enjoying continuing levels of very high popular support was one of the stranger aspects of the Czechoslovak political scene. (Another was that, despite the accelerating drift to national separation, polls showed that a decided majority of Slovaks continued to support the idea of some form of common state.) Virtually all of the legislative initiatives made by Havel during 1991 were rejected, although he continued to be the most popular politician in Czechoslovakia and attracted a 71 per cent approval rating in November 1991.

Following publication of further proposals for constitutional reform at the end of the year, Havel had the support of 82 per cent of Czechoslovak citizens in early 1992. Nevertheless, after the elections of June 1992, greater importance was assumed by regional leaders who had already shown themselves to be distinctly out of sympathy with Havel's vision. Václav Klaus, whose CDP won 30 per cent of the Czech vote in their National Council, immediately conferred with Mečiar, whose Movement for a Democratic Slovakia gained 37 per cent of the Council votes there, and, in view of the conditions now prevailing, insisted on rapid severance of the regional link. The number of seats gained by the CDP and the MDS in the Federal Assembly was also high (and broadly equivalent to those won in the National Councils) and this would have guaranteed further wrangling and constitutional stalemate.[27] The defeat suffered by President Havel in this area – the hero of the revolution only two-and-a-half years earlier and still an immensely popular figure – could hardly have been more apparent. He submitted his resignation as President of Czechoslovakia on 17 July 1992, immediately after the Slovak National Council adopted the Slovak Republic's declaration of sovereignty, which was a direct challenge to his authority. A matter of weeks after this the distinguished Slovak politician Alexander Dubček, elected chairman of the Federal Assembly in December 1989 and still held in considerable esteem for the position he had taken in 1968, was involved in a serious car crash and died on 7 November 1992.

The life of the post-communist Czechoslovak state was therefore a short one. In view of the political *impasse* and the conflicting expectations that could still be detected in the Czechoslovak population, it was decided simply to form a grand coalition of the major forces (which was duly done on 2 July) and work towards the least harmful break that could be arranged – a 'velvet divorce' to succeed the relatively calm revolution of three years earlier. The federation was thus dissolved on 1 January 1993, although the preparations did not run quite so smoothly as had originally been hoped. Slovak representatives showed some intransigeance on a number of financial issues, while arguments broke out in the Czech Republic on several questions arising from the new constitution. Václav Havel announced his intention to run for the Czech presidency but also argued for constitutional provisions to give the president more influence over domestic affairs. He appeared to have had some success in this, but the election of the new Czech president turned out to be unexpectedly contentious and it was only after extensive wrangling that Havel was elected on 26 January 1993. Similar problems attended the election of a Slovak president, and Michal Kovač was only elected to that post after a second vote held on 15 February 1993.

Some uncertainty and several areas of conflict seemed to lie ahead for the independent Slovakia, and these were not just restricted to its internal affairs. The existence of a 600,000-strong Hungarian minority in the small country of some 5 million people was a source of considerable tension, both domestically and in relations with Hungary itself. Views expressed by Mečiar and the newly formed Slovak government suggested that ethnic relations would not be treated with great delicacy. Relations with Hungary were further troubled by disagreements over the long-drawn out Gabčíkovo hydro-electric dam project, which finally brought about the diversion of Danube waters in October 1992. The role of Slovakia in regional affairs more generally, as well as in relations with the European Community (in connection with which the position of the new Czech Republic would also require clarification), raised further questions and made it clear that a number of important issues were ripe for consideration in the near future.

NOTES AND REFERENCES

1. Mason, *Revolution in East-Central Europe*, p. 69.
2. Berglund and Dellenbrandt, *The New Democracies*, pp. 220–22.
3. For example, Konrád, *Antipolitics*, and Havel, 'Anti-political politics'.
4. Schapiro, *Totalitarianism*.
5. Lewis, *Democracy and Civil Society in Eastern Europe*.
6. Lewis, 'Democracy and its future', pp. 304–7.
7. Huntington, 'Will more countries become democratic ?'
8. Glenny, *The Rebirth of History*.
9. Batt, *East Central Europe*, p. 37.
10. Hankiss, 'What the Hungarians saw first', p. 19.
11. Barany and Vinton, 'Breakthrough', p. 203.
12. Hawkes, *Tearing Down the Curtain*, p. 82.
13. East, *Revolutions in Eastern Europe*, p. 76.
14. Merritt, *Eastern Europe and the USSR*, pp. 192–97.
15. Bujak, 'West of Centre', pp. 10–11.
16. Korzeniowski, 'Anomia polityczna a preferencje wyborcze'.
17. Dehnel-Szyc and Stachura, *Gry polityczne*, p. 15.
18. Gebethner, 'Sejm rozczłonkowany', p. 78.
19. East, *op. cit.*, p. 79.
20. Lengyel, 'New ingredients in the goulash', p. 38.
21. *RFE/RL Research Report*, 3 January 1992.
22. Frydman et al, *The Privatization Process*, p. 125.
23. *Rzeczpospolita*, 28 May 1993.
24. *East European Reporter* vol. 4, 4 (1991), p. 42.
25. Wolchik, *Czechoslovakia in Transition*, p. 53.
26. Novak, 'The last communist party', p. 28.
27. Wightman, '1992 parliamentary elections', pp. 296–97

CHAPTER THIRTEEN
Conclusion: the Weight of History

THE RE-EMERGENCE OF CENTRAL EUROPE

The sudden collapse of communism throughout Central Europe in 1989 marked a clear turning-point in the course that events had taken in the region since the end of the Second World War. While the implications of this development for existing patterns of political rule and forms of economic organization seemed clear-cut, its bearing on subsequent developments was less apparent. The initial outcome at least was relatively obvious and unambiguous in its implications. The power that the Soviet Union had exercised since the 1940s was abruptly curtailed; the ties that had linked the region's economies was severed; and the ever-present threat of military intervention from the sizeable Soviet military contingents stationed in the area were removed. The finality of this change was later underlined by the terminal crisis that afflicted the Soviet Union itself and led to the abolition of the federal state in 1991.

The further meaning and implications of the changes for Central Europe were by no means so clear, however. The Iron Curtain suddenly disappeared and obstacles to broader European integration seemed to be removed. It was generally felt that artificially imposed barriers had been raised and the path opened for the countries of Central Europe to rejoin the main trajectories of political, economic, cultural and social development from which they had been cut off for several decades.

Precisely where Central Europe was returning to and the destination of its course of post-communist development remained somewhat uncertain. The countries involved were of small or medium size, economically vulnerable, and engaged in a process of political transition whose end point was unknown. One starting point was growing emphasis on a new identity within the post-communist context: Central Europe had become more prominent as a regional entity and re-emerged as an attractive framework within which the recently emancipated, post-communist countries could be anchored. Poland, however, had not generally been a major participant in the traditions of early twentieth-century Central Europe (which were more strongly rooted in the areas of former Austro-Hungarian rule). This had to some extent changed, though, with the growing cross-frontier awareness of the post-Helsinki civil rights movement, and the increasing influence of political dissidence during the later stages of communist rule.

National friction was not absent from the region, although Polish-Czech relations were considerably better than they had been before the Second World War. Certain elements of competition emerged in relations with potential economic partners and in negotiations with the European Community. Ethnic tensions seemed likely to worsen with the formation of separate Czech and Slovak states, particularly because the latter had a significant Hungarian minority within its relatively small territory and the new Slovak government did not appear to approach the issue with much caution or tact. Specific points of international tension, like the fate of the Gabčíkovo hydro-electric scheme, were also likely to exacerbate relations.

Nevertheless, the re-emergence of the Central European idea was a significant factor in the immediate post-communist situation and a further example of the growing differentiation within the Soviet empire that was becoming apparent well before the upheavals of 1989.[1] The 'return to diversity', of which the re-emergence of Central Europe proved to be an emphatic confirmation, also represented more than just a revival of interest in the inde-pendence, sovereignty and dignity of the interwar period that Rothschild was able to identify. 1989 may have seen an 'end to history' in the sense suggested by Fukuyama – that of the disap-pearance of the Marxist-Leninist challenge to liberal democracy as an alternative model of social development – but it also meant a resumption of historical tradition for the countries of Central Europe in terms of enhanced national independence and greater room for manoeuvre in the exercise of political and social choice. The resurrection of national traditions and the re-emergence of Central Europe were, further, associated with two other conceptions that implied a higher level of integration and greater participation in the mainstream international developments of the late twentieth century. These were summed up in the ideas of a return to Europe – that of the West, from which Central Europe had been separated with the descent of the Iron Curtain – and a return to democracy and the more liberal political practices of the immediate post-war period, which the imposition of communist dictatorship had brought to an abrupt halt.

These ideas also contained strong elements of ambiguity. Many influential Central Europeans might well have felt themselves to be distinct and different in culture and tradition from the Russians, but this was a view whose implications were not uncontested and which provided a source of considerable controversy in the period immediately preceding the collapse of the communist regime.[2] Much of the debate about Central Europe and the conditions of its contemporary identity hinged, indeed, on perceptions of the relationship of Russia itself with Europe.[3] While the inhabitants of Central Europe were undoubtedly European in a general sense, too, the degree to which they and their ancestors had been full participants in the mainstream of European developments – which had tended to be concentrated in the west of the continent – was, in at least some cases, debatable. Nevertheless, a strong orientation towards Europe and what were perceived to be the values of European civilization was evident during 1989 and the early years of post-communist transition. This perspective was undoubtedly due in part to the success of Western Europe, and the Community which many of its members had formed, in upholding and extending democratic practices at the same time as a relatively effective economic growth pattern was maintained – a combination that stood in striking contrast to the experience of the years leading up to the Second World War.

Firmer European ties, culminating in eventual membership of the European Community, have been understood in some way to underpin Central Europe's return to democracy and its adoption of a sustainable model of economic growth, and to provide – under contemporary conditions – a firmer basis for its survival than they did in the interwar years. Ideas of a return to democracy and a return to Europe are, then, interlinked and both dependent on commitment to a particular course of future development. Thus the real meaning of the 'return' lies some way in the future and, in many ways, depends on how and with what degree of success the legacy of the past is coped with. The weight of history, both of the recent communist past and that of the pre-Second World War period, is likely to be critical in determining the possibility of any return to Europe and the establishment of the liberal democracy and market economies with which it has been associated.

RESURGENT TRADITIONS

Among the resurgent traditions of Central Europe and the themes of the region's history that have surfaced during the relatively brief post-communist period, the most important has been that of nationalism and the growing emphasis placed on ethnic identity. The strength of national feeling was, of course, important in preserving elements of civil society during the years of communist rule and reinforced the expression of democratic sentiments against Soviet-backed dictatorship. It remained strong in both Hungary and Poland and was associated with the persistence of reformist tendencies in those countries. It was less evident in Czechoslovakia, apart from a brief period in 1968 and 1969, but remained latent during the long period of normalization and re-emerged under the more positive conditions present in 1988–89. It is in this sense ironic that it is precisely Czechoslovakia that has been unable to maintain its territorial integrity since 1989 and has, in a sad reflection of developments during the Second World War, split into its major constituent parts – even if the process was fed more by the political ambitions of Vladimír Mečiar and his associates than by nationalist feelings held by Slovaks or, even less, by Czechs.

In the formerly more nationalistically inclined countries of Poland and Hungary, state borders and a reasonable level of social order have been maintained, not least because the demographic consequences of the Second World War left them with a relatively homogeneous population. Nevertheless, nationalism has certainly not been absent from post-communist Hungary and Poland and the influence of pre-war traditions has not been unimportant. This is significant in more than one sense. Most directly, of course, nationalism feeds ethnic tensions and produces fertile ground for diverse forms of social and political conflict. In one case, many of these centre on the numerous Hungarians living beyond the borders of the contemporary state. The responsibility felt by the Budapest government for the treatment of Hungarians in Romania has already been a source of considerable tension, while the position of Hungarians in Serbia's Vojvodina could become the source of more dangerous conflict if the political and military gaze of Belgrade shifts from the other conflicts surrounding the republic's borders.

With the establishment of an independent Slovak state, too, the position of its 600,000–strong Hungarian minority has become considerably more sensitive, particularly in view of the burgeoning nationalism apparent in the Mečiar government. Any mention of autonomy from the Hungarian minority has brought accusations of separatist tendencies from the Slovak government and claims of irredentism directed against Hungary. Prime Minister Mečiar will not accept ethnic Hungarian deputies elected to the Slovak National Council as true representatives of the minority (in combination with the Coexistence party, the Hungarian Christian Democratic Movement won 7.4 per cent of votes cast in the 1992 election) and has refused outright to hold discussions with them. Certain tensions have also arisen from the treatment of the Polish minority in Lithuania, although this was on a much reduced scale from that surrounding the Hungarian minorities.

Such conflicts and potential sources of friction have concerned ethnic minorities within individual countries and relations across national borders and, in some cases, both equally. Other legacies of the pre-war period direct attention more to internal minorities than to international relations. A number of such groups have come into considerably greater prominence since the collapse of the communist order. The German minority in Poland, for example, was estimated at the relatively low level of 50,000 in the early 1980s (see Chapter 3). By 1990, however, some 250,000 Germans were registered in Opole (Oppelen Silesia) alone, and it was suggested that the final total might well exceed 300,000. (In early 1993, indeed, it emerged that the German minority number between 308,000 and 350,000).[4] In the 1991 elections, seven representatives of the German Minority party (as well as those of other ethnic and regional groups) were elected to the Polish *Sejm* and the minority had achieved a far higher level of visibility and social importance. The risks of admitting to a German identity in the past have been referred to in explanation for this sudden change. New sources of conflict have achieved public prominence, one example being an insistence on commemorating German war casualties in Polish cemeteries.

While by no means absent during the communist period, deeply rooted sentiments of anti-semitism have again resurfaced in Poland and Hungary. In the latter case, MDF vice-president Csurka attacked a supposed alliance of 'Jews and communists' and deplored the inability of Hungarian populism to evoke feelings of allegiance to the people – or *Volk*, as some were tempted to put it in this context.[5] There could, indeed, have been a very small number of Jews left in either Hungary or Poland (and certainly extremely few who led anything like an identifiable Jewish way of life or practised the Orthodox religion). Nevertheless, such appeals and attacks were able to draw on lengthy traditions of anti-semitism, which could be adroitly manipulated for contemporary political causes, as intellectuals of whole or part Jewish origin were certainly identifiable in liberal circles and amongst particular political groupings allied with former dissidents (although Csurka did not identify himself as anti-semitic).

Similar prejudices, particularly strong in Hungary and Slovakia, fuelled resentment of, and in some cases attacks on gypsies, tendencies that were strengthened with the increasing presence of Romanian refugees. Racially motivated attacks on Germans were recorded (with at least one death in Poland during 1992 as a result), events not unconnected with attacks in Germany itself on immigrants, refugees or simple travellers (amongst them Poles leaving and travelling to enter their own country). The resurgence of the extreme right in Germany as a whole was in some ways the most threatening of all the pre-war traditions which surfaced as a result of the changes seen in 1989–90. It showed once more that movements fuelled by racial intolerance and nationalism were by no means restricted to post-communist Central Europe and the countries of the east.

The prejudice and intolerance such movements reflected and the conflicts they produced in themselves constituted obstacles to the establishment of a pluralist order, and impeded the development of democratic processes. They were also significant in another sense, as they showed the extent to which solidary conceptions of the political order had persisted throughout the communist period. They highlighted the nature of the problems that needed to be tackled if processes of compromise and bargaining were to be accepted as valid components of the post-communist political system, and the principles of institutionalized conflict characteristic of democracy established. Political abstractions and impassioned allegiance to national symbols were often all that could be deployed in expressing opposition to communist dictatorship; they were, however, not just insufficient to advance the process of democratization but were often counterproductive to its advance. It was, as Francis Fukuyama later acknowledged, precisely the newly liberated nationalisms of Eastern Europe that were likely to delay the 'end of history' in that region.[6]

Such forms of political commitment and casts of mind were not limited to areas of ethnic tension. Similar tendencies of allegiance with comparable political consequences could be seen in the sphere of religion in Hungary and, particularly, Poland. Its association with nationalism could easily be traced in the latter case and the political consequences could be equally authoritarian, as questions of faith and its social implications are generally not accessible to processes of negotiation. The issue of abortion has thus occupied a critical place in Polish political life since the early post-communist period and has exerted a major influence on the capacity of Poland's fragmented parliament to produce a viable government coalition. Such problems of democratic efficacy are closely linked with other themes that can be traced to pre-war political life and traditions that took root in that or earlier periods. The fissiparous character of Polish political life gave rise to demands for 'strong government' at an early stage of the inter-war republic and prepared the ground for the authoritarian rule of Marshal Piłsudski. A related debate has arisen around the figure of President Wałęsa, and there has been persistent discussion of his being tempted to extend his political base by creating a presidential party that could promise to sustain more effective government.

THE LEGACY OF COMMUNISM

The collapse of communist rule and the emergence of new patterns of political behaviour did not necessarily mark a sharp break with the practices of state socialism and the values associated with it. The role of social movements in Central Europe, like those of Solidarity in Poland and Civic Forum in Czechoslovakia have suggested, as we have seen, the emergence of forms of participation in political life very different from those characteristic of liberal and representative democracy. This was, further, followed by fragmentation of the broad social forces that formed during the period of communist decline and oversaw the early months of democratic transition. The role of elites in the Central European democratic transition continued to emerge as a particularly critical one, not just because of the negotiated character of the early cases of regime change, but also because of the political flux and institutional vacuum left behind after the collapse of communist power.

The legacy of communism was not restricted to general characteristics and tendencies in post-communist political life. It also provided specific topics of controversy and produced areas of major parliamentary conflict. There were, in particular, fiery debates and controversies throughout Eastern Europe about the status and continuing influence of the former elites, and the adoption of policies of more thoroughgoing 'decommunization'. Despite the collapse of the communist system and the crumbling of its official structures, many communist functionaries were still very much around and connected with centres of power and influence. There was, in practical as well as in political and moral terms, major uncertainty about what should be done in this area, as the revolutions of 1989 – if that is what they were – were partial ones. They had to cope not just with a broadly historical and general legacy of the former regime, but also with its personnel and institutions, its bureaux and system of administration. In many ways such individuals were still those best placed to maintain the administrative structures and machinery of state whose continuing existence and operation was a necessary condition of any process of development and controlled social change.

The consequences of the partial nature of the Central European revolutions were particularly noticeable in Poland, where the elections of 1989 produced what was very much a halfway house, led by a Solidarity prime minister but presided over by a communist president. All this, of course, soon changed as other countries followed suit and carried out a more thorough overhaul of the political system. This placed in some doubt Mazowiecki's original policy of the 'thick line' which he suggested should be drawn under the experience of the communist period – thus signing it off as if it were a closed period of accounting.

That, however, was far from sufficient for many Poles or for those in other countries of Central Europe. In Poland Wałęsa was quick to harness the issue of 'acceleration' to his campaign for the presidency, and questions of decommunization have rarely left the political agenda for any length of time anywhere in Central Europe. The massive extent of *Stasi* activities in the GDR prompted a popular onslaught on their headquarters and the ransacking of their files in the first weeks of 1990. Of more direct political significance, however, were the extensive and persistent allegations made of prominent politicians and public figures that they had been employees, informers or general associates of the security agency. They put an end to the political career of, amongst others, the last prime minister of the GDR, Lothar de Maizière, after he had become a member of the all-German parliament. The consequences of similar suggestions have been somewhat less clear-cut in the other countries of Central Europe, but they have often been of considerable political significance and regarded as a powerful resource for use in political conflict.

In Poland, where the process of government formation has encountered greatest difficulty and political instability has been most pronounced, questions of security involvement were instrumental in bringing the Olszewski government to an end in 1992. Regardless of the fact that no valid evidence was actually produced and that the issue was confused by the speed with which the political initiatives were mounted, the sensitivity of the political process to such allegations and matters arising from the recent communist past, demonstrated their significance in the course of contemporary political change. The question of security involvement has the capacity, among other things, to harness the crusading enthusiasm of those who suffered for their beliefs during the communist period with the guilt and frustration of those who submitted to its dictates and now wish to vindicate their behaviour. What George Konrád has called the 'clear conscience messianism of the revolution or counter-revolution' carries the possibility of encouraging new forms of oppression.[7] In a further development, the security associations of President Wałęsa have also been placed on the agenda, and, more recently the role played during the communist period by members of his entourage (like Mieczysław Wachowski, a key aide) have been raised by political activist Jaroslaw Kaczyński in what has appeared to be an intensifying crusade against the person and actions of the president.

The most concrete and far-reaching steps in this area were taken by the Czechoslovak government which, in October 1991, passed a Screening Act. This not only banned prominent advocates of the former regime from high public office but also established a principle of implied collective guilt in which individual responsibility in the suppression of human rights did not have to be fully proved. Membership of a party body or the appearance of a supposed collaborator's name in security files became proof enough. It was a form of negative *nomenklatura* in which lists of former security agents, members of the People's Militia and those on the control commissions set up after 1968 were drawn up in order that those individuals (who numbered at least 300,000) should not be considered for appointment to major functions in the state administration, cultural institutions, education, etc. It prompted considerable criticism, including that of President Havel and also attracted the attention of the Council of Europe. In the attempt to divest itself of the unwanted legacy of the recently abandoned communist system, then, Czechoslovak legislators chose (by, in fact, a minimal majority) to cut the links with a dictatorial past by methods whose democratic content was itself open to question and which did little to facilitate a return to Europe. The Screening Act also appeared to be a sore point in the independent Slovak Republic, and public suggestions that Mečiar's government was considering its abolition to preserve the careers of some of the officials of the new state played a part in the actions taken to restrict the freedom of the Slovak media.

Hungarian experience has again been different. In the attempt to open the way to prosecution of those accused of having committed murder or treason during 1956, in November 1991 parliament passed a bill lifting the 30–year statute of limitation on capital offences. It evoked rather more protest than the Czechoslovak act and in March 1992 the Hungarian Constitutional Court ruled unanimously against the law. The lack of government action in this area, however, helped strengthen criticism from radical populists and intensified conflict within the elite. It was only a few months later, in August, that István Csurka published his tract attacking HDF weakness in dealing with the opposition. He argued that, if the HDF was to have any chance of winning the 1994 elections, it would have to be resolute in severing ties with members of the former political system and eliminate those in the party and government apparatus who prevented the leadership getting on with its proclaimed national agenda. The issue was once more prominent in the proceedings of the HDF Congress in January 1993 and it was agreed that new legislation would have to be drafted to call to account members of the communist party who committed acts that, under contemporary conditions, would generally be deemed criminal. Issues of decommunization were clearly not going to be allowed to pass into oblivion, but whether their further pursuit would really strengthen processes of democratization and assist the return to Europe remained open to some question.

PROBLEMS OF SOCIAL RECONSTRUCTION

The resurgence of nationalist traditions combined with the persistence of populism and authoritarian tendencies, as well as major frustration and uncertainties about the approach to be taken to the political legacy of the immediate communist past, point to high levels of social dislocation and diverse orientations to the norms and symbols of the different periods of the Central European past. They indicate centrifugal tendencies within society which bode ill for the achievement of a certain level of consensus and constitutional order that have proved to be necessary for the growth of democratic processes and institutions. The still uncertain prospects of democracy in Central Europe may, then, also be linked with the problematic development of civil society and the role of contending social forces. With reference to Central Europe during the 1980s, 'civil society' became more of a slogan than an analytical concept. Its role in undermining the foundations of communist power and even its very existence in any meaningful sense was by no means fully established.[8] Yet civil society, Ralf Dahrendorf has argued, can also be regarded as the key to the effective constitutional and economic development that alone can provide the social foundations for a free society and the growth of a firmly based democracy; 'it pulls the divergent time scales and dimensions of political and economic reform together. It is the ground in which both have to be anchored in order not to be blown away'. To lay these foundations, however, 'sixty years are barely enough'.[9]

From this perspective, the development and consolidation of stable democracies is a very long-term process – although one that, in comparison with the lengthy period over which democracy developed in Britain or France, is by no means unrealistic or unduly pessimistic. At issue here, though, is the existence of a developed and firmly rooted civil society that has the capacity to nurture and promote liberty – and even in the view of those who did argue for the development of an effective civil society during the slow decline of communist rule it is clear that this is by no means the situation in contemporary Central Europe. This is partly due to the fact that the apparent victory of civil society over communist dictatorship could be construed as being conducive less to liberal democracy than to populism. In this situation there is direct political dominance by 'the people' with little regard for constitutional arrangements, the institutional mediation of power relations, or any protection of minority rights. It has been an outcome seen in societies not unlike those of Central Europe where political processes have been, at least initially, relatively unconstrained and political transformation has been accelerated by rapid socio-economic change. The desires and aspirations of a greater proportion of society might indeed be better satisfied by the arrangements of such a political order – but this is not the same thing as the establishment of liberal democracy or of a constitutional order which conforms to the principles subscribed to in the European Community.

In this context it is the character of state power in relation to social preferences that becomes the prime issue. The question of minority rights has certainly been firmly placed on the political agenda of a country like Poland, where the civil society that did emerge was significantly sustained by religious faith and supported organizationally by a strong Catholic Church. It was a situation in which a Polish liberal was driven to argue that 'a state in which morality forms the law is a totalitarian state'.[10] It is, indeed, constitutional order and stable institutions that promise some solution to the problems of early democratization,[11] and it is in this area that the prospects for democracy in much of Central Europe can appear rather bleak.

The emphasis on personality and deep-rooted mistrust of the state and its agencies throughout the region militate against the development of democracy and leave new institutions locked in a cycle of relative weakness.[12] Structures such as viable parties and effective parliaments are in the early stages of development, and their consolidation and growth seem likely to be dependent on the emergence of effective post-communist elites and integrated groups of politically influential individuals who share some common vision of the region's future. However, the background of post-communist elites often does little to inspire confidence in their capacity to form an effective governing group; their's was an experience 'formative of the new political elites as resisters. It in no way equipped them for power'.[13] In the absence of established elites or effectively operating institutions, the political situation remains an unstable one and at times the process of democratization seems to threaten to stall.

Perhaps the greatest problem of all is that institutional weakness and the actions of ineffective and self-regarding elites then feed back into social perceptions. This further divides and distances the populations of Central Europe from their rulers and impedes the development of the civil societies that offer the greater hope for the development of stable democracy. People grow disillusioned both with the slow development of democratic processes and the distance of the promise of eventual economic recovery. (For many, indeed, the latter necessitates a significant short- or even medium-term worsening of their material situation.) There is, then, further withdrawal from political processes, more scepticism about what they can deliver and a progressive demobilization of social forces.

The construction of a modern civil society is bound, in any case, to be a major long-term undertaking and, in a broader comparative framework, the post-communist experience of Central Europe has been less arduous and the impact of regional history less destructive than that seen elsewhere. The 'velvet divorce' in Czechoslovakia is, thankfully, a distant relation of the explosive fragmentation of Yugoslavia; the economic travails of Poland have not mirrored the degree of poverty and disruption seen in not so distant areas of the former Soviet Union. Nor have the problems of civil society exerted quite the destructive impact that have been feared. The weakness of Poland's party system and the fragility of its government have not so far tempted frustrated social forces to gather and re-form as authoritarian movements aiming to impose stronger government. Hungarian society, too, has seen increasing impatience but also political caution and the capacity to maintain stable structures.

THE INTERNATIONAL CONTEXT

Historical influences on the contemporary Central European situation, the difficulties surrounding a problematic civil society in Central Europe and the roles played by specific social groupings, are by no means the only factors that bear on the contemporary prospects for democracy there. The democratization of the post-communist countries, as well as the processes of economic recovery and development which are intended to accompany it, are critically dependent on international support and processes of regional and global integration. The granting of associate EC status to Czechoslovakia, Hungary and Poland in December 1991 thus represented a significant change in their international status. As in the case of Spain, this might eventually help consolidate the progress already made towards democracy and improve prospects of economic development. While it might be admitted that Central Europe is likely overall to face the same political and economic problems of poor capitalism as countries in Latin America, with political instability and uneven economic growth, it at least has the benefits of geography which give it some chance of participating in the advantages of Western Europe.[14]

Nevertheless, some of the less positive consequences of regionally, or even globally, structured capitalism may already be detected in the emerging post-communist environment of Central Europe. The evolution of political structures under conditions of transnational economic incorporation can confront developing states with major problems in terms of political integration and the consolidation of their structures of rule.[15] If replicated in Central Europe, such a pattern could lead to the further weakening of national elites and continuing problems in establishing relations with the appropriate social constituencies, leaving them with a relatively weak position from which to spearhead the thrust towards democracy. The critical role of finance minister Leszek Balcerowicz in sustaining international (and notably IMF) support for Poland and the substantial resentment he provoked in domestic political circles provided an early example of this tendency in post-communist Central Europe. The rise of Mečiar in Slovakia and the development of a separatist movement there showed the strengthening of similar tendencies in response to the actions of Czechoslovak prime minister Václav Klaus. As the prominence of nationalist currents and activity suggested, critical lines of division within radically changing societies under contemporary conditions were often drawn across the national community and integrated some politicians and groups more successfully with international institutions than with domestic constituencies.[16]

On balance, however, the introduction of closer relations between European countries has been a positive factor in the Central European democratization process and promises to provide a favourable framework for future developments. Whatever the problems involved in the transition, the existence of a relatively robust political framework and established economic mechanism in the west in the form of the European Community provides a major objective and point of reference for countries which are still politically uncertain, economically weakened and lacking any other regional centre from which to co-ordinate post-communist developments. It has, indeed, been a factor promoting integration amongst the Central European countries on their own account in terms of the association formed as a result of the Visegrad agreement in February 1991. This was intended to set a course for greater regional co-operation and to provide a framework for the co-ordination of efforts to strengthen links with the EC. The association agreements reached at the end of 1991 with the Community and membership of the Council of Europe (granted to Poland only after the elections of October 1991) had, however, little more than symbolic meaning. Concrete substance of any great significance in terms of EC membership appears to lie some distance in the future.

It is, indeed, important to recognize the extent of the progress made so far, but also not to minimize the efforts that need to be made to take the processes of regional and international integration as far as many hope will eventually be the case. Developments within the EC itself since German unification and the signature of the Maastricht Treaty in 1991 are eloquent testimony to the nature of the problems that can arise to disrupt the apparently smooth development of an existing integration process. (The difficulties in question were, moreover, closely linked with the solutions applied to problems in the former communist portion of Germany.) Unwarranted optimism and excessive emphasis on the role of co-operative institutions would itself be dangerous. Unsuccessful and over-ambitious regional institution-building can damage both West and East by drawing the former into a complex of problems it is incapable of solving, and the latter by raising expectations that cannot be satisfied, and undermining the islands of social stability that have remained since the traumatic collapse of the communist regime.[17]

Interventions of foreign states and the role of neighbouring powers in influencing the course of events in Central Europe in the not-so-distant past have, to put it mildly, not been generally benevolent. The weight of history lies, in this sense, as much on regional and international relations as it does on domestic affairs. It may be concluded that, after the experience of prolonged German and Russian hegemony over Central Europe for much of the twentieth century, the essential elements for solutions to the region's problems of post-communist transition are most likely to be found in its own community and the strength derived from its own historical experience.

NOTES AND REFERENCES

1. Rothschild, *Return to Diversity*, pp. 218–22.
2. See Schöpflin and Wood, *In Search of Central Europe*.
3. Rupnik, *The Other Europe*, p. 21.
4. *Rzeczpospolita*, 11 March 1993.
5. *East European Reporter* (Budapest), September/October 1992.
6. Fukuyama, *The End of History and the Last Man*, pp. 268–75.
7. Konrád, 'Authority and tolerance', p. 41.
8. Lewis, *Democracy and Civil Society*, pp. 6–8.
9. Dahrendorf, *Reflections on the Revolution in Europe*, p. 93.
10. *Polityka*, 29 September 1990.
11. Przeworski, *Democracy and the Market*, p. 39.
12. Schöpflin, 'Post-communism', p. 239.
13. Hirst, 'State, civil society', p. 231.
14. Przeworski, *op. cit.*, p. 190.
15. Lewis, 'Democracy and its future in Eastern Europe', p. 308.
16. *Polityka*, 18 January 1992.
17. Snyder, 'Averting anarchy in the new Europe'.

Guide to Further Reading

This guide is intended to provide information for those seeking further reading on the topics covered in this book, either in terms of more detailed coverage of particular countries and historical periods, or of specific events and the individuals who played a leading part in them. It is restricted to works in English, although those eager to locate foreign-language sources will find further references in some of the specialized works identified here. Titles only are provided in this guide; fuller publication details can be found in the list of references that follows.

Amongst general surveys of the region, some place it in a broader historical context, like J. Held (ed.) in *The Columbia History of Eastern Europe in the Twentieth History* and R. Okey's *Eastern Europe: 1740–1980*. Most dealing with the region in the post-1945 period also locate it in a broader 'Eastern Europe' that generally refers to the countries that fell under Soviet influence soon after the end of the war. This is the case with L. P. Morris, *Eastern Europe Since 1945*; J. F. Brown, *Eastern Europe and Communist Rule*; G. Swain and N. Swain, *Eastern Europe since 1945*; and J. Rothschild, *Return to Diversity. A Political History of East Central Europe since World War II* (although the GDR was excluded from the last work as it was, in the words of the author, 'not a nation and less than half a country'). A comprehensive treatment of the early post-Stalin period was offered by F. Fejtö in his *History of the People's Democracies*, and a more critical view from the years of the Soviet empire's evident decline can be found in J. Rupnik's *The Other Europe*. Z. Zeman also offers a distinctive historical perspective in *The Making and Breaking of Communist Europe*. D. Turnock's *Eastern Europe. An Economic and Political Geography* is particularly strong in the areas indicated by its title.

Those interested in discussion and contrasting perspectives on the nature of Central Europe as a more distinctive part of this post-war Eastern Europe might turn first to G. Schöpflin and N. Woods (eds.), *In Search of Central Europe*. R. Okey's article 'Central Europe/Eastern Europe: behind the definitions' provides an instructive historical perspective on the development of the different regional identities, while A. Judt outlines 'The rediscovery of Central Europe' from the point of view of the West. T. Garton Ash's *The Uses of Adversity* also contains a number of articles written during the 1980s reflecting the character of the period during which the idea of Central Europe began to re-surface within parts of the Soviet empire. Insights into recent developments in this area can be found in the *East European Reporter*, which commenced publication in London during 1985 and is currently produced as a bi-monthly in Budapest. A sound historical survey of pre-war developments in the area is presented by J. Rothschild in *East Central Europe between the Two World Wars* while H. Seton-Watson's *Eastern Europe between the Wars*, though dated, is an authoritative account written closer to the period by one of the most eminent Western observers.

There are numerous histories of the individual countries dealt with in this book, many of which set post-1945 developments in a broader historical context. J. Korbel presents an account of *Twentieth Century Czechoslovakia: The Meaning of its History*, and D. W. Paul has produced *Czechoslovakia: Profile of a Socialist Republic at the Crossroads of Europe*. A more recent general study which covers the period dealt with in this book is H. Renner, *A History of Czechoslovkia Since 1945*. A book-length bibliographical survey dealing with diverse aspects of Czechoslovak history, society and culture and which therefore gives a comprehensive guide to yet further reading is D. Short's *Czechoslovakia: World Bibliographical Series vol. 68*.

A solid account of Hungarian developments may be found in P. Ignotus *Hungary*, and a work directing attention to the regional context of post-war Hungarian history is C. Gati's *Hungary and the Soviet Bloc*. A more recent account which covers the whole period is N. Swain's *Hungary: the Rise and Fall of Feasible Socialism*. A book which takes a longer view, starting with the establishment of the Dual Monarchy of Austria-Hungary, is J. K. Hoensch's *History of Modern Hungary 1867–1986*. A full bibliographical survey has been compiled by T. Kabdebo, *Hungary: World Bibiliographical Studies vol. 15*.

The relatively short life of the German Democratic Republic as a separate entity is most comprehensively covered by D. Childs in *The GDR. Moscow's German Ally.* M. McCauley presents another general overview in *The German Democratic Republic since 1945.* A recent account which covers the GDR's demise as well as the course of its overall history is A. McElvoy's *The Saddled Cow. East Germany's Life and Legacy.* The division of Germany was, naturally, an important condition of the GDR's development, and this factor is dealt with in H. A. Turner's *The Two Germanies since 1945.*

Poland has been particularly well served in terms of historical treatment. In view of the strong influence exerted on recent developments in Poland by the nation's turbulent history and the significance of its national traditions, it is not surprising that some of the best works dealing with its modern history set it in a broad temporal context. R. F. Leslie's edited *History of Poland since 1863* is one such authoritative volume, and N. Davies's *Heart of Europe. A Short History of Poland* another that provides considerable historical detail (and, while eminently readable, is not quite so short as its title suggests). A well-presented account that focuses more sharply on the modern period is *Poland in the Twentieth Century* by M. K. Dziewanowski. A further bibliographic survey is that by R. C. Lewarski, *Poland: World Bibliographical Series vol. 32.*

To return to the sequence of developments presented in this work and the immediate context in which post-1945 Central Europe was formed, a number of works that deal with the circumstances of the extension of Soviet power towards the west and the post-war division of Europe should be noted. The Soviet side and the evolution of its perceptions are particularly well covered by V. Mastny in *Russia's Road to the Cold War.* In relation to the countries whose post-war borders and international status provoked most contention, A. Phillips' *Soviet Policy toward East Germany Reconsidered: The Postwar Decade* and S. M. Terry's *Poland's Place in Europe. General Sikorski and the Origin of the Oder-Neisse Line, 1939–1943,* provide informed and well-documented guidance. A classic account of the communist assumption of power is H. Seton-Watson's *The East European Revolution.* A more recent, and historically comprehensive compendium, of the origins of communist domination over Central Europe (and elsewhere) is *The Anatomy of Communist Takeovers,* edited by T. T. Hammond. The same editor has assembled a range of personal views and memoirs of the process in *Witnesses to the Origins of the Cold War.* Some country studies, like K. Kaplan's *The Short March. The Communist Takeover in Czechoslovakia 1945–48,* also deserve attention in this context. The evolution of regional relations and the pattern of Soviet behaviour during this period, as well as that which followed, is ably presented by Z. K. Brzezinski in *The Soviet Bloc. Unity and Conflict.* The account from this perspective is carried further forward by H. Carrère d'Encausse in *Big Brother. The Soviet Union and Soviet Europe* and R. L. Hutchings *Soviet-East European Relations. Consolidation and Conflict.*

The nature of the system that was then installed in Central Europe is best introduced in R. C. Tucker's edited volume, *Stalin. Essays in Historical Interpretation.* The most characteristic features of full-blown Stalinism were mass purges and the show trials mounted to demonstrate the ruthless nature of the newly installed dictatorship; J. Pelikan's *The Czechoslovak Political Trials 1950–1954* provide ample evidence of what was involved. The trials, of course, affected the communist parties and their leading cadres more than the societies as a whole. It was in the parties that the key processes of political evolution and the major conflicts of the communist period were in many ways located, and in terms of politics the histories of the parties can be regarded as key accounts of the period. Major works in this area are Z. Suda's *Zealots and Rebels: A History of the Ruling Communist Party of Czechoslovakia* and K. Kaplan's *The Communist Party in Power: A Profile of Party Politics in Czechoslovakia* (which offers a view of the party from within); M. McCauley's *Marxism-Leninism in the German Democratic Republic;* B. Kovrig's *Communism in Hungary: From Kun to Kádár* and M. Molnár's *A Short History of the Hungarian Communist Party,* and M. K. Dziewanowski's *The Communist Party of Poland* and J. B. de Weydenthal's *The Communists of Poland: An Historical Outline.* A comprehensive guide to the political analysis of the communist period in Central Europe is provided in the relevant chapters of R. C. Taras (ed.) *Handbook of Political Science Research on the USSR and Eastern Europe.*

The effects of communist rule, of course, extended far beyond the organization and membership of the communist parties and exerted a critical influence over the shape of the economy and social structures. M. Kaser's edited *Economic History of Eastern Europe* provides the most comprehensive account of developments in this area. Individual countries are covered in A. Teichova *The Czechoslovak Economy 1918–1980;* M. Myant *The Czechoslovak Economy, 1948–1988;* I. Jeffries and M. Melzer (eds.) *The East German Economy;* I. Berend and T. Ranki *The Hungarian Economy in the Twentieth Century* and Z. Landau and J. Tomaszewski *The Polish Economy in the Twentieth Century.* There is, of course, an enormous range of specialist economic literature, but of greater interest to a general readership are likely to be works that focus on some of the more distinctive features of economic development in the countries of Central Europe. W. Robinson's *The Pattern of Reform in Hungary*, for example, focuses on the distinctive policies adopted to cope with the problems of running a communist economy in that country. J. Batt develops this theme and compares Hungarian and Czechoslovakian experience in this area in *Economic Reform and Political Change in Eastern Europe*. A succinct presentation of Poland's economic problems towards the end of the communist period can be found in R. A. Clarke (ed.) *Poland: the Economy in the 1980s*. Details of the regional structure within which economic development was pursued are given in M. Kaser *Comecon: Integration Problems of the Planned Economies* and van Brabant *Economic Integration in Eastern Europe*.

Characteristics of the different national solutions adopted to cope with the demands of a more traditional economic sector are investigated in A. Korbonski *The Politics of Socialist Agriculture in Poland: 1945–1960* and, for Hungary, N. Swain *Collective Farms Which Work?* An unusually direct insight into the conditions of work in communist industry is given by Hungarian writer M. Haraszti in *A Worker in a Worker's State*. The consequences for Central European society of communist rule and the economic policies pursued under it for Central European society is a complex subject and one that involves some controversy. D. Lane's *The End of Social Inequality? Class, Status and Power under State Socialism* represents one comprehensive and succinct approach to the subject. Treatments of the nature and consequences of social change in particular countries include Z. Ferge *A Society in the Making. Hungarian Social and Societal Policy 1945–75*; J. Krejci *Social Change and Stratification in Postwar Czechoslovakia*, J. Krejci *Social Structure in Divided Germany* and D. Lane (ed.) *Social Groups in Polish Society*. A series of books on the theme of Marxist regimes also focused on the shape of politics, economics and society in the later phase of the communist period, the list including M. Dennis on the *German Democratic Republic*, H-G. Heinrich on *Hungary*, and G. Kolankiewicz and P. G. Lewis on *Poland*.

Social change in Central Europe was not just expressed in structural transformations and broad tendencies of group development. Nor was political life restricted to the activities of the communist party. Periodically the Central European societies threw up their own movements against communist rule and their populations responded in direct ways to the changes occurring within society. Each of these crisis points has been well documented, the conflicts they reveal illuminating the nature of the historical development that was taking place beneath the surface of communist dictatorship. The first of these occurred in East Germany during 1953 and was described in S. Brant *The East German Rising* and A. Baring *Uprising in East Germany: June 17, 1953*. Three years later came the Hungarian Revolution, which saw the production of a more extensive literature including F. A. Vali *Rift and Revolt in Hungary: Nationalism Versus Communism*; P. Kecskemeti *The Unexpected Revolution: Social Forces in the Hungarian Uprising*; P. E. Zinner *Revolution in Hungary* and M. Molnár *Budapest 1956: A History of the Hungarian Revolution*. The revolution retained a major political significance throughout the communist period and the events surrounding it were a matter for regular reappraisal, an important later contribution being that of B. Lomax in *Hungary 1956*.

The events of the same year in Poland were somewhat less violent but none the less significant in forcing the Soviet Union to accept a party chief backed by the local leadership and the Polish nation. This was reflected in the relatively optimistic titles of books like K. Syrop's *Spring in October: The Polish Revolution of 1956*; F. Lewis's *The Polish Volcano: A Case of Hope* and K. S. Karol's *Visa for Poland*. An alternative, and ultimately more accurate view, was expressed in F. Gibney's *The Frozen Revolution, Poland: A Study in Communist Decay*. The next revolt was that expressed in the Czechoslovak reform movement and this, too, prompted a stream of publications. The most comprehensive, and suitably extensive, was H. Gordon Skilling's *Czechoslovakia's Interrupted Revolution*. But there were also others, like V. Kusin's *The Intellectual Origins of the Prague Spring: The Development of Reformist Ideas in Czechoslovakia, 1956–67* and *Political Groupings in the Czechoslovak Reform Movement*; *The Czechoslovak Reform Movement: Communism in Crisis, 1962–1968* and *Reform Rule in Czechoslovakia: The Dubcek Era, 1968–1969* by Galia Golan, and B. W. Jancar's *Czechoslovakia and the Absolute Monopoly of Power: A Study of Political Power in a Communist System*. Somewhat later, and providing a valuable first-hand account of the end of the reform movement and the political machinations that followed the Soviet invasion, appeared Z. Mlynář's *Night Frost in Prague: The End of Humane Socialism*.

The more isolated, but clearly significant, revolt of Polish workers in 1970 did not give rise to so many publications in English, although A. Bromke and J. Strong's edited *Gierek's Poland* contained some useful material on this episode as well as on the early period of Gierek's rule. The rise of Solidarity and the protracted challenge to communist rule it presented until the declaration of martial law was, on the other hand, documented in a considerable number of books. The political and intellectual precursor of the free trade union, the defence committee formed after the 1976 demonstrations, received a full historical treatment in J. J. Lipski's *KOR. A History of the Workers' Defense Committee in Poland 1976–1981.* As had been the case with communist Poland's earlier crisis period, most of the books on the formation and activity of Solidarity itself were by journalists and quite general in nature, although they contained useful insights and much valuable documentation. Early example's were K. Ruane's *The Polish Challenge*; J-Y Potel's *The Summer Before the Frost*; T. Garton Ash's *The Polish Revolution: Solidarity 1980–82* and M. Myant's *Poland: A Crisis for Socialism.* Different in approach and more sociological in content was the work conducted by A. Touraine's team and published as *Solidarity: Poland 1980–81.* The struggle was described from the side of the party in G. Sanford's *Polish Communism in Crisis,* while the broader context of party rule and apparatus domination in which the Solidarity crisis was set is outlined in P. Lewis's *Political Authority and Party Secretaries in Poland, 1975–86.*

In between these outbreaks of unrest and instability, public life in communist Central Europe tended to be dominated by a succession of party leaders whose careers, while often not particularly dramatic or spectacular in their own right, nevertheless typified the form of political rule that prevailed, and shed considerable light on the course of developments in the individual countries. C. Stern's *Ulbricht: A Political Biography*; H. Lippmann's *Honecker and the New Politics of Europe* as well as E. Honecker's *From My Life* all, therefore, help with coverage of the German Democratic Republic. Orthodox party leaders in Czechoslovakia received less attention, although *Dubček* was portrayed by W. Shawcross as was the Hungarian leader in the same author's *Crime and Compromise: Janos Kádár and the Politics of Hungary Since Revolution.* Imre Nagy's views were presented in his own account in *On Communism: In Defense of the New Course.* For Poland, N. Bethell presented *Gomułka: His Poland and His Communism,* while T. Torańska's fascinating interviews with Stalinist leaders in Poland was translated and published as *Them – Stalin's Polish Puppets.* The views of diverse historical actors and observers are also presented in M. Charlton's *The Eagle and the Small Birds. Crisis in the Soviet Empire: from Yalta to Solidarity.*

Alongside the official careers and expressions of communist orthodoxy, though, independent voices came to be heard more often in Central Europe and publications from unofficial sources became increasingly available during the late 1970s and 1980s. They were quite plentiful, even in the English language, and only a few major examples will be noted here. Perhaps the most significant statement of the opposition was that of V. Havel, future president of Czechoslovakia, in his *Power of the Powerless: Citizens Against the State in Central and Eastern Europe*. Similar sentiments with regard to the party domination of public life were expressed in Hungary by G. Konrád *Antipolitics*, while A. Michnik's *Letters From Prison and Other Essays* gives a good sample of writings by a leading Polish activist and intellectual. Useful insights into the career of the free trade union organizer and future president of Poland can be gained from the autobiography by L. Wałęsa, *A Path of Hope*. The later surge in the GDR may be sampled in D. Philipsen's *We Were the People. Voices from East Germany's Revolutionary Autumn of 1989*.

The collapse of communism and the circumstances which surrounded it have, not surprisingly, been the subject of a rapidly growing number of publications. Journalists were again first off the mark and a number of dramatic and illuminating accounts were produced, among them M. Frankland's *The Patriots' Revolution*; T. Garton Ash's *We, the People*; N. Hawkes (ed.) *Tearing Down the Curtain* and D. Selbourne's *Death of the Dark Hero: Eastern Europe 1987–90*. M. Glenny's *The Rebirth of History: Eastern Europe in the Age of Democracy* also contains useful insights into the process of democratization that the events of 1989 set into motion. Factual guidance to the changes, details of the key figures involved and information on electoral and governmental change can be found in K. Sword (ed.) *The Times Guide to Eastern Europe* and R. East's *Revolutions in Eastern Europe*. Diverse Central European perspectives were included in G. Prins' edited book, *Spring in Winter: the 1989 Revolutions*, while J. F. Brown's *Surge to Freedom: the End of Communist Rule* contains a blend of historical description and analysis. Of a somewhat more academic nature and particularly useful for developing insights into the dynamics of communism's failure in Central Europe and its implications for future developments are J. Batt's *East-Central Europe from Reform to Transformation*; R. Dahrendorf's *Reflections on the Revolution in Europe*; E. Hankiss' *East European Alternatives* and J. Staniszkis' *Dynamics of the Breakthrough in Eastern Europe*. S. Wolchik's *Czechoslovakia in Transition. Politics, Economics and Society* replicated the focus of the earlier Marxist

Regimes volumes but appeared at a time when it was possible to give full attention to the transitional period. A useful overview of the communist period and the nature of the subsequent changes is provided by D. Mason in *Revolution in East-Central Europe. The Rise and Fall of Communism and the Cold War.*

Bibliography

Alton, T. P., 'Comparison of overall economic performance in the East European countries', in *The Economies of Eastern Europe Under Gorbachev's Influence* (ed. R. Weichhardt), Brussels (1989).

Andrzejewski, J. (ed.), *Gomułka i inni: dokumenty z archiwum KC*, London (1987).

Ash, T. G., *The Polish Revolution: Solidarity 1980–82*, London (1983).

Ash, T. G., *The Uses of Adversity*, Cambridge (1989).

Ash, T. G., *We, the People*, Cambridge (1990).

Barany, Z. D. and Vinton, L., 'Breakthrough to democracy: elections in Poland and Hungary', *Studies in Comparative Communism* vol. 23, 2 Los Angeles (1990), pp. 191–212.

Baras, V., 'Beria's fall and Ulbricht's survival', *Soviet Studies* vol. 27, 3 Glasgow (1975), pp. 381–395.

Baring, A., *Uprising in East Germany: June 17, 1953*, Ithaca (1972).

Batt, J., *Economic Reform and Political Change in Eastern Europe*, London (1988).

Batt, J., *East Central Europe from Reform to Transformation*, London (1991).

Bauman, Z., 'Twenty years after: the crisis of Soviet-type systems', *Problems of Communism* vol. 20, 6 Washington, DC (1971), pp. 45–53.

Berend, I., 'The historical evolution of Eastern Europe as a region', *International Organization* vol. 40, 2, Los Angeles (1986), pp. 329–46.

Berend, I., and Ranki, T., *The Hungarian Economy in the Twentieth Century*, London (1985).

Berglund, S., and Dellenbrandt, J. A. (eds.), *The New Democracies in Eastern Europe. Party Systems and Political Cleavages*, Aldershot (1991).

Bethell, N., *Gomułka: His Poland and His Communism*, Harmondsworth (1972).

Bielasiak, J., 'Inequalities and politicization of the Polish working class', in Nelson (1983).

Blondel, J., *Contemporary France. Politics, Society and Institutions*, London (1972).

Botsas, E. N. 'Patterns of trade', in Fischer-Galati (1981).

Bradley, J. F. N., *Politics in Czechoslovakia, 1945–1971*, Washington, DC (1981).

Brant, S., *The East German Rising*, London (1955).

Bromke, A., 'Poland under Gierek: a new political style', *Problems of Communism* vol. 21, 5, Washington, DC (1972), pp. 1–19.

Bromke, A. and Strong, J. (eds.), *Gierek's Poland*, New York (1973).

Brown, J. F., 'The East European setting', in *Eroding Empire: Western Relations with Eastern Europe* (ed. L. Gordon *et al.*), Washington, DC (1987).

Brown, J. F., *Eastern Europe and Communist Rule*, Durham (1988).

Brown, J. F., *Surge to Freedom: the End of Communist Rule*, Twickenham (1991).

Brus, W., 'Stalinism and the People's Democracies', in Tucker (1977).

Brus, W., 'Aims, methods and political determinants of the economic policy of Poland 1970–1980', in *The East European Economies in the 1970s* (eds. A. Nove, H-H. Höhmann, G. Seidenstecher), London (1982).

Brzezinski, Z. K., *The Soviet Bloc. Unity and Conflict*, Cambridge, MA, (1967).

Bujak, Z., 'West of Centre', *East European Reporter* vol. 4, 3, Budapest (1990), pp. 10–11.

Bunce, V., 'Neither equality nor efficiency', in Nelson (1983).

Bunce, V., 'Decline of a regional hegemon: the Gorbachev regime and reform in Eastern Europe', *Eastern European Politics and Societies* vol. 3, 2, Berkeley (1989), pp. 235–67.

Bunce, V., 'The empire strikes back', *International Organization* vol. 39, 1 (1985), pp. 1–46.

Calvocoressi, P., *Resilient Europe 1870–2000*, London (1991).

Carnovale, M., 'The Warsaw Pact at thirty: Soviet and East European successes and failures', in Carnovale and Potter (1989).

Carnovale, M. and Potter, W. C. (eds.), *Continuity and Change in Soviet-East European Relations*, Boulder (1989).

Carr, E. H., *What is History?*, Harmondsworth (1987).

Carrère d'Encausse, H., *Le grand frère*, Paris (1983).

Carrère d'Encausse, H., *Big Brother. The Soviet Union and Soviet Europe*, London (1987).

Charlton, M., *The Eagle and the Small Birds. Crisis in the Soviet Empire: from Yalta to Solidarity*, London (1984).

Checinski, M., *Poland: Communism, Nationalism, Antisemitism*, New York (1982).

Childs, D., *The GDR. Moscow's German Ally*, London (1988).

Clarke, R. A. (ed.), *Poland: the Economy in the 1980s*, Harlow (1989).

Cohen, S. F., 'Bolshevism and Stalinism', in Tucker (1977).

Connor, W., *Socialism's Dilemmas. State and Society in the Soviet Bloc*, New York (1988).

Crane, K., 'Soviet economic policy towards Eastern Europe', in Carnovale and Potter (1989).

Dahrendorf, R., *Reflections on the Revolution in Europe*, London (1990).

Davies, N., *Heart of Europe. A Short History of Poland*, Oxford (1986).

Dawisha, K., *Eastern Europe, Gorbachev and Reform*, Cambridge (1988).

Dehnel-Szyc, M., and Stachura, J., *Gry polityczne: orientacje na dziś, Warsaw (1991)*.

de Nevers, R., 'The Soviet Union and Eastern Europe: the end of an era', *Adelphi Papers* 249, London (1990).

Dennis, M., *German Democratic Republic. Politics, Economics and Society*, London (1988).

de Weydenthal, J. B., *The Communists of Poland: an Historical Outline*, Stanford (1986).

Djilas, M., *Conversations with Stalin*, Harmondsworth (1963).

Djilas, M., *The New Class. An Analysis of the Communist System*, London (1966).

Draper. T., 'A new history of the velvet revolution', *New York Review of Books* 14 January 1993.

Dziewanowski, M. K., *The Communist Party of Poland*, Cambridge, MA (1959).

Dziewanowski, M. K., *Poland in the Twentieth Century*, New York (1977).

East, R., *Revolutions in Eastern Europe*, London (1992).

East European Reporter (London/Budapest).

Elleinstein, J., *The Stalin Phenomenon*, London (1976).

Erickson, J., *The Road to Berlin, Stalin's War with Germany volume 2*, London (1985).

Fallenbuchl, Z. M., 'Comecon integration', *Problems of Communism* vol. 22, 2, Washington, DC (1973), pp. 25–39.

Fejtö, F., *A History of the People's Democracies*, Harmondsworth (1974).

Ferge, Z., *A Society in the Making. Hungarian Social and Societal Policy 1945–75*, Harmondsworth (1979).

Fischer-Galati, S. (ed.), *Eastern Europe in the 1980s*, Boulder (1981).

Frank, P., 'The CPSU local apparat', in *The Soviet State. The Domestic Roots of Soviet Foreign Policy* (ed. C. Keeble), London (1985).

Frankland, M., *The Patriots' Revolution*, London (1990).

Franklin, S. H., *Rural Societies*, London (1971).

Frydman, R., *et al.*, *The Privatization Process in Central Europe*, London (1993).

Fukuyama, F., 'The end of history?', *The National Enquirer* 16 1989), pp. 3–18.

Fukuyama F., *The End of History and the Last Man*, Harmondsworth (1992).

Gaddis, 'The emerging post-revisionist synthesis on the origins of the Cold War', *Diplomatic History*, vol. 7, Washington, DC (1983), pp. 171–90.

Gati, C., *Hungary and the Soviet Bloc*, Durham (1986).

Gebethner, S., 'Sejm rozczłonkowany: wytwór ordynacji wyborczej czy polaryzacji na polskiej scenie politycznej', in *Wybory '91 a polska scena polityczna* (S. Gebethner and J. Raciborski), Warsaw (1992).

Gibney, F., *The Frozen Revolution, Poland: A Study in Communist Decay*, New York (1959).

Glenny, M., *The Rebirth of History. Eastern Europe in the Age of Democracy* (2nd edn.), Harmondsworth (1992).

Golan, G., *The Czechoslovak Reform Movement: Communism in Crisis, 1962–1968*, Cambridge (1971).

Golan, G., *Reform Rule in Czechoslovakia: The Dubček Era, 1968–1969*, Cambridge (1973).

Gömöri, G., 'The political and social setting of the contemporary arts', in Schöpflin (1970).

Gorbachev, M., *Perestroika. New Thinking for Our Country and the World*, London (1988).

Griffith, W. E. (ed.), *Central and Eastern Europe: The Opening Curtain*, Boulder (1989).

Griffith, W. E., 'Central and Eastern Europe: the global context' in Griffith (1989).

Guardian (London).

G.U.S., *Rocznik Statystyczny*, Warsaw.

Halliday, F., *The Making of the Second Cold War*, London (1986).

Hammond, T. T. (ed.), *The Anatomy of Communist Takeovers*, New Haven (1975).

Hammond, T. T., *Witnesses to the Origins of the Cold War*, Princeton (1982).

Hankiss, E., *East European Alternatives*, Oxford 1990.

Hankiss, E., 'What the Hungarians saw first', in Prins (1990).

Harasymiw, B., 'Nomenklatura: The Soviet Communist Party's leadership recruitment system', *Canadian Journal of Political Science* vol. 2, 4 (1969), pp. 493–512.

Haraszti, M., *A Worker in a Worker's State*, Harmondsworth (1977).

Harbutt, F. J., *The Iron Curtain*, New York (1986).

Havel, V., *The Power of the Powerless: Citizens Against the State in Central and Eastern Europe*, London (1985)

Havel, V., 'Anti-political politics', in *Civil Society and the State* (ed. J. Keane), London (1988).

Hawkes, N. (ed.), *Tearing Down the Curtain*, London (1990).

Heath, R. E., 'Education', in Fischer-Galati (1981).

Heinrich, H-G., *Hungary. Politics, Economics and Society*, London (1986).

Held, J. (ed.), *The Columbia History of Eastern Europe in the Twentieth Century*, New York (1992).

Herspring, D. R., 'The Warsaw Pact at 25', *Problems of Communism* vol. 29, 5, Washington, DC (1980), pp. 1–15.

Herspring, D. R., 'The Soviets, the Warsaw Pact, and the East European militaries', in Griffith (1989).

Hirst, P., 'State, civil society and the collapse of Soviet communism', *Economy and Society* vol. 20, 2, London (1991), pp. 217–42.

Hoensch, J. K., *A History of Modern Hungary 1867–1986*, London (1988).

Holden, G., *The Warsaw Pact: Security and Bloc Politics*, Oxford (1989).

Holmes, B., 'Education in Eastern Europe', in Schöpflin (1970).

Honecker, E., *From My Life*, New York (1981).

Hough, J., *Russia and the West*, New York (1990).

Huntington. S., 'Will more countries become democratic?', *Political Science Quarterly* vol. 99, 2, New York (1984), pp. 193–218.

Hutchings, R. L., *Soviet-East European Relations. Consolidation and Conflict*, Madison (1987).

Ignotus, P., *Hungary*, New York (1972).

Ito, T., 'Eastern Europe: achieving legitimacy', in Rozman (1992).

Jancar, B. W., *Czechoslovakia and the Absolute Monopoly of Power: A Study of Political Power in a Communist System*, New York (1971).

Jasiewicz, K. and Żukowski, T., 'The elections of 1984–89 as a factor in the transformation of the social order in Poland', in

Democratization in Poland, 1988–90 (ed. G. Sanford), London (1992).

Jeffries, I. and Melzer, M. (eds.), *The East German Economy*, London (1987).

Johnson, A. R., 'The Warsaw Pact: Soviet military policy in Eastern Europe', in Terry (1984).

Jones, C. D., 'Soviet hegemony in Eastern Europe', *World Politics* vol. 29, 2, Baltimore (1977), pp. 216–41.

Jones, C. D., 'Agencies of the alliance: multinational in form, bilateral in content', in *Security Implications of Nationalism in Eastern Europe* (eds. J. Simon and T. Gilberg), Boulder (1986).

Jones, C. D., *Soviet Influence in Eastern Europe*, New York (1981).

Jones, C. D., 'Gorbachev and the Warsaw Pact', *Eastern European Politics and Societies* vol. 3, 2, Berkeley (1989), pp. 215–34.

Judt, A., 'The rediscovery of Central Europe', *Daedalus* vol. 119, 1 (1990), pp. 23–54.

Kabdebo, T., *Hungary: World Bibliographical Studies vol. 15*, Oxford (1980).

Kaplan, K., *The Communist Party in Power: A Profile of Party Politics in Czechoslovakia*, Boulder (1987).

Kaplan, K., *The Short March. The Communist Takeover in Czechoslovakia 1945–48*, London (1987).

Karol, K. S., *Visa for Poland*, London (1959).

Kaser, M. C., *Comecon: Integration Problems of the Planned Economies*, London (1967).

Kaser, M. C., (ed.), *The Economic History of Eastern Europe. Volume 3: Institutional Change within a Planned Economy*, Oxford (1986).

Kecskemeti, P., *The Unexpected Revolution: Social Forces in the Hungarian Uprising*, Stanford (1961).

Khruschev, N., *Khruschev Remembers*, trans. S. Talbot, London (1971)

Kolankiewicz, G., 'The working class', in Lane (1973).

Kolankiewicz, G. and Lewis, P. G., *Poland. Politics, Economics and Society*, London (1988).

Konrád, G., *Antipolitics*, London, 1984.

Konrád, G., 'Authority and tolerance', *East European Reporter* vol. 5, 2, Budapest (1992), pp. 40–41.

Konrád, G. and Szelényi, I., *The Intellectuals on the Road to Class Power*, Brighton (1979).

Kopelev, L., *No Jail for Thought*, Harmondsworth (1979).

Korbel, J., *Twentieth Century Czechoslovakia: The Meaning of its History*, New York (1977).

Korbonski, A., *The Politics of Socialist Agriculture in Poland: 1945–1960*,

New York (1965).

Korbonski, A., 'Cmea, economic integration, and *perestroika* 1949–1989', *Studies in Comparative Communism* vol. 23, 1, Los Angeles (1990), pp. 47–73.

Korybutowicz, Z., *Grudzień 1970*, Paris (1983).

Korzeniowski, K., 'Anomia polityczna a preferencje wyborcze w pierwsze turze wyborów', in W. Z. Daab *et al.*, *Polska wyborca '90, tom 1*, Warsaw (1991).

Kovaly, H. M., *Prague Farewell*, London (1988).

Kovrig, B., *Communism in Hungary: From Kun to Kádár*, Stanford (1979).

Kramer, M., 'Beyond the Brezhnev doctrine', *International Security* vol. 14, 3, Cambridge, MA (1989/90), pp. 25–67.

Krejci, J., *Social Change and Stratification in Postwar Czechoslovakia*, London (1972).

Krejci, J., *Social Structure in Divided Germany*, New York (1976).

Kukliński, R. J., 'Wojna z narodem widziana od środka', *Kultura* (Paris) April 1987.

Kusin, V., *The Intellectual Origins of the Prague Spring: The Development of Reformist Ideas in Czechoslovakia, 1956–67*, Cambridge (1971).

Kusin, V., *Political Groupings in the Czechoslovak Reform Movement*, New York (1972).

Ladygin, B., *CMEA: Achievements, Problems and Prospects*, Moscow (1987).

Landau, Z. and Tomaszewski, J., *The Polish Economy in the Twentieth Century*, London (1985).

Lane, D., (ed.) *Social Groups in Polish Society*, London (1973).

Lane, D., *The End of Social Inequality? Class, Status and Power under State Socialism*, London (1982).

Lavigne. M., *The Socialist Economies of the Soviet Union and Europe*, London (1974).

Lengyel, L., 'New ingredients in the goulash', *East European Reporter* vol. 4, 3, Budapest (1990), pp. 36–38.

Leslie, R. F. (ed.), *The History of Poland since 1863*, Cambridge (1980).

Lewarski, R. C., *Poland: World Bibliographical Series vol. 32*, Oxford (1984).

Lewis, F., *The Polish Volcano: A Case of Hope*, London (1959).

Lewis, P. G. (ed.), *Eastern Europe: Political Crisis and Legitimation*, London (1984).

Lewis, P. G. 'Legitimation and political crises: East European developments in the post-Stalin period', in Lewis (1984).

Lewis, P.G. *Political Authority and Party Secretaries in Poland 1975–1986*, Cambridge (1989).

Lewis, P. G., 'Non-competitive elections and regime change: Poland 1989', *Parliamentary Affairs* vol. 43, 1, Oxford (1990), pp. 90–107.

Lewis, P. G., 'The long goodbye: party rule and political change in Poland since martial law', *Journal of Communist Studies* vol. 6, 1, London (1990), pp. 24–48.

Lewis, P. G., *Democracy and Civil Society in Eastern Europe*, London (1992).

Lewis, P. G., 'Soviet and East European relations', in Rozman(1992).

Lewis, P. G., 'The anatomy of ruling parties: dissecting the vital organs', *Journal of Communist Studies* vol. 8, 3, London (1992), pp. 8–26.

Lewis, P. G., 'Democracy and its future in Eastern Europe', in *Prospects for Democracy* (ed. D. Held), Cambridge (1993).

Libération (Paris).

Lippmann, H., *Honecker and the New Politics of Europe*, New York (1992).

Lipski, J. J., *KOR. A History of the Workers' Defense Committee in Poland, 1976–1981*, Berkeley (1985).

Lomax, B., *Hungary 1956*, London (1976).

Lomax, B., 'Hungary – the quest for legitimacy', in Lewis (1984).

Lovenduski, J. and Woodall, J., *Politics and Society in Eastern Europe*, London (1987).

Lynch, A., 'Changing contours of Soviet-East European relations', *Journal of International Affairs* vol. 42, 2, New York (1989), pp. 423–34.

McAdams, A. J., *East Germany and Detente. Building Authority after the Wall*, Cambridge (1985).

McCauley, M., *Marxism-Leninism in the German Democratic Republic The Socialist Unity Party (SED)*, London (1979).

McCauley, M., *The German Democratic Republic since 1945*, London (1983).

McCauley, M., 'Legitimation in the German Democratic Republic', in Lewis (1984).

McElvoy, A., *The Saddled Cow. East Germany's Life and Legacy*, London (1992).

Makowski, W. (ed.), *Wydarzenia czerwcowe w Poznaniu*, Poznań (1981).

Malia, M. (Z), 'To the Stalin Mausoleum', *Daedalus* vol. 119, 1, Cambridge, MA (1990), pp. 295–344.

Marer, P., 'The political economy of Soviet relations with Eastern Europe', in Terry (1984).

Marer, P., 'The economies and trade of Eastern Europe', in Griffith (1989).

Marrese, M., 'CMEA: effective but cumbersome political economy', *International Organization* vol. 40, 2, Los Angeles (1988), pp. 287–327.

Mason, D. S., 'Policy dilemmas and political unrest in Poland', *Journal of Politics* vol. 45, 2, Austin (1983) pp. 397–421.

Mason, D. S., *Revolution in East-Central Europe. The Rise and Fall of Communism and the Cold War*, Boulder (1992).

Mastny, V., *Russia's Road to the Cold War*, New York (1979).

Merritt, G., *Eastern Europe and the USSR. The Challenge of Freedom*, London (1991).

Michnik, A., *Letters From Prison and Other Essays*, Berkeley (1985).

Mlynář, Z., *Night Frost in Prague: The End of Humane Socialism*, London (1980).

Molnár, M., *Budapest 1956: A History of the Hungarian Revolution*, London (1971).

Molnár, M., *A Short History of the Hungarian Communist Party*, Boulder (1978).

Morris, L. P., *Eastern Europe since 1945*, London (1984).

Myant, M., *Poland: A Crisis for Socialism*, London (1982).

Myant, M., *The Czechoslovak Economy, 1948–1988*, Cambridge (1989).

Nagy, I., *On Communism: In Defense of the New Course*, New York (1987).

Narkiewicz, O. A., *Petrification and Progress. Communist Leaders in Eastern Europe, 1956–1988*, London (1990).

Nelson, D. N. (ed.), *Communism and the Politics of Inequalities*, Lexington (1983).

Nelson, D. N., 'Leninism and political inequalities', in Nelson (1983).

Novak, A., 'The last communist party in Central Europe', *East European Reporter* vol. 5, 3, Budapest (1992), pp. 28–29.

Nove, A., *An Economic History of the USSR*, Harmondsworth (1989).

Okey, R., *Eastern Europe: 1740–1980* (2nd edn.), London (1986).

Okey, R., 'Central Europe/Eastern Europe: behind the definitions', *Past and Present* 137, Oxford (1992), pp. 102–33.

Paul, D. W., *Czechoslovakia: Profile of a Socialist Republic at the Crossroads of Europe*, Boulder (1981).

Pearson, R., *National Minorities in Eastern Europe 1848–1945*, London (1983).

Pelikan, J., *The Czechoslovak Political Trials 1950–1954*, Stanford (1971).

Pethybridge, R. W., *A History of Postwar Russia*, London (1966).

Philipsen, D., *We Were the People. Voices from East Germany's Revolutionary Autumn of 1989*, Durham (1993).

Phillips, A., *Soviet Policy toward East Germany Reconsidered: The Postwar Decade*, Westport (1986).

Pick, M., 'Quo vadis - homo sapiens? Results and alternatives for the transformation strategy of the CSFR', *Europe-Asia Studies*, vol 45, 1, Glasgow (1993), pp. 103–14.

Piontkowsky, A. A., 'The Russian sphinx: hope and despair', in Prins (1990).

Polityka (Warsaw).

Polonsky, A., *The Little Dictators*, London (1975).

Potel, J-Y., *The Summer Before the Frost*, London (1982).

Prins, G. (ed.), *Spring in Winter: the 1989 Revolutions*, Manchester (1990).

Prybyla, J., 'The great malaise: economic crisis in Eastern Europe', in *The Uncertain Future. Gorbachev's Eastern Bloc* (eds. N. N. Kittrie and I. Volgyes), New York (1988).

Przeworski, A., *Democracy and the Market*, Cambridge (1991).

Rayski, A., *Nos illusions perdues*, Mesnil (1985).

Remington, R. A., *The Warsaw Pact: Case Studies in Communist Conflict Resolution*, Cambridge, Mass. (1971).

Renner, H., *A History of Czechoslovakia Since 1945*, London (1989).

RFE/RL Research Report (Munich).

Richet, X., *The Hungarian Model: Markets and Planning in a Socialist Economy*, Cambridge (1989).

Robinson, W., *The Pattern of Reform in Hungary*, New York (1973).

Rothschild, J., *East Central Europe between the Two World Wars*, Seattle (1974).

Rothschild, J., *Return to Diversity. A Political History of East Central Europe since World War II*, New York (1989).

Rozman, G., *Dismantling Communism. Common Causes and Regional Variations*, Washington/Baltimore (1992).

Ruane, K., *The Polish Challenge*, London (1982).

Rupnik, J., *The Other Europe*, London (1988).

Rzeczpospolita (Warsaw).

Sanford, G., *Polish Communism in Crisis*, London (1983).

Schapiro, L., *Totalitarianism*, London (1972).

Scharf, C. B., *Politics and Change in East Germany*, Boulder (1984).

Schöpflin, G. (ed.), *The Soviet Union and Eastern Europe. A Handbook*, London (1970).

Schöpflin, G., 'The Stalinist experience in Eastern Europe', *Survey* vol. 30, 3 (1988), pp. 124–47.

Schöpflin, G., 'The end of communism in Eastern Europe', *International Affairs* vol. 66, 1, London (1990), pp. 3–16.

Schöpflin, G., 'Post-communism: constructing new democracies in Central Europe', *International Affairs* vol. 67, 2, London (1991), pp. 235–50.

Schöpflin, G. and Wood, N. (eds.), *In Search of Central Europe*, Cambridge (1989).

Schulz, E., 'Recent changes in the policy of the GDR towards the Federal Republic of Germany', in Carnovale and Potter (1989).

Selbourne, D., *Death of the Dark Hero: Eastern Europe 1987–90*, London (1990).

Seton-Watson, H., *Eastern Europe between the Wars* (3rd edn.), Hamden (1962).

Seton-Watson, H., *The East European Revolution*, London (1956).

Shawcross, W., *Crime and Compromise: Janos Kádár and the Politics of Hungary Since Revolution*, London (1974).

Shawcross, W., *Dubček*, London (1970).

Short, D., *Czechoslovakia: World Bibliographical Series vol. 68*, Oxford (1986).

Šimečka, M., *The Restoration of Order. The Normalization of Czechoslovakia*, London (1984).

Skilling, H. G., *Czechoslovakia's Interrupted Revolution*, Princeton (1976).

Skilling, H. G., 'Stalinism and Czechoslovak political culture', in Tucker (1977).

Smith, K., *Berlin: Coming in from the Cold*, Harmondsworth (1991).

Snyder, J., 'Averting anarchy in the new Europe', *International Security* vol. 14, 4, Cambridge, MA (1990), pp. 5–41.

Staniszkis, J., 'The obsolescence of Solidarity', *Telos* 80, New York (1989), pp. 37–50.

Staniszkis, J., *Dynamics of the Breakthrough in Eastern Europe*, Berkeley (1991).

Stent, A., 'Technology transfer to Eastern Europe: paradoxes, policies, prospects', in Griffith (1989).

Stern, C., *Ulbricht: A Political Biography*, New York (1965).

Stokes, G., *From Stalinism to Pluralism. A Documentary History of Eastern Europe since 1945*, New York (1991).

Suda, Z., *Zealots and Rebels: A History of the Ruling Communist Party of Czechoslovakia*, Stanford (1980).

Swain, G. and Swain, N., *Eastern Europe since 1945*, London (1993).

Swain, N., *Collective Farms Which Work ?*, Cambridge (1985).

Swain, N., *Hungary: the Rise and Fall of Feasible Socialism*, London (1992).

Sword, K. (ed.), *The Times Guide to Eastern Europe* (2nd edn.), London (1991).

Syrop, K., *Spring in October: The Polish Revolution of 1956*, London (1957).

Talbot, S., *Deadly Gambits. The Reagan Administration and the Stalemate in Nuclear Arms Control*, London (1985).

Taras, R. C. (ed.), *Handbook of Political Science Research on the USSR and Eastern Europe*, Westport (1992).

Tarniewski, M., *Płonie komitet*, Paris (1982).

Taylor, J. R., 'Cinema', in Schöpflin (1970).

Teichova, A., *The Czechoslovak Economy 1918–1980*, London (1988).

Terry, S. M., *Poland's Place in Europe. General Sikorski and the Origin of the Oder-Neisse Line, 1939–1943*, Princeton (1983).

Terry, S. M., (ed.), *Soviet Policy in Eastern Europe*, New Haven (1984).

Thomas, H., *Armed Truce. The Beginnings of the Cold War 1945–46*, London (1988).

Tigrid, P., 'The Prague coup of 1948', in Hammond (1975).

Torańska, T., *Oni*, London (1985), translated as *Them - Stalin's Polish Puppets*, London (1987).

Touraine, A., *et al.*, *Solidarity: Poland 1980–81*, Cambridge (1983).

Trilling, O., 'Theatre', in Schöpflin (1970).

Trofimenko, H. A., 'Soviet policy vis-à-vis Europe: a Soviet view', in *The Changing Soviet Union in the New Europe* (ed. J. Iivonen), Aldershot (1991).

Tucker, R. C., *The Soviet Political Mind*, London (1972).

Tucker, R. C., *Stalin. Essays in Historical Interpretation*, New York (1977).

Turner, H. A., *The Two Germanies since 1945*, New Haven (1987).

Turnock, D., *Eastern Europe. An Economic and Political Geography*, London (1989).

Ulam, A., 'Europe in Soviet eyes', *Problems of Communism* vol. 32, 3, Washington, DC (1983), pp. 22–30.

Urban, J., 'Czechoslovakia: the power and politics of humiliation', in Prins (1990).

Urwin, D. W., *Western Europe Since 1945. A Political History*, London (1989).

Vali, F. A., *Rift and Revolt in Hungary: Nationalism Versus Communism*, Cambridge, Mass. (1961).

van Brabant, J., *Economic Integration in Eastern Europe*, New York (1989).

Volgyes, I., 'The Warsaw Pact: changes in structure and functions', *Armed Forces and Society* vol. 15, 4, Chicago (1989), pp. 551–70.

Wałęsa, L., *A Path of Hope*, London (1988).

Wąsowicz, W. and Socha, L., 'Z archiwum Bolesława Bieruta', *Krytyka* 8 (1981).

Wat, A., *My Century*, New York (1990).

White, S. (ed.), *Political and Economic Encyclopaedia of the Union and Eastern Europe*, London (1990).

White, S., *Gorbachev and After*, Cambridge (1991).

Wightman, G., 'The 1992 parliamentary elections in Czechoslovakia', *Journal of Communist Studies* vol. 8, 4, London (1992), pp. 296–97.

Wiskeman, E., *Europe of the Dictators 1919–1945*, Glasgow (1966).

Wolchik, S. L., *Czechoslovakia in Transition. Politics, Economics and Society*, London (1991).

Wright, M., 'Ideology and power in the Czechoslovak political system', in Lewis (1984).

Young, J. W., *Cold War Europe 1945–1989*, London (1991).

Zambrowski, R., 'Dziennik', *Krytyka* 10, Warsaw (1980).

Zeman, Z. A. B., *The Making and Breaking of Communist Europe*, Oxford (1991).

Zinner, P. E., *Revolution in Hungary*, New York (1962).

Zinner, P. E., (ed.), *National Communism and Popular Revolt in Eastern Europe*, New York (1956).

Maps

Map 1 Physical features of Eastern Europe

Map 2 Territorial Changes as a result of the Second World War

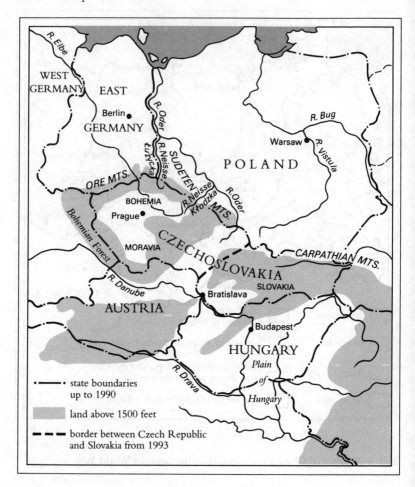

Map 3 Eastern Europe in 1945

Index